In Memory of Gunnar Hedlund

This book is dedicated to the memory of Gunnar Hedlund, a great contributor in the management field, who was born on 14 December 1949 in Skellefteå, Sweden, and passed away on 18 April 1997 at a hospital in Stockholm. Gunnar studied at the Stockholm School of Economics (SSE), where he received his master's degree in 1972. He completed his PhD in 1976, at the age of 27. That same year, a new institute was formed at SSE: the Institute of International Business (IIB), founded by the leading Swedish industrialists Ruben Rausing and the two brothers Marcus and Jacob Wallenberg. Gunnar was committed to the Institute from the very beginning, and in 1980 he became the Director of IIB, a position he held for 10 years over the 20-year period he was active at IIB. Gunnar led the Institute to the internationally renowned position it enjoys today.

Gunnar became a full Professor at SSE in 1988 where, amongst other accomplishments, he actively participated in creating two other important institutes at SSE: the European Institute of Japanese Studies and the Centre for Advanced Studies in Leadership. Over the years, Gunnar sat on the boards of numerous academic institutes and organizations, and served on the editorial board of some 10 academic journals. He spent long periods at the Wharton School, University of Pennsylvania, and Stanford University. Gunnar published many important books and articles in the area of international business and organization theory. He was the father of important management concepts that have had a great influence on many of us. He constantly sought new perspectives and had a unique ability to cross over disciplines – seeing new research opportunities. We will remember Gunnar as a truly exceptional scholar. While his research has come to an end, his spirit and works will live on in the continuing efforts of the Institute.

KNOWING IN FIRMS

*Understanding, Managing and
Measuring Knowledge*

edited by
Georg von Krogh, Johan Roos
and Dirk Kleine

SAGE Publications
London • Thousand Oaks • New Delhi

First published 1998

 SAGE Publications Ltd
6 Bonhill Street
London EC2A 4PU

SAGE Publications Inc.
2455 Teller Road
Thousand Oaks, California 91320

SAGE Publications India Pvt Ltd
32, M-Block Market
Greater Kailash – I
New Delhi 110 048

British Library Cataloguing in Publication data

A catalogue record for this book is available
from the British Library

ISBN 0 7619 6013 9
ISBN 0 7619 6014 7 (pbk)

Library of Congress catalog card number 98–61329

Typeset by Mayhew Typesetting, Rhayader, Powys
Printed and bound in Great Britain by Athenaeum Press, Gateshead

CONTENTS

NOTES ON EDITORS AND CONTRIBUTORS

Editors

Georg von Krogh was born on 24 May 1963 in Norway. He is Professor of Management at the University of St Gallen and member of the board of directors at the Institute of Management. He studied engineering at the Norwegian Institute of Technology where he graduated in 1986. In 1990 he received his PhD from the Division of Organization and Work Science at University of Trondheim. From 1991 to 1994 he was an Associate Professor of Strategy at the Norwegian School of Management and Director of the School's MSc programme in international strategy and marketing. Professor von Krogh has been Assistant Professor at SDA Bocconi, Milano. He has been a Research Fellow at the University of Munich and the University of Aachen, and Visiting Professor at the London School of Economics and Political Science and Hitotsubashi University, Japan. He has also worked as a management consultant at the Center for Applied Strategy in Zug, Switzerland, and he is an active adviser to European and American firms in the area of corporate and competitive strategy. His present research interests are in the area of strategic management: cooperative strategies; strategic processes including knowledge and competence development; strategic management practices in emerging industries; and the foundations of qualitative research in the field of strategy. He has published several books as well as some 30 articles in international scientific journals.

Johan Roos is a Professor at the International Institute for Management Development (IMD), Switzerland. He researches how companies become and remain healthy enough to keep adapting to and shaping their own environments. Related areas of research include: knowledge development and ways of knowing in companies; concepts and practices of intellectual capital; the firm as a complex adaptive system; and effective strategy processes in emerging industries. Professor Roos has consulted widely on these issues for both US and European corporations and associations, and frequently presents these ideas at international conferences for both management scholars and practitioners. Professor Roos is the author, or co-author, of more than 40 articles and book chapters, and 12 books. He is Swedish.

Before joining IMD as a Professor of Strategy and General Management, he was affiliated with the Norwegian School of Management, the Wharton School of the University of Pennsylvania, and the Stockholm School of Economics. He was awarded a PhD degree in international business in 1989, and a MSc degree in agriculture in 1985.

Dirk Kleine is a Research Associate and doctoral candidate at the University of St Gallen, Institute of Management, in Switzerland. He holds a bachelor degree from Berufsakademie Mannheim, Germany, and an MBA from Lancaster University, United Kingdom. He has been working on different research projects with major European multinationals. Those projects have mainly focused on the pharmaceutical industry and cooperative strategies. Currently he is conducting empirical research on the changing roles and functions of strategic planning departments, involving companies such as BMW, Bayer, Hewlett-Packard and Siemens. He is co-author of a book on environmental information systems and has co-authored articles on knowledge transfer, the pharmaceutical industry and argumentation theory.

Contributors

Thomas Bertels is a consultant with Rath & Strong and helps clients accelerating organizational learning through process design efforts involving teams. He is co-author of the book *The Intelligent Enterprise: Faster Learning as a Competitive Advantage* and several articles on organizational learning and knowledge management. Prior to consulting Mr Bertels was with Asea Brown Boveri, managing a customer service organization.

Frank Blackler is Professor of Organizational Behaviour at Lancaster University Management School. He trained in philosophy and psychology before specializing in organizational psychology and organizational theory. His research has included studies of job design, organizational change and the introduction of new technologies. Currently he is undertaking a major study of innovation in high-technology organizations which involves an analysis of knowledge, learning processes and competitiveness. His books include *Job Redesign and Management Control* and *Whatever Happened to Shell's New Philosophy of Management* (with Colin Brown), *Applying Psychology in Organizations* (with Sylvia Shimmin), *Information Technology and People* (with David Osborne) and an edited collection *Social Psychology and Developing Countries*. A collection of papers entitled *Organizations and Knowledge* edited jointly with Bente Elkjaer and David Courpasson is soon to be published by Sage.

Bettina Büchel holds a degree in public administration from the University of Constance, Germany, and a master's degree from Rutgers University. After finishing her PhD at the University of Geneva she became an Assistant Professor at the Asian Institute of Technology (AIT) in Bangkok, Thailand. She is currently teaching MBA students from 25 different Asian countries. Her research interests include cooperative strategies, organizational learning and knowledge management. Dr Büchel is a consultant to several multinational corporations and international organizations, including AT&T, Hewlett-Packard and the World Health Organization. In 1995 she co-founded the Geneva Knowledge Group.

Norman Crump is a research fellow at Lancaster University Management School. He has a degree in organization studies from Lancaster University, following a former career in the public sector. He is currently involved in a major research project looking at the innovative management of innovation in high-technology industries. His research interests include knowledge, learning and the influences of globalization on organizations.

Peter Gomez was born in 1947 in St Gallen, Switzerland. He followed graduate and doctoral studies at the University of St Gallen. From 1977 to 1978 he was Visiting Professor at the State University of New York; from 1978 to 1989 he was Senior Vice-President of Switzerland's leading publishing house Ringier Group and press distribution house Distral Group; and in 1989 he became founding partner of Valcor, consultants for strategic management and M&A. Since 1990 he has been Professor for Management and Organization and Director of the Institute of Management at the University of St Gallen, and from 1995 to 1997 Dean of the Business Administration Faculty. He is the author of 10 books and over 50 other publications on strategic management, systems thinking in management and creating shareholder value.

Lars Huemer is a PhD candidate in business administration at the Umeå Business School, Umeå University, Sweden. He graduated with a BS in business marketing and organizational theory from Umeå University in 1989. His research interests include the nature and roles of trust in business relationships, and the link between trust and knowledge development and knowledge transfer in organizations.

Tom Housel specializes in telecommunications, information technology, value-based business process reengineering and knowledge value management. He is currently Visiting Associate Professor for Information Management at the University of Southern California. He has been the Chief Business Process Engineer for Pacific Bell and his last assignment in the corporate world was as the Chief of Consumer Market Research for Telecom Italia in Venice. He is Managing Partner for Business Process Auditors, a firm which specializes in management development using a methodology for measuring the return generated by business processes and corporate knowledge assets. He received his PhD from the University of Utah. Dr Housel won the prestigious Society for Information Management award for the best paper, and his work on measuring the value of intellectual capital has been featured in a *Fortune* cover story and *Investor's Business Daily* articles.

Kazuo Ichijo is an Associate Professor of the Faculty of Social Sciences at Hitotsubashi University, Tokyo. He received a BA (social sciences) and an MA (social sciences) from Hitotsubashi University, and a PhD (business administration) from the University of Michigan. His research interests are focused on knowledge development and management in organizations, and on innovation at three levels: the project level, the organization level and the industry level. Professor Ichijo has published papers in Japan and the US, and has conducted numerous management seminars.

Valery Kanevsky is currently Senior Industry Consultant at Hewlett-Packard, and was the Lead Member of Technical Staff at Pacific Bell Telephone in San Ramon, California. He is an expert in the application of complexity theory to fundamental business problems such as calculating the value added by component processes and information technology. He is also an internationally recognized authority in mathematical modelling and simulation.

Rodrigo Magalhães is currently Research Fellow and PhD candidate at the London School of Economics, Department of Information Systems. His research topic is the impact of information systems implementation on the organization's knowledge system. Other research interests include information systems and organizational change, and inter-cultural management. He is faculty member of the Department of Economics and Management at the Portuguese Catholic University in Lisbon. He holds an MBA from the University of Sheffield, an MA from the Leeds Metropolitan University, and a BA from the University of Natal, South Africa.

Donald A. Marchand (PhD, MA, UCLA) is Professor of Information Management at the International Institute for Management Development (IMD). He was formerly Dean and Professor of Information Management at the School of Information Studies, Syracuse University and Professor of IS and Director, Institute for Information Management, Technology and Policy, College of Business Administration, University of South Carolina. Professor Marchand is a consultant and speaker to numerous corporations and government organizations on the strategic management of information and technology. His research interests include the strategic role of IT in enterprise transformation and business process redesign, managing information and knowledge assets, and reengineering IS/IT strategies and organizations.

Seonaidh McDonald is a research fellow at the University of Lancaster Management School. As an undergraduate she studied management science at Stirling University, where she later undertook a PhD in the waste management field. Following a period at the Department of Management Science at the University of Strathclyde, evaluating group decision support methods with Professor Colin Eden, she joined a multi-disciplinary research team at Lancaster looking at the management of innovation. Seonaidh is interested in how boundaries between different specialists and interest groups can be successfully managed, and in teaching the realities of research.

Günter Müller-Stewens studied business administration at the University of Regensburg. He was Research Assistant at the Department of Statistics and at the Institute for Organizational Science at the University of Munich. He did a research stay at both Harvard Business School and Stanford

Business School. He was Professor of Strategic Planning, Organization and Human Resource Management at Duisburg University. Since 1991 he has been Professor of Management and Organization at the University of St Gallen and Director of its Institute of Management. He is author of several books and publications on statistics, strategic management and organization. He is editor of the *M&A Review* and member of the editorial board of the *CEMS Business Review*. He is consultant to several international companies.

Ikujiro Nonaka is a Professor and Director of the Institute of Business Research at Hitotsubashi University, Tokyo. He received MBA and PhD degrees from the Haas School of Business, University of California at Berkeley. Professor Nonaka's research on the management of innovation and organizational structure has been widely published in English and Japanese journals and books, and he has conducted numerous seminars for Japanese and English scholars and managers. His recent work *The Knowledge-Creating Company* (co-author, Oxford University Press, 1995) was awarded the Best Book of the Year in Business and Management.

Gilbert Probst is Professor for Organization and Management and Director of the MBA programme at the University of Geneva, Switzerland. He did his PhD and *habilitation* at the University of St Gallen, Switzerland. Professor Probst has written more than 20 books and over 80 journal articles, mainly in the fields of systemic and cybernetic thinking in management, problem solving, organizational learning, developmental management and knowledge management. He is a member of the board of Neue Warenhaus AG (EPA/UNIP), SKU and Kuoni Travel (all in Switzerland) and a consultant to many multinational corporations, including Hewlett-Packard, Ciba-Geigy, Winterthur Insurance, Hilti and Swissair. In 1995 he was a co-founder of the Geneva Knowledge Group.

Steffen Raub holds degrees in business administration from the University of Mannheim (Germany) and ESSEC (France). Since 1994 he has been a Research Assistant with Professor Probst at the University of Geneva, Switzerland. His research focuses on organizational learning and knowledge management, strategic management (in particular organizational capabilities) and qualitative research methods. Publications include two books and several journal articles. He is a consultant to a variety of national and multinational corporations, including Falke (Germany), Hewlett-Packard, AT&T, Swiss Bank Corporation and Coop (Switzerland). In 1995 he co-founded the Geneva Knowledge Group.

Keigo Sasaki is a Senior Lecturer at the Department of Economics and Business Administration, Yokohama City University. He received a BA (economics) from Kyushu University, Fukuoka, Japan, and an MA (commercial science) from Hitotsubashi University, Tokyo, Japan. His current research interests are focused on organizational technological knowledge and individual skill, and knowledge creation and learning in organizations.

Charles Savage is President of Knowledge Era Enterprises, Inc. in Wellesley, Massachusetts, and author of the newly revised edition of *Fifth Generation*

Management: Co-Creating through Dynamic Teaming, Virtual Enterprising and Knowledge Networking.

Jürgen Schüppel was born in 1963. He is partner of the Munich-based Pi Group (Partner for Change and Innovation). The main focus of his work as a consultant is on strategy, business process reengineering and systemic aspects to realize the fundamental management of change. In 1997 he was appointed Professor for Strategy and Organization at the Kolping-Fachhochschule in Riedlingen. He studied business administration and psychology at the University of Munich, Germany, and received his doctoral degree for his dissertation on knowledge management at the University of St Gallen, Switzerland.

Gabriele Troilo holds a PhD in business administration and is Assistant Professor of Marketing at University L. Bocconi. His main research areas are focused on resource-based marketing, cognitive mapping and environmental management. He is author of several articles and books.

Katsuhiro Umemoto obtained a BA in economics, Kyushu University, Fukuoka, Japan, studied information science at Syracuse University in New York and communication science at the University of Southern California in Los Angeles. He holds a PhD in public policy from Washington University, USA. Currently Dr Umemoto is Professor of Social Systems at the Graduate School of Knowledge Science, Japan Advanced Institute of Science and Technology. His major research interests include epistemology of public policy and indigenous peoples' knowledge systems.

Markus Venzin is Assistant Professor at Bocconi University of Milan, Italy. He got his doctoral degree at the University of St Gallen (HSG) and is working with a number of innovative firms in the field of strategic management, focusing on knowledge processes in strategic conversations. His research concentrates on the development of a knowledge-based model to understand and create the company's future.

Salvatore Vicari is Professor of Business Administration at Bocconi University, Milan, and the Director of Human Resources Development at SDA Bocconi, the Graduate School of Business Administration. He has published extensively in the fields of strategy, marketing and organization theory. His current research interests cover the new sciences as they apply to firms, among them autopoiesis and chaos theory. Professor Vicari is a member of several editorial boards and also an active management consultant in the areas of strategy and management.

INTRODUCTION

Georg von Krogh, Johan Roos and Dirk Kleine

This volume is a collection of chapters that explore the emergent body of research on knowledge management in the field of strategic management. It is our conviction that knowledge management is one of the most exciting areas of inquiry in the field of strategic management. Thus, we have tried to select chapters that contribute with new concepts, issues and ideas to the understanding, management and measurement of knowledge in organizations. We have also attempted to bring together some of the leading researchers on knowledge management from a wide range of academic institutions in the US, Japan and Europe. As the reader will notice, all contributors share our view that knowledge is at the centre stage of organizational life. Hence, we hope to offer much food for thought for further advancing into the knowledge economy. It is our aim that this book serves as an important resource for researchers and reflective practitioners interested in knowledge management.

We want to acknowledge the support of our institutions, the University of St Gallen and the International Institute for Management Development (IMD), in preparing this book. It has also been a considerable pleasure working with all of the authors in the book and we thank them for their patience and contribution. We are grateful as well to the people at Sage Publications, especially to Rosemary Nixon and Hans Lock for their help in turning our manuscript into a form that makes a real contribution to the realm of knowledge management.

Structure of the Book

The contributions in the book are arranged in two main parts:

Part I: Understanding Knowledge in Organizations
Part II: Managing and Measuring Knowledge in Organizations.

Before we start to think about knowledge management, we need to clearly understand how 'knowing in firms' takes place. Therefore Part I 'Understanding Knowledge in Organizations' covers topics such as how and why individuals and organizations come to know, images and types of knowledge and the potential links of concepts of organizational learning and trust with theories of knowledge. The contributions in Part I aim to uncover and discuss the theoretical assumptions underlying research on knowledge in organizations and to conceptualize future research in the field.

Having understood the nature of knowledge, we can proceed to discuss methods and tools of knowledge management. Knowledge management is so challenging because we need to discard our very ingrained notions of 'control', 'structure' and 'goal rationality'. Taking these challenges into account, Part II 'Managing and Measuring Knowledge in Organizations' brings forth practical ways of managing knowledge. The contributions outline different models of knowledge development and some contributions illustrate their application through case studies of various organizations. A wide range of issues is covered in Part II such as knowledge enablers and drivers, knowledge creation processes and clustering knowledge management tools. Furthermore, the issue of how to determine and leverage the value of knowledge in organizations is explored. The authors outline concepts such as intellectual capital and the value of core processes in the organization.

The key concepts and ideas of the different chapters are summarized in the table shown.

Key ideas and concepts in the contributions

Chapter	Author(s)	Ideas and concepts
1	Bertels/Savage	Highlighting the tough questions to inspire research
2	Venzin/von Krogh/Roos	Contextualizing research; epistemological assumptions; knowledge appearances; knowledge applications
3	Blackler/Crump/McDonald	Images of knowledge; knowing as a process
4	Magalhães	Epistemological foundations of organizations; autopoiesis; languaging
5	Huemer/von Krogh/Roos	The nature of trust; linking trust and epistemology
6	Nonaka/Umemoto/Sasaki	Theory of knowledge creation; knowledge spiral; five-phase model of knowledge creation
7	Ichijo/von Krogh/Nonaka	Knowledge enablers; knowledge intent; care; conversations
8	Vicari/Troilo	Innovation; error production; learning process
9	Schüppel/Müller-Stewens/Gomez	Knowledge spiral; instruments for knowledge development
10	Probst/Büchel/Raub	Resource-based view; organizational learning

On the Contributions

In Chapter 1, T. Bertels and C. Savage develop a research agenda for the field of knowledge management. They argue that the challenge for research is to get the questions right in order to advance into the 'knowledge era'. The questions centre around assets and aspirations, boundaries and boundarylessness, change and continuity, contribution and coherence, culture and context, information and infostructures, leadership and language, learning and leveraging, measurement and motivation, transfer and transparency, and values and valuation. One set of questions can open a new frontier in a seemingly unrelated area. Rather than giving definitive answers, this chapter poses tough questions about where further research and scholarship are needed to help build a theoretical and practical base for a knowledge-based economy.

In Chapter 2, M. Venzin, G. von Krogh and J. Roos explore the concept of knowledge within the field of strategic management. A research map is developed that facilitates further theory building and gives an overview of existing literature in this field. Arguments on why the issue of knowledge is important for strategy are matched with underlying epistemological assumptions, knowledge appearances and applications. The authors argue that the epistemological positioning of new concepts and the retrofitting of existing concepts will facilitate scientific (and managerial) conversations because they enhance the connectivity of existing work and open up research in underexplored areas.

Chapter 3 also offers an overview and critique of common approaches to understanding knowledge in organizations. F. Blackler, N. Crump and S. McDonald first review common images of knowledge, as embodied, embedded, embrained, encultured and encoded. They argue that the thrust of much of the recent literature on knowledge, competency and learning has been to suggest that embrained, encultured and encoded knowledge is of increasing significance to wealth creation. Further, this chapter develops a critique of the common approaches to understanding knowledge by suggesting that knowledge is better analysed as an active, pragmatic process that is culturally situated, artefact mediated and socially distributed and which occurs within communities of practice. The authors conclude with a discussion of what this approach means for the management of knowledge in organizations. Six key themes are highlighted: knowledge acquisition, knowledge planning, domain innovation, boundary innovation, organizational learning and new approaches to collaboration.

In Chapter 4, R. Magalhães aims to clarify various trends and 'schools of thought' from the relevant literature in organization theory by bringing together three metaphors which are usually dealt with separately: organizational learning, organizational knowledge and organizational memory. A new and unifying approach to organization knowledge based on autopoiesis theory is introduced and the increasingly relevant role of language in organizational discourse is emphasized. Another objective of the chapter is to highlight contributions to these issues which are outside the mainstream positivist research paradigm in the organization sciences. These contributions are gaining ground around a new pole of attraction that can broadly be described as the postmodern movement.

Chapter 5, written by L. Huemer, G. von Krogh and J. Roos, focuses on the managerial issue of trust. At present, there is no consensus on how to approach or view this conceptually complex concept within the realms of strategic management and organization theory. The authors suggest that conditions of trust are essential for organizational knowledge development and transfer to occur. Thus, one of the most important roles which trust may play focuses on issues related to corporate epistemology. Guided by different epistemological perspectives, the aim is to develop an understanding of trust and the dynamic relationship between trust and knowledge.

In Chapter 6, I. Nonaka, K. Umemoto and K. Sasaki present three cases of Japanese companies, namely Sharp, National Bicycle and Seven-Eleven Japan. They first introduce their theory of organizational knowledge creation. This is followed by case descriptions that outline how these three companies have developed business process innovations as knowledge-creating systems to acquire consumers' latent wants. The authors argue that those knowledge-creating systems are not the results of often inhumane reengineering activities, which to a large extent rely on information technology, but are based on human beings' intellectual ability and mutual trust.

The goal of Chapter 7 is to develop a richer understanding of the problem of creating, capturing and capitalizing on knowledge-based competences in firms. K. Ichijo, G. von Krogh and I. Nonaka argue that despite the growing interest in the management of knowledge in firms, there is a lack of knowledge with respect to the micro-level process of how knowledge is enabled in firms. While providing insights on the subject, the chapter is still exploratory and at the stage of theory building rather than theory testing. The authors study this topic – enabling the management of knowledge in firms – by pursuing the discovery of theory, i.e. grounded theory, intending to provide theoretical and management implications for knowledge management in firms based on a case study on MYCOM, a corporate brand for Maekawa Seisakujo (Maekawa Manufacturing Company). The primary result of this approach is a conceptual model which highlights key knowledge enablers and shows how they will contribute to the management of knowledge-based competences in firms.

In Chapter 8, S. Vicari and G. Troilo propose a new way to face complexity and, consequently, a new role for management. The firm is considered as a cognitive system which enacts and makes sense of its own environment from its individual point of view. Following the idea that the environment and the market are cognitive constructions of the firm, a new model of innovation as a learning process is developed. The relevance of the concept of error and a taxonomy of error production in management are described. These topics raise a number of organizational issues which are briefly discussed in the last part of the chapter.

In Chapter 9, J. Schüppel, G. Müller-Stewens and P. Gomez argue that knowledge management has to comprise all activities regarding production, reproduction, distribution, utilization and multiplication of relevant knowledge. In concrete, knowledge management can be implemented as a process along the following four dimensions. First, the process has to focus on the subjects of knowledge by optimizing the ratio of internal and external knowledge elements within the value chain and internalizing necessary external knowledge into the organization. Second, the process has to focus on the relevance of knowledge in a competitive environment. Thereby the company needs to identify the present and future knowledge potentials for building sustainable competitive advantages. Third, the process must increase the availability, communication and transfer of knowledge by focusing on both implicit and explicit forms of knowledge. Fourth, the richness and validity of knowledge have to be determined. This can be discussed using a dichotomy of knowledge experience and knowledge of rationality. The authors argue that the goal of systematic knowledge management must be seen in the modelling of a dynamic knowledge spiral that builds on the four process dimensions by using specific, knowledge-oriented instruments.

The purpose of Chapter 10 by G. Probst, B. Büchel and S. Raub is to link 'the organizational learning perspective' and the 'resource-based view' in order to show how the development of organizational knowledge through learning can lead to a competitive advantage. From the perspective of the resource-based view, the possession of unique knowledge can be seen as a strategic resource which provides the foundation of competitive advantage. From the organizational learning perspective, knowledge can be seen as the product of a learning process which ensures continuous adaptation. Propositions are offered which show how learning to develop organizational knowledge can be a means of ensuring a sustainable competitive advantage.

In Chapter 11, D. Marchand argues that in many discussions of 'the learning organization', 'change management' and 'competitive advantage', the practical links between what managers think about these concerns and how they 'manage' knowledge and information are often weak to non-existent. This is the managerial issue addressed in this chapter. The intent is, first to suggest a framework for the continuous conversion from information to knowledge and knowledge to information, and second to illustrate the business value of managing these conversion processes through the pioneering efforts of one company – Skandia – in visualizing and measuring 'intellectual capital'.

In Chapter 12, V. Kanevsky and T. Housel claim that the understanding of how to accelerate the conversion of knowledge into value (i.e. money) is the real challenge in the information age. The 'knowledge payoff' occurs when a corporation's most valuable intangible asset – knowledge – is converted into bottom-line value in the form of a concrete, saleable product. The value of an organization's core processes can be derived from the amount of knowledge required to reproduce their outputs. Process knowledge becomes a surrogate for the final process output. This chapter focuses on the fundamental relationship between the returns that an organization derives from its processes and the knowledge embedded therein.

PART I

UNDERSTANDING KNOWLEDGE IN ORGANIZATIONS

1

TOUGH QUESTIONS ON KNOWLEDGE MANAGEMENT

Thomas Bertels and Charles M. Savage

In a very short time, industry has discovered *knowledge, intellectual capital* and *knowledge management*. Tom Stewart of *Fortune* magazine was one of the first to chronicle this development in his articles on 'brain-power' (Stewart, 1991) and 'intellectual capital' (Stewart, 1994). Word is out and the conference factories have begun to schedule conferences on knowledge management. They sense business process reengineering (BPR) has lost its lustre and they want to be the first to offer the new topic. Surely consulting firms will suddenly proclaim they are also in the knowledge management business, and incorporate the latest buzzwords into their brochures, just as they did with BPR. More and more CIOs will change their title to CKO, chief knowledge officer.

Then, after three years of intense fluff, the lemmings will be on to their next topic, without ever having really mined the subject of knowledge. Quick solutions will be bandied around, as if a few silver bullets will do the trick. When they do not work, people will claim the knowledge business is a sham, try to clear the mess the consultants left behind and return to business as usual.

What if we agreed at the outset to do our homework, even if it were to take 5 or 10 years? What if we follow Albert Einstein's insight that the world we have made, as a result of the level of thinking we have had thus far, creates problems that we cannot solve at the same level of thinking at which we created them? What if we approached knowledge and intellectual capital with a sober and humble realization that, if we do our work right, we will indeed be laying the foundation for the next economy? The stakes are much higher than just increasing productivity by 30% or even 300%. What does this mean?

We face a major transition, as we begin to leave the industrial era behind and enter the knowledge era. Remember, it took from 50 to 150 years to move from the agricultural to the industrial era. Agriculture did not die. We just brought an industrial approach to agriculture so that 5% of our population farms instead of 65%. In the future we will still have industry, but we will understand and manage it from a new perspective, that of the knowledge era.

In other words, we are beginning on a 10- to 50-year transition to a knowledge-based economy. Likely we will find that all our goods can be produced by less than 10% of our population. What do the others do?

In addition, we are learning that we need to be more responsible with our natural resources. We cannot continue to abuse nature's resources or to pile high our rubbish for future generations to tend.

As we produce more with fewer people, our income distribution mechanisms are breaking down. Persistent high unemployment is one indication. And it cannot be solved just by more government transfer payments. Instead, we need to awaken people to the value of their own knowledge, energy and aspirations, so they feel genuinely excited about initiating their own entrepreneurial efforts (Handy, 1990). A four-person company can have almost the same presence on the Internet as a large multinational one.

It is unlikely the industrial era is sustainable in the form we have known it. We now realize that narrowly defined tasks and command-and-control hierarchies may work fine in stable environments. They are hopelessly out of date for the emerging knowledge era. The danger is that with the ever increasing pace of change, we may spend so much time on redesigning the old corporate structures that we have no time left to capitalize our efforts and deliver results. Some may wonder whether somebody has changed the rules of the business game and forgotten to tell.

Moreover, we are discovering how poorly the industrial era model was designed from a human perspective. We have designed into our companies a culture of distrust. Instead of valuing people, we have fostered a climate where people do not feel valued for what they know or what they can do. We have focused on hands and not heads and hearts. If we want to move into the knowledge era, our biggest challenge is a cultural one. And as we know, cultural change does not come easy.

We are convinced that our first challenge is to get our questions right. Only as we probe, test and experiment will we begin to uncover the real wealth of the knowledge era. We can also envision a close working partnership between the universities and industry, services and governments, similar to the Fraunhofer model in Germany.

We will have to develop new capabilities and a fresh understanding to create new opportunities. The challenge is not to adapt existing concepts to new situations, but to generate creative ideas about business and values. The dominant logic of the industrial era is a barrier to reaching an understanding of the knowledge era. Perhaps we are again standing with Galileo, realizing the contradictions of traditional wisdom, and reaching for a new order?

What are some of the questions which will help us co-create the knowledge era? Rather than giving definitive answers, we have formulated some of the tough questions on which further research and scholarship are needed. Our goal is to inspire industrial and academic researchers to help build a theoretical and practical base for a knowledge-based economy.

We have developed a wide range of questions centred on the following interrelated topics:

- assets and aspirations
- boundaries and boundarylessness
- change and continuity
- contribution and coherence
- culture and context
- information and infostructures
- leadership and language
- learning and leveraging
- measurement and motivation
- transfer and transparency
- values and valuation.

One set of questions can open a new frontier in a seemingly unrelated area. Honest probing is needed now, rather than glib answers.

Assets and Aspirations

Typically *assets* are recognized items of worth. We count our assets on our balance sheet, we put asset numbers on machinery and we recognize that these assets depreciate. As we move into the knowledge era we are faced with more than just things. Ideas begin to take on major business significance. Yet, we hardly know how to put asset numbers on them, unless they be patents or trademarked items.

Gordon Petrash and his colleagues at Dow Chemical have done an excellent job in developing an information asset management programme which reviews patents and other nuggets of know-how. They are anchoring these within the concrete business context of the enterprise. Their work is leading to a better understanding of the valuation of their patent portfolio, and hence to increased profitability.

This is just the start. We are beginning to understand that good ideas, processes and infostructures can appreciate with usage. Likewise, we are beginning to realize that as we as individuals get better at recognizing and valuing the positive experience and capabilities of our colleagues, we can generate value for the company.

These developments beg a whole series of new questions:

- Are ideas assets?
- How do we account for ideas which appreciate with usage?
- How do we measure depreciation of ideas that have outlived their usefulness?
- How do we value the knowledge and time of our customers?
- Are these assets which accrue to our benefit?

We have just been through a period of extreme downsizing and asset-stripping to improve financial ratios. These practices often ignore the *hidden value* in business units and capabilities in terms of core knowledge. How can we better visualize the hidden intellectual capital within and between our organizations so we can move out of the traps of short-term financial thinking? How can we learn from the excellent work of Professors Ikujiro Nonaka and Hirotaka Takeuchi (1995) on 'the knowledge-creating company'?

We are finding that it is not enough just to focus on what we know. It is also important to understand what we as individuals, functions or companies do with what we know. In other words, our *aspirations* are also very important. Our aspirations are rooted in our deep values. They are the things for which we have a passion.

They are the energy sources of our actions. They are the drives for innovation, creativity and excellence. They point us to the future and its possibilities.

- How do we learn to listen to one another's aspirations, especially as we launch new teaming efforts?
- What models can support expression of aspirations so that they become visible and valued 'idea assets'?
- How do we learn to listen not just to our customers' needs and problems, but also to their aspirations?
- What are they trying to do to better respond to their customers, and how can we support them best?
- What is our contribution to the total value chain?

- How do we stop the vicious circles of mistrust which destroy our capabilities to learn, to live our expectations and to create new products and services?

If we can find answers, it is likely that our genuine human aspirations will fuel a new renaissance of economic activity.

Boundaries and Boundarylessness

The marketplace has become global, and the effects are visible everywhere. Instead of a limited number of competitors in our domestic markets we now face countless enterprises that offer the same or something similar. The niches have lost their exclusive touch, and it seems there is no place left to hide. As long as we could oversee the market it was enough to be better than the competition. Where do we position our business within the global context of the knowledge era? How can we set organizational *boundaries* that best utilize our specific set of competencies and best match that of our partners in the value chain? What is our vision, and where are our strengths? Instead of focusing on our present product range, what business activities will best suit our knowledge portfolio? Instead of using competition as the only measurement, we need to focus our efforts by improving our ability to deliver unique contributions.

Focus is needed to create uniqueness. We must search for excellence to be able to create something that nobody else can offer. Some questions might describe the challenges we face:

- How do we identify our core competencies, our unique abilities, our core knowledge, and what does it take to sustain and develop these capabilities further than everybody else?
- What business activities contain our most valuable ideas and knowledge? The ability to focus organizational activity and knowledge creation is crucial for survival.
- We are able to identify our core business and core markets, but how do we assess our core ideas?
- In the global village, how can we be focused and committed to our specific capabilities, and at the same time be able to see the whole picture?

ABB's Percy Barnevik translates *boundarylessness* into 'think global, act local'. Matching of local competence with global ideas calls for participation and communication across functional, organizational and cultural frontiers. In an era where cross-organizational and cross-cultural teaming will become an important means to create value and generate new ideas, we must unlearn our beliefs about 'us and them'. How can we understand our contribution and best match our abilities to our partners within the value chain? This requires dialogue and trust, confidence in our skills, and valuing and recognition of others and their work.

The same boundaryless sense is needed when we work with our internal customers. How can we see the larger context when communicating across functional barriers in order to best match our efforts instead of optimizing our job box? This will affect leadership as well as structure. The role of executives will shift from controlling their turf to initiating real dialogue so that tacit knowledge can be made explicit. How do we create double-win situations which transcend simple compromise? What models and tools will support boundaryless behaviour?

We must match our uniqueness to others' unique abilities. This is only possible when we see others' contribution to the value chain, built on a common set of values and on a culture of valuing. Traditionally, we have limited our thinking to the border of our job box. What can we do to support workers in understanding their position within the overall context whilst getting a strong sense of pride out of what they are doing?

Change and Continuity

Every new business book begins with a mantra on *change*. Change management is the battle-cry of every consultant. And yet, change is tremendously threatening, because when things change, people's worlds come unstuck. All that seemingly made them important is disappearing. It is little wonder that, in spite of the cries for change, constant change and more change, resistance is unbelievably strong in our organizations. Perhaps the problem starts with the concept of 'change'. Perhaps we should think in terms of *transformation*.

Transforming our organizations into knowledge-based businesses asks for much more than developing a new set of buzzwords. The task to solve is similar to Otto Neurath's metaphor of sailors on the open sea who must reconstruct their ship but are never able to start from the bottom; they must make use of some of the drifting timber from the old structure, but they cannot put the ship into dock to start from scratch. During the transformation we must stay on the old structure and will have to deal with new problems that at present we can only envision.

In going through the transformation we need help in terms of both guidelines and models. We need ideas to experiment with, which help to build on existing ground and yet are stable enough to carry over to the new economy.

- What strategies can we apply to prepare today's organizations for the shifts to be expected?

- How do we weave the ideas of knowledge and its value into the organization and be nevertheless able to function in the present business situation?
- What difficulties can be expected?

How is *continuity* possible in a fast-moving business world? What gives us a sense of consistency and security, what makes it possible to continually let go in order to reach for the next trapeze bar? It may well be that change becomes livable when we change our corporate cultures from a culture of devaluing to one of valuing. If people were to feel they are taken seriously by their colleagues, subordinates and superiors, then would they have less need to hold on to the outer signs of importance, such as title, office size and parking space?

We are in desperate need of a model allowing for quick change that is based on firm, stable beliefs. We need corporate cultures where values are strong and firm enough to encourage everybody to participate and contribute. Brian Hall (1993) has been doing a wonderful job of helping companies make explicit the tacit values of individuals and organizations so they can create a more collaborative and creative environment.

The present realities show the complete reverse picture: we build cultures on values that are vague and counterproductive, we try to manipulate our culture in order to achieve better financial results, but we ignore the need for consistent and shared values. Using culture as a weapon to increase productivity has failed, and it has resulted in fear and resentment towards quick-fix solutions.

Cynics might say that we are pretty good at reflecting the pace of outside change in our efforts to publish mission statements and develop lists of values. But these cynics know we are ready to abandon them as soon as we have to change our behaviour in accordance with them. Are there ways companies are able to make cultural change stick?

A business based on sharing individual ideas and beliefs calls for a supportive and open culture, such as Oticon's in Denmark. How do we develop stability in our values and valuing, so that we can be extremely dynamic in allocating and reallocating our resources? In short, how do we create stability and consistency in our values so we can dynamically respond to ever changing business opportunities?

Contribution and Coherence

Although Adam Smith understood the value of the division and subdivision of labour, he also saw its potential negative effect. Buried deep in his *The Wealth of Nations* (1987), way past the model of the pin-making factory, is a comment to the effect that this mode of work could potentially be detrimental for the human spirit. The continuous repetition of work will draw on such a small portion of the person's capabilities that they will likely atrophy. In essence, this model had the possibility, as Smith understood it, of making workers stupid. What kinds of *contribution* can workers make if their capabilities are significantly underutilized and their spirits are ignored?

In his book *Jobshift*, William Bridges (1994) documents the shift away from narrowly defined jobs into a model of organizations which begin to excel at teaming and reteaming capable people. Significantly, we are moving to an approach which needs to use the whole person, and all the person's talents.

Moreover, no one person has all the insights, so we are finding it is very important to be aware of the richness of diversity in the workplace, facing questions like:

- How do we better understand this shift?
- How do we work with human resources and information systems to build this dynamic workplace?
- What infostructure is needed, and how do rewards and recognition change?

We are finding real value in building upon the diversities of backgrounds of our people, be they educated as engineers, in finance or in the humanities. Each has a significant contribution to make. Moreover, we are finding diverse workforces offer a richness of insight. And as we begin to work more closely with other companies through virtual enterprising, we learn to build upon the diversity of cultures in one another's organizations.

Typically we want to know what makes workers satisfied. There have literally been thousands of employee satisfaction studies and surveys over the last 50 years. Unfortunately satisfaction can been very ethereal. I may be hungry, i.e. dissatisfied with my physical condition, but then when I eat I am satisfied, at least for a short while. Studies of worker satisfaction made sense when they were doing hand work. But when we are involved in head work, then satisfaction may not be the best theme. Instead of asking, am I *satisfied* with my work, it would be more appropriate to ask, am I *significantly involved* in what I am doing? How can I contribute?

Traditionally, we did not care about contribution: we defined the output and then we could calculate the required input. This model only works when the definitions are clear and the conditions are stable. The more we deal with vague ideas and knowledge, the more we realize that we cannot define the input any longer, that we depend on the contribution and that we cannot enforce the contribution, because that force is counterproductive. Contribution asks for common values and supportive sharing. What cultural values will support contribution but avoid the lowest common denominator? How can we match individual talents so that we create something nobody can achieve on their own, involving the best of everyone, making best use of this input?

We might even ask ourselves if we need to unlearn our obsession with competition as the driving economic force. What does it take to bring together the individual capabilities? When we compete we try to exclude, to position ourselves, we fight to make our point. For sure, the knowledge era will know competition, but the definition of 'us and them' is likely to change towards a more dynamic understanding, spanning across functional and organizational barriers.

How do we link the individual with the organization to create *coherence*? Realizing that we will have to abandon fundamental beliefs about business raises the question of whether such soft, fragile bonds as culture, values and language will tie an organization together in the face of organizational realities, where individual and functional egoism can only be mastered by applying pressure and dependence. It seems obvious that a new kind of organization will have to offer more to its co-workers than it did before. The conflict between unleashing the full potential of the human spirit and at the same time achieving corporate goals asks for a new quality of relationship. How can we reflect this kind of relationship? How can organizational focus and individual goals be matched?

Maybe we will have to unlearn our ideas about employment and work contracts in order to be able to reflect this new type of relationship. When knowledge becomes the dominant resource we must face the fact that the worker is the owner of the resource. This touches the roots of capitalistic theory and of established beliefs about ownership and dependence.

Ownership of resources equals power. How can we translate this into structures that address this fact? Maybe we will have to rethink our organizations as partnerships or as coalitions that are sustained only for a limited period?

The traditional organization was bound together by power and pressure, and the damage was covered by monetary compensation. But what is the equivalent in the knowledge era that ties the organization together? What can organizations offer, when the success of an organization relies on its capability to involve every brain it can reach as much as possible? How do we create common sense and direction when everybody is involved? How do we achieve coherence in the diverse demands of an ever changing market?

Culture and Context

The 1980s raised the idea of corporate *culture*, but the topic soon vanished from the agenda when it was realized how much effort it takes to turn a company around. The serious attempts of many to change the fundamental beliefs of a whole enterprise have been seen to fail, and yet there are too few examples like GE, Oticon in Denmark and Metler-Toledo in Germany where the mechanisms of large-scale change can be studied (Warnecke, 1995). We have developed powerful solutions to change structures and processes but we have failed to address the cultural dimensions.

Now as we enter the knowledge era the challenge is back. This time we cannot postpone the issue any longer. We are now challenged to create organizations based on cultures of trust which support the dynamic teaming of ever changing constellations of capable individuals and companies and add to the knowledge creation process (Savage, 1996).

To what extent do we have to sacrifice holy cows in order to create an environment where organizational members create new knowledge, share their knowledge and support each other? How do we lay the groundwork for trust and common sense despite the fact that the economic rat race is still with us? How do we value knowledge in the organization, and how can we create an atmosphere where established but outdated knowledge can be challenged?

How can an organization change its culture from mistrust to trust and valuing, from direct control by rewards and punishments towards self-responsibility and intrinsic control? In short, how can we support major cultural shifts?

Back when the industrial era was just beginning, there was a struggle as to how best to deal with complexity. It was decided that the best way was to break complex processes into little bits. Adam Smith's pin-making factory is the prototype example of this line of thinking. Although one or two individuals might understand the whole process, those in the little boxes, and there were 18 boxes in Smith's model, knew only their little bit of the process.

Now as we move more to a teaming environment, people are expected to come together to solve a problem or seize an opportunity. If they do not understand the larger business *context*, they will likely suboptimize from their limited perspective and miss the mark.

It used to be the top management group that kept the corporate strategy very close to their chests. This approach makes it difficult for those at lower hierarchical levels in the organization to understand the context and business background of their actions. How can we change this? Could we learn some valuable lessons from the work on holonic management being developed by the world-wide Intelligent Manufacturing System project, or the fractal factory work of Professor Hans-Juergen Warnecke of the Fraunhofer Institute in Germany?

To be sure, in a climate of distrust, it was best to say as little as possible, but in a dynamic and ever changing business environment, internal openness becomes a necessity. This means new strategies are needed to deal with complexity. Luckily, complexity theory has been evolving and now we are learning how to spot the significant patterns in chaotic situations. But what will be the impact on management studies? We can envision that multi-disciplinary education for business leaders will supersede the traditional MBA, that new, holistic approaches will overcome our current obsession with specialization.

Information and Infostructures

It is often said that we are in the information age. It certainly seems like it. In fact, the abundance of *information* can be overwhelming. We need to sort this out. How do we find the significant patterns? The important insights? The key points?

We begin to understand that information only comes alive by our interpretation, that we create meaning by distinguishing and valuing information. The industrial era did not really challenge our beliefs and patterns of thought. In this era, the flow of information has been typically slow and we did not need to understand and rethink our interpretation schemes. The world has been changing, and now we need to explore these patterns that sort and give meaning to the pieces.

We sense that information has a limited life span in terms of relevance. The numerous reports that occupy the armadas of corporate staff too often display outdated thoughts, while at the same time we lack the significant facts which can help to support our decisions. How do we reflect this when seeking information?

We seem to drown in the ocean of data – and die of thirst for relevant information at the same time. We sense that there is nothing like facts, that information derives its importance only because of our judgement. How do we make our implicit patterns and beliefs explicit?

Understanding the interplay between data, information and meaning will ask for much more than sophisticated models of data storage and will force us to understand the process of creating meaning.

Dan Burrus, author of *Technotrends*, calls our information infrastructures *infostructures* (Burrus and Gittines, 1993). The task is not just to structure the information, but to structure the whole process of acquiring, processing and sorting out this information and discovering its meaning. In other words, we need to put whole systems together from which we can effectively see the patterns and act in a timely manner.

Infostructures are fast becoming critical to effective knowledge management. In the development of the Internet and intranets we can begin to see infostructures taking shape. There are massive amounts of information, but with hypertext and search engines we are able to sort out and find the essential, and systems thinking can help us to understand the multiple connections and cause–effect loops.

Leadership and Language

There is a tremendous amount of work to be done in rethinking the traditional management and *leadership* models. The old 'command-and-control' model is no longer adequate. What do we put in its place?

In many ways, the old management model was based on fear and manipulation. In the new organizational model we need trust and respect. What is the source of new leadership power?

As we start to work more with the core competencies of individuals, functions and companies, what leadership and management style do we need to facilitate the teaming and reteaming of these capabilities in ever changing constellations within and between companies? How can future and knowledge-oriented leadership be taught and trained?

The global village will leave no space to hide. The chances to survive with second-best solutions will be few. The call for excellence in terms of unique and flexible solutions is out. Our task is to rethink the traditional management ideas based on the belief in best practices. How can we create unique products, new markets, fresh ideas if we stick to common beliefs embedded in the 7-S model, three generic strategies and two-by-two portfolios? How can we differentiate if we use approaches available to everyone able to read and understand an MBA textbook?

The need for creative and unique ideas to market differentiation brings new demands. Instead of management's role being just managing resources, distributing cash and administrating SBU portfolios, isn't the real task to excel in creating strategic intent, motivating the whole organization and building upon our unique intellectual capital to create new business opportunities?

There are already the first signs of change in the *language* of business. Instead of just physical capital (property, plant and equipment), we are beginning to talk of 'intellectual capital'. As Leif Edvinsson of Skandia or Hubert St. Onge of the Canadian Imperial Bank of Commerce define it, intellectual capital is composed of human capital, structural capital and customer capital. Human capital is the knowledge and experience in people's heads and hands; structural capital is embodied in software, databases, policies, procedures and techniques, the things that stay in the company when people go home at night; and customer and supplier capital represent the value and strength of the organization's relationships.

Are these terms correct? Instead of structural capital, could we be talking about infrastructural capital, or even infostructural capital? Shouldn't we better speak of potential instead of capital, stressing that this kind of capital is not an asset with a fixed value but an ever changing resource with its importance and value depending on constant development and improvement? Is human capital an asset or a liability? Are human talents owned or are they on loan to the organization?

How do we understand the interplay between human, structural and customer capital? Our suspicions are that wealth is generated in the dynamic interaction of these three elements. What leadership and management style do we need to help facilitate these interactions?

Can we quickly develop a glossary of the new terms and work at some provisional definitions? We should be careful, however, not to try to freeze any definitions, because we are still learning about this whole area.

We may even have to look at the grammar of relationships. For example, in the traditional hierarchical model the subordinate works 'for' the boss. In the new model, where the leader is coach and mentor, it is more likely that they work 'with' one another. What is the significance of moving from a 'for' model of relationships to one characterized by 'with' relationships?

In the industrial era we developed a language focusing on the physical transformation of raw material into finished goods. How can we develop a language which focuses on the transformation of raw ideas into well-developed products and services? We worry about 'inventory turns', but should we not also be working on our 'idea turns' or 'knowledge turns'? How can this new language keep up with the constant change around us? What kind of language can mirror the intangible and unstable aspects of knowledge and nevertheless enable communication?

Learning and Leveraging

There has been a lot of talk about the learning organization over the past several years. Although there have been few visible results the idea of organizational *learning* deserves some attention. Individual learning seems to be the input when talking about knowledge. Up to now, the discussion has taken knowledge in terms of individual and organizational knowledge as something given. The main idea was how tacit knowledge can be converted into explicit knowledge. But should we not also look at the process of creating individual knowledge in order to understand the value chain as a whole? Does organizational knowledge creation comprise organizational learning? Is it the same or something different? Learning can be understood as a process, knowledge as the result of that process. What help can the ideas of organizational learning offer to understand the process of gaining and sharing organizational knowledge?

We need to understand individual and collective learning processes much better than we do at present. What happens when we learn? What impulses drive learning? How can we increase our awareness of early signals that stimulate learning? How can we unlearn outdated beliefs and insights?

Yet, how can we talk about learning when we cannot see it happen? We only realize that something has changed, and we attribute the difference to something called learning, confusing process and result (Bateson, 1972).

Until now, the concepts of knowledge management and organizational learning have not really been interrelated. Maybe we could take a step forward by treating both topics as different perspectives on the same topic and by integrating research rather than using different labels to compete against each other? The point of view that organizational learning takes might help us to understand how the raw material in the knowledge era – ideas – is generated. Knowledge management might help to transform the raw material into competitive advantage.

Until now the discussion on knowledge management has centred on turning tacit knowledge into explicit knowledge, or on making individual knowledge available for the organization (Nonaka and Takeuchi, 1995).

We are beginning to suspect that knowledge exists in several layers. When we look at organizational change we see that fundamental change is based on changing the culture and its values, which has a lasting effect on product development and relationships with customers and suppliers. We also sense that knowledge creation on the R&D level is not enough to ensure competitive advantage that lasts. We feel that knowledge on the product or technology level is much easier to discuss than knowledge on a cultural level.

Yet, we can observe a *leveraging* effect of knowledge at deeper levels. Values and cultural characteristics can foster knowledge creation in terms of product development and customer skills; abilities to learn from customers can enhance relationships; and the ability to learn how knowledge is shared and insights are gained can help to improve communication.

There seems to be a relationship between the level or depth of knowledge and its impact on the organization over time (Bertels and Walz, 1995). Maybe we can create a model explaining the impact of knowledge that exists at different levels? What levels are useful to distinguish? What effect has knowledge at these levels on the organization in terms of competitive advantage? Does the difference in impact on the organization enforce different approaches and instruments or even language to deal with it? How can these layers be addressed? At present, we can only observe that although companies create the same products or use the same technology, their foundations are somehow different. We sense that there is something that makes a difference, but we lack the language to address that difference.

Measurement and Motivation

In the industrial era, *measurement* became the master. We managed what we measured. That which could not be measured was often ignored. Yet companies like GE and ABB realize that it is the softer issues which are really the hard issues. How does an organization measure its level of trust? How can we measure the potential for ideas and products hidden in the brains of individuals? Microsoft's real assets are not reflected by established accounting principles. The shift from manufacturing to 'ideafacturing' enforces the pressure to reflect and revise traditional lessons learned from dealing with tangible inputs and outputs.

A few companies like Skandia in Sweden and S.A. Armstrong in Canada are beginning to measure some of the elements of intellectual capital. Skandia is even issuing an intellectual capital supplement to its traditional balance sheet (Skandia, 1995). This has awakened the interest of the Securities and Exchange Commission in the United States, as well as countless accounting firms. They all realize it is much too early to set any definitive guidelines, but there is a growing recognition that this is a fruitful area of study. It would be wonderful if we could have a goodly number of doctoral dissertations in this area, as we need some fresh ideas and probing thought to find answers to questions like:

- How can we develop adequate measures for these intangibles?
- Is double-entry book-keeping really capable of accounting for ideas, especially ideas which appreciate with usage?
- Do we have to create a fresh set of measurements?
- How can these measures be standardized to allow comparison of companies?

In the industrial era, *motivation* is too often rooted in manipulation. Managers seldom tell their workers how well they are doing, because it is easier to motivate by fear than through praise. As a result, companies devise elaborate reward systems to motivate workers to do more in less time. Unfortunately, these systems often function as punishment systems, and even when they work they develop their own dynamics, encouraging dysfunctional behaviour that is limited to the extent of monetary compensation, ignoring the overall purpose of the organization. Although most HRM systems are designed with the corporate objectives in mind, they seem to provoke suboptimization, functionalism and distrust as a consequence of being reduced to their technical function, failing to recognize the 'soft factors' that cannot be measured directly.

The traditional approaches might get people to work faster, but do they really serve to inspire minds to work together?

The industrial era is closely knit with the mechanisms of motivating people by monetary means. How can we motivate people to use their brains and hearts for the organization, instead of simply applying their hands? GE and other companies struggle hard to develop systems that reflect the importance of quality and teamwork without being able to measure these factors.

How do employees, managers and executives learn to motivate one another through genuine interest in one another's ideas, capabilities and aspirations? How can we develop a fundamentally redefined approach to motivation in the knowledge era?

Transfer and Transparency

Some may assume our challenge in the knowledge era is simply to *transfer* already existing knowledge from one location to another, or one person to another. To be sure, this is one element, and an important one, but it is certainly only part of the picture.

Companies have gigabytes of storage capability and high-bandwidth local and wide-area networks. Should this not be enough to store and utilize existing knowledge, to manage corporate memory and to integrate data files?

The answer is that technology represents only one side of the coin. Our ability to track down explicit knowledge in databases, guidelines or organizational charts is only the tip of the iceberg. An organization's real knowledge is often embodied in the experience, skills, knowledge and capabilities of individuals and groups. It is shaped by beliefs and metaphors. Too often we try to change our organizations without understanding tacit knowledge and beliefs. We know these elements have value, but how do we probe them with our existing information systems infrastructures?

Nonaka (1991) has brought the interplay between tacit and explicit knowledge to the fore. That leads us to an understanding of the context in which something is understood. This is certainly more than a physical transfer issue, a transfer of bits and bytes from one location to another. Instead, might it be a question of transferring our understanding based on the context of the situation? How can we create the openness where people are willing to discover and share their basic beliefs? The toolbox of scientific management tried to erase the human element as a source of irritation. Utilizing knowledge is based on the ability to involve the human element far more than we can imagine. How do we do this?

We begin to understand the differences between knowledge and traditional economic resources. Knowledge gains value when being shared with others. This will impact behaviour significantly as we have to learn how to handle this. How we can support the sharing of knowledge? The management of explicit knowledge asks for administrative skills, for efficiency in utilization and distribution. Creating and sharing tacit knowledge demands creative and social competence. It challenges us to transfer our perspectives from the tacit to the explicit and back to the tacit, to move between levels of abstraction no matter what level we are at in the organization.

The traditional hierarchical organizational chart creates the impression of *transparency*, giving us the impression that we can easily see everything. We know who is in charge and can orient ourselves by looking at the organizational charts and process maps. We quickly know where all the boxes are and who reports to whom.

Yet, in reality, too often we find this organization anything but transparent. Instead, it is very opaque. It is not easy to see what is happening in the box to the right or left, above or below. Despite that, the importance of informal structures is not reflected by the official version. Today organizations struggle hard to map their processes. Introducing new accounting systems such as activity-based costing often reveals the complex structure not capable of being allocated to boxes.

Do we lose this organizational transparency when we move to a dynamic team-based organization which is continually teaming and reteaming competent individuals? How do we maintain responsibility? If people are no longer seen by their 'bosses' because they are off on this team or that, will they get recognized for their contributions and knowledge? How do we create transparency and establish communication if we have to forget our ideas about hierarchy and responsibility (meaning chain of command)? How do we develop ways to understand complex issues and to stay in context and control even while giving individuals more freedom than ever before?

And what happens when we open the cage of the job box? Will the organization break apart? We have become comfortable with the ideas of accountability and objective standards. Have we lost the sense of the invisible bonds that tie teams together, that create new and fascinating ideas? What do we put in place of these lines that connected the job boxes? What models will help us to understand our processes when the narrowly defined tasks are gone? If the machine metaphor is no longer adequate, what is a proper metaphor for dynamic organizations which are continually in flux? Are they hypertext organizations, as Nonaka and Takeuchi (1995) suggest? Are they like fractals, as Warnecke (1993) has written? Or are they like spaghetti, as Lars Kolind (1994), President of Oticon in Denmark, has reasoned?

The mechanisms of how knowledge is created, converted and communicated within the organization are yet unexplored. We need to achieve a far deeper understanding of the most valuable resource for the coming era quite soon in order to make full use of this new value chain.

Values and Valuation

In the industrial era we have been interested in value in terms of what things cost, how much we have to pay, and how we can increase something's price.

On the other hand, in the industrial era *values* have not been very important. There was a time not long ago when we heard the phrase 'customer beware'. It hardly represents a valuing attitude towards customers.

Hubert St Onge, VP and Director of the Canadian Imperial Bank of Commerce's Leadership Centre in Toronto, and Brian Hall, President of Values Technology in Santa Cruz, have asked, 'Are values necessary to create value?' Their question deserves a lot more thought and reflection.

Some companies are generating a list of 4 to 10 key values they would like everyone to adopt. Even though they publish on wall posters and in the company newsletter, it is unlikely that there will be much of a cultural change. Why?

As long as values are listed as nouns, everyone can agree that they are important, but values only come alive when they become verbs. You and I can agree that 'trust' (noun) is important, but only as you feel I am 'trusting' (verb) of you does it count. How do we identify values (nouns) and turn them into active verbs?

The industrial era focused primarily on people's hands. Were they doing their assigned work in the job box? In the knowledge era we are working not just with raw materials, but also with raw ideas. Values and valuing are the lubrication which makes good idea refinement possible. The gears which refine insight need this kind of lubrication. Brian Hall (1993) has developed, over the last 30 years, a way of helping individuals and organizations to make their values more explicit. They can then make choices about their further development. He is finding that values and valuing help organizations to build a much more solid foundation of trust and respect so that they begin to reach new levels of productivity together.

Valuation is generally assumed to refer to the aggregate worth of an entity. Often comparisons are used to establish this worth. What is the value of our product in relation to the selling price of other manufacturers? What is the value of our service in relationship to competing offers? The stock market is making these judgements all the time, based on objective and subjective factors. We are finding that companies who invest in understanding and mastering their own 'knowledge management' capabilities are not only improving time to market, but also increasing their corporate valuation. For example, as Monsanto has been able to bring several applications through the FDA process in the US within one year because of its improved skills in knowledge management, its valuation as perceived by the market has increased noticeably. We are beginning to suspect there is a strong interconnection between values, valuing, value and valuation, which will play an increasingly important role in our business environment. But much more study is needed in this area.

Conclusion

In this short chapter we have covered many topics relating to 'knowledge', all closely interrelated with one another. We need an approach where academia and business work closely in what might be called an 'action research learning and implementation' approach. It would be wonderful to have master's and doctoral theses in many of these areas where the issues are probed deeply, but within the larger context. If our brief set of questions has helped uncover some of the relevant themes, we feel we have accomplished our purpose. This work needs a deep foundation, because we are building the basis for the next economy which may well last the next 200 or 2000 years. In this chapter we have posed more questions than answers, and we would like to invite researchers to consider the range of interrelated topics which are emerging as we move towards the knowledge era. It would be wonderful to tap the intellectual capabilities of the next generation to rebuild the foundations of our economies.

References

Bateson, G. (1972) *Steps to an Ecology of Mind*. New York: Dutton.

Bertels, T. and Walz, H. (1995) *Das intelligente Unternehmen: schneller lernen als der Wettbewerb*. Landsberg am Lech: Moderne Industrie.

Bridges, W. (1994) *Jobshift: How to Prosper in a Workplace without Jobs*. Reading, MA: Addison-Wesley.

Burrus, D. and Gittines, R. (1993) *Technotrends: 24 Technologien, die unser Leben revolutionieren werden*. Wien: Ueberreuter.

Hall, B. (1993) *Values Shift*. Rockport, MA: Twin Lights.

Handy, C. (1990) *The Age of Unreason*. Boston, MA: Harvard Business School Press.

Kolind, L. (1994) Thinking the unthinkable: the Oticon revolution. *Focus on Change Management*, 3: 7–9.

Nonaka, I. (1991) The knowledge-creating company. *Harvard Business Review*, November–December: 96–104.

Nonaka, I. and Takeuchi, H. (1995) *The Knowledge-Creating Company: How Japanese Companies Create the Dynamics of Innovation*. New York: Oxford University Press.

Savage, C.M. (1996) *Fifth Generation Management: Co-Creating through Virtual Enterprising, Dynamic Teaming and Knowledge Networking*. Newton, MA: Butterworth-Heinemann.

Skandia (1995) Renewal and development: intellectual capital. Supplement to Skandia's *1995 Interim Report*.

Smith, A. (1987) *The Wealth of Nations*. London: Dent.

Stewart, T.A. (1991) Brainpower: how intellectual capital is becoming America's most valuable asset. *Fortune*, 3 June: 44–60.

Stewart, T.A. (1994) Your company's most valuable asset: intellectual capital. *Fortune*, 3 October: 68–74.

Warnecke, H. (1993) *Die fraktale Fabrik: Revolution der Unternehmenskultur*. Berlin: Springer.

Warnecke, H. (1995) *Aufbruch zum Fraktalen Unternehmen: Praxisbeispiele für neues Denken und Handeln*. Berlin: Springer.

2

FUTURE RESEARCH INTO KNOWLEDGE MANAGEMENT

Markus Venzin, Georg von Krogh and Johan Roos

In this chapter we pursue two goals. First, we aim at giving the reader an overview of the concept of knowledge within the management literature. We thereby concentrate on four major layers. We start by explaining why the concept of knowledge is important for strategic management. Then we explore the basic assumptions about knowledge and knowledge development. Three different epistemologies are outlined that enable us to better understand the various contributions to knowledge. Based on these epistemological distinctions, we then proceed to explore various categories and applications of knowledge.

The second goal of this chapter is to give an example of 'contextualized' research on knowledge. We will show how the previously mentioned four layers are closely connected to each other. Contextualizing theory building therefore is a research methodology that pays homage to this close link between epistemological assumptions, knowledge appearances, knowledge applications, and the question of why the issue of knowledge is addressed. Isolated statements about one of these four layers have to be treated with caution. As an example, we will take the concept of 'tacit' knowledge and show on the basis of three articles how this knowledge category is closely linked to each layer and how it is influenced and modified, depending on the epistemological assumptions the articles are based on.

Nonaka and Takeuchi (1995) will be used to explain some of the autopoietic assumptions, whereas Simon's (1993) article is marked by more cognitivistic assumptions. The connectionistic epistemology will be clarified by the work of Kogut and Zander (1992; Zander and Kogut, 1995). We will show how it is often problematic to place an entire article in one of the epistemologies described. Hence, we see the three epistemologies as a continuum, knowing that most articles cannot be

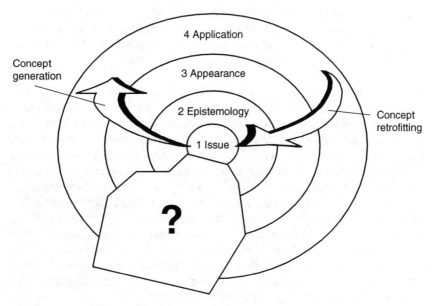

Figure 2.1   *Generic research map*

attributed solely to one epistemology. We chose these examples to illustrate how differences in epistemological assumptions influence the appearance and the application of knowledge.

Resulting from this chapter is a research map (see Figure 2.1) that facilitates further theory building on the concept of knowledge within the field of strategic management. It is a generic tool for other academic work that contextualizes arguments as to why the issue of knowledge is important, with underlying epistemological assumptions, knowledge appearances and applications.

Contextualized Theory Building

Contextualizing theory building means revealing and clarifying the research issues, the epistemological origins of the concepts discussed, and their appearances and applications. Activities of concept creation and retrofitting alternate; while 'walking on the research map', new concepts have to be consistent with the researcher's epistemology and legitimated by a research issue. If an existing concept is used, it has to be carefully retrofitted, which means that application, appearance, epistemology and the issue as such have to be matched with one's own work. This notion of retrofitting further expands the work done by von Krogh and Roos who perceive retrofitting as 'making ideas adjust to old design principles' (1996b: 730). Representing a modest effort to push the field in the direction of more intensive research on the concept of knowledge, this chapter suggests the four-step approach illustrated in Figure 2.1. Theory building consists of exploring the research issue, the epistemological roots, the appearances and the applications.

STEP 1: ISSUE   Knowledge as a theoretical issue has to be explored. Researchers have to explain why it becomes increasingly important to carry out research on knowledge within the field of strategic management. The goal is to validate the need to adapt strategic management theory to the contemporary challenges of a knowledge-based economy. Resulting from step 1 are research questions that steer further theory building. This chapter suggests six reasons why strategic management would profit from exploring the concept of knowledge. Mostly implicitly, the research interests are closely tied to epistemological assumptions. Consequently, researchers have to position themselves in step 2 within the epistemologies to be able to see the limitations of their own ways of thinking and to gain inspiration for new, interesting research questions derived from other epistemological areas. This constant alternation is a sustainable source for further theory building.

STEP 2: EPISTEMOLOGY   Theory building requires a careful investigation of fundamental assumptions. We claim that before researching into the concept of knowledge itself, the process of knowledge development has to be explored by revealing its epistemological roots. We argue that concepts take different forms depending on the epistemology they are based on. To understand these basic assumptions, on which the concepts and theories addressed are based, is therefore essential for new concept generation, but also for the integration and comparison of existing concepts, which will be shown by means of articles by Simon (1993), Zander and Kogut (1995) and Nonaka (1994).

STEP 3: APPEARANCE   Here the appearance of knowledge, or how previous studies have conceived of knowledge in strategic management studies, is discussed. By 'appearance', we mean the different forms that knowledge can take, expressed by numerous adjectives of knowledge (e.g. tacit, explicit, embedded, social or encoded). These appearances differ fundamentally between the three epistemologies. We will outline these differences by means of one example: we will retrofit the concept of 'tacit knowledge'. We argue that in respect of this concept the articles researched can be clearly positioned, except the article by Herbert Simon, where tacit knowledge is not explicitly mentioned. In that case, it has to be explored to what extent knowledge in the cognitivistic epistemology might be tacit, and how this is expressed.

STEP 4: APPLICATION   It has to be explored how the concept of knowledge is applied to the field of strategic management. Currently, we are experiencing an explosion of knowledge management approaches, which are partly contradictory in their results. The diverging managerial responsibilities that result from the three epistemologies may serve as an example: most cognitivist studies consider the identification, collection and central dissemination of information as the main knowledge development activity. The connectionists, on the other hand, believe that knowledge resides in the connections and hence focus on the self-organized dispersed information flow. Contrary to the previous two epistemological lines of thought, autopoietic epistemology stresses the interpretation and not the gathering of information as a major managerial responsibility. Consequently, strategic models differ fundamentally, because they are partly based on different epistemological assumptions, and aim at structuring different issues. We will see how different notions of 'tacit knowledge' (Polanyi, 1958; 1966) result in different ways to transfer knowledge, because they are based on distinct epistemologies and the studies address different issues.

Both the retrofitting and the generation of concepts would benefit from discussion of these four steps. The question mark in Figure 2.1 stands for the undiscovered area of the map that has to be revealed while working with ('walking on') the map. This can be done by new concept creation (e.g. new research streams in cognitive science or philosophy). A considerable potential for theory building lies in the retrofitting of concepts. By taking existing concepts and retrofitting them within a different epistemology, the map is expanded. We argue that careful retrofitting of existing concepts adds more value to the understanding of knowledge in strategic management than the uncontextualized invention of more and more new concepts.

The research methodology presented in this chapter represents an opportunity to structure the academic conversation about knowledge and strategy. The various concepts can be related to each other, which makes them comparable. Again, transparency is vital. It is then up to each individual to decide in what situations one or the other epistemology might be more appropriate. The following sections attempt to draw the research map focusing on knowledge in strategic management, and to show how researchers may use a small part of the map while researching strategic management in the knowledge era. The overview of the tables presented is given in Figure 2.2.

Strategizing in the Knowledge Economy

Recent contributions to the field of strategic management have pointed out that 'knowledge', in one form or another, is of central importance to the development of sustainable competitive advantage of companies. But why is knowledge an issue in strategic management, and how can it

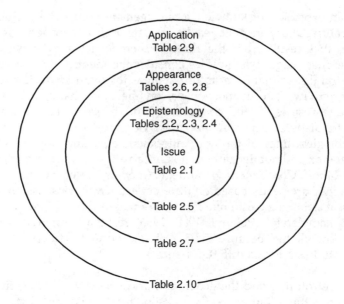

Figure 2.2   *Overview of tables in Chapter 2*

potentially influence the field? In order to be able to answer this question, it is of great importance to integrate the economic and sociological perspectives, because only both together create a profound understanding of the nature of the knowledge society (Stehr, 1994).

The following arguments are intended to move the concept of knowledge from an exogenous variable in economic analysis to an endogenous one, while at the same time shedding more light on the potential for strategic management scholars to rethink the role of knowledge in their own work according to their very own epistemology. In sum, knowledge is important for the theoretical realm of strategic management for the following six reasons (and possibly more).

Knowledge Implies Sustainable, Heterogeneous Resource Distribution

As mentioned in the first chapter, strategic management has been dominated by an external factors approach which attributed more significance to a company's environment than to the company itself. Over the last 15 years, however, researchers in the field have brought a second point of reference into focus: 'the resource-based view' (Selznik, 1957; Penrose, 1959; Mahoney and Pandian, 1992). This approach, mostly viewed as complementary to the 'environment-based view' (Hamel and Heene, 1994a; Henderson and Cockburn, 1994), explains competitive advantage as a result not of product–market positions but of differences in equipment and combinations of critical organizational resources (Wernerfelt,

1984; Dierickx and Cool, 1989; Amit and Schoemaker, 1993). This theoretical view allows for sustainable differences in resource endowment,
since there are certain resources that are in limited supply for a company
(Peteraf, 1993). Characteristics for such resources are that they are hard
to substitute, imitate and transfer (Barney, 1991). Owing to the complex
and idiosyncratic nature of knowledge, which we will elaborate more
profoundly below, strategy development based on the company's valuable knowledge is likely to lead to sustainable competitive advantage.

The increased relevance of intangible resources, and knowledge in
particular, for sustainable differentiation has led to an explosion of new
publications on knowledge and knowledge management. Knowledge
measurement is a good example of a new branch in the field of strategic
management. Eccles (1991) pointed out the importance of knowledge
measurement: he described the trend towards qualitative performance
measurement tools (innovation, personnel, customer satisfaction etc.)
instead of mere financial evaluation. Kaplan and Norton (1992; 1993)
expanded upon this idea and introduced with their 'balanced scorecard' an instrument which combines performance measurements from
different perspectives (i.e. knowledge development perspective, customer perspective and financial perspective). The Swedish insurance
company Skandia was inspired by this idea and developed its own
instrument to evaluate their intellectual and financial assets: the 'Business Navigator' (Skandia, 1994; Brooking, 1996). Since then, much effort
has been devoted to research on the measurement of (core) competences
(Klavans, 1994; McGrath et al., 1995), of abilities (Klein and Hiscocks,
1994) and of technological knowledge (Bohn, 1994), and on the meaning
of employee know-how and other 'intangible resources' (Hall, 1992;
1993).

Besides the measurement of knowledge, other research questions arise
from the observation that knowledge implies sustainable, heterogeneous
resource distribution. How long is competitive advantage 'sustainable'?
How can investments in knowledge be passed on to stakeholders? How
can they be informed about the value of the hidden assets? What is the
future role of traditional resources? Who owns intangible resources?
Where is the balance between knowledge exploitation and development? To what extent can alliances promote the development of unique
knowledge combinations? How quickly can new knowledge be
developed?

Knowledge Changes the Nature of Resource Investment Decisions

The above research questions point in one direction: how can intangible
resources be managed? How can we know what knowledge we have
and what we will need in the future? The low predictability of the
impact that knowledge has on the performance of an economy leads to
the question of how these resource bundles that are connected with

knowledge might be observed and understood. Friedrich von Hayek (1975: 434) pleads for distinct scientific methods to approach complex phenomena (he refers to markets) that can hardly ever be fully known or measured. He argues that in most cases it is enough to develop 'imperfect true knowledge' (1975: 438) about a phenomenon that is characterized by organized complexity (i.e. the character of the structure depends not only on the properties of the individual elements and their relative frequency of occurrence, but also on their interconnections). Hayek suggests focusing on mere pattern predictions 'of some of the general attributes of the structures that will form themselves, but not containing specific statements about the individual elements of which the structures will be made up' (1975: 436).

Consequently, strategic management needs new tools to see emergent patterns in knowledge endowments. A company has to be able to identify current knowledge inside and outside the company, and to decide upon knowledge development projects. Strategic knowledge management will be of high importance, because the formation of knowledge is a lengthy process, which brings us directly to the next point. Decisions on investments in particular knowledge areas are increasingly difficult to make, because knowledge is only partly transferable or tradable.

Path Dependency in the Knowledge Economy Increases

Path dependency refers to the phenomenon that organizations are restricted in their evolutionary scope. Past decisions and actions to a large extent prescribe the future development of the company. We argued that resource endowment in the knowledge economy is sustainable, heterogeneous and reinforced through positive feedback. This means that it is very difficult for companies to develop fundamentally new resources. The probability increases that the economy will gradually lock itself 'into an outcome not necessarily superior to alternatives, not easily altered, and not entirely predictable in advance' (Arthur, 1989: 128). Leonard-Barton (1992) observed that excellence in the dominant discipline (e.g. marketing) reinforces the development of this particular field, but at the same time inhibits the development of other expertise (e.g. technology). A similar argument is outlined in Cohen and Levinthal's (1990) study on 'absorptive capacity' in which the authors show that innovative performance is path-dependent. They argue that an early lack of investment in an area of expertise may foreclose the future development of a technical capability in that area (1990: 128).

Although increased path dependency leads to a narrower set of options, on the other hand it lends increased importance to strategic management. Because the company is, at least on the knowledge level, path-dependent, it is more important to blaze a trail in advance. New ways to cope with the increased danger of being locked onto a specific path have to be further explored, e.g. experimentation (Leonard-Barton, 1995). The ability to recognize, imagine and create patterns, and thus to develop knowledge foresight, may be the distinguishing factor in a knowledge economy, because it stakes out *ex ante* limits to competition' (Peteraf, 1993).

Knowledge Triggers Positive Feedback Loops Rather Than Negative Ones

As already mentioned, classical economic theory is based on the assumption of diminishing returns resulting in predictable equilibrium for prices and market shares, yet the parts of the economy that are knowledge-based are largely subject to increasing returns (Arthur, 1994: 3). Increasing returns therefore allow for a variety of possible equilibrium points. The challenge in the knowledge society therefore is to select a path that may lead to a *preferred* equilibrium point, knowing that the 'best' solution from an economic and technical point of view is not always the most successful.

A second implication of the increased importance of knowledge is that the positive feedback mechanisms widen the gap in the two-class society, i.e. between knowledge workers and blue-collar workers (Drucker, 1994). The more knowledge one has, the faster it will develop. The traditional conceptual distinction between the three economic sectors becomes more and more obsolete. What will be more important to study is the emergence of a social division into blue-collar and knowledge workers. Consequently, Reich (1991: 174) sees the future of work in three distinct categories: routine production services, in-person services and symbolic-analytic services. We need to understand how knowledge-based work differs from material-based work (Drucker, 1986), and how organizational forms may change and so influence strategic decisions.

Knowledge Changes the Nature of Work and Property

In the past decades, our societies have experienced a shift towards the post-industrial society (Bell, 1973). Inherent in the terms 'postmodernism', 'post-capitalism' or 'post-industrial society', is the suggestion that a crisis, a radical break or a *coupure* (Jameson, 1992) in existing concepts triggers the creation of something entirely new. 'Most *goods* purchased are intended to provide a service or a function, and there are few "pure" *services* unconnected to certain commodities' (Stehr, 1994: 135, italics his). The partial replacement of traditional resources by knowledge gives rise to new work forms.

Property is distributed and not identical with the possession of objects. Rather it is increasingly intangible and invisible (1994: 84). This shift weakens Marx's criticism of the division of labour (and his concept of the revolutionary reserve) because the critical resources reside to a large extent in the individuals themselves. Furthermore, as the benefits from knowledge start to surpass the benefits from physical capital (Lane, 1991: 415), the attempts to measure and evaluate knowledge have been intensified (Stewart, 1994). But the more widely complex knowledge is distributed among loosely connected workforces, the more difficult becomes the attribution of intellectual property to any individual owner. Intellectual property is often controlled by corporate actors, and cannot be sold, given away or inherited (Stehr, 1994: 85).

This embeddedness of individual knowledge in the corporate knowledge system explains the importance of continuous employment. Both employee and employer benefit from a close and sustainable work relationship, because it encourages the development of firm-specific knowledge (i.e. knowledge that is valid only within a specific company). This particular knowledge type enables the firm to differentiate itself from the competitors and hence generates competitive advantage. On the other hand, the emphasis on firm-specific knowledge forces the employee into dependence on the employer, because the most important asset that the employee could offer to a new employer would in most cases be firm-specific knowledge. Hence, the responsibility of managers in the knowledge economy is to ensure the employability of the organizational members instead of guaranteeing them lifelong employment. Employees need to be given the opportunity to acquire knowledge that is not only valuable within one firm. If knowledge is the most important asset, companies attract the best knowledge workers only if they offer them interesting knowledge development projects that increase their value on the job market (von Krogh and Venzin, 1997).

Knowledge Emphasizes the Social Context

Although the ownership of knowledge is not entirely confined to the individual, the number of institutions which create meaning (and knowledge) in any society has increased. Whereas in the Middle Ages the Church and some Greek philosophical texts were the most important sources for the creation of meaning, nowadays individuals draw on different sources when they interpret events, and by doing so create knowledge. 'Meaning is the result of *my* explanation of past lived experiences which are grasped reflectively from an actual now and from an actually valid reference schema' (Schutz and Luckmann, 1974: 16, emphasis added).

Thus, we move away from controlled 'production' of meaning through a few institutions towards a pluralistic, self-referential and context-sensitive way of meaning creation. As knowledge develops through the social creation of new meanings of concepts, it has lost its universal character. Today, we have to cope with conflicting and often paradoxical knowledge, leading to the phenomenon that in a knowledge society the number of 'best' solutions to well-defined problems decreases. In some situations it will be very difficult to attain a shared *meaning* of an issue, because meanings are idiosyncratic: they develop over time and are related to prior experience. 'If people want to share meaning, then they need to talk about their shared experience in close proximity to its occurrence and hammer out a common way to encode it and talk about it' (Weick, 1995: 188).

Consequently, one might argue that strategic processes involve a broad group of organizational members. Yet they engage in meaning creation within small teams that have the possibility to establish common ground.

Table 2.1   *Strategic issues in the knowledge economy*

Issue 1	Knowledge implies sustainable, heterogeneous resource distribution
Issue 2	Knowledge changes the nature of resource investment decisions
Issue 3	Path dependency in the knowledge economy increases
Issue 4	Knowledge triggers positive feedback loops rather than negative ones
Issue 5	Knowledge changes the nature of work and property
Issue 6	Knowledge emphasizes the social context

To sum up, the emergent importance of knowledge as a source of competitive advantage summarized in Table 2.1 makes it necessary to rethink strategic concepts fundamentally. The link between knowledge and strategy has to be further developed, because the nature of knowledge is different from that of traditional resources. Knowledge cannot be fully owned by the company: it is not easy to transfer or to imitate, it is context-sensitive and it is observer-dependent. Existing strategic tools that partly claim to have universal relevance to all industries and managerial situations are of limited use. Strategic management theory needs to explore new ways of observing emergent equilibrium points of a resource that cannot be fully measured or described. Thereby, decisions on knowledge development and exploitation are facilitated. Being the intellectual leader does not necessarily also mean being ahead of one's competitors. Timing of exploitation and exploration of knowledge becomes increasingly important, because there is no single equilibrium point that can be targeted.

Uncovering Epistemological Assumptions

Given that the concept of knowledge is so important for strategic management theory, we have to advance our understanding of the nature of knowledge and knowledge processes as described in the following quotation:

> Knowledge is constituted by the ways in which people categorize, code, process and impute meaning to their experiences. . . . Knowledge emerges out

of a complex process involving social, situational, cultural and institutional factors. The process takes place on the basis of existing conceptual frameworks and procedures and is affected by various social contingencies, such as skills, orientations, experiences, interests, resources and patterns of social interaction characteristic of the particular group or interacting set of individuals, as well as those of the wider audience. (Arce and Long, 1992)

Frank Blackler (1995) presents different categories of knowledge which all describe the nature of knowledge but refer back to the process by which it was acquired. Encultured knowledge, for example, refers to the process of achieving shared understandings (1995: 1024), whereas embodied knowledge is acquired by doing and requires physical presence. Hence, in order to grasp the nature of knowledge, it is first of all important to understand the *process of knowledge development*. This section provides a brief introduction to the most influential contributions to epistemology that have shaped management thinking.

Reasons to Discuss Epistemological Assumptions

Differences in the personal epistemology are manifested in different ways to categorize knowledge, such as the use of different analytical techniques, and/or different ways to define the boundaries of the processes of knowledge development. By uncovering the epistemological roots of current strategic management theories, we hope to bridge over controversial discussions about the nature and practices of strategy as mentioned in the previous section. Hence, besides the importance of epistemology for contextualized theory building, we study epistemological assumptions for several other, more practice-oriented, reasons.

First, understanding epistemological assumptions ensures effective knowledge management. The managerial tools and practices employed in a company have to match the specific nature of knowledge (von Krogh and Roos, 1996a). As knowledge becomes more and more important in our society, the ability to manage knowledge is critical: 'In order to manage knowledge assets, we need not merely to identify them but to understand them – in depth – in all their complexity: where they exist, how they grow or atrophy, how managers' actions affect their viability' (Leonard-Barton, 1995: xii).

Distinct managerial responsibilities and practices arise from each epistemology. *Consequently, being familiar with a different possible epistemology means having a larger knowledge management repertoire, and a better understanding of the limitations of each approach.*

Second, because knowledge development is contingent (i.e. dependent on the context), researchers as well as managers need to interpret and understand changes in corporate epistemology. Individuals and organizations can hardly be assigned to one single way of knowing. Distinct epistemologies emerge from the connection to a specific task or situation. Knowing more about existing epistemologies facilitates understanding of the context. Following Deborah Tannen's (1995) work on conversational styles, we support her plea for mutual understanding of a different way of developing knowledge rather than to obtrude on one's epistemology. *Knowing more about the current epistemological mode, and that of the co-worker, will decrease misunderstandings.*

Third, if we are able to recognize different epistemologies, we might also be able to choose a distinct mode depending on the current situation. We claim that – similarly to the active choice of a speech style – it is also possible to choose and apply a distinct epistemology. Mary Crawford states that 'speakers do not speak in a vacuum. They attempt to choose language that will "work" interactionally. Their use of language is situational and strategic. And what "works" depends on the social status of the speaker and the power relations between speaker and listener' (1995: 44). Hence, ways of thinking can be assigned to specific tasks, or vice versa. *The conscious choice of an epistemological mode is a critical success factor for research and management.*

In the rest of this section, we would like to help the reader to reflect upon his or her own epistemology, and in turn to assess the epistemology of others in order to contextualize, better understand, and retrofit contributions in the field of strategic management. This facilitates the ongoing conversation within the strategy research community, and may generate a mutual understanding for other epistemologies.

The epistemological distinction that we suggest as a basis for positioning, concept development and retrofitting is based on the contributions of Varela et al. (1991) and von Krogh and Roos (1995b). These authors refer back to cognitive science because it has been most influential for scientists studying organizational knowledge – although it has not yet been established as a mature science (Varela et al., 1991: 4). Also, building as it does on neuroscience, biology, philosophy, linguistics, artificial intelligence and cognitive psychology, cognitive science combines insights from various fields. The distinctions made by cognitive science allow for a positioning within distinct epistemological areas. The following sections will provide a brief overview of the three epistemologies discussed in Varela et al. (1991), and von Krogh and Roos (1995b). To keep the overview parsimonious we assumed that the claims made are valid on several organizational levels, from the individual to the industry.

Cognitivist Epistemology

The beginning of cognitivist epistemology can be traced back to the mid 1950s, when Herbert Simon, Noam Chomsky, Marvin Minsky, John McCarthy and others developed a particular way of knowing. Organizations are considered to be open systems which develop knowledge by formulating increasingly accurate 'representations' of their pre-defined worlds. Because knowledge is seen as a representation of these worlds, data accumulation and dissemination are the major knowledge development activities in organizations: the more data organizations can gather, the closer the representation will be to reality. *Hence, most cognitivist approaches equate knowledge with information and data.*

When gathering information from the external environment the brain stores *facts*, relates them to existing experiences and creates a picture of the world. The world is considered to be a pre-given object, event or state which can be perceived in an objectivistic way. What varies from one person to another is the ability to represent reality. The 'truth' of knowledge is understood as the degree to which inner representations correspond to the world outside. As new things are learned, this 'truth' will be constantly improved. Learning in the traditional epistemology means taking information from the environment and relating it to the previously acquired frames of reference, to the cognitive map (Varela, 1979). This is the way in which representations can be improved. Because the cognitivists view the human brain – and the organization – 'as a "machine" of logic and deduction' (von Krogh and Roos, 1995b: 14), knowledge is believed to be developed by processing incoming data according to 'universal' rules. The whole organization essentially follows the same 'login gate' as a mainframe computer, which consists of various propositions using 'if . . . then', 'not', 'and', and 'or' as connections for statements or propositions. The cognitivistic profile is summarized in Table 2.2.

EXAMPLE: SIMON   In the article by Herbert Simon (1993) the properties of the cognitivistic epistemology are – in our view – predominant. He states that in order to survive in an uncertain world, companies have to anticipate the shape of the future, generate alternative options for effective operation, and implement new plans rapidly and efficiently (1993: 134). The first step – the anticipation of the future – calls for representation: 'anticipation is of value to the degree that it is as accurate as, or more accurate than, the anticipation of the other players, and accompanied by implementation as effective as theirs or more effective' (1993: 136). Accuracy is an important concept in Simon's work. This shows that he somehow refers to a pre-given world that has to be portrayed as precisely as possible in order to ensure a solid basis for action. Therefore, as many data as possible have to be gathered – as early as possible: 'If a prospective major factor is detected early, and monitored as it approaches closer to realization, estimates of lead times can be modified, and planning and preparation times change accordingly' (1993: 134).

Once the world is represented, the generation of alternatives has to follow certain rules: 'One severe test of a theory of alternative generation or design is to see whether the theory can be converted into a computer program that carries out the process automatically and successfully' (1993: 138). Simon substitutes intuition or subjective insights by objective, explicit data (e.g. customer databases, memos, codified rules, experience

Table 2.2 *Cognitivistic profile*

Profile criteria	Theoretical statement	Managerial statement
View of one's own organization	'An organization works like a mainframe computer; it is open for information that is collected and stored centrally. Action is steered by the "main frame" of the top management.'	*Marketing manager*: 'Our company is formed by the founder. He still makes the important decisions.'
Perception of the environment, and positioning in it	'The environment is pre-given. The main task for the organization is to represent/ picture it and to adapt to it universally.'	*Head of strategy department*: 'I am responsible for depicting the actual situation and for developing options for the top management.'
Notion of knowledge	'Knowledge is a fixed and representable entity (data) universally stored in computers, databases, archives and manuals. Knowledge can be easily shared across the organization.'	*Human resource manager to a new employee*: 'We have a large documentation of what our knowledge is. If you spend some time reading it, you will understand how the company works.'
Knowledge development	'The cognitivist develops knowledge through the assimilation and dissemination of incoming information. Inner representations that partly or fully correspond to the outer world are created.'	*Head of research*: 'The number of new patents is our most important indicator for our knowledge development. We have to bargain for knowledge.'
Characteristics of truth	'Truth is the degree to which our inner representations correspond to the world outside. Truth is defined as dependent on the amount of information.'	*Employee*: 'The more information we have, the more truth we have.'

reports, books, manuals or policy descriptions). He does not distinguish between data, information and knowledge, or between 'to be informed' and 'to know' (1993: 135). The implementation process as described by Simon makes it even clearer that the organization operates according to universal rules that have to be reinforced continually. These rules have one main frame of reference: the top management. Herbert Simon talks about the 'absorption of strategic plans' (1993: 141) – which means that it is possible to reach consensus about policies and to *implant* 'them firmly in the hundreds of heads' (1993: 139).

Connectionistic Epistemology

Representationism as it has been described in the cognitivist epistemology is still prevalent in the connectionistic epistemology, but the process of representing reality is different. In connectionism, the rules on how to process information are not universal, they vary locally. Organizations are seen as self-organized networks composed of relationships, and driven by communication. The main method in the connectionistic epistemology is to look at relationships and not to focus on the individual or the entire system. Thus, the connectionist's models are built up on a large number of interacting units that are able to influence one another by sending activation signals down interconnecting pathways. Organizations are seen as networks.

Like the cognitivists, the connectionists consider information processing the basic activity of the system. The connectionists see the process of shaping an organization as dependent not only on the stimuli entering the system but also on the system itself. Relationships and communication are the most important issues of cognition. Another essential difference between these two cognitive models is that the connectionists make no distinction between structures that store information and others that process information. Both functions are embodied in the connections between the units. Organizational knowledge is a state in a system of interconnected individuals. Thus, the number of connections, the dynamics of the information flow, and the capacity to store this information characterize the network (which is similar to a computer network). The rules of these connections therefore form an essential part of knowledge. The connectionistic profile is summarized in Table 2.3.

EXAMPLE: ZANDER AND KOGUT   Zander and Kogut (1995) suggest that knowledge of the firm 'can be characterized into "information" and "know-how". It consists of the competence of the individuals and of the organizing principles by which relationships among individuals, groups, and members to an industrial network are structured and coordinated' (1995: 77). Information, as the authors describe it in an earlier article (Kogut and Zander, 1992: 386), stands for knowledge which can be transmitted without loss of integrity once the syntactical rules required for deciphering it are known. Know-how, on the other hand, is a description of knowing how to do something. Put differently, knowledge is 'held by the individual, but is also expressed in regularities by which members cooperate in a social community' (1992: 383).

Consequently, Kogut and Zander (1992) argue that firms exist only because they are better at transferring and sharing knowledge than the market. In other words, organizations can make more accurate representations of the environment, because they can process and store a higher amount of data than an individual: 'Firms exist because they provide a social community of voluntaristic action structured by organizing principles that are not reducible to individuals' (1992: 384). Kogut and Zander differ from the cognitivists because they believe that these rules may vary throughout the company: 'It is the persistence in the organizing of social relationships in which knowledge is embedded' (1992:

Table 2.3   *Connectionistic profile*

Profile criteria	Theoretical statement	Managerial statement
View of one's own organization	'The virtual organization consists of individuals who are connected mostly through information technology. Action is self-organized and steered by local rules that refer to several frames of reference.'	*Treasurer*: 'The key feature of our company is the strong network that allows us to solve complex problems.'
Perception of the environment, and positioning in it	'Clusters of the organizational network produce different pictures of the pre-given world that form the basis for a differentiated adaptation.'	*CFO*: 'We analyse the different regional market trends in our company. The different financial goals of our subunits are set according to these results.'
Notion of knowledge	'Knowledge resides in the connections of experts and is problem-solution oriented. Knowledge is dependent on the state of the network of interconnected components.'	*CEO*: 'My knowledge has developed through the interaction with others, mostly over ICT. If I lost my laptop, I guess that I would lose about 70% of my knowledge.'
Knowledge development	'Local rules in a network of individuals determine how knowledge is accumulated. This allows self-organized groups to develop specific knowledge in order to represent their own environment.'	*Sales manager*: 'I develop knowledge by establishing new connections and thereby extending my network. I have to bargain for a central position in the network.'
Characteristics of truth	'Different experts who have accumulated information about parts of the objective reality bargain about the truth.'	*CEO*: 'Our experts define what we consider to be the truth in our company.'

385). Further they state that 'it is the sharing of a common stock of knowledge, both technical and organizational, that facilitates the transfer of knowledge within groups' (1992: 389). Hence, the capability of sharing knowledge throughout the company is dependent on existing knowledge that is shared. In order to increase the knowledge transfer capacity, Kogut and Zander suggest developing higher-order organizing principles that act as mechanisms by which technologies can be codified into a language accessible to a wider circle of individuals (1992: 389).

Autopoietic Epistemology

Autopoietic epistemology provides a fundamentally different under-standing of the input coming from outside a system. Input is regarded not as information, but as data, the smallest units of potential informa-tion. Information itself is data put into a certain context. It is the first process step by which knowledge is acquired. Thus, autopoietic systems are simultaneously open and closed: open with regard to data, but closed to information and knowledge. Knowledge cannot be directly conveyed from one individual to another, because data have to be interpreted. Signals from outside can stimulate processes within the system, but they always follow the self-defined rules of the system. To be operationally closed regarding information is the central aspect of an autopoietic system that organizes itself. The boundaries of the system are defined by these rules. Thus, only data can pass these frontiers.

As an example, Maturana and Varela (1980) take the cell as a living system that is self-referring, which means that the cell is an autonomous entity where everything happens in reference to itself (Varela et al., 1991: 121). Components of the cell produce other components which produce the units that produced them. The membrane is the border of the cell that limits the diffusion. By doing so, the membrane facilitates the internal production which keeps the membrane alive. This cycle of self-production characterizes the theory of autopoiesis, a name derived from the Greek words *auto* (self) and *poiesis/poein* (production). The auto-poietic profile is summarized in Table 2.4.

EXAMPLE: NONAKA AND TAKEUCHI   The analysis of the epistemological assumptions of Nonaka and Takeuchi (1995) results in their being positioned closer to the autopoietic epistemology: in their work, the world is not perceived as a fixed and objective entity, for it is not possible to represent reality. Nonaka and Takeuchi state that 'Japanese intellectual tradition suggests that ultimate reality for the Japanese lies in the delicate, transitional process of permanent flux, and in visible and concrete matter, rather than in eternal, unchanging, invisible and abstract entity' (1995: 31–2). The organization is seen as a living organism rather than a machine for processing information (1995: 9). In contrast to 'Western thinking', Nonaka and Takeuchi explain how the Japanese intellectual tradition focuses on the 'oneness' of humanity and nature, body and mind, and the self and other. The 'oneness' between humanity and nature expressed in the Japanese language and their flexible view of time and space 'clearly illustrates a Japanese tendency to deal with sensitive emotional movements rather than to abide by any fixed worldview or metaphysics' (1995: 29). Hence, the world in this view is not pre-given as in the previous epistemologies.

The denial of the separation between mind and body leads to the emphasis on physical experience. That means that each individual has to *create* his or her own knowledge through experience: formal data lose their determinative role in knowledge creation. Knowledge is perceived as 'justified true belief' (1995: 21).[1] Inherent in this definition is the rejection of the assumption that 'truthfulness' is the major attribute of knowledge, as it is to be found in the epistemologies previously outlined. Two additional characteristics of knowledge are added. First, by

Table 2.4 *Autopoietic profile*

Profile criteria	Theoretical statement	Managerial statement
View of one's own organization	'The autopoietic company is an autonomous and observing system that is simultaneously open for data but closed for information. It is a group of individuals who have created an emergent frame of reference.'	*Human resource manager*: 'Everybody in our organization is a free agent. We try to develop opportunities and support the organizational members by putting them into action.'
Perception of the environment, and positioning in it	'The world is brought forth in conversations. The environment and the organization are coevolving systems.'	CEO: 'We try to create new businesses/industries, and we are constantly searching for discontinuity as a source of innovation.'
Notion of knowledge	'Knowledge resides in mind, body, and the social system. It is observer- and history-dependent, context-sensitive and not directly shared, only indirectly through discussions.'	*Controller*: 'Our knowledge is private. We respect each other as individuals who have undergone different experiences and who come from different cultures.'
Knowledge development	'The process of interpreting incoming data in conversations is the cornerstone in knowledge development. This enables the autopoietic systems to make distinctions and to create meaning according to observations and previous experiences.'	*Production employee*: 'From time to time we talk about our production processes and allocate a considerable part of our time to developing knowledge about other activities. I have to make an effort to gain inspiration from others.'
Characteristics of truth	'Truth is not a main issue. By accepting that there is not an objective reality, different standpoints are possible. Reality is socially created.'	*Secretary*: 'We all create our own reality. There are many truths in our company – and they are respected by everyone.'

considering knowledge to be a personal or social 'belief' the subjective character of knowledge is highlighted. In order to be knowledge, a statement must be true (objective truth), and in addition, individuals have to believe that it is true (subjective attitude towards the truth). Hence, the 'belief condition' reveals the individual attitude towards knowledge (e.g. a statement/proposition) which denies the existence of one true representation of reality. Second, the 'justification condition' requires sources of evidence of truth. By distinguishing between the traditional epistemology and the theory of knowledge creation, 'the former naturally emphasizes the absolute, static, and non-human nature of knowledge, typically expressed in propositional forms in formal logic, whereas the latter sees knowledge as a dynamic human process of justifying personal beliefs as part of an aspiration of "truth"' (Nonaka,

1994: 15). Hence, knowledge has to be validated, although it is known that absolute 'truth' can never be attained.

Relating Emerging Knowledge Strategy Issues to the Epistemologies

What we have attempted to show in this section is that cognitivistic, connectionistic and autopoietic epistemologies vary in their perceptions of concepts like 'organization', 'knowledge' and 'truth'. These differences allow of the positioning of scientific contributions within these epistemologies. Tables 2.2, 2.3 and 2.4 summarized the three epistemologies and aimed at supporting the positioning of new statements within these epistemologies. Practical statements are distinguished from theoretical statements to show the relevance of epistemological profiling for academics as well as for managers. Table 2.5 in turn reveals how the issues presented in the previous section vary in their very nature depending on their epistemological assumptions.

Issue 1 (i.e. knowledge implies sustainable, heterogeneous resource distribution), for example, takes a different shape in scientific contributions that can be positioned within the cognitivistic epistemology compared with work based on connectionistic or autopoietic epistemological assumptions. From a *cognitivistic point of view*, knowledge is a fixed and representable entity (data) universally stored in computers, databases, archives and manuals. This in turn implies that knowledge can be easily shared within the organization, and across organizational boundaries. Hence, from a cognitivistic viewpoint, issue 1 has little relevance, i.e. sustainable differences in the resource endowment hardly exist, because it is not very difficult to transfer and imitate knowledge.

For the *connectionists*, knowledge resides in the expert links. Knowledge is dependent on the state of the network of interconnected components. Local rules in a network of individuals determine how knowledge is accumulated. Barriers to the transfer of knowledge would essentially come from the lack of knowledge about the expert network resulting in inefficient search rules. Kogut and Zander (1992), for example, consequently focus on the importance and at the same time on the difficulties of discovering the procedural rules that are needed to reveal the required data hidden somewhere in the organization. Now, using the words of Kogut and Zander, one might say that it is more difficult for another organization to discover the procedural rules of a targeted competitor, and therefore knowledge can imply sustainable heterogeneous resource endowment. In addition, it is not very likely to succeed in transferring knowledge by transferring single individuals, because knowledge resides in the connections between experts. This might also explain why investment companies, for example, started to entice away entire teams from their competitors.

From an *autopoietic viewpoint*, knowledge is always private and is never 100% equal from one individual to another. Hence, sustainable

Table 2.5 *Retrofitting emerging knowledge strategy issues*

	Cognitivistic epistemology	Connectionistic epistemology	Autopoietic epistemology
Issue 1 Knowledge implies sustainable, heterogeneous resource distribution	There is no significant impact of knowledge on the heterogeneity of the resource distribution, because knowledge can be transferred as easily as a commodity. It is accessible for all companies in the same way	Knowledge implies sustainable heterogeneous resource endowment, because the search rules and the connections are not directly accessible to competitors	Knowledge implies sustainable heterogeneous resource endowment because knowledge is individually created by a process of internalization and externalization
Issue 2 Knowledge changes the nature of resource investment decisions	Knowledge is visible and easy to measure. Resource allocation decisions for knowledge development projects are therefore similar to investment decisions made in more tangible areas	It is not easy to observe the knowledge status and flow in organizations. Resource allocation decisions therefore have to include effects on the dynamic knowledge links within and outside an organization	It is not easy to evaluate knowledge and knowledge development, because it is not directly observable. Resource allocation decisions for knowledge development therefore cannot always be made explicit, and they are hard to communicate
Issue 3 Path dependency in the knowledge economy increases	Because knowledge is easy to transfer, path dependency does not necessarily increase in the knowledge economy. If a company wants to change the path, new knowledge can be easily bought from outside	Path dependency increases in the knowledge economy, because it takes more time to redirect the development or transfer of resources, i.e. to identify and change the network with its locally varying dynamics	As knowledge is deeply idiosyncratic and hard to transfer or imitate, path dependency increases in an economy where knowledge is the decisive production factor

continued overleaf

Table 2.5 (cont.)

	Cognitivistic epistemology	Connectionistic epistemology	Autopoietic epistemology
Issue 4 Knowledge triggers positive feedback loops rather than negative ones	It is most probable that along with an increasing amount of knowledge comes a position/task assignment closer to the main frame (i.e. top management), which in turn would lead to a increased access to data flows	The more knowledge a company has, the more links have been established that in turn reveal several other connections in the expert network. Thus, a new connection potentially triggers positive feedback	Knowledge triggers positive feedback loops as new distinctions enable the autopoietic system to make further observations, which in turn leads to new distinctions
Issue 5 Knowledge changes the nature of work and property	Because knowledge is seen as a commodity that can be identified, measured and traded, neither the nature of property nor the nature of work changes	If organizations are seen as a network of experts who are more or less replaceable, more flexible work forms gain in impact, and organizational and industry boundaries vanish. Knowledge can only be partially revealed, and property therefore depends on the accessibility of one's own knowledge	As knowledge resides in the individual and is to a large extent tacit (i.e. it cannot be articulated and transformed into structural capital), property is distributed, and long-term physical and emotional experiences in groups become more important
Issue 6 Knowledge emphasizes the social context	Knowledge is universal and is not context-dependent	Knowledge is partly dependent on the context: the state of the network	Knowledge is individually developed, and meaning creation is dependent on previous experiences and the current situation

differences in resource (knowledge) distribution exist as organizations consist of a divergent group of individuals. To make these differences apparent in a competitive context, we need to explore to what extent individual knowledge is different from social knowledge, and in turn, to what extent it is less difficult to share knowledge with organizational members compared with individuals outside the organization. The example of the violin-maker Stradivarius shows that although he wanted to convey his knowledge about making a violin to his students, he never fully succeeded in doing so. Nonaka et al. (Nonaka, 1994; Nonaka and Takeuchi, 1995) describe the transfer of knowledge therefore as a process of internalization and externalization, where the student–teacher relationship in the form of an apprenticeship or work groups with physical experiences is stressed. Consequently, it is more difficult to transfer knowledge from organization to organization, because organizations normally do not work together in such an intensive way.[2]

Table 2.5 reveals the epistemological position of this chapter. The issues discussed in the previous section best conform to the autopoietic assumptions. The following section will show how differences in fundamental epistemological assumptions result in considerable variances in appearances and applications of knowledge, a subject which has already been briefly touched upon in the last few pages.

Knowledge Appearances

We start out by strengthening the connection between strategy and knowledge, by reviewing different appearances of knowledge, and knowledge-related concepts. As an example, 'tacit knowledge' will be retrofitted. As it might not be sufficient to identify appearances of knowledge, in order to understand and to manage knowledge the epistemological roots are explored in the following paragraphs. We show how retrofitting as a method works by means of the concept of 'tacit knowledge'.

Selected Categories of Knowledge

Various authors have elaborated with subtle distinctions on the concept of 'knowledge'.[3] This is a manifestation of the ongoing knowledge development on this issue. The variety of terms a language contains for certain aspects of life can serve as an indicator of the significance and the extent of knowledge in that field. The vocabulary of the Eskimo language, for example, contains about 40 different words for snow. There is no doubt that snow is an integral part of Eskimo life, since it is at times vital for them to know the exact category of snow they are confronted with. Table 2.6 lists a summary of frequently used categories of knowledge.[4]

Table 2.6   *Categories of knowledge*

References	Knowledge	Explanation
Polanyi (1958; 1966; 1969); Spender (1993)	Tacit	A person knows more than he can express in words (Polanyi). A painter, for example, cannot describe in detail how he goes about drafting a new picture. This category explores the development of knowledge as well as knowledge transfer relative to the interaction of explicit and tacit knowledge
Zuboff (1988); Blackler (1995); Nonaka and Takeuchi (1995); Collins (1993)	Embodied	Knowledge in this category results from experiences of physical presence (i.e. project work). The emphasis lies on the process of knowledge development. Prahalad and Bettis (1986) call this 'unique combinations of business experience'
Zuboff (1988); Blackler (1995); Collins (1993)	Encoded	Knowledge that remains in the company after all employees have gone home (Skandia, 1994), i.e. notebooks, data banks containing information on customers and employees, product catalogues, codified rules and regulations, itineraries, training materials, etc.
Blackler (1995); Prahalad and Bettis (1986); Argyris and Schön (1978); Fiol and Lyles (1985); Collins (1993)	Embrained	This category of knowledge depends on the cognitive abilities which allow of the recognition of underlying patterns (for example of a new industry), the reflection of basic assumptions (see 'dominant logic' by Prahalad and Bettis; and 'double loop learning' by Argyris and Schön or abstractions synthesizing
Berger and Luckmann (1966); Astley and Zammuto (1992); Brown and Duguid (1991); Badaracco (1991); Collins (1993)	Embedded	The emphasis lies on the process of knowledge construction. Knowledge is here embedded in a variety of contextual factors and not objectively pre-given. Shared knowledge is generated in different language systems, (organizational) cultures and (work) groups
	Event	This category describes knowledge of events but also trends within and outside the organization (for example, company A buys company B, or the number of accidents has dropped by 20%)
Zander and Kogut (1995); Bohn (1994); Winter (1987); Ryle (1958)	Procedural	Contrary to the knowledge of events, this category encompasses knowledge of processes and as opposed correlations. Examples include 'if . . . then' scenarios, knowledge of product processes or procedural knowledge, for example contract negotiations

Of course, the table is not a complete list. Researchers in the field of knowledge and knowledge management have created and used more terms than those mentioned. 'Strategic' knowledge is, for example, not listed in the table because it represents higher-order knowledge categories – 'meta-knowledge'. Strategic knowledge is knowledge about knowledge: where it is located, how it is stored, how it is transferred, what type of knowledge it is and how swiftly it changes over time. Reflection on knowledge develops strategic knowledge. .

The various definitions of knowledge from the last section may have given the reader an impression of how difficult it is to develop a definition of knowledge that is uniformly accepted in the management realm. Despite the many words employed to describe knowledge, it is often difficult to conduct a conversation about knowledge with these words. Winter (1987: 180) notes that words like information, innovation, transfer, diffusion, learning, knowledge and competence are parts of the realm of discourse, but are not really conducive to it. The differentiation between 'tacit knowledge' (Polanyi, 1966) and 'embodied knowledge' (Zuboff, 1988; Nonaka, 1991; Hedlund and Nonaka, 1992; Hedlund, 1994) may serve as an example. Embodied knowledge is only partially articulated and results from physical presence. Zuboff puts it this way:

> For it was also through the body's exertions that learning occurred and for those who were to become skilled workers, long years of physically demanding experience were an unavoidable requirement. . . . Where the skilled worker was concerned, the body's sentience was also highly structured by a felt knowledge of materials and procedures. (1988: 36)

Embodied knowledge refers more to the process of knowledge development, and where knowledge actually resides. Tacit knowledge, on the other hand, describes the more inherent attributes, the condition of the knowledge category, so to speak. A closer examination of the knowledge types led to the following four criteria for clustering the knowledge categories: objects of knowledge development; processes of knowledge development; location of knowledge; and knowledge-related concepts.

Clustering Knowledge Categories

Most commonly, knowledge is categorized according to the *object of knowledge development* (i.e. biotechnology, mathematics or linguistics). Procedural knowledge, for instance, encompasses knowledge of processes and correlation, which include 'if . . . then' scenarios, knowledge of product processes, or contract negotiations. Event knowledge is another example of this kind. It refers to knowledge of what happens within the environment (e.g. mergers, new legal restrictions, product launches) or within the company (e.g. purchase of new computers, company profile on Internet). On the meta-level, if knowledge itself becomes the object of knowledge development, we may find strategic knowledge concerning itself with questions like where specific knowledge can be found, how knowledge develops, or how knowledge is mediated.

In the literature on knowledge, categorizations can be found that put strong emphasis on the *process of knowledge development*. As mentioned at the beginning of the previous section, encultured knowledge is one example of this category, because it refers back to the process by which shared understandings have been achieved. Another example of a knowledge category that is closely related to the process by which knowledge is developed is embedded knowledge. As such, it is embedded in a variety of contextual factors, and is constructed by a social system. Shared knowledge is generated in different language systems, (organizational) cultures and (work) groups. If the context changes (e.g. culture), knowledge also changes. Concepts that can be summarized as embrained knowledge are other examples of this category. Embrained knowledge depends on the cognitive abilities which enable one to see underlying patterns (for example of a new industry), the reflection of basic assumptions (see 'dominant logic' by Prahalad and Bettis, 1986; and 'double loop learning' by Argyris and Schön, 1978), or abstractions and synthesizing.

Another way to approach the nature of knowledge is to research the *location of knowledge*. Although embodied knowledge also refers back to the process of how knowledge developed, namely through physical experiences, we put more emphasis on the result of this knowledge development process and categorize embodied knowledge under locations of knowledge. The reason is that the result of this physical knowledge development process is that the knowledge thereby created is partly tacit and therefore closely related to an ontological entity. Distinctions between individual, group, company, inter-company, customer or industry knowledge indicate the carrier of knowledge (Walsh, 1995). The same close connection to a specific location can be found in encoded knowledge. If knowledge is stored in some form in addition to the human body, we call this category encoded knowledge. If knowledge is encoded, it has been stored in some form (e.g. text, sound, graphics) and can be easily located (e.g. in notebooks, manuals, videotapes).

Retrofitting Knowledge Categories

The challenge that researchers face now is to retrofit the knowledge appearances they intend to borrow from other academics with their own work. This requires a careful exploration of the basic assumptions they are constructed on. The notion of 'tacit knowledge' may serve as an example. We chose tacit knowledge because we think that a profound understanding of this concept is essential for most researchers who explore the issues outlined earlier, and because our understanding of this form is so limited. Table 2.7 summarizes an attempt to retrofit the different knowledge categories with the epistemologies. Procedural and event knowledge have not been retrofitted, because we believe that objects of knowledge development do not fundamentally differ in nature except in one respect: within autopoietic epistemology, observations focus more on the collation of context data than in the other two epistemologies.

In the following we will briefly describe the first category of Table 2.7: tacit knowledge. The concept of tacit knowledge can be traced back to Michael Polanyi (1958; 1966; 1969) who suggested that individuals know more than they can say. Polanyi suggests that knowledge that can be expressed is only a small part of the whole body of knowledge.

EXAMPLE: SIMON   Herbert Simon has been positioned in the cognitivistic realm, where tacit knowledge is not explicitly mentioned. As we understand his work, there is no knowledge that cannot be codified. Hence, is it impossible to retrofit the concept of tacit knowledge with cognitivistic epistemology? Is there any knowledge that cannot be made explicit from a cognitivistic point of view? Here we have the chance to expand the research map: if the organization works like a computer, one might speculate that tacit knowledge exists if the amount of data is too high and too complex to be presented on one screen. Even though data are available in fragments, it is not possible for the system to connect the various parts. Imagine a map containing some information about a region: roads, religions, precipitation, topography, languages, political orientation, population. If the map is well designed, it might still be possible to retrieve the information required. But at some point, a map will not be able to represent all available information. Hence, the tacit dimension of knowledge – in the cognitivistic epistemology – might be rooted in the limitations of analogue data perception.

EXAMPLE: KOGUT AND ZANDER   Kogut and Zander (1992) adapted Polanyi's work to connectionistic assumptions. They rephrased Polanyi's well-known statement and argue that: 'organizations know more than contracts can say. The analysis of what organizations are should be grounded in the understanding of what they know how to do' (1992: 383). Further, they state that:

> an interpretation of his [Polanyi's] argument is that tacit knowledge consists of search rules, or heuristics, that identify the problem and the elements consisting of the solution (Polanyi, 1966, pp. 23–24). The act of solving a problem rests on a sense of how the phenomena function; the formal

Table 2.7 *Retrofitting knowledge categories*

	Cognitivistic epistemology	Connectionistic epistemology	Autopoietic epistemology
Tacit knowledge	Knowledge is not very likely to be tacit. Only if the amount of data is too high and complex for a representation by some means, might it be the case that knowledge is only partially explicit	Knowledge can be tacit if the search rules for knowledge that hide somewhere in the organization are not fully transparent	Tacit knowledge is physical and subjective, being created in a specific practical context. It can only be partly conveyed by processes comparable to master–apprentice relations
Embodied knowledge	All knowledge can be gained without practical experience, only through cognitive learning; this category is not of high importance	All knowledge can be gained without practical experience, only through cognitive learning: this category is not of high importance	As knowledge resides in mind, body and the social system, bodily experiences are of high importance
Encoded knowledge	It is possible to encode 100% of existing knowledge	It is possible to encode 100% of existing knowledge	Encoded knowledge represents only a small part of existing knowledge
Embrained knowledge	Embrained knowledge refers to the capacity to centrally collect data from within and outside the system, and to identify universal rules and patterns that influence this data flow	Embrained knowledge is the ability to identify and map the relevant network of interrelated components that influence one's own operations and to recognize the higher-order rules and dynamics of this network	Embrained knowledge refers to the ability to scale up, to observe experiences from various contexts, and to recognize patterns in the interpretation processes involved in these experiences
Embedded knowledge	Knowledge is universal, and embedded knowledge is therefore not a relevant knowledge category	Knowledge is embedded in a distinct state of the network of interconnected components of individuals	Embedded knowledge explains the phenomenon that knowledge changes its meaning across different cultural and contextual systems

expression of the solution is unlikely to capture fully this procedural knowledge, or even the data and information (or clues, as Polanyi describes it) leading to the solution. Thus, even in the arena of problem identification and solving, the know-how of heuristic search precedes the formal knowledge of the solution. (1992: 389)

From this quote, we learn that within the connectionistic view, tacit knowledge exists because the appropriate search rules cannot be revealed. In contrast to Nonaka, Kogut and Zander argue that it is 'unlikely' – but theoretically possible – that knowledge can be made entirely explicit. On the one hand, data have to be made explicit. The challenge to articulate knowledge might reside in the difficulties of grasping data in their very nature, which shows that they are close to – or even partly in – the autopoietic epistemology. They abandon the idea that the human brain works like a computer and admit that there might be parts that cannot be codified. From an autopoietic point of view, there is some knowledge that can never be entirely conveyed to others, because the sum of experiences that an individual undergoes throughout time is unique. The knowledge created resides partly in the body. But on the other hand, the authors do not further investigate this. Instead, they stress the importance of discovering the procedural rules that are needed to reveal the required data hidden somewhere in the organization.

EXAMPLE: NONAKA AND TAKEUCHI   The way in which Nonaka characterizes tacit knowledge is very much in line with Polanyi's original notion: knowledge of experience tends to be tacit, physical and subjective, since it is created in a specific practical context and has analogue qualities. Analogue processes are typically found in the master–apprentice relationship, where the student shares the experience of his teacher by carrying out the same task at the same time. Nonaka differs from Polanyi in the way power is perceived. In Nonaka's work, the relationship between the master and the apprentice is not described as determined by authority, as is the case with Polanyi. For Nonaka, power and authority are not major issues.

After having studied the underlying assumptions of the different appearances of knowledge, the next step is to identify these appearances in their hidden forms. In management literature, knowledge often appears wrapped up in *related constructs* as shown in Table 2.8, such as competence, invisible assets, intangible assets, strategic assets, absorptive capacity, architectural competence, organizational memory, capabilities, and skills. In most contributions to the strategic management literature, authors use several of these concepts simultaneously, and often interchangeably, or without clearly distinguishing and retrofitting them.

Table 2.8   *Knowledge-related constructs*

References	Construct	Explanation
Itami and Roehl (1987); Skandia (1994)	Invisible assets, intellectual capital	Resources based on information (i.e. customer trust, trade name, distribution control, organizational culture, capacity of management)
Hall (1992; 1993; 1994)	Intangible resources	Intangible assets which can belong to a legal person are distinguished from capabilities (competences can here be used as a synonym) which are not easily transferable (i.e. the know-how of the employees, suppliers and customers, and the culture of the organization)
Amit and Schoemaker (1993); Winter (1987)	Strategic assets	Combination of resources and capabilities which are difficult to imitate or transfer, rare, appropriate and specialized to generate competitive advantage in the organization
Cohen and Levinthal (1990)	Absorptive capacity	A firm's capacity to develop new knowledge in interaction with its environment
Henderson and Cockburn (1994)	Architectural competence	Ability to integrate new knowledge into the organization
Prahalad and Hamel (1990); Hamel and Heene (1994b); Rumelt (1994)	Core competences	Combination of abilities and technology which is based on explicit and tacit knowledge and characterized by durable stability and cross-product influence. Moreover, core competences create value for the customer, are unique among competitors, allow of access to new markets, are not easily imitable or transferable and are synergetically linked to other competences
Walsh and Ungson (1991); Pautzke (1989); Lyles and Schwenk (1992)	Organizational memory	Capacity for storing organizational knowledge (in knowledge structures)
Zander and Kogut (1995); Amit and Schoemaker (1993); Stalk et al. (1992); Grant (1991)	(Core) capabilities	Capacity of an organization to use resources. It is based on organizational principles which structure, coordinate and communicate knowledge
Aaker (1989); Klein et al. (1991)	Skills	'Capabilities' and 'competences' are often used synonymously and refer to social systems. 'Skills' describe the individual capabilities on which competences are based

Knowledge Applications

Currently, we are experiencing an explosion of knowledge management approaches and themes. In this section, we will not discuss each category in detail. Instead, we will focus on the knowledge application 'knowledge transfer' which is retrofitted with the previously presented various notions of tacit knowledge in the articles by Simon, Kogut and Zander, and Nonaka.

Selected Knowledge Applications

Based on the observations from the previous section, Table 2.9 categorizes knowledge applications. By the term 'knowledge application' we refer to the way knowledge is managed, and applied to the field of strategic management.

Retrofitting Knowledge Applications

The brief overview of knowledge applications might have given the reader an impression of how broad the emerging area of knowledge management is. An intensive discussion of all applications would exceed the scope of this chapter. We limit the following discussion therefore to retrofitting the application 'knowledge transfer' with the category 'tacit knowledge'.

EXAMPLE: SIMON   The cognitivists established quite a clear-cut understanding of how knowledge is transferred. Data – as a synonym for knowledge – can be transferred from one element of the system (e.g. individuals in an organization) to another with a controlled, computable loss of content. Because data are universal, specific characteristics of the sender, the receiver or the context do not change the content of data. In Herbert Simon's article, it is stated that in order 'to be effective, a mission statement or a description of the organization's comparative advantage must become part of the mind-set of every member of the organization who is responsible for making or helping to make decisions of any consequence' (1993: 138). Only if knowledge, for example 'a few concise documents' (1993: 139), has been firmly implanted in the heads of the organization, can a shared understanding (or consensus) of the fundamental concepts be reached. This is necessary if an organization is to be effective and efficient: 'A new member of the organization has not been assimilated successfully until he or she has acquired the concept of what the organization is seeking to accomplish and how it proposes to go about it' (1993: 138–9).

EXAMPLE: KOGUT AND ZANDER   From a connectionistic point of view, knowledge transfer (information processing) in an organization is determined not only by stimuli from the environment, but also by stimuli

Table 2.9   *Selected knowledge applications*

References	Research focus	Explanation
Nonaka (1991; 1994); Nonaka and Takeuchi (1995); Hedlund (1994); Hedlund and Nonaka (1992); Gomez and Probst (1995); von Krogh and Venzin (1995)	Knowledge management models	Different epistemological and ontological dimensions are integrated into phased models. These describe both processes of knowledge development and their impact on organizational activities
von Krogh and Roos (1995a; 1995b); Astley and Zammuto (1992); Brown and Duguid (1991); Kogut and Zander (1992); Müller-Stewens and Pautzke (1991)	Knowledge, conversations and cooperation	Knowledge is developed over language and symbolic communication. Conversations and the modes of cooperation therefore significantly influence the process of knowledge development
Eccles (1991); Kaplan and Norton (1992; 1993); Stewart (1994); Skandia (1994)	Knowledge measurement and evaluation	The tendency is towards measuring qualitative constructs mainly related to the evaluation of existing, task-specific knowledge. The significance of knowledge evaluation evolved from its merely communicative function for the shareholders into a strategic instrument
Badaracco (1991); Winter (1987); Richter and Vettel (1995); Hamel (1991); Zander and Kogut (1995); Reed and DeFillippi (1990); Amit and Schoemaker (1993); Black and Boal (1994)	Knowledge transfer	Two themes dominate the literature: intended knowledge transfer and imitation of knowledge by competitors. Main points of research are knowledge classifications according to transferability, codification of knowledge, as well as the dilemma of simultaneous transfer and imitation
Huff (1990); Walsh and Ungson (1991); Lyles and Schwenk (1992); Sandelands and Stablein (1987); Weick and Roberts (1993); Pautzke (1989); Walsh (1995)	Knowledge and cognition	Representation, acquisition, storage and retrieval of knowledge in organizations are expanded upon
Winograd and Flores (1986); Zuboff (1988); Davenport (1989); Davenport et al. (1989; 1992); Blackler et al. (1993); Scarborough (1993)	Knowledge and information technology	Points of focus are the impact of 'new' information and communication technologies on knowledge development in virtual organizations, the effects of mechanisms of control and organizational structures, and the management of incoming information

Table 2.9 *(cont.)*

References	Research focus	Explanation
Pfeffer (1981; 1992); Lane (1991); Gergen (1995); Hosking (1995); Ibarra (1993)	Knowledge and power	Explores the influence of power on the legitimization of knowledge. It is discussed to what extent existing power structures determine what knowledge is accepted as 'real'. Power therefore does not necessarily influence the search for truth in a negative way, but it definitely is an important factor in the construction of 'reality'
Perry (1993); Knights et al. (1993); Kiesler and Sproull (1982); Tushman and Moore (1988)	Knowledge, networks and innovation	Examines the cooperation of experts in physically separated networks aimed at generating innovation. Topics are the application of IT and the role of trust and power

from the organization itself. As opposed to the cognitivist viewpoint, data are not thought to be processed by universal rules. Local differences in the rules *and* the stock of knowledge may exist. Hence, the transfer of knowledge requires a shared stock of knowledge, shared language, shared coding schemes and a set of common values that facilitate the transfer of knowledge within groups (Kogut and Zander, 1992).

Whereas from the cognitivistic viewpoint knowledge transfer is independent of prior knowledge and knowledge process rules, the connectionists look upon these organizational features as the central aspect. Kogut and Zander distinguish, as already described, between information and know-how. Information 'implies knowing what something means' and 'can be transmitted without loss of integrity once the syntactical rules required for deciphering it are known' (1992: 386). Know-how 'is a description of what defines current practice inside a firm' (1992: 387). Kogut and Zander therefore mention two dimensions that strongly influence the transferability of knowledge: codifiability and complexity. The former refers to the firm's ability to structure knowledge into a set of identifiable rules and relationships that can be easily communicated (1992: 387), the latter to the number of operations required to solve a task (1992: 388). Further, the authors state that complexity can be accommodated at a certain cost (1992: 388).

Even though it is sometimes hard to codify and manage the complexity of knowledge, Kogut and Zander assume that it is always possible to transfer knowledge without loss. They argue that knowledge is socially constructed, and this embeddedness of knowledge in social relationships is what makes knowledge sometimes not easily transferable.[5] Hence, the major managerial task is to establish a set of higher-

order organizing principles that act as codification mechanisms of technologies into a language accessible to a wider circle of individuals (1992:
389). Once the information process rules are known (i.e. a way has been
found to articulate tacit knowledge), knowledge can be easily transferred.

EXAMPLE: NONAKA AND TAKEUCHI   Moving away from a representatio-
nistic way of thinking, autopoietic epistemology provides a different
understanding of how knowledge may be transferred. Knowledge
develops in an autonomous manner for the human being because it is
not abstract, and thus cannot be transferred directly to other people (von
Krogh and Roos, 1995a: 50). The embodiment of knowledge – a key
property of knowledge in the autopoietic epistemology – is the reason
why knowledge has its tacit dimension, which can never be made
entirely explicit.

Consequently, Nonaka and Takeuchi (1995) use the word 'conversion'
instead of 'transfer' of knowledge. Because knowledge cannot be directly
transferred, it is always created anew. Knowledge conversion has four
different dimensions: socialization (from tacit to tacit knowledge), externalization (from tacit to explicit knowledge), internalization (from
explicit to tacit knowledge) and combination (from explicit to explicit
knowledge). Nonaka and Takeuchi stress the relational aspect in knowledge conversion: 'It should be noted that this conversion is a "social"
process *between* individuals and not confined *within* an individual' (1995:
61, emphasis theirs). Even in the case of knowledge combination, new
knowledge is created because explicit knowledge is combined with other
explicit knowledge: it is a process of systematizing concepts into a
knowledge system (1995: 67). In the other three conversion modes,
physical experience and interpretation of data play a key role.

Table 2.10 summarizes an attempt to retrofit a selected knowledge
management activity (knowledge transfer) with the concept of tacit
knowledge. This table is a further exploration of what has been written
in the previous text. A specific kind of knowledge (tacit knowledge) is
retrofitted. To gain a more comprehensive picture of the generic research
map on knowledge in the field of strategic management, other rows
would have to be added to Table 2.10 retrofitting the concept of tacit
knowledge within the other knowledge applications. In addition, new
tables like 2.10 would be needed, dealing with the other knowledge
categories mentioned in Table 2.6 instead of the category of tacit knowledge. However, it can be said that because knowledge, and tacit
knowledge in particular, has a different definition within the three
epistemologies, knowledge is differently applied. Cognitivists fuel the
organization with data and process them according to universal rules.
The connectionists stress the importance of shared information processing rules, and create higher-order organizing principles to ensure

Table 2.10 *Retrofitting the knowledge application 'knowledge transfer' with the concept 'trait knowledge'*

	Cognitivistic epistemology	Connectionistic epistemology	Autopoietic epistemology
Knowledge transfer	Because knowledge might be tacit owing to a lack of representation capacity, the transfer of tacit knowledge would imply raising the representation capacity or the redefinition of data selection mechanisms. Tacit knowledge is thereby made explicit and is then easy to transfer	Knowledge transfer can be facilitated by the identification of key experts in the network who have mastered the search rules in their area. Knowledge that has been hidden (tacit) in the organization can thereby be accessed and transferred	Tacit knowledge is only partly transferable. Intensive bodily experiences in work forms such as master–apprentice relations may facilitate the transfer of explicit knowledge

the connection between different self-organizing subunits. Researchers who argue within autopoietic assumptions reject the notion that knowledge can be transferred. Hence, they focus on shared experiences through mainly face-to-face conversations (Nonaka and Takeuchi, 1995: 85).

Advancing Research on Knowledge in the Field of Strategic Management

Given the transformation into a knowledge economy, many current strategic management theories and practices are, to put it baldly, bent on a course of self-destruction. The numerous special issues, articles and books questioning the relevance of theories for companies; the recent focus on 'new sciences' and philosophy as sources of inspiration; and the many new ideas emerging from managers rather than business school professors, are some indicators of the gradual demise of strategic management theory as we know it. The logic is straightforward: if knowledge is the key to competitiveness, which it seems to be in an increasing number of companies, industries, industrial networks, countries and regions of the world, then strategic management theories and practices must incorporate epistemological considerations.

But we are not in search of a universal epistemology. Instead, we argue that strategic management theory needs to consider different epistemologies at the same time in order to understand how an organization knows in different contexts. We argue that considerable efforts should be made to advance strategic management within autopoietic assumptions, and thereby complement existing theories. We believe that value could be added to our understanding of what strategy means in the knowledge economy by taking an anti-representationistic viewpoint. We do not plead for one epistemology as 'the best'. Instead, we argue that autopoietic assumptions within the field of strategic management have long been neglected, and this one-sidedness has implications. We attempted to show that the appearance of knowledge (e.g. tacit knowledge) and the application of knowledge (e.g. transfer – or conversion – of knowledge) strongly depend on the epistemological assumptions these concepts are based on.

The academic challenge thus consists of three parts. First, the epistemological assumptions of a scientific contribution have to be made explicit. Researchers have to position themselves within the epistemological continuum: cognitivistic, connectionistic and autopoietic epistemology. It is often not easy to position one's work clearly within one of these epistemologies. Also, we do not insist upon one epistemology as being superior to others. Some phenomena might be better understood and explained within the cognitivistic epistemology – but some are not, and so call for a new epistemology. Second, researchers have to retrofit the knowledge-related concepts they borrow from other epistemological areas. We have shown how the concept of 'tacit knowledge' may be retrofitted with the different epistemologies. This process is essential in order to grasp the explanatory limits of the concepts researched in the current epistemology. Third, because most strategic theories and practices still rest on the assumptions of knowledge inherited from the industrial era, advances in this realm call for a new epistemology. We outlined the basic ideas of the autopoietic epistemology, which is a venture in this direction that has to be further developed. But where does the inspiration for such a development come from?

The development of different epistemologies within the realm of strategic management has strong implications for empirical research – because methodology is intimately connected with epistemology. The managerial and business issues involving knowledge require research methods that allow us to observe and interpret social processes in organization at leisure over long periods of time. Inevitably, this leads us to ethnography to obtain dense descriptions. And when scholars acknowledge the Heisenbergian link between the observer and the observed, the step to fully fledged action research is a short one. Then, as scholars, we might realize that we cannot observe knowing managers, just our relationship with these managers in a relational context. The observer is thus absorbed into the observed. The article by von Krogh et al. (1994) was a step in this direction. The authors labelled their methodology a 'matching process' between the two professors' 'grand theory' of autopoiesis, and the businessman's 'local theory' of strategic management. More than two years of intensive conversations unified their languages, i.e. the concepts and meaning of these, into one language system that was used to convey their message. But we urge the reader to go further along this route. This implies, of course, that scholarly journals also face 'relevance extinction' unless they move beyond today's self-validating practices, and strive for this transition by contextualized theory building.

We think that the discussion in this chapter concerns everyone: a claim that a researcher has no epistemology would only reveal an epistemology that does not include self-awareness. This would be unfortunate, since the knowledge economy, as we have discussed above, increasingly probes for *the researcher's* view of knowledge. In this chapter, we have tried not to promote one of the three epistemologies. Rather, we plead for a pluralistic view on different ways of knowing. Epistemological positioning and retrofitting will facilitate scientific (and managerial) conversations. Knowing more about the epistemological assumptions of the conversation partner may increase mutual under-standing. From our point of view, the academic challenge is to develop epistemological profiles (i.e. positioning of concepts such as 'organiza-tion', 'knowledge', 'environment', 'truth', 'power' within the three epis-temologies) within scientific contributions before using the concepts in one's own work. In sum, it is important to discuss the epistemological assumptions *before* the appearances and applications of a concept.

Notes

1 The authors refer back to Plato. The discussion about the analysis of knowledge will be continued in Chapter 5.

2 In Japan there are a few exceptional firms that send some employees out to their customers or suppliers to work in their factories in order to share their knowledge.

3 We attempt to categorize knowledge concepts to facilitate the discussion on knowledge management. The proposed categories might enable the reader to see patterns in the theoretical contributions and to link existing concepts. However, we are aware of the risk that those categories, and the way the authors are assigned to them, have a tentative character.

4 A more inclusive overview of knowledge categories can be found in Blackler (1993; 1995), Collins (1993) or Winter (1987).

5 Even though the authors refer to the work of Berger and Luckmann (1966), it would interesting to further explore how Kogut and Zander retrofitted the concept of 'social constructivism', from an anti-representationistic world-view to representationism.

References

Aaker, D.A. (1989) Managing assets and skills: the key to a sustainable com-petitive advantage. *California Management Review*, 31 (2): 91–106.

Amit, R. and Schoemaker, P.J.H. (1993) Strategic assets and organizational rent. *Strategic Management Journal*, 14: 33–46.

Arce, A. and Long, N. (1992) The dynamics of knowledge: interfaces between bureaucrats and peasants, in N. Long and A. Long (eds), *Battlefields of Knowledge: the Interlocking of Theory and Practice in Social Research and Development*. New York: Routledge. pp. 211–46.

Argyris, C. and Schön, D.A. (1978) *Organizational Learning: a Theory of Action Perspective*. Reading, MA: Addison-Wesley.

Arthur, B. (1989) Competing technologies, increasing returns, and lock-in by historical events. *The Economic Journal*, 99 (March): 116–31.

Arthur, B. (1994) *Increasing Returns and Path Dependence in the Economy*. Ann Arbor: University of Michigan Press.

Astley, G. and Zammuto, R. (1992) Organization science, managers, and language games. *Organization Science*, 3 (4): 443–60.

Badaracco, J.L. (1991) *Knowledge Link: How Firms Compete through Strategic Alliances*. Boston, MA: Harvard Business School Press.

Barney, J.B. (1991) Firm resources and sustained competitive advantage. *Journal of Management*, 17: 99–120.

Bell, D. (1973) *The Coming of Post-Industrial Society*. New York: Basic Books.

Berger, P. and Luckmann, T. (1966) *The Social Construction of Reality: a Treatise in the Sociology of Knowledge*. London: Penguin.

Black, J. and Boal, K. (1994) Strategic resources: traits, configurations and paths to sustainable competitive advantage. *Strategic Management Journal*, 15: 131–48.

Blackler, F. (1993) Knowledge and the theory of organizations: organizations as activity systems and the reframing of management. *Journal of Management Studies*, November: 863–84.

Blackler, F. (1995) Knowledge, knowledge work and organizations: an overview and interpretation. *Organization Studies*, 16 (6): 1021–46.

Blackler, F., Reed, M. and Whitaker, A. (1993) Editorial introduction: knowledge workers and contemporary organizations. *Journal of Management Studies*, November: 851–62.

Bohn, R. (1994) Measuring and managing technological knowledge. *Sloan Management Review*, Fall: 61–73.

Brooking, A. (1996) *Intellectual Capital: Core Asset for the Third Millennium Enterprise*. London: International Thomson Business Press.

Brown, J.S. and Duguid, P. (1991) Organizational learning and communities-of-practice: toward a unified view of working, learning, and innovation. *Organization Science*, 2 (1): 40–57.

Cohen, W. and Levinthal, D. (1990) Absorptive capacity: a new perspective on learning and innovation. *Administrative Science Quarterly*, 35: 128–52.

Collins, H.M. (1993) The structure of knowledge. *Social Research*, 60 (1): 95–116.

Crawford, M. (1995) *Talking Difference: on Gender and Literature*. London: Sage.

Davenport, T. (1989) The case of the soft software proposal. *Harvard Business Review*, May–June: 12–24.

Davenport, T., Eccles, R. and Prusak, L. (1992) Information Politics. *Sloan Management Review*, Fall: 53–65.

Davenport, T., Hammer, M. and Metsisto, T. (1989) How executives can shape their company's information systems. *Harvard Business Review*, March–April: 130–4.

Dierickx, I. and Cool, K. (1989) Asset stock accumulation and sustainability of competitive advantage. *Management Science*, December: 1504–14.

Drucker, P. (1986) The changed world economy. *Foreign Affairs*, 64: 768–91.

Drucker, P. (1994) The age of social transformation. *The Atlantic Monthly*, 274 (5): 53–80.

Eccles, R. (1991) The performance measurement manifesto. *Harvard Business Review*, January–February: 131–37.

Fiol, C. and Lyles, M. (1985) Organizational learning. *Academy of Management Review*, 10: 803–13.

Foucault, M. (1978) *Der Wille zum Wissen*. Frankfurt am Main: Suhrkamp.

Gergen, K.J. (1995) Relational theory and the discourses of power, in D.-M. Hosing, H.P. Dachler and K.J. Gergen (eds), *Management and Organization: Relational Alternatives to Individualism*. Avebury: Aldershot. pp. 29–50.

Gomez, P. and Probst, J.B. (1995) *Die Praxis des Ganzheitlichen Problemlösens: vernetzt denken, unternehmerisch handeln, persönlich überzeugen*. Bern: Haupt.

Grant, R. (1991) The resource-based theory of competitive advantage: implications for strategy formulation. *California Management Review*, Spring: 114–35.

Hall, R. (1992) The strategic analysis of intangible resources. *Strategic Management Journal*, 13: 135–44.

Hall, R. (1993) A framework linking intangible resources and capabilities to sustainable competitive advantage. *Strategic Management Journal*, 14: 607–18.

Hall, R. (1994) Intangible sources of sustainable competitive advantage, in G. Hamel and A. Heene (eds), *Competence Based Competition*. Chichester: Wiley, pp. 149–69.

Hamel, G. (1991) Competition for competence and inter-partner learning within international strategic alliances. *Strategic Management Journal*, 12: 83–103.

Hamel, G. and Heene, A. (eds) (1994a) *Competence Based Competition*. Chichester: Wiley.

Hamel, G. and Heene, A. (1994b) Introduction: competing paradigms in strategic management, in G. Hamel and A. Heene (eds) *Competence Based Competition*. Chichester: Wiley. pp. 1–7.

Hedlund, G. (1994) A model of knowledge management and the N-form corporation. *Strategic Management Journal*, 15: 73–90.

Hedlund, G. and Nonaka, I. (1992) Models of knowledge management in the West and Japan, in P. Lorange, B. Chakravarthy, J. Roos and A. van de Ven (eds), *Strategic Processes: Learning, Adaptation and Innovation*. London: Basil Blackwell.

Henderson, R. and Cockburn, J. (1994) Measuring competence? Exploring firm effects in pharmaceutical research. *Strategic Management Journal*, 15: 63–84.

Hosking, D. (1995) Constructing power: entitative and relational approaches, in H.P. Dachler, D.M. Hosing and K. Gergen (eds), *A Relational Perspective of Organizing: Alternatives to Individualism*. New York: Avebury Aldershot.

Huff, A.S. (1990) *Mapping Strategic Thought*. Chichester: Wiley.

Ibarra, H. (1993) Network centrality, power, and innovation involvement: determinants of technical and administrative roles. *Academy of Management Journal*, 36 (3): 471–501.

Itami, H. and Roehl, T. (1987) *Mobilizing Invisible Assets*. Cambridge, MA: Harvard University Press.

Jameson, F. (1992) *Postmodernism, or, the Cultural Logic of Late Capitalism*. London: Verso.

Kaplan, R. and Norton, D. (1992) The balanced scorecard – measures that drive performance. *Harvard Business Review*, January–February: 71–9.

Kaplan, R. and Norton, D. (1993) Putting the balanced scorecard to work. *Harvard Business Review*, September–October: 134–47.

Kiesler, S. and Sproull, L. (1982) Managerial response to changing environments; perspectives on problem sensing from social cognition. *Administrative Science Quarterly*, 27 (December): 548–70.

Klavans, R. (1994) The measurement of a competitor's core competence, in G. Hamel and A. Heene (eds), *Competence Based Competition*. Chichester: Wiley, pp. 171–82.

Klein, J.A., Edge, G.M. and Kass, T. (1991) Skill-based competition. *Journal of General Management*, 16 (4): 1–15.

Klein, J.A. and Hiscocks, P.G. (1994) Competence-based competition: a practical toolkit, in G. Hamel and A. Heene (eds), *Competence Based Competition*. Chichester: Wiley. pp. 183–212.

Knights, D., Murray, F. and Hugh, W. (1993) Networking as knowledge work: a study of strategy development in the financial services industry. *Journal of Management Studies*, 30 (6): 975–95.

Kogut, B. and Zander, U. (1992) Knowledge of the firm, combinative capabilities, and the replication of technology. *Organization Science*, 383–97.

Lane, R. (1991) *The Market Experience*. Cambridge: Cambridge University Press.

Leonard-Barton, D. (1992) Core capabilities and core rigidities: a paradox in managing new product development. *Strategic Management Journal*, 13, Special Issue (Summer): 111–25.

Leonard-Barton, D. (1995) *Wellsprings of Knowledge*. Boston: Harvard Business School Press.

Lyles, M. and Schwenk, C. (1992) Top management, strategy and organizational knowledge structures. *Journal of Management Studies*, 29 (March): 155–74.

Mahoney, J.T. and Pandian, J.R. (1992) The resource-based view within the conversation of strategic management. *Strategic Management Journal*, 13 (5): 363–80.

Maturana, H. and Varela, F. (1980) *Autopoesis and Cognition: the Realization of the Living*. London: Reidl.

McGrath, G., MacMillan, I. and Venkatataman, S. (1995) Defining and developing competence: a strategic process paradigm. *Strategic Management Journal*, 16: 251–75.

Müller-Stewens, G. and Pautzke, G. (1991) Organisatorisches Lernen und Führungskräfteentwicklung, in T. Sattelberger (ed.), *Die Lernende Organisation*. Wiesbaden: Gabler. pp. 183–205.

Nonaka, I. (1991) The knowledge-creating company. *Harvard Business Review*, November–December: 96–104.

Nonaka, I. (1994) A dynamic theory of organizational knowledge creation. *Organization Science*, 5 (1): 14–37.

Nonaka, I. and Takeuchi, H. (1995) *The Knowledge-Creating Company: How Japanese Companies Create the Dynamics of Innovation*. New York: Oxford University Press.

Pautzke, G. (1989) *Die Evolution der organisatorischen Wissensbasis: Bausteine zu einer Theorie des organisatorischen Lernens*. Herrsching: Kirsch.

Varela, F. (1979) *Principles of Biological Autonomy*. Amsterdam: North-Holland.

Varela, F., Thompson, E. and Rosch, E. (1991) *Embodied Mind: Cognitive Science and Human Experience*. Cambridge, MA: MIT Press.

von Hayek, F.A. (1975) Pretence of knowledge. *Swedish Journal of Economics*, 433–42. Nobel Memorial Lecture held 11 December 1974.

von Krogh, G. and Roos, J. (1995a) Conversation management. *European Management Journal*, 13 (4): 390–4.

von Krogh, G. and Roos, J. (1995b) *Organizational Epistemology*. New York: Macmillan and St Martin's Press.

von Krogh, G. and Roos, J. (1996a) Five claims of knowing. *European Management Journal*, 14: 423–6.

von Krogh, G. and Roos, J. (1996b) A tale of the unfinished. *Strategic Management Journal*, 17: 729–37.

von Krogh, G., Roos, J. and Slocum, K. (1994) An essay on corporate epistemology. *Strategic Management Journal*, 15: 53–71.

von Krogh, G. and Venzin, M. (1995) Anhaltende Wettbewerbsvorteile durch Wissensmanagement. *Die Unternehmung*, 6: 417–36.

von Krogh, G. and Venzin, M. (1997) Chancen durch firmenunabhängiges Wissen: Erhöhte Beschäftigungsfähigkeit statt Arbeitsplatzsicherheit. *Neue Zürcher Zeitung*, 23. 28 January.

Walsh, J.P. (1995) Managerial and organizational cognition: notes from a trip down memory lane. *Organization Science*, 6 (May–June): 280–321.

Walsh, J.P. and Ungson, G.R. (1991) Organizational memory. *Academy of Management Review*, 16 (1): 57–91.

Weick, K.E. (1995) *Sensemaking in Organizations*. London: Sage.

Weick, K. and Roberts, H. (1993) Collective mind in organizations: heedful interrelating on flight decks. *Administrative Science Quarterly*, 38: 357–81.

Wernerfelt, B. (1984) A resource-based view of the firm. *Strategic Management Journal*, 5: 171–80.

Winograd, T. and Flores, F. (1986) *Understanding Computers and Cognition: a New Foundation for Design*. Norwood, NJ: Ablex.

Winter, S.G. (1987) Knowledge and competence as strategic assets, in D.J. Teece (ed.), *The Competitive Challenge: Strategies for Industrial Innovation and Renewal*. New York: Ballinger. pp. 159–84.

Zander, U. and Kogut, B. (1995) Knowledge and the speed of the transfer and imitation of organizational capabilities: an empirical test. *Organization Science*, 6 (1): 76–92.

Zuboff, S. (1988) *In the Age of the Smart Machine: the Future of Work and Power*. New York: Basic Books.

Penrose, E.T. (1959) *The Theory of the Growth of the Firm*. New York: Wiley.

Perry, N. (1993) Scientific communication, innovation networks and organization structures. *Journal of Management Studies*, 30 (6): 957–73.

Peteraf, M. (1993) The cornerstones of competitive advantage: a resource-based view. *Strategic Management Journal*, 14: 179–91.

Pfeffer, J. (1981) *Power in Organizations*. Marshfield: Pitman.

Pfeffer, J. (1992) *Managing with Power: Politics and Influence in Organizations*. Boston, MA: Harvard Business School Press.

Polanyi, M. (1958) *Personal Knowledge: towards a Post-Critical Philosophy*. Chicago: University of Chicago Press.

Polanyi, M. (1966) *The Tacit Dimension*. London: Routledge and Kegan Paul.

Polanyi, M. (1969) *Knowing and Being*. Chicago: University of Chicago Press.

Prahalad, C.K. and Bettis, R.A. (1986) The dominant logic: a new linkage between diversity and performance. *Strategic Management Journal*, 7: 485–501.

Prahalad, C.K. and Hamel, G. (1990) The core competence of the corporation. *Harvard Business Review*, May–June: 71–91.

Reed, R. and DeFillippi, R. (1990) Causal ambiguity, barriers to imitation, and sustainable competitive advantage. *Academy of Management Review*, 15: 88–102.

Reich, R.B. (1991) *The Work of Nations: Preparing Ourselves for 21st-Century Capitalism*. New York: Knopf.

Richter, F.J. and Vettel, K. (1995) Successful joint ventures in Japan: transferring knowledge through organizational learning. *Long Range Planning*, 28 (3): 37–45.

Rumelt, R. (1994) Foreword, in G. Hamel and A. Heene (eds), *Competence Based Competition*. Chichester: Wiley. pp. xv–xix.

Ryle, G. (1958) *The Concept of Mind*. London: Hutchinson.

Sandelands, L. and Stablein, R. (1987) The concept of organization mind, in S. Bacharach and N. DiTomaso (eds) *Research in the Sociology of Organizations*. Greenwich, CT: JAI Press. pp. 135–61.

Scarborough, H. (1993) Problem-solutions in the management of information systems expertise. *Journal of Management Studies*, 30 (6): 939–55.

Schutz, A. and Luckmann, T. (1974) *The Structures of the Life-World*. London: Heinemann.

Selznik, P. (1957) *Leadership in Administration: a Sociological Interpretation*. New York: Harper and Row.

Simon, H.A. (1993) Strategy and organizational evolution. *Strategic Management Journal*, 14: 131–42.

Skandia (1994) *Visualizing Intellectual Capital in Skandia*.

Spender, J.C. (1993) Competitive advantage from tacit knowledge? Unpacking the concept and its strategic implications. Working Paper, Graduate School of Management, Rutgers University.

Stalk, G., Evans, P. and Shudman, L. (1992) Competing on capabilities: the rules of corporate strategy. *Harvard Business Review*, March–April. 57–69.

Stehr, N. (1994) *Knowledge Societies*. London: Sage.

Stewart, T. (1994) Your company's most valuable asset: intellectual capital. *Fortune*, 11 (123): 42–60.

Tannen, D. (1995) The power of talk: who gets heard and why. *Harvard Business Review*, September–October: 138–48.

Tushman, M. and Moore, W. (eds) (1988) *Readings in the Management of Innovation*. New York: Harper Business.

3

KNOWLEDGE, ORGANIZATIONS AND COMPETITION

*Frank Blackler, Norman Crump and
Seonaidh McDonald*

Economic Changes and New Approaches to Management

The list of changes occurring in advanced economies is long. It includes the proliferation of centres of capital, the mutual interpenetration of regional economies, world-wide networks of communication based on advanced information and communication technologies, the emergence of 'global cities', trends towards a world-wide division of labour, a reduced role for governments in the redistribution of wealth, a weakening of trade unionism, and new approaches to management and organization.

A range of terms have been proposed to describe such trends, including 'post-Fordism' (Piore and Sabel, 1984), 'disorganized capitalism' (Lash and Urry, 1994), 'the informational mode of development' (Castells, 1989) and 'late modernity' (Giddens, 1990). While there are important differences in the detail of the explanations that different commentators suggest to account for these trends, there is widespread agreement that capitalism is moving into a new phase where the pace and extent of social change are greatly magnified. As Giddens explains in his account of the underlying dynamics of modernity, human activity has been, and is being, transformed by the mechanisms through which it is mediated. Activities have been disengaged from local contexts as people's sense of place and time has been dislocated from their immediate surroundings. Expertise has been abstracted from particular situations to be incorporated and developed within complex institutional, organizational and technological systems. New sources of meaning have been created (wealth, consumption, mobility) that differ fundamentally from those of traditional societies. The doubt that has been created from knowledge has undermined tradition as a guide to behaviour, and the self-awareness that is associated with this process continually provokes a search for new possibilities. Indeed, the internal dynamics of change which are a feature of contemporary societies have led to the emergence of economic and social systems that are extraordinarily complex. Giddens's image of modernity as a juggernaut that is out of control dramatically captures some of the dangers of this situation.

At the level of the organization the extent and pace of contemporary developments have provoked considerable interest in new approaches to organizing. Indeed it is not difficult to see how the developing pre-occupations of writers on organizational change have reflected broader social problems. From the mid 1960s to the mid 1970s the literature on organizational change focused on the need to manage *continuity*. Theorists argued that those affected by changes need to understand what was happening and that managerial decisions should be tempered by employee involvement. Concepts which were common within the management literature at this time included 'participation', 'leadership style' and 'motivation'. The focus was on feelings and relationships; organizational change was seen as an incremental process to ensure that changes should not be introduced in a way that would violate the core values and meanings of those involved. From the late 1970s to the late 1980s, however, the literature on organizational change developed in new ways. Economic problems in Europe and America had provoked an urgent search for new approaches to management and the key theme of this period was the management of *transition*. Common concepts during the 1980s included 'corporate culture', 'commitment' and 'trans-formative leadership'. The preoccupation was with strategic change and organizational redirection; the focus was on the power of symbols and the need to communicate a sense of mission that would rapidly move organizations from one paradigm of practice to another. In the 1990s, however, people began to find themselves less inclined to assume that one stable state will be replaced by another. The prospect of a future without certainty and of perpetual paradigmatic developments is being emphasized as commentators highlight the need to manage *continuing change*. Key concepts in the management literature at the present time include 'organizational learning', 'managing chaos' and, above all, 'knowledge management' and 'knowledge creation'. Esoteric expertise and innovation are the preoccupation of the moment; in complex and volatile markets the priority is the production of goods and services for which customers will pay a premium.

Images of Knowledge in Organizations

The notion that specialist knowledge and know-how and their develop-ment is becoming ever more central to the process of wealth creation has been proposed by a range of commentators including management journalists, marketing and business strategists, political economists, cross-cultural management theorists, information technology theorists, geographers and historians. Knowledge work, as Boland and Tenkasi (1995) explain, 'creates new understandings of nature, organisations or markets and applies them in valued technologies, products or processes'. The suggestion is that, in one form or another, intellectual capabilities and mental skills are becoming ever more significant to wealth creation, replacing reliance on physical skills and the bureaucratic control of resources, and enabling creative and flexible responses to the uncertainties of the global economy.

Examples of the arguments that have been proposed along these lines include the following. Shortly before his appointment as US Secretary of State for Labor, the political economist Robert Reich (1991) suggested that the American economy now depends crucially upon the skills and abilities of its most highly trained citizens rather than upon the size and power of America's conglomerates. Reich believes that American corporations are increasingly building their strategies not around particular products as such, but around the competitive advantage that the knowledge of their specialist employees can provide. The knowledge which commands high rewards is difficult to duplicate, he points out, and crucially it involves a high level of conceptual skill. Reich's 'symbolic analytical' workers are the contemporary entrepreneurs, with skills of problem identification (e.g. marketing, advertising, consulting), brokerage (e.g. financing, networking, contracting), and problem solving (e.g. research, product design and production). In a similar vein Drucker (1993) argued that the economies of Western social democracies are transforming themselves into what he calls 'knowledge societies'. Drucker suggests that just as during the early years of this century a shift took place away from a dependence on craft skills to a dependence on skills that had been captured in technological and organizational routines, a shift of similar proportions is occurring today. Nowadays, he suggests, wealth generation is becoming dependent on the creative insights of 'knowledge workers', that is, people who are able to exploit the competitive advantage that their specialized insights provide.

Related arguments have been developed at the organizational level of analysis. Following Nelson and Winter's (1982) analysis of organizational capabilities as a complex mix of interpersonal, technological and socio-structural routines, Prahalad and Hamel's (1990) notion of 'core competency' has been influential in the business strategy literature. The core competencies of an organization, they argue, will incorporate both tacit and explicit knowledge and should be conceived as a mix of skills and technologies. Organizational success depends less on particular products, more on the appropriate use and development of an organization's distinctive capabilities. They argue that organizations should identify, select, develop and protect the capabilities which distinguish them from competitors; marketing- and production-oriented competencies are, they suggest, becoming less important than the competencies which enable organizations to produce products or services tailored to particular customer needs. Others have developed similar positions. The Swedish academics Wikstrom and Norman (1994) argue that organizations should be thought of as knowledge systems, and their key activities should be analysed in terms of knowledge creation, transformation and utilization. And in his analysis of what he calls 'knowledge-creating' companies the Japanese commentator Nonaka (1994; Nonaka and Takeuchi, 1995) suggests that the 'true' core competence of an organization is its ability to create new knowledge to solve changing problems. This is, he argues, 'a way of behaving, indeed a way of being, in which everyone is a knowledge worker – that is to say, an entrepreneur'.

Developing a related point Peters (1992) points to the central role that conversations play in expert consultancies. Taking McKinsey as an example he describes the way in which energetic efforts are made to share key reports in the organization, to maintain a data bank of project lessons, to make experienced consultants routinely available to other staff for guidance, and generally to create a lively internal 'marketplace' of readily accessible ideas. And in her analysis of how new information and communication technologies are disrupting embodied skills, replacing what she calls 'action-oriented skills' by a heavy dependence on cognitive understanding, Zuboff (1988) makes a similar point. Talk about computer-mediated information is crucial; rather than working at isolated screens, staff working with computer-mediated information systems should work in ways that support shared interpretations of relevant data.

While writers such as these share the view that knowledge is becoming of increased importance to capitalism and needs careful handling, it does not require a close reading of their arguments to see that that the term 'knowledge' is being treated in a variety of ways. Some take strongly individualistic approaches to the nature of knowledge, contrasting the conceptual skills of the new generation of knowledge workers with the skills of previous eras. Others also assume that knowledge is an individual matter but point to the significance of interpersonal engagements for its development. A third group emphasize the significance of language to knowledge, and feature the significance of dialogue and the social construction of meanings.

The concept of knowledge is, of course, notoriously complex and it should really be no surprise that management theorists use the term in various ways. One of this chapter's authors recently reviewed popular uses of the term in the management literature, concentrating on the literature on organizational learning (Blackler, 1995). Five images of knowledge feature within this literature. Different writers emphasize the significance of knowledge that is embodied, embedded, embrained, encultured or encoded.

Embodied knowledge is action-oriented and, theorists agree, is likely to be only partly explicit (what Ryles, 1949, called 'knowledge how'). The knowledge of the expert craftsperson provides an excellent example of embodied knowledge, although Zuboff (1988) presented a contemporary account of its central importance in other settings. Such knowledge, she says, depends on people's physical presence, sentient and sensory information, physical cues and face-to-face discussions, is acquired by doing, and is rooted in specific contexts. Other contemporary accounts include Hirschhorn's (1984) analysis of mechanization and his conclusion that operators' tacit understandings of machine systems are more important than their general knowledge.

Embedded knowledge is knowledge which resides in systemic routines. Embedded knowledge is analysable in systemic terms, in the relationships between, for example, technologies, roles, formal procedures and emergent routines. This is how Nelson and Winter (1982) analysed an organization's capabilities. They noted that an individual's skills are composed of subelements which become coordinated in a smooth execution of the overall performance, impressive in its speed and accuracy, with conscious deliberation being confined to matters of overall importance. An organization's skills can be analysed in exactly the same way, they maintain, except that in addition to the physical and mental factors that comprise individual skills, organizational skills include also technological and socio-structural factors. Similar approaches to Nelson and Winter's include Levitt and March's (1988) development of the notion of organizational routines, which, they suggest, make the lessons of history accessible to subsequent organizational members, and Prahalad and Hamel's (1990) notion of organizational competencies referred to above.

Embrained knowledge is the knowledge that is dependent on conceptual skills and cognitive abilities (what Ryles, 1949, called 'knowledge that'). Within Western culture abstract knowledge has enjoyed a privileged status, and in the organizational learning literature a number of commentators have similarly accorded it privileged status. In their landmark paper on organizational learning, for example, Fiol and Lyles (1985) contrasted 'routine' behavioural adjustments with what they termed 'higher-level' abilities to develop complex rules and to understand complex causations.

Encultured knowledge refers to the process of achieving shared understandings. Relevant theorists point out that cultural meaning systems are intimately related to the processes of socialization and acculturation; such understandings are likely to depend heavily on language, and hence to be socially constructed and open to negotiation. As Swidler's (1986) general analysis indicated, in periods of social transformation explicitly formulated ideologies become the main vehicle for promoting new recipes for action. Following Pettigrew's (1979) and Ouchi's (1980) discussions of organizational culture there has, of course, been considerable interest in the relevance to organizations of such processes and, in the tradition of Wittgenstein, many contemporary theorists of organizational culture emphasize the intimate relationship between language and thought. Language is understood not as a way of representing knowledge and thought but as knowledge and thought itself; utterances are analysed as practical acts through which meanings are shaped and negotiated.

Finally, *encoded* knowledge is information conveyed by signs and symbols. To the traditional forms of encoded knowledge, such as books, manuals and codes of practice, has been added information encoded and transmitted electronically. Zuboff's (1988) analysis of the 'informating' power of information technologies explores the significance of this point for organizations: information encoded by decontextualized, abstract symbols is inevitably highly selective in the representations it can convey. Poster's (1990) thesis on how the new information technologies may be 'culturally alien' and Cooper's (1992) analysis of the significance of technologies of representation for the theory of organization are other contributions to such a line of analysis.

One way or another, contributors to the knowledge work debate are suggesting that, in the emerging global economy, knowledge that is embrained, encultured and encoded knowledge is of growing significance compared with knowledge that is embodied or embedded. Figure 3.1 summarizes the situation. Organizations that concentrate on familiar problems are distinguished from organizations that concentrate on unfamiliar ones, and organizations that depend on the contributions of key individuals are distinguished from organizations that depend upon collective endeavour. The resulting two-by-two matrix distinguishes: (a) 'expert-dependent organizations', such as craft-based organizations or professional bureaucracies, that rely heavily on the embodied knowledge of key individuals; (b) 'knowledge-routinized organizations', such as machine bureaucracies, that depend heavily on knowledge that is embedded in routines, technologies and procedures; (c) 'symbolic-analyst-dependent organizations', such as esoteric consultancies, that rely heavily on the embrained knowledge of star members; and (d) 'communication-intensive organizations', such as adhocracies, that depend heavily on encultured knowledge and communal understandings. The arrows on Figure 3.1 summarize the general trends that, it is suggested, are occurring in advanced economies as embrained and encultured knowledge become especially important. Note also that new forms of encoded knowledge supported by advanced information and communication technologies are of considerable interest at this time and that they are impacting on all these types of organization in various ways: see the detailed notes on Figure 3.1.

Two related conclusions can be drawn from this analysis. First, the variety of images of knowledge identified here indicates that it would be a mistake to assume that only so-called 'knowledge workers' or 'knowledge-intensive firms' depend upon knowledge. Knowledge in its

(b) Knowledge-routinized organizations *Emphasis on knowledge embedded in technologies, rules and procedures* Typically capital, technology, or labour intensive Hierarchical division of labour and control Low skill requirements *Example* 'Machine bureaucracy' such as a traditional factory *Current issues* Organizational competencies and corporate strategies Also: the development of computer integrated work systems	**(d) Communication-intensive organizations** *Emphasis on encultured knowledge and collective understandings* Communication and collaboration the key processes Empowerment through integration Expertise is pervasive *Example* 'Adhocracy', 'innovation-mediated production' *Current issues* 'Knowledge creation', dialogue, sensemaking processes Also: the development of computer supported cooperative work (CSCW) systems
(a) Expert-dependent organizations *Emphasis on the embodied competencies of key members* Performance of specialist experts is crucial Status and power from professional reputation Heavy emphasis on training and qualifications *Example* 'Professional bureaucracy' such as a hospital *Current issues* Nature and development of individual competency Also: computer displacement of action skills	**(c) Symbolic analyst-dependent organizations** *Emphasis on the embrained skills of key members* Entrepreneurial problem solving Status and power from creative achievements Symbolic manipulation is a key skill *Example* 'Knowledge-intensive firm' (KIF) e.g. a software consultancy *Current issues* Developing symbolic analysts, the organization of KIFs Also: information support and expert systems design

Emphasis on collective endeavour

Emphasis on contribution of key individuals

Focus on familiar problems   Focus on novel problems

Figure 3.1   *Organizations and knowledge types: arrows summarizes trends suggested in the knowledge work literature (after Blackler, 1995)*

various forms is an integral feature of *all* individuals and collectivities; very much as Giddens indicates in his analysis of modernity, knowledge is an everyday feature of modern life that pervades human activities.

At the same time, however, knowledge is highly complex and for this reason it remains something of an enigma. While it can be helpful to contrast different knowledge types as in Figure 3.1, it must also be emphasized that it would be misleading to divorce the categories of knowledge presented there. Knowledge is multifaceted. It is both explicit and implicit, abstract and situated, individual and collective, encoded and verbal, mental and physical, and static and developing. Although, as the figure suggests, organizations depend differentially on the knowledge types identified in the figure, *all* organizations depend upon *all* the forms of knowledge identified there. In the highly complex situations facing many businesses at the present time, analysis of the relationships *between* different manifestations of knowledge is, in the opinion of the writers, at least as important as the delineation of their differences.

Knowing as a Process

At first sight the development of a more holistic analysis of knowledge appears to be a daunting task. There has, however, been much interest in rethinking knowledge in recent years and a range of contributions to this task have been made. As several writers have suggested (Starr, 1992; Jowitt, 1992; Lave, 1993; Serres, 1995) a consensus is beginning to emerge around new approaches to understanding knowledge and its management. In this section key aspects of this emerging orientation are summarized.

Key to understanding the new approach is the point that questions that have tended to dominate the management literature (such as 'how and where is knowledge stored?') have been superseded by a series of new concerns. There has been a shift away from thinking about knowledge as a commodity that individuals and organizations have or may acquire, towards the study of knowing as something that they do. The key question arising from this perspective is: *how do people do their knowing?* As is sketched out below, answers to this question have highlighted the link between knowing and social processes, a finding that has drawn attention to the importance of two further questions. These are: 'who do people do their knowing with?' and 'can people learn to collaborate with people schooled in other communities of knowing?'

In place, therefore, of an analysis of knowledge as located in bodies, brains, routines, technologies, cultures and symbols, the new orientation analyses knowing as a process. Knowledge has been analysed as (1) provisional and reflexive, (2) mediated by linguistic and technological infrastructures, (3) situated and pragmatic as well as distanciated and abstract, (4) contested and political, and (5) emotional as well as rational.

KNOWLEDGE IS PROVISIONAL AND REFLEXIVE   In recent years it has become commonplace in philosophy to challenge assumptions that knowledge is a timeless phenomenon and to suggest instead that truth is a story that is actively and creatively constructed (see, for example, Lawson's 1989 review). This approach suggests that there·is no one true account of physical, social or psychological events. Rather than searching for fundamentals and eternal verities the issue becomes how to differentiate good stories about the world from poor stories. Interest, plausibility and believability are as important as logicality, coherency and consistency.

KNOWLEDGE IS MEDIATED BY LINGUISTIC AND TECHNOLOGICAL INFRASTRUC-TURES   The vocabulary people have makes objects and experiences available to them in particular ways, providing a horizon of understanding which guides what they will accept as fact. As noted above, Wittgenstein's pioneering analysis of language indicated how patterns of discourse facilitate and inhibit actions and imaginations. Language does not passively mirror the world, rather speech is a practical act that shapes and negotiates meanings. Organizational members operate within interpretive or discourse communities (in Wittgenstein's terminology they play 'language games'); for example, concepts like 'chain of command', 'subordinate', 'manager' only make sense within a network of familiar words that guide understandings and actions. Barrett et al. (1995) illustrate how the language of a group can change over time in their case study of how total quality management was introduced into the American Navy. As people grasp for new insights they experiment with new metaphors in their talk, which in turn make possible patterns of action that would have been unimaginable under previous rules of discourse. And just as thought is mediated by language and discourse, actions are mediated also by routines and technologies. Zuboff's studies of the changes associated with the introduction of computerized work systems, touched on above, clearly illustrate the point.

KNOWLEDGE IS SITUATED AND PRAGMATIC   In Giddens's (1990) terms, it is also *distanciated and abstract*. Traditional approaches to expert knowledge have assumed that after many years of specialized study professionals learn how to execute standardized skills that, once learned, they will practise throughout their professional careers. Polkinghorne (1992) offers an alternative interpretation. Claims of timeless knowledge are, he suggests, no more (and no less) than historically situated conversations. The knowledge of the expert is a tentative, fragmented and essentially pragmatic social construction. Scribner's (1986) description of 'practical thinking', i.e. problem-solving techniques which depend on an intimate knowledge of a situation rather than abstract rules, Suchman's (1987) studies of how people spontaneously construct interpretations of technologies as they interact with them, and Lave and Wenger's (1991) analysis of learning and socialization, provide well-worked accounts of related processes.

KNOWLEDGE IS CONTESTED AND POLITICAL   As Foucault's (1980) notion of a 'discourse of perversions' dramatically indicates, patterns of discourse reflect and produce relations of power. Claims to the possession of decontextualized knowledge are, as Lave (1993) points out, often no more than a 'power play', as experts stake out their claims to be respected against the rival claims of other interest groups. Contemporary analysis of the nature of knowledge underlines the point that the relationships between culture, knowledge and power are impossible to disentangle.

KNOWLEDGE IS EMOTIONAL AS WELL AS RATIONAL   Finally it is important to emphasize that cognitive and affective states should not be treated as if they are distinct. Main (1990) makes the point. At the level of the individual the acquisition of new knowledge may be associated with feelings of opportunity and mastery. But it may also be asssociated with feelings of loss as cherished practices are displaced. At the level of the group and organization similar processes operate. Ideas that were born at a time of excitement and discovery may later come to be passed on impatiently, with no appreciation of the learning needs of newcomers.

A Partial Synthesis: Knowing as Culturally Situated, Technologically Mediated and Socially Distributed

The general style of analysis illustrated by the suggestion that knowledge is provisional, mediated, situated, contested and emotional marks a major departure from traditional approaches to understanding knowledge. The implications for practice promise to be considerable. Nonetheless, because of the complexity and unfamiliarity of the issues touched on here it is not easy to find a way of representing the complexities of such insights in a direct and straightforward way.

One approach, however, which captures many of the points summarized above (in particular it features suggestions that knowledge is provisional, mediated and situated) is Engestrom's (1987) general model of activity systems (see Figure 3.2). The model represents the relationships between personal knowledge and the cultural infrastructure of knowledge and between individual actions and the broader pattern of activities of which they are a part.

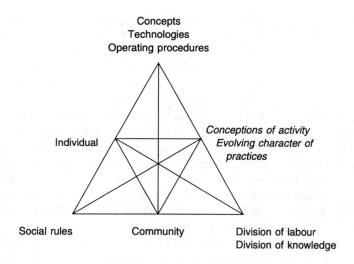

Figure 3.2   *General model of activity systems (adapted from Engestrom, 1987)*

Relationships between three central factors provide the basis for Engestrom's model. These are the individual, his or her work or professional colleagues, and the conceptions they have of their joint activity. These core relations are represented by the inner triangle on Figure 3.2. In any particular situation the relationships between workers, colleagues and the conceptions they have of their activities are mediated by a number of other factors. First, a worker's relationship to his or her work is mediated by the technologies he or she is using (compare, for example, the impact on worker–work relationships of contemporary computer-centred banking systems with that of manual book-keeping techniques) and by the discourse, knowledge and skills that he or she employs in the execution of the work role (compare, for example, the medical training of a nurse with that of a doctor). Second, the relationship between work colleagues and their work activities is mediated by the ways in which roles are structured, i.e. by the division of labour and the division of knowledge (compare hierarchical structures with matrix organizations and professional bureaucracies with organizations that rely heavily on multi-disciplinary teams). Third, the relationship between a worker and his or her colleagues is mediated by the implicit and explicit rules of the organization (compare organizations that are characterized by formal and competitive relationships with those that have open and confronting relationships).

Note that the mediations illustrated on Figure 3.2 are intended to indicate that technologies, structures or processes intimately affect the relationships they mediate between workers, work and colleagues. New technologies, new ways of distributing work roles and responsibilities, or shifts in interpersonal processes do not merely make it easier to do things that were going to get done anyway but will precipitate wholly new relationships and developments. Examples of this have been touched on above, and include the power of new patterns of discourse and linguistic images and the ways in which technologies based on microelectronics have transformed the experience of work.

Note also that it would be a mistake to assume that the relationships between intentional, technological, structural and processual factors illustrated on Figure 3.2 are tidy and clear-cut. Incoherencies, inconsistencies, tensions and paradoxes are integral features of activity systems. The point is represented by the wavy lines on Figure 3.2. It is the explicit, but often tacit, conceptions of activity that people have of their activities, featured in italics on the right of the internal triangle, that give coherence to their individual actions. Through the consistency and determination with which people enact their understandings of what is appropriate in the contexts in which they find themselves, the tensions which regularly arise within activity systems are, as a matter of course, overcome.

Knowledge does not appear as a separate phenomenon in Engestrom's model. The suggestion is that the appropriate unit of analysis is neither individuals nor cultures but activity systems, that is, the interdependency of individuals and cultures. People act on the world, with others, utilizing (and contributing to the development of) the linguistic, material and social resources available for supporting collective endeavours. Engestrom's model depicts the interdependency of thinking and doing on the one hand and of knowing and the cultural infrastructure of knowledge on the other. Further it features the dynamics of knowing: the balance within an activity system changes constantly as participants employ their situated knowledge in a situation that is itself constantly evolving.

To conclude this section, traditional approaches to knowledge emphasize the importance of individual cognitive processes and consider knowledge to be a personal matter involving a passive assimilation of ideas. New knowledge is developed cumulatively and learning is understood to depend on individual abilities and motivations and to involve the development of particular skills and actions. Like the approaches to knowledge in organizational settings reviewed earlier, such approaches segment and divorce issues that are intimately related, such as bodies and brains, individuals and communities, thought and action. The approach outlined here is very different. While it does not deny the value of traditional approaches entirely it approaches knowledge in a new way. The analysis of activity systems involves the identification of the linguistic, social and material infrastructures that make knowing possible. It emphasizes that knowledge is culturally situated, technologically mediated and socially distributed, and that it occurs within and between 'communities of knowing'. Knowing is analysed as an active achievement, and knowledge development is analysed as a process that does not just involve incremental developments but may also involve paradigm shifts as activity systems are reconfigured. Such shifts can be stimulated by the questioning and collective experimentation that occur as attempts are made to resolve the contradictions that (inevitably) develop within and between activity systems.

Changes in Capitalism and in the Infrastructure of Knowing

The impact of the changes in contemporary capitalism that were touched upon at the start of this chapter can be reinterpreted using this approach and fresh insights can be gained into the nature of knowledge and competition. In short, organizations can be analysed as networks of interrelated activity systems.

Activity theory suggests that the tensions and instabilities that inevitably arise within and between activity systems have several origins. Mismatches can develop between related activity systems, e.g. the output of one organization may not be what is required as an input to another. Tensions can develop between the constituent elements of any particular activity system, e.g. new work technologies may not produce the results that were expected of them, and paradoxes and contradictions may develop within the particular elements of a system, e.g. expanded work roles can be experienced both as an opportunity for personal development and as the cause of pressure and stress. Importantly also, alternative or emerging conceptions of work priorities may clash, e.g. the desire for engineering excellence may conflict with the aim of business profitability, and short-term business objectives may conflict with long-term ones. In a sense therefore activity systems can be thought of as *tension producing* systems: incoherencies, inconsistencies, paradoxes and contradictions within and between them are normal. While such tensions provide both the motive and the opportunity for collective development, the significance of particular tensions is not always easy to assess. Moreover, the issues they raise may be difficult to resolve and, as a result, the opportunities they present for experimentation and learning can be ignored.

While it is commonplace for activity systems to include tensions and incoherencies, the economic, legislative and technological changes of recent years have provoked an unusually extensive range of tensions within many organizations. As outlined at the start of the chapter, globalizing markets, post-Keynesian economic and social policies, new technologies, and the development of new approaches to organization appear to be creating a new era in capitalism's history. As noted, ongoing and extensive change is the expectation of the day. Indeed, most of the new approaches to organization and management that have been proposed in recent years can be understood as attempts to help organizations to respond to the increasing complexity and instability of their activity systems. Described in activity theoretical terms, *the activity systems of many organizations have become markedly more complex and interrelated in recent times and correspondingly less stable.*

The extent and the visibility of current tensions and incoherencies within organizations are striking. It is now quite commonplace, for example, to find that managerial priorities which, in previous times, would have been regarded as incompatible must now be met simultaneously. Examples include the way manufacturing organizations have had simultaneously to reduce lead times, to reduce costs and to achieve higher quality and customer responsiveness; the way public sector organizations have had to learn to respond to fiscal disciplines as well as to their responsibilities to provide public services; and the way in which a great many organizations have sought to concentrate on core competencies and have substantially reduced staff numbers, whilst at the same time staff have been asked to innovate and to generate organizational learning.

The new approaches to knowledge suggest two key points with regard to the contemporary situation. First, complex though the tensions are within many activity systems it would usually be a mistake to conclude that they present *irresolvable* problems. Rather, as activity systems become more complex internally and more interdependent externally, solutions to the resulting complexities are likely to be only partial and temporary. Plans will continually fall short of expectations. The need to develop temporary solutions to emerging tensions presents a major ongoing challenge for individual and collective learning. It is no accident that theorists have urged that the key expertise of senior managers in fast-moving environments is less their ability to interpret trends and identify solutions, i.e. to plan, and more their ability to make sense of surprises, disappointments and failures, i.e. to create new knowledge and through debate and dialogue to involve others in the process (see, for example, Weick, 1995). Organizations in complex environments must expect to find themselves continually puzzling about evolving tensions, and reorganizing and rethinking.

Second, organizations that compete through knowledge tend to be made up of multiple communities of experts. In the jargon of the new approach to understanding knowledge, knowledge is *distributed* within them. Traditional ways of integrating different domains of expertise within organizations do not function well in the fast-moving environments of the present day. Organizations that depend on knowledge work and organizational learning need to move away from coordination through rules and hierarchies and to create 'self-managing' systems of collaboration where different specialists interact directly and jointly regulate their shared efforts.

The trend towards multi-disciplinary working is widespread. For example, Gibbons et al. (1994) suggest that many of the most significant contemporary developments in knowledge creation are not the result of collaboration between discipline-based researchers but are the result of multi-disciplinary groups that are organized in non-traditional ways. Certainly, multi-disciplinary groupworking has been widely promoted in the manufacturing industry. The high levels of mutual adjustment, improvization and learning that groupworking promises offer perhaps the only way in which the conflicting objectives of, for example, product quality and customer responsiveness, short development periods and low costs can all be met.

Nonetheless, as Ancona and Caldwell's (1992) review of American experiences with multi-disciplinary groupworking suggests, the successful integration of experts from different fields is exceptionally difficult to arrange. The new approaches to understanding knowledge in general, and activity theory in particular, help explain why this is the case: tensions within multi-disciplinary teams are likely to be more intense and more intractable than the tensions within the activity systems of single-disciplinary teams.

Orr's (1990) analysis of the strong bonds between specialists (in his study of photocopier maintenance technicians) helps explain the point. Orr discovered that the stories shared by maintenance personnel responsible for servicing complex machinery are an integral and essential aspect of their activity. Classroom instruction can only do so much to alert photocopier maintenance staff to the mix of technological problems they are likely to encounter, and the stories the technicians tell each other not only compensate for this problem but help create the identity of their engineering specialism. First, community stories provide an informational function, preserving and circulating news about current problems that are occurring. Second, they serve an educational function: not only do the technicians learn from each other about current fault patterns but the stories help community members to develop their problem-solving skills. Third, by contributing their own stories engineers become established as useful members of the community. As Brown and Duguid (1991) point out, learning is a social understanding that emerges from practical collaboration. Different experts not only have internalized the cognitive styles associated with their expert peers but, typically, will identify strongly with this community.

The problems of developing understandings between different communities of experts in an organization are demonstrated in Dougherty's (1992) discussion of the differing outlooks of technical experts, sales people, manufacturing engineers and business planners. She points out that, from the outside looking in, it is easy to pick up the conventional stereotypes of these various functions: technical people keep changing their designs, sales people have short-term orientations, manufacturing people are inclined to say 'no', planners appear to be very conceptual, etc. etc. Yet from *within* each of these perspectives each appears to be firmly grounded in good sense. As specialists all argue, their particular

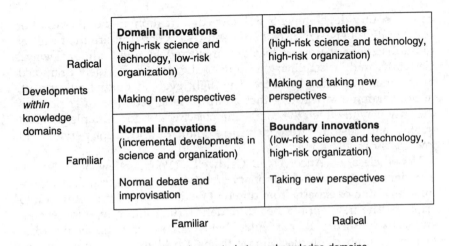

Figure 3.3 *Disciplinary and cross-disciplinary knowledge and innovation*

orientation is essential to the organization's success; yet such an orientation may routinely be challenged by the alternative understandings of other groups. The fact that multi-disciplinary groups are often uncomfortable and unsettling is not surprising therefore; the skills they demand may be counter-intuitive and life within them can be conflictual. Members of multi-disciplinary groups can find themselves torn between apparently competing communities.

As activity systems become more complex and interrelated, participants need to develop an expanded sense of their activities and an ability to work across communities and in new contexts. Such attitudes and skills are not easily acquired. Figure 3.3 sketches out some of the challenges that such developments involve. The figure features two kinds of innovation: developments that experts need to make *within* their specialist areas as they address novel problems, and developments that they must make in collaboration with experts from *other* specialisms. The amount of innovation either within or between specialist areas can vary considerably, of course. This is represented on the figure by the distinction between familiar and radical developments. In this way a fourfold classification is presented: 'normal innovations' for small developments that are an everyday event, 'domain innovations' for significant developments within an area of specialization, 'boundary innovations' for developments that involve cross-disciplinary interactions, and 'radical innovations' for developments involving significant specialist and cross-disciplinary advances.

Both domain and boundary innovations are likely to demand reflexivity and an ability to step beyond the familiar. But while domain innovations are likely to benefit from the single-mindedness and motivation of the expert, from clear thinking, inspiration and hard work, boundary innovations require open-mindedness and a willingness to question, appreciate, combine, negotiate and experiment. Adopting Boland and Tenkasi's (1995) terminology, domain innovations require experts to make a new perspective of their own; boundary innovations require them to take the perspective of others. 'Perspective taking' presents particular challenges: it raises the possibility of cognitive uncertainties, interpersonal misunderstandings, and issues of power and emotion. A new expanded sense of activity and community needs to emerge, born of an awareness of the changing context and a willingness to construct new meanings and methods.

Conclusion: Managing Knowledge

Whilst the practical implications of the issues discussed in this chapter have yet fully to be worked out, key themes are not difficult to identify. In terms of the management of knowledge some, long-recognized, priorities remain unchanged. Organizations which compete through knowledge must recruit suitably trained and experienced personnel who need to be supported by appropriate procedures and technologies. Such people need to be utilized appropriately, mentored and trained. They should be supported by a culture of enquiry in their efforts to innovate and to keep up to date with new developments in their domains of knowledge.

In addition to such factors, however, a new series of priorities for the management of knowledge can be identified. First is the need to support an expanded sense of activity and boundary innovations. As we have noted, effective collaboration across different knowledge domains cannot be taken for granted. Barriers to the development of expanded priorities and collaborative relationships with other experts are likely to include linguistic, ideological, cognitive and social factors. Collaborative relationships often require staff to spend as much time understanding what they are doing as actually doing it. Multi-disciplinary collaboration can be inhibited by a shortage of appropriate forums for dialogue, the mismanagement of such forums, and inadequate procedural infrastructures.

Second, the long-term effectiveness of organizations that compete through knowledge depends crucially on their organizational learning, that is, upon the speed and effectiveness with which they can mobilize their established and emerging knowledge bases. For rapid mobilization of knowledge to be possible, lessons from key past developments need to be reviewed and to be shared within the organization. Barriers to organizational learning are likely to include inappropriate infrastructures (from organizational discourse to technologies and procedures), competitive rather than collaborative attitudes between functions or project groups, time pressures, and a lack of appropriate forums for intragroup discussion and debate.

Finally, new skills are demanded of senior managers as activity networks within organizations become more complex. Organizations inevitably signal a preference for how tensions within and between activity systems should be resolved. One key role of senior managers is to ensure that appropriate signals are conveyed and to find a new balance between centralized direction and local inventiveness. Moreover, the support of group and intergroup learning, tolerance of uncertainty, the management of anxiety, and shifting patterns of power and politics are amongst the key responsibilities of senior managers in organizations that compete through knowledge.

To conclude, we have argued that the extent and pace of change in advanced economies have grown significantly in recent years. Changes in the way wealth is generated have placed a premium on certain forms of knowledge. Familiar approaches to theorizing knowledge need revision however; in particular, images of knowledge as embodied, embedded, embrained, encultured and encoded are overly compartmentalized. Knowing is better conceptualized as an active process, for knowledge is provisional, mediated, situated, political and emotional. As activity systems become more complex and interrelated, new demands are falling on the knowing of both individuals and of organizations. Debate, improvization, learning and collaboration are of primary importance in the emerging circumstances. In the difficult and demanding environment of contemporary economies the key insight for management is that knowledge is a collective achievement.

Notes

Work reported here was supported by two grants. An EU Human Capital and Mobility Project 'European Competitiveness in a Knowledge Society' supported the review of changing approaches to knowledge in the management literature. An ESRC Innovation Programme 'Innovation in High Technology Organizations' supported the development of the theoretical framework based on activity theory.

References

Ancona, D. and Caldwell, D. (1992) Cross functional teams: blessing or curse for new product development?, in T. Kochan and M. Useem (eds), *Transforming Organisations*. Oxford: Oxford University Press.

Barrett, F., Thomas, G. and Hocevar, S. (1995) The central role of discourse in large scale change: a social construction perspective, *Journal of Applied Behavioural Science*, 31: 352–72.

Blackler, F. (1995) Knowledge, knowledge work and organisations, an overview and interpretation. *Organisation Studies*, 16: 1021–46.

Boland, R. and Tenkasi, R. (1995) Perspective making and perspective taking in communities of knowing. *Organisation Science*, 6: 350–72.

Brown, J. and Duguid, P. (1991) Organisational learning and communities of practice. *Organisation Science*, 2: 40–57.

Castells, M. (1989) *The Informational City: Information Technology, Economic Restructuring and the Urban–Regional Process*. Oxford: Basil Blackwell.

Cooper, R. (1992) Formal organization as representation: remote control, displacement and abbreviation, in M. Reed and M. Hughes (eds), *Rethinking Organization: New Directions in Organization Theory and Analysis*. London: Sage.

Dougherty, D. (1992) Interpretive barriers to successful product innovation in large firms. *Organisation Science*, 3: 179–202.

Drucker, P. (1993) *Post-Capitalist Society*. Oxford: Butterworth-Heinemann.

Engestrom, Y. (1987) *Learning by Expanding: an Activity Theoretical Approach to Developmental Research*. Helsinki: Orenta-Konsultit.

Fiol, C. and Lyles, M. (1985) Organizational learning. *Academy of Management Review*, 10: 803–13.

Foucault, M. (1980) *The History of Sexuality*, Vol. 1. New York: Vintage.

Gibbons, M., Limoges, C., Nowotny, H., Schwartzman, S. Scott, P. and Trow, M. (1994) *The New Production of Knowledge: the Dynamics of Science and Research in Contemporary Societies*. London: Sage.

Giddens, A. (1990) *The Consequences of Modernity*. Cambridge: Cambridge University Press.

Hirschhorn, L. (1984) *Beyond Mechanization: Work and Technology in a Post-Industrial Age*. Cambridge, MA: MIT.

Jowitt, K. (1992) *New World Disorder*. Berkeley, CA: University of California Press.

Lash, J. and Urry, S. (1994) *Economics of Signs and Space*. London: Sage.

Lave, J. (1993) The practice of learning, in S. Chaiklin and J. Lave (eds), *Understanding Practice: Perspectives on Activity and Context*. Cambridge: Cambridge University Press.

Lave, J. and Wenger, E. (1991) *Situated Learning: Legitimate Peripheral Participation*. Cambridge: Cambridge University Press.

Lawson, H. (1989) Stories about stories, in H. Lawson and L. Appignanesi (eds), *Dismantling Truth: Reality in the Postmodern World*. London: Weidenfeld and Nicolson.

Levitt, B. and March, J. (1988) Organizational learning. *American Review of Sociology*, 14: 319–40.

Main, T. (1990) Knowledge, learning and freedom from thought. *Psychoanalytic Psychotherapy*, 5: 59–78.

Nelson, R. and Winter, S. (1982) *An Evolutionary Theory of Organizational Change*. Cambridge, MA: Harvard University Press.

Nonaka, I. (1994) A dynamic theory of organisational knowledge creation. *Organization Science*, 5: 15–37.

Nonaka, I. and Takeuchi, H. (1995) *The Knowledge-Creating Company*. Oxford: Oxford University Press.

Orr, J. (1990) Sharing knowledge, celebrating identity: community memory in a service culture, in D. Middleton and D. Edwards (eds), *Collective Remembering*. London: Sage.

Ouchi, W. (1980) Markets, bureaucracies and clans. *Administrative Science Quarterly*, 25: 129–41.

Peters, T. (1992) *Liberation Management: Necessary Disorganization for the Nanosecond Nineties*. New York: Knopf.

Pettigrew, A. (1979) On studying organizational cultures. *Administrative Science Quarterly*, 24: 570–81.

Piore, M. and Sabel, C. (1984) *The Second Industrial Divide*. New York: Basic Books.

Polkinghorne, D. (1992) Postmodern epistemology of practice, in S. Kvale (ed.), *Psychology and Postmodernism*. London: Sage.

Poster, M. (1990) *The Mode of Information: Poststructuralism and Social Context*. Cambridge: Polity.

Prahalad, C. and Hamel, G. (1990) The core competence of the corporation, *Harvard Business Review*, May–June: 79–91.

Reich, R. (1991) *The Work of Nations: Preparing Ourselves for 21st-Century Capitalism*. London: Simon and Schuster.

Ryles, G. (1949) *The Concept of Mind*. London: Hutchinson.

Scribner, S. (1986) Thinking in action: some characteristics of practical thought, in R. Sternberg and R. Wagner (eds), *Practical Intelligence: Nature and Origins of Competence in the Everyday World*. Cambridge: Cambridge University Press.

Serres, M. (1995) *Genesis*. Ann Arbor, MI: University of Michigan Press.

Starr, S. (1992) The Trojan door: organizations, work, and the 'open black box'. *Systems Practice*, 5: 395–410.

Suchman, L. (1987) *Plans and Situated Actions*. Cambridge: Cambridge University Press.

Swidler, A. (1986) Culture in action: symbols and strategies. *American Sociological Review*, 51: 273–86.

Weick, K. (1995) *Sensemaking in Organisations*. London: Sage.

Wikstrom, S. and Norman, R. (1994) *Knowledge and Value: a New Perspective on Corporate Transformation*. London: Routledge.

Zuboff S. (1988) *In the Age of the Smart Machine: the Future of Work and Power*. New York: Basic Books.

4

ORGANIZATIONAL KNOWLEDGE AND LEARNING

Rodrigo Magalhães

> We human beings are human beings only in language. Because we
> have language, there is no limit to what we can describe, imagine, and
> relate. It thus permeates our whole ontogeny as individuals: from
> walking to attitudes to politics. (Maturana and Varela, 1992: 212)

The issue of core competencies has been brought to the fore in the
business literature in the last few years (Prahalad and Hamel, 1990; Stalk
et al., 1992; Collis and Montgomery, 1995) and organizational knowledge
has been construed as the basic capability behind such competencies.
Some authors refer to organizational knowledge as the only source of
advantage for business organizations in the future given that, unlike all
the other sources, knowledge is endogenous to the company and cannot
be copied. This trend was also identified, but under a different guise,
early in the 1990s in a high-profile meeting that brought together academics, researchers and practitioners at MIT, to discuss the challenges of
the decade ahead, in view of the radical changes taking place in the
global economy. A passage from the conclusion of that meeting is the
following:

> Rational decision making, traditional design principles, power- and leadership-
> based models, shareholder- or financial market-driven change, organizational
> development and the stakeholder view of the corporation all came in for
> criticism. None of these served as a comfortable metaphor for describing the
> challenges facing contemporary organizations, for either academics or
> practitioners. . . . Instead, what emerged were two overriding themes. The
> first was an emphasis on change that challenges and reconfigures the tacit
> knowledge or deep assumptions about how organizational boundaries,
> technologies, strategies and human resources should be arranged. . . . Second,
> most participants found a consensus on the concept of the 'learning

organization'. This metaphor captured the vision of individuals, groups, and organizational networks committed to and capable of continuous learning through information, exchange, experimentation, dialogue, negotiation and consensus building. (Kochan and Useem, 1992: 391)

The different guise we have referred to is the 'learning organization' which has since been sold, mainly in the popular business literature, as the key to achieving superior business performance. However, the notion of the learning organization means different things to different people, depending on the books which are consulted. What does it mean? How is it achieved? What changes will it imply? The approaches in the popular business literature usually have little to do with the research output from academia, and academics have difficulty in relating to the recipes put forward for the consumption of management practitioners. So, the logical question to ask is: is there a relationship between the notion of the learning organization and the academic research and writing on organizational knowledge and learning?

To talk about organization knowledge and learning implies also talking about organizational memory, not only because all three concepts are very much linked both in popular and in scientific discourse, but also because the view that organizations are capable of cognition has been taking shape (Gioia and Sims, 1986). Organizational memory too is rapidly becoming a favourite topic in the literature in view of the obvious implications of information technology in organizations (Huber, 1990; Walsh and Ungson, 1991; Stein and Zwass, 1995). The arguments are straightforward, i.e. the more information technology is implemented in an organization, the more information processing and storage capacity it will possess *as an organization*. But, is really that straightforward? Do we know enough about what the organization's memory is and how it works? And, worst of all, have we learned anything over the years about the impact of information technology on the organization's memory and on organizations in general? Years of accumulated research seem to indicate that we have not (Robey, 1977; Attewell and Rule, 1984; Markus and Robey, 1988; Orlikowski and Robey, 1991; Orlikowski, 1992; Robey, 1995).

So, what are we to make of all this? Are we confusing the practitioners? Are we confusing ourselves? As Jones puts it: 'If the concept of organizational learning is not to be rapidly discredited, then it would seem necessary that writers on the subject include a more explicit discussion of the particular interpretation they are using than is typically the case at present' (1995: 75). We strongly agree with this statement, and believe that one of the reasons for the confusion in which the field finds itself has been precisely the lack of awareness among researchers about the incompatibility of the reality of management 'out there', with the intense changes it is undergoing, and the intellectual biases and approaches that are being brought to bear on the same problems 'in the laboratory'. As we see it, the problem is of an epistemological nature. On the one hand, a soft and very subjective notion of the 'learning organization' is put forward as being the way into the future, as opposed to the 'rational decision making, traditional design principles, power- and leadership-based models, shareholder- or financial market-driven change, organizational development and the stakeholder view of the corporation' (Kochan and Useem, 1992: 391) referred to earlier. But, on the other hand, there seems to be no change in the hard and highly objective epistemological assumptions behind mainstream organization and management theory. This seems to be the main source of the confusion that Jones is alluding to.

In this chapter it is proposed to contribute, from an academic point of view, towards a clarification of the field, especially regarding its usefulness for management practice. This will be achieved by bringing together conceptual issues which are usually dealt with separately – organizational knowledge, organizational learning and organizational memory – into a single framework and analysing them from the point of view of three major poles of influence in the literature: the individual view, the social view and the critical and alternative views. The first has an emphasis on learning and a bias towards psychology and the traditional cognitive sciences, such as mainstream artificial intelligence; the second emphasizes knowledge and memory, instead of learning, and shows a strong influence from sociology and systems theory; and the third, which highlights both knowledge and learning, has a mixture of intellectual influences, with management and the organization sciences as prevailing ones. The classificatory framework, featuring the three major poles of influence, each subdivided into either schools of thought or individual works which are considered particularly influential, can be seen in Figure 4.1.

The other contribution, it is hoped, will emerge from the discussion on the third pole of influence – critical and alternative views. Such a discussion features views from students and researchers of organizations which so far have been outside the mainstream theoretical positions on organizational knowledge and learning, but which are the basis for important new epistemological departures. The discussion will be supported not only by the historical trends in the management and organization sciences literatures, but also by key arguments from new epistemological underpinnings, emerging from a unifying theoretical lens: *the theory of autopoiesis applied to organizations and management, which will also be referred to as organizational autopoiesis.*

Autopoiesis (Maturana and Varela, 1992) is a theoretical framework which has been developed, for the last 30 years, in the fields of cognitive science and systems theory and has been brought into the organization sciences in the form of a new epistemology for organizations (von Krogh and Roos, 1995a). This new epistemology brings a fresh view to the field of organization knowledge and learning which, so far, has been under

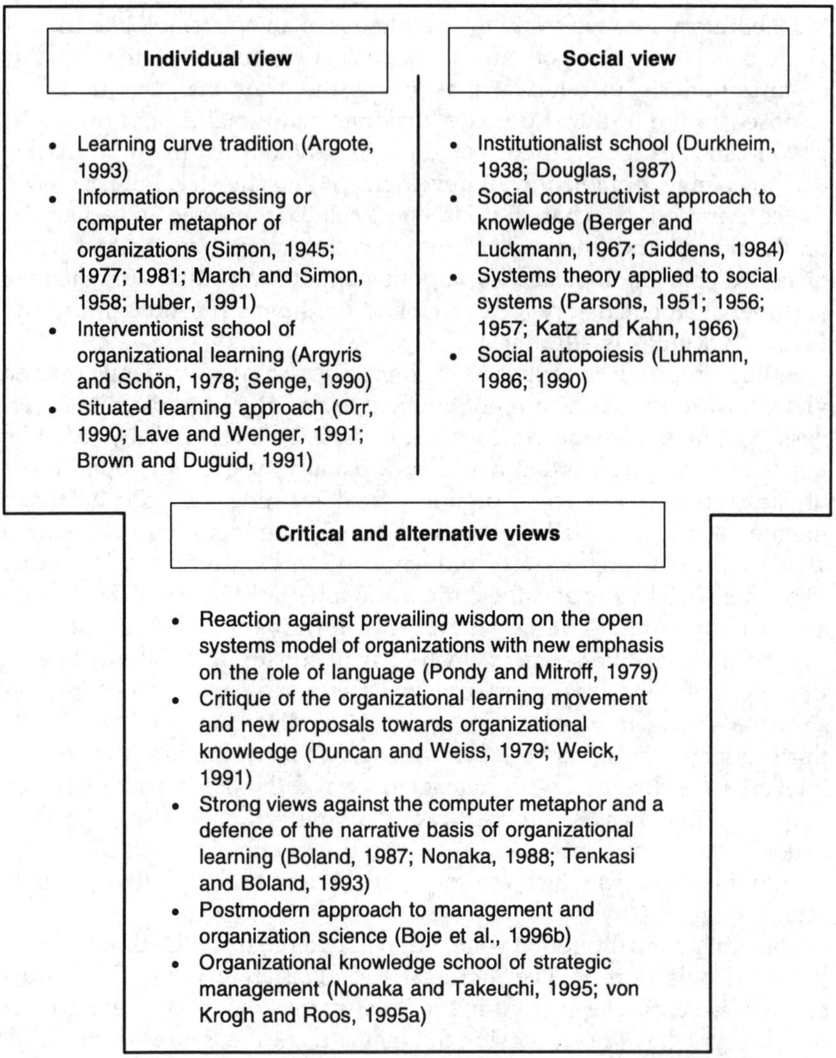

Individual view	Social view
• Learning curve tradition (Argote, 1993) • Information processing or computer metaphor of organizations (Simon, 1945; 1977; 1981; March and Simon, 1958; Huber, 1991) • Interventionist school of organizational learning (Argyris and Schön, 1978; Senge, 1990) • Situated learning approach (Orr, 1990; Lave and Wenger, 1991; Brown and Duguid, 1991)	• Institutionalist school (Durkheim, 1938; Douglas, 1987) • Social constructivist approach to knowledge (Berger and Luckmann, 1967; Giddens, 1984) • Systems theory applied to social systems (Parsons, 1951; 1956; 1957; Katz and Kahn, 1966) • Social autopoiesis (Luhmann, 1986; 1990)

Critical and alternative views

- Reaction against prevailing wisdom on the open systems model of organizations with new emphasis on the role of language (Pondy and Mitroff, 1979)
- Critique of the organizational learning movement and new proposals towards organizational knowledge (Duncan and Weiss, 1979; Weick, 1991)
- Strong views against the computer metaphor and a defence of the narrative basis of organizational learning (Boland, 1987; Nonaka, 1988; Tenkasi and Boland, 1993)
- Postmodern approach to management and organization science (Boje et al., 1996b)
- Organizational knowledge school of strategic management (Nonaka and Takeuchi, 1995; von Krogh and Roos, 1995a)

Figure 4.1 *Major strands of influence on the literature on organizational knowledge and learning*

the prevailing influence of other epistemologies. Organizational knowledge (which, in this chapter, includes also the notions of learning and memory) has been treated as very much an abstract phenomenon, revealing the influence of a cognitivist or representationist epistemology. The autopoietic view treats organizational knowledge not as an abstract phenomenon, but as one embodied in the people and the groups that make up the organization. Autopoiesis affords a new epistemological lens for many of the issues which have been dividing students and researchers of organizations, such as: a psychological view of learning versus a sociological approach to knowledge; a view of management activity essentially based on rational thought versus an approach based on organizational power; a top-down view of business strategy as opposed to a bottom-up, emergent approach; and a positivist approach to research versus a purely interpretivist stance.

In this chapter, it is not intended to tackle all these issues. The focus is on organizations as learning entities, with knowledge and memory capabilities, but because these issues are directly concerned with the essence of the organization, the discussion naturally leads to the epistemological foundations of organizations. And all the other issues become immediately relevant as well. In the last section, some conclusions are drawn which extend beyond the narrower focus of the chapter and encompass some of the broader organizational issues mentioned above. The chapter focuses mainly on the third pole of influence – critical and alternative views – as it is within it that the new and unifying trends in organizational knowledge learning are to be found. The remaining two poles of influence – the individual and the social views – will only be touched upon in the next section. A fuller treatment of these can be found elsewhere (Magalhães, 1996).

A Psychological View of Organizational Learning versus a Sociological View of Organizational Knowledge

The Individual View

This pole of influence, which has dominated much of the research and writing in the organization sciences, contains the whole of the organizational learning movement. It can be subdivided into four strands. Chronologically, the earliest is probably the learning curve tradition (reviewed in Argote, 1993), influenced by classical individual psychology but still very active especially among social psychologists (Yelle, 1979; Spence, 1981; Epple et al., 1991). The second strand, and by far the most representative in terms of volume of output, is one we have labelled the 'information processing view', greatly influenced by the work of H. Simon (1945; 1977) and March and Simon (1958). This strand is really the initiator of the organizational learning movement in the 1960s with the work of Cyert and March (1963), followed by authors such as Cangolesi and Dill (1965), Hedberg (1981), Fiol and Lyles (1985), Cohen and Levinthal (1990), Cohen (1991), Huber (1991) and Lyles and Schwenk (1992). A third strand, labelled the 'interventionist school', found its inspiration in systems theory applied to individual learning (Bateson, 1972) and was later developed by Argyris and Schön (1978; 1996) and Senge (1990). Lastly, there is the 'situated learning' approach where the work of Lave and Wenger (1991) has been the dominant source, with Orr (1990) and Brown and Duguid (1991) applying it to

organizational learning. Although substantially different from the previous three approaches, the situated learning approach has in common
with them an emphasis on the individual and individual learning, as
opposed to organizational learning.

The Social View

The second major pole of influence is very different from the first in
terms of its research tradition and academic affiliations. Given its sociological roots, we have labelled it the social view. This pole starts with an
influence from the early studies on social knowledge (Durkheim, 1938)
and the application of this social theory to the study of institutions and
institutional memory (Douglas, 1987). This strand was later developed
into a stream of research known as 'organizational cognition' (Gioia and
Sims, 1986). Second, there is the social constructivist approach which is
part of a sociological tradition on the social construction of reality and
knowledge (Berger and Luckmann, 1967), later influenced by Giddens's
(1976; 1984) structuration theory. A third strand features the application
of systems theory to social systems (Parsons, 1951) and to organizational
systems (Katz and Kahn, 1966). This strand has been central to the work
of Luhmann (1986; 1990) which, in its later stages, has been influenced by
autopoiesis theory. Given that this theoretical framework is also fundamental for understanding the language-based approaches which are the
foci of this chapter, special attention will be devoted to it further on.

Critical and Alternative Views

The third pole of influence has been roughly subdivided into two major
blocks. The first stands for the critical views, a line of research and
writing which represents to a large degree a minority voice, having as a
unifying feature a critical stance about the overly positivist and
empiricist orientation of the mainstream literature in the organization
and administrative sciences. These views find some support among the
proponents of a postmodern organization and management theory (Boje
et al., 1996b). The second block stands for what is perceived as some
convergence in the form of alternative approaches, coming into the field
from the literature on strategic management. A new development
behind these alternative views is the new approach to business strategy
that has been taking shape over the last few years: the resource-based
approach. This approach holds that the key to business advantage in the
twenty-first century rests upon the development of internal organizational capabilities, among which is the development of organizational
knowledge. Two different ways of looking at organizational knowledge
have been identified. First, Nonaka and Takeuchi (1995), building on the
work of Polanyi (1973) on the role of tacit knowledge, start from an
individual perspective and develop a new theory of organizational
knowledge creation. Nonaka and Takeuchi's dynamic theory hinges on

the interplay between tacit and explicit knowledge and the means by which the organization can make better use of the wealth of tacit knowledge within it. Second, we go into the work of von Krogh and Roos (1995a), which contains the bulk of the new proposals which are being endorsed and expanded in this chapter. It starts from a social perspective using autopoiesis theory and Luhmann's approach to social systems, and goes on to put forward a new organizational epistemology.

The Critique of Open Systems Theory

The open systems model of organization has been enormously influential in the organization and management sciences in the last 30 years or more. However, along the way there have been some authors who have tried to draw attention to some fundamental problems that the open systems orthodoxy can bring, especially in so far as it ties research down to a very narrow and often overly mechanistic paradigm. Two of the earliest authors to warn about such dangers were Pondy and Mitroff, in a remarkable article which starts off as follows: 'Inventing the future for organization theory is the intention of this article' (1979: 4). Unfortunately, the article has been forgotten to a large degree and the future for organization theory has been delayed somewhat. In their article, Pondy and Mitroff go back to basics in systems theory and review Boulding's hierarchy of systems, in which all types of existing systems are ranked according to their complexity. The hierarchy is as follows: level 9, systems of unspecified complexity; level 8, multi-cephalous systems; level 7, symbol processing systems; level 6, internal image systems; level 5, blueprinted growth systems; level 4, open systems; level 3, control systems; level 2, clockworks; level 1, frameworks.

One of Pondy and Mitroff's major arguments is that even though human systems start at level 7, the study of organizations is still fixated, to a large extent, at level 4, and in many cases at level 3, in strictly controlled cause-and-effect research models. The conceptual difference between control systems and open systems is that whereas the former tend towards equilibrium in response to externally prescribed targets (e.g. thermostats or economic cycles in centrally controlled economies), thereby producing uniformity, the latter resist uniformity while also tending towards equilibrium but using their internal capacity for self-maintenance (e.g. the biological cell). Pondy and Mitroff argue that 'we have seriously misunderstood the nature of open systems and have confused them with natural or control systems' (1979: 22) and their endeavour is to show how the (still) current formulation of the open systems criteria for organizational modelling leave out important organizational phenomena, such as language and meaning.

For the purposes of our discussion, the major achievement of Pondy and Mitroff's paper has been to show the reality of how far apart have been studies of the more measurable aspects of organizations, such as structure and control systems, and studies of intangible aspects, such as organizational knowledge and learning. Using Boulding's hierarchy of systems as an aid, it is seen that knowledge and learning in organizations are, first and foremost, attributes of complex systems which can only be studied in the higher echelons of the hierarchy. 'Organization theories seem to have forgotten that they are dealing with human organizations, not merely disembodied structures in which individuals play either the role of in-place metering devices or the role of passive carriers of cultural values and skills' (1979: 17) and they go on to say that the models we use to study organizations must take into account the capacity that people have for self-awareness, for the use of language and for learning from their experience.

Specifically regarding the use of language, Pondy and Mitroff treat language as a kind of technology for processing data and meaning and, as is the case with any production technology, language will also determine what inputs will be accepted and what transformations will be permitted. Here, a strong influence from the individual/psychological view of organizational learning is clearly felt. These authors identify four distinct roles for language in organizational behaviour:

Control of perception Those events for which language expressions do not exist tend to be filtered out of consciousness.

Attribution of meaning By categorizing streams of events, language gives meaning to our experiences.

Facilitation of communication Old and new meanings can be communicated better.

Provision of a channel of social influence Language is essential in the organization's power games.

Although not addressing specifically the issue of organizational knowledge, Pondy and Mitroff provided a major contribution, in their article, to the study of organizations as knowledge systems, perhaps by stating how this issue *should not* be approached. In other words, they have shown how a lower-level model, especially with a very mechanistic interpretation such as the open systems orthodoxy, is not suited to researching complex systems such as knowledge systems, and also how a critical organizational resource such as language should play a central role in this discussion.

The Critique of the Organizational Learning Movement

From within the organization sciences there have been some 'doubts', over the years, about the appropriateness of the research models which have been used under the label of 'organizational learning'. Such doubts have been few and far between and the 'movement' as such is still going strong, as can be seen from the compilation of readings recently edited by Cohen and Sproull (1996). However, there is a small set of authors who have had something different to say and, although they have not made much of an impact, their views are still very relevant today.

Duncan and Weiss (1979) addressed the problem of *what* the main-stream organizational learning movement was trying to achieve, within the contingency perspective which was dominant in organization theory at the time. The contingency perspective stated that organizational effectiveness should be directly related to the degree of 'fitness' between the characteristics of the environment and the design of internal organizational structures and processes. According to these authors, a great deal of the organizational learning literature revolves around the basic questions of how the organization is designed (or adapted) to deal with the environment. The need for such changes, how they should be detected, appraised and applied, is obviously the responsibility of the organization's dominant coalition, thus making organizational learning a central concern for top management. However, they are very critical of the way that the literature fails to offer 'any insight into how this learning takes place, what the specific outcomes of learning are, who in the organization learns, or how the dominant coalition can utilize this learning process' (1979: 78). Another critical note made by these two authors concerns the way that much of the discussion on organizational learning is centred around individual learning in an organizational setting and the organizational dimension *per se* is lost.

Duncan and Weiss's contribution is also important because it was one of the first in the organization sciences to talk of organizational knowl-edge as opposed to organizational learning. Even today there seems to be a careful avoidance of the word *knowledge* in this field, which again may say something about the 'scientification' of management. Nonaka and Takeuchi (1995) use the expression 'scientification of business strategy' to explain the gradual taking over of the field by frameworks and models, such as the Boston Consulting Group (BCG) matrix, the profit impact of marketing strategy (PIMS) method of business fore-casting or Porter's five-forces model of industry analysis. These authors claim that this 'scientification' has created major limitations in the field of strategy, given that (1) it is not able to deal with questions of value and belief (i.e. cultural values); (2) it presupposes a top-down manage-ment style where only top management is assumed to manipulate explicit information; (3) it ignores the role of knowledge, especially tacit knowledge, as a source of competitiveness. This position is very close to Mintzberg's (1990) criticism of the 'design school' of strategic manage-ment.

Duncan and Weiss (1979) focus on knowledge as the outcome of learning, in their case, knowledge about action–outcome relationships and the effects of the organizational environment on such relationships. Furthermore, they treat learning as a process of knowledge develop-ment towards these objectives. They recognize that the learning or the knowledge development is achieved by individuals and that there must be organizational processes by which the individual knowledge becomes organizational knowledge. 'This process need not be formal. Indeed we would argue that it is a natural process driven by the need for organizational knowledge. The overall organizational knowledge base emerges out of this process of exchange, evaluation and integration of knowledge. . . . But it is a social process, one that is extraindividual. It is composed of the *interaction* of individuals and not their isolated behaviour' (1979: 89).

Duncan and Weiss' s formulation brings together to the organizational level, for the first time, the individual *and* the social dimensions of the problem, whereas other formulations before and after theirs saw the problem from either one *or* the other perspective. They put forward that 'frameworks exist within organizations and are to a large extent particular to a specific organization. That is, a given organization is characterized by a paradigm that is shared by organizational members in their socialization. Indeed, an organizational member must learn the system of concepts used within the organization if (s)he is able to communicate and understand the actions they are to take and the actions taken by others' (1979: 91).

The other author we have singled out as having had a significant contribution in the critical view of organizational learning is Karl Weick (1991; 1995). Weick casts some doubts upon the basic stimulus–response paradigm focused on behavioural change, which has guided much of the research in this area (i.e. the individual/psychological view). He starts off his earlier article by stating 'It has always bothered me that people in organization theory began to talk about learning just about the time psychologists began to desert the concept' (1991: 116), and he opens up the question of whether the traditional definition of individual learning should be kept and somehow applied to an organizational setting or whether a new definition should be adopted. Although the answer to the question is inconclusive and very conciliatory, Weick does show an inclination towards a wider understanding of the problem, namely by referring to the advantages of the second possibility. Replacing the traditional definition of organizational learning would mean to steer learning away from its individual component and towards the properties of organization and also to pursue the idea that organizations are interpretation (or knowledge) systems (Daft and Weick, 1984). By taking this approach, the expression 'learning' could be used interchangeably with 'knowledge development' because, as Weick recognizes, if there is a change in knowledge a change in behaviour becomes unnecessary.

The Critique of the Computer Metaphor

Another reason why 'learning' instead of 'knowledge' has become the dominant construct in the organization sciences has to do with the prevalence of the 'cognitive revolution', which can be summed up in two equivalent metaphors: the 'information processing' and the 'computer' metaphors of the human mind. Such metaphors of the mind have dominated much of the thinking in cognitive psychology, artificial intelligence and organization science over the last 40 years. According to this view, which has been deeply influenced by the ideas and concepts of H. Simon (1945; 1977; 1981), our brain acts like a computer, as an information processing mechanism which takes inputs from the environment, processes them according to pre-established rules and turns the inputs into outputs. Also according to this view, the brain contains representations of the environment, which it will retrieve and process as and when needed. Likewise, the organization, as an extension of the brain, also contains representations of the environment and is able to store and retrieve organization-wide knowledge structures.

The 'information processing' view has been a major influence on the mainstream organizational learning movement since it was introduced to the field in the early 1960s by Cyert and March's (1963) work on the behavioural theory of the firm. According to this view, organizations are treated as objective entities, rather than as concepts, endowed with a capability for cognition through some type of collective mind. Organizations are, therefore, seen as capable of containing representations of the environment in which they operate, very much in the same fashion that the human brain is said to contain representations of the outside (objective) world. Following this line of reasoning to its logical conclusion, it can easily be accepted that organizations are capable of learning, with adaptation to the environment as the main evidence of such learning. The information processing or cognitivist view has maintained its influence throughout the 1980s and 1990s. Hedberg states that 'There are many similarities between human brains and organizations in their roles of information processing systems' (1981: 6); and Huber, in a major review of the field, defends that 'an entity learns if, through its processing of information, the range of its potential behaviours is changed. This definition holds whether the entity is a human, a group, an organization' (1991: 89).

The cognitivist view of organizations has been challenged by many authors and from many points of view. One of the more outspoken has been Boland (1987). Boland centres his criticism around the notion of information (which is closely related to knowledge) and on the way that the computer metaphor paradigm has created a mindset in organizational and managerial parlance about information. Such a mindset is embodied in five *fantasies of information* which show the misconceptions which he attributes to the prevailing influence of the cognitivist paradigm. The first and leading fantasy is that *information is structured data*. This fantasy, according to Boland, is the most pernicious of all 'because it undermines the possibility for taking the problem of language seriously' (1987: 370). It originates in the Simonian notion that it is possible to create information simply by manipulating data and decision premises and that, when structured in certain ways, data acquire meaning. The next logical step along this line of thinking is to use the expressions *structured data* and *meaning* interchangeably. This is the same as saying that meaning can be established independent of the receiver of the data and, therefore, independent of the use of language. The remaining four fantasies are all consequences and elaborations of the first. They are as follows: *organization is information; information is power; information is intelligence;* and *information is perfectible.*

Tenkasi and Boland (1993) propose an alternative to the information processing metaphor. They state that 'as an alternative to the prevailing representational focus, we identify the making of narratives by organizational actors as the site for understanding processes of sensemaking, learning and change in organizations' (1993: 80). These authors bring together Giddens's structuration theory and Bruner's (1990) notion of the narrative as being the organizing principle of human cognition, and they propose a new approach to organizational learning and change. According to Bruner, 'our capacity to render experience in terms of narrative is not just child's play, but an instrument for making meaning that dominates much of life in culture – from soliloquies at bed time to the weighing of testimony in our legal system' (1990: 97).

By joining Bruner's approach (i.e. the individual view) with Giddens's structuration theory (i.e. the social view), the process of making narratives becomes an ongoing and interactive process with narratives being created and re-created continuously: 'as narratives change, structures change; narratives are the generative process in cognition' (Tenkasi and Boland, 1993: 97). This approach, which is in line with many aspects of an autopoietic view of knowledge and learning, as will be seen further on, is especially useful in pointing to new directions for a research methodology in organizational knowledge. Tracking organizational narratives is a more straightforward task than identifying abstract notions such as cognitive maps, or measuring elusive variables which purportedly reflect, for example, the degree of organizational learning.

The Postmodern View of Organizations and Management

Boje et al. (1996a), after a very interesting review of 40 years of literature and of the successive attempts to 'ward off the postmodern barbarians' from *Administrative Science Quarterly*, suggest that the time has come to revitalize the organizational disciplines by reconnecting them with their pluralistic roots. They state:

> Every body of knowledge has some particular epistemological and ontological assumptions that ultimately shape our existential, social, political and economic relations. A postmodern re-reading [of the administrative sciences] aims to expose these unchallenged assumptions and to submit them to a

critical analysis in order to expose the putative facticity or 'naturalness' of administrative science as timeless and universal truths. (1996a: 91)

In order to achieve this, Boje et al. (1996a) announce a 'critical post-modernist manifesto' and suggest a variety of methods and methodologies to carry out research in organization and management, ranging from critical ethnography to power/knowledge discourse analysis and from deconstruction methods to methods of ecological science.

This intellectual stance, which comes from within the organization sciences, is very much in accordance with the views outlined above about the narrative basis of organizational knowledge (Tenkasi and Boland, 1993). It is also in accordance with what philosophers and social psychologists have called the 'linguistic' or 'discursive' turn (Flick, 1995) which came after two other epistemological turns: in chronological order, the 'behaviourist' turn and the 'cognitivist' turn. Behaviourism, emphasizing observable behaviour and the stimulus–response relationship, treats the mind basically as a black box. The behaviourist stance, which is in general inadequate in explaining human behaviour, is present in most of the strands which characterize the individual view, mainly through the adoption of the stimulus–response paradigm by the mainstream organizational learning movement. Cognitivism was conceived as a way of making sense of the black box of the mind, and this was done mainly by the adoption of the computer metaphor, whereby the functioning of the human mind was modelled after the functioning of a computer. The notions held by the cognitivism para-digm that information processing and the making of meaning can be used interchangeably have come under intense criticism on the grounds that computers cannot assign meanings to events (Winograd and Flores, 1987). From a computational point of view, meanings are pre-assigned to messages through a system of pointers, but if the pointers are removed the meanings will be lost. From a human cognitive point of view pointers are not needed and there are many paths for the same meaning to be assigned to a given message. The cognitivist turn too seems to be coming to the end of its influence on many of the social sciences, including the organization sciences.

Thus, the discursive or linguistic turn appears as one of the epistemological underpinnings for some of the views grouped under the critical and alternative pole of influence. These views all share the concern, though to varying degrees, that undue weight is being given to positivist and quantitative research methods in the field and that not nearly enough attention is being given to interpretivist and qualitative methods, including narrative and language-based research. At first, they were just seen as dissenting voices by the mainstream organization science establishment, but gradually they seem to be gaining credibility and legitimacy among this community. Such credibility might also be associated with the momentum that the postmodern movement, with its defence of the analysis of discourse as a method of enquiry, is gaining in the organization sciences (Boje et al., 1996b).

The main issue which has been raised by the postmodern movement in management and organization science concerns the different interpretations that organizational events have for different organizational actors. Postmodernists claim that it is pointless to try to establish general laws for behaviour in organizations when all reality is socially constructed and, therefore, the meaning that organizational members ascribe to organizational events is always 'emergent'. In other words, there are no regularities in organizational life and each event has to be analysed on its own merit. However, organizations are not just made up of social structures. They are made up of management structures and systems as well. Managers construct reality through authoritative acts: that is, when they create rules and procedures, they take 'undefined space, time and action and draw lines, establish categories and coin labels that create new features of the environment that did not exist before' (Weick, 1995: 31). Hence, organizational events are not just ontologically 'emergent', but are 'enacted' as well, that is, in organizational life people produce part of the environment they face (1995: 31). From this, it can be posited that some regularities can be expected in some instances of organizational life, even though such regularities might be short-lived.

The point of the short discussion above is that even though the postmodernist movement in the management and organization sciences is right in drawing attention to the overly positivist stance taken by the mainstream research in the field and calling for alternative methods based on the analysis of discourse, it ignores the 'enactive' dimension which may be amenable to more objective-oriented methods of investigation.

The Organizational Knowledge Approach from Strategic Management

The last strand of influence to be looked at in this literature review comes mainly from the field of strategic management, but it is part of a broader view which has been named the resource-based approach to strategy (Wernerfelt, 1984). This approach also marks an important turn in business and management thinking in the 1990s, in the form of a change in focus from looking outward to market conditions in general in order to find a better competitive positioning for the firm, to looking inward and achieving more competitiveness starting from within the company. It is a shift from a position that everything begins and ends out there in the market to a position of everything begins and ends right here in the company. It is not a new approach, as it can be traced back to Penrose (1959) and the notion that what makes a firm grow is the accumulated experience and knowledge from within the company. But the approach has been dormant, certainly during the period of economic growth and the euphoria that followed in the 1960s and part of the 1970s, until more recently the work on evolutionary economics by Nelson and Winter (1982) has provided a more solid foundation for the resource-based view to develop.

Nelson and Winter's views are centred on knowledge and competence as assets and their endeavour is in finding which knowledge states are amenable to description and quantification and also which control variables can be used to alter such knowledge states. In attempting this, one of the problems they have encountered has to do with the terminology at our disposal to deal with this type of issue. On this particular point, Winter complains that:

> Within each microcosm of expertise or skill there is of course a specialized language in which that subject can be discussed. At the opposite extreme, there is terminology of very broad scope. There are words like information, innovation, skill, technology transfer, diffusion, learning and (of course) knowledge and competence. These name parts of the realm of discourse but do not do much to point the way towards advancing the discourse. The problems of managing technological and organizational change surely lie between these two extremes of low and high generality and in that range there seems to be a serious dearth of appropriate terminology and conceptual schemes. (1987: 180)

The above comment summarizes very accurately one of the major issues we have tried to emphasize in this chapter, which is the reigning confusion in the discussions around the theme of organizational learning and knowledge and the need for an integrative framework.

The following quote from Prahalad and Hamel (1990) illustrates well the need to talk about core competencies in strategic management. It also explains quite clearly why it became crucial for business organizations in particular to understand the importance of getting to grips with the issue of managing their knowledge resources.

> Of course, it is perfectly possible for a company to have a competitive product line up but be a laggard in developing core competencies – at least for a while. If a company wanted to enter the copier business today, it would find a dozen Japanese companies more than willing to supply copiers on the basis of an OEM [original equipment manufacturer] private label. But when fundamental technologies changed or if its supplier decided to enter the market directly and become a competitor, that company's product line, along with all of its investments in marketing and distribution, could be vulnerable. Outsourcing can provide a shortcut to a more competitive product, but it typically contributes little to building the people-embodied skills that are needed to sustain product leadership. (1990: 84)

Nonaka and Takeuchi (1995) set out to create a new theoretical framework for the resource-based approach to strategy, starting from the premise that business advantage will come from the internal capacity of organizations to create new knowledge, that is, to create something new and unique which will set them apart from the competition. They argue that although the literature keeps referring to the importance of knowledge and learning in the post-industrial society, very few studies have been carried out on the specific issue of how knowledge is created within or between business organizations. The main reason for this failure, according to Nonaka and Takeuchi, is the Cartesian dualism between subject and object or mind and body which is still very prevalent in Western thinking. To talk about knowledge in Western organizations is to talk about the explicit and objective aspects of knowledge while the tacit and subjective dimensions are almost completely neglected. He explains this state of affairs as the result of the growing 'scientification' of business strategy, where models upon models have tried to point the way to more cost cutting, excellent optimization of resources and increased market share, but still with no guarantee of success.

Nonaka and Takeuchi put forward a model where the various elements of knowledge creation are identified and interrelated in a dynamic whole which incorporates three basic dimensions: epistemological, ontological and temporal. The epistemological dimension, which is perhaps the major breakthrough of this theory, draws on the dichotomy of tacit versus explicit knowledge, a theme scholarly expounded upon by Michael Polanyi (1973). Tacit knowledge is personal and context-specific and hard or sometimes impossible to articulate in language. Examples of tacit knowledge are playing the piano or riding a bicycle; it is not easy to explain what you actually do when undertaking these activities, although they can be taught or explained by means of analogy or metaphors. Explicit knowledge refers to knowledge which is codifiable and transmittable in formal language. Nonaka (1994), Hedlund (1994) and Nonaka and Takeuchi (1995) argue that the processes of knowledge conversion, operating interactively and spirally between tacit and explicit knowledge, lie at the heart of knowledge creation. Thus, they are able to construct a two-by-two table containing all the possible modes of knowledge conversion: from tacit to tacit (socialization); from tacit to explicit (externalization); from explicit to tacit (internalization); and from explicit to explicit (combination).

The ontological dimension considers four different levels of knowledge creation: individual, group, organization and inter-organization. Organizational knowledge creation 'should be understood as a process that "organizationally" amplifies the knowledge created by individuals and crystallizes it as part of the knowledge network of the organization. This process takes place within an expanding "community of interaction" which crosses intra- and inter-organizational levels and boundaries' (Nonaka and Takeuchi, 1995: 59). As regards the temporal dimension, it concerns two types of movement, respectively along the ontological and the epistemological axes. Along the ontological axis, the movement starts with the individual's tacit knowledge, is amplified through the four modes of knowledge conversion and is finally crystallized at higher ontological levels (organizational or inter-organizational). This creates a spiral effect which becomes wider as it progresses along the ontological axis, that is, from the individual to the inter-organizational level, with increasing interaction between tacit and explicit knowledge. The second temporal movement takes place along the epistemological axis and it concerns the conversion of tacit into explicit knowledge put to organizational use, for example, in the form of advertisements, patents, products or services. This temporal movement also takes the form of a spiral with five stages: sharing tacit knowledge, creating concepts, justifying concepts, building an archetype and cross-levelling of knowledge. Nonaka and Takeuchi (1995) claim that it is through the transformation processes within these spirals and through their interaction over time that innovation occurs.

The framework put forward by these authors for creating or developing organizational knowledge is very different from the mainstream organizational learning movement. One of the reasons for this is the explicit attempt to break away from the Cartesian dualism of mind and body that prevails in the Western academic tradition and to follow a line of thought closer to the Japanese intellectual tradition. It is a very rich framework built upon examples and cases from Japanese companies, which also helps in placing this work outside the current schools of thought in Western organizational and management literatures. While this is not the place to write a critical review of these new proposals, it is our intention to place them within the framework of our thesis, that is, that language and languaging are central to an understanding of organizational learning and knowledge. Thus, the objective is not to look at this framework in detail but simply to ask the question: how is it achieved? Or, in other words, what are the basic mechanisms for achieving the major goal of the model, i.e. making much better use of tacit knowledge at the organizational level? The answer to this question is found in what Nonaka and Takeuchi (1995) call the 'three characteristics of knowledge creation': (1) the use of metaphor and analogy, that is figurative language, to help in the articulation of tacit knowledge; (2) the use of dialogue and discussion to maximize the sharing of personal knowledge, thereby helping in its conversion into organizational knowledge; and (3) the use of ambiguity and redundancy to help create new and common ways of thinking among organizational members.

All of the three basic mechanisms outlined above revolve around language and language use and, once more, they prove the point that Pondy and Mitroff (1979) made about how language should not be left out of models of organization, namely the open systems model. But they also show a great deal of convergence with the ideas that other writers have put forward when looking for features which help or hinder organizational knowledge development (or learning). The use of dialogue in organizational learning, for example, is one of the tenets of the 'interventionist school' of organizational learning (Magalhães, 1996). Isaacs (1993a; 1993b) has emphasized the importance of dialogue in organizational learning, and Normann (1985) has introduced the notion of 'rich language' as a way of promoting discussion among organizational members, in opposition to poor language which creates vicious learning circles. Von Krogh and Roos (1995b) see the issue of 'conversation management' as being a powerful means of creating and sustaining business advantage. Understanding that each organization has its own unique set of concepts and phrases and unique uses of them, and also the ability to create new language, are seen as essential components of the business strategy of the future. For these authors 'language and knowledge go hand in hand' and 'the currency of knowledge development is language' (1995b: 391). Eccles and Nohria (1992) have expressed the same view when talking about the need to manage the 'language cycle', i.e. the recognition that language also has a life cycle and that new words have to be introduced and old words discarded from the organization's vocabulary.

Thus far, we have attempted to show that there is a trend in current strategic management thinking which is moving away from the 'managerial rationality' of the past and towards a 'communicative rationality'. This is not new in management thinking, but it seems to have been forgotten in the euphoria of the 'scientification' movement, discussed by Nonaka and Takeuchi (1995). Peter Drucker (1954) was one of the first to point out the relevance of communication in management: 'Managers have to learn to know language, to understand what words are and what they mean. Perhaps most important, they have to acquire respect for language as our most precious gift and heritage. The manager must understand the meaning of the old definition of rhetoric as the "art which draws men's hearts to the love of true knowledge".'

Henceforth, the discussion will focus on specific proposals, at the epistemological level, which add further strength to the critical views reviewed so far and will underpin them with powerful alternative views of organizations and organizational knowledge. This will be based on the theory of autopoiesis, as put forward by its creators Maturana and Varela (1992), and on its application to management and the organization sciences by von Krogh and Roos (1995a), which in turn received some influence from the application of autopoiesis to the social sciences by Niklas Luhmann (1986; 1990).

What is Autopoiesis?

Autopoiesis is a concept developed more than 30 years ago in biology through the pioneering work of Maturana and Varela (1980; 1992), primarily as a construct which enabled them to make the distinction between living and non-living systems. Autopoiesis is a Greek word which means 'self-production'. An autopoietic system, therefore, is characterized as one that contains within its own boundaries the mechanisms and processes that enable it to produce and reproduce itself. The biological cell is the paradigmatic example of an autopoietic system as it possesses all the features that define a first-order autopoietic system, that is, it is autonomous, it is operationally closed, it is self-referential, it has its own organization and its own structure, and it is capable of structural coupling with its environment. As organisms evolve and become more complex, other forms of autopoiesis arise, namely second-order and third-order autopoiesis, where the same basic characteristics or criteria apply but in higher orders of complexity.

As organisms evolve and in some cases develop nervous systems, the possibilities for the organism to exhibit behaviour are expanded dramatically. The nervous system emerges in the history of living beings as a network of a special type of cell (neurons) which is embedded in the organism in such a way as to couple points in the sensory surfaces with points in the motor surfaces. It participates in the operation of a metacellular organism as a mechanism that maintains its structural changes within certain limits (for example, changes in the heartbeat following an upsurge in the flow of adrenaline). Thus the presence of a nervous system allows behaviour to become observable which, in turn, makes interaction between living beings possible. Such interactions, which can also be called social phenomena, are at the basis of a higher level of autopoietic activity. 'We call social phenomena those phenomena that arise in the spontaneous constitution of third order couplings and social systems the third order unities that are thus constituted' (Maturana and Varela, 1992: 193). Third-order autopoiesis is especially relevant for the purposes of this chapter as it forms the basis of languaging – the essence of the organization's knowledge system – and for this reason it is worth dwelling on it a little longer.

Social systems are of course not exclusive to the human species. They are to be found in all species endowed with a nervous system and vary in sophistication in close relationship with the species' nervous system complexity. However, what all species have in common is an internal phenomenology which is unique to that species and which causes uniform patterns of behaviour (even if to last a very short time) to appear among the members of that particular third-order unity. Such behaviour patterns usually require reciprocal coordination among the group and it is this coordinated behaviour triggered among the members of a social unity which Maturana and Varela (1992) call *communication*. Among social insects, for example, the mechanism of structural coupling and of coordination of behaviour takes place through the interchange of chemical substances, called *trophallaxis*. Trophallaxis, then, is communication for social insects. It is worth noting here that in autopoiesis theory, communication is not defined, as is traditional, as exchange of information, but instead means *doing* something. Communication has to imply action – in this case, coordinating action.

Communication can be innate or acquired. Innate communicative behaviour depends on structures that arise in the development of the organism independent of its particular history of social interactions, whereas acquired communicative behaviour does depend on such history of social interactions. Learned communicative behaviour constitutes a *linguistic domain*. A linguistic domain, however, is not to be confused with language. Human beings are not the only animals who are capable of generating linguistic domains in their social life. Many other species are capable of developing linguistic domains, that is, learned communicative behaviour. There are many well-known examples of highly developed communicative behaviours among, for example, primates or dolphins. In the words of Maturana and Varela, 'linguistic domains arise as cultural drift in a social system with no pre-established design. The process is one of behavioural transformation contingent on conservation of the social system through the behaviour of its components' (1992: 209), but such transformation of behaviour does not give rise to language.

The domain of language is uniquely human, first of all because it coordinates all social action. Language stands for human beings as trophallaxis stands for social insects: 'social unity is based on "linguallaxis" (a linguistic trophallaxis): a linguistic domain constituted as a domain of ontogenic coordinations of actions' (1992: 212). Second, language is unique to the human species because it is closely related to the notions of consciousness and reflection. To operate in language means to be able to make linguistic distinctions of linguistic distinctions. In other words, it means to be conscious that a word (for example *profit*) carries a linguistic distinction (for example the contrary of *loss*) and to reflect such awareness back in action. Language enables those who operate in it to (1) develop and maintain 'an ongoing descriptive recursion which we call the *I*' (1992: 231), i.e. consciousness and (2) 'describe themselves and their circumstances' (1992: 210), i.e. reflection.

Third, language is uniquely human because it generates meaning. Language does not exist as isolated items of behaviour, but must be seen as an ongoing process of *languaging*. 'To an observer, linguistic coordinations of actions appear as distinctions, linguistic distinctions. They describe objects in the environment of those who operate in a linguistic domain. Thus when an observer operates in a linguistic domain, he operates in a domain of descriptions' (1992: 211). The notion of observer and observing is crucial in autopoiesis. An autopoietic process can never be observed from the inside and it must always depend on one (or more) observers for its description. So, languaging arises when two (or more) observers engage in an exchange of linguistic distinctions which, in turn, gives rise to *meaning* being created and re-created. And 'meaning becomes part of our domain of conservation of adaptation' (1992: 211), as members of the human species.

Social Autopoiesis

The later work of the philosopher Niklas Luhmann (1986; 1990) has been greatly influenced by autopoiesis theory. Following the original work of Maturana and Varela, Luhmann has also developed a three-level classi-fication of autopoietic systems: living systems, psychic systems and social systems. The first level pertains to the functioning of cells and meta-cellular organisms. Individual human beings belong to the second level, and groups of individuals are placed on the third level. The first level uses life as its mode of reproduction while the second and third levels use meaning, which is produced and reproduced over time, also as a mode of reproduction. The basic difference between psychic and social systems, as regards their mode of functioning, is that the first uses consciousness and the second uses communication as the means to produce and reproduce meaning over time. Consciousness, communication and the production and reproduction of meaning are processes which are entirely dependent on language.

For Luhmann (1986) social systems are systems of meaning produced autopoietically, that is, produced by the social group itself. Meaning is produced primarily by individuals, as psychic systems, through the use of language. But in interacting with other individuals, in the social system, a different meaning may arise around the same object or con-cept, and the new meaning which holds true for the group may not exactly hold true for the individual. Interpretations of the same event may differ (and they often do) between the group and the individual. In other words, social groups develop their own systems of meaning and, because social systems are third-order autopoietic systems, they also become autonomous, operationally closed and self-referential. Social groups acquire their own knowledge and, in this sense, individuals are not part of the autopoietic system which the group constitutes but are observers placed in the system's environment.

Organizational Autopoiesis

First and foremost, von Krogh and Roos (1995a) are influenced by the writings of Maturana and Varela and especially by their views on the nature of knowledge. They assume a clearly anti-cognitivist position in the cognitive sciences debate, that is, they reject the notion that the world is a pre-given and that the task of the cognitive system is to represent it as accurately as possible. They equally reject that knowledge is abstract in the sense of being uncoupled from functions performed by the human body. Alternatively, they defend that knowledge *is embodied*, and also that knowledge and the world are structurally coupled and *coevolve*, that is, the world is not represented in the human mind or brain, but *comes forth* as a result of actions or observations by human beings. The key concept here is one by Maturana and Varela (1992): *knowledge is what brings forth a world*. These notions become clearer if they are built into an example, and von Krogh and Roos achieve this brilliantly with the following passage:

> Imagine that you are about to enter an office that is new to you. Your experience (knowledge) tells you to take an initial sweeping look in order to locate the reception desk, your assumed point of entry into the inner circles of the office. Having located what you believe is the reception desk (world) you take the first steps towards the desk. In doing this you get a glimpse of a corridor on your right-hand side in which you see a door and on which you locate a name plate (world). You recognize the name on the door to be the person you are supposed to visit (knowledge). (1995a: 52)

The notions that the world is not represented but brought is forth in knowledge, and that knowledge is not something abstract but is embodied, elicit the discussion about individual versus organizational knowledge. In keeping with the autopoietic view, knowledge construction is a very personal experience, and this of course applies to any organizational setting where new and old employees continuously learn (i.e. develop knowledge) about the organization, its objectives, its routines and its values. However, not only is such learning personal and individualized, but also there is no means for it to be directly transferred to other employees. Furthermore, it is not possible for any organizational member to know at any point in time what other organizational members know, except in a very limited way and to the extent that organizational members are willing to reveal what they know. Hence there are serious difficulties surrounding the notion of organizational cognition whereby the organizational 'mind' or 'brain' would be the sum total of all the minds or brains of the people working in that organization. Also, and by the some token, many of the traditional organizational learning theories would find it very difficult to defend their view that an organization is capable of adapting to the environment by learning and acting *en bloc*.

In order to resolve the problem of how individualized organizational knowledge becomes socialized, von Krogh and Roos turn to Luhmann (1986; 1990) among others. In his view of social systems, Luhmann maintains that social groups (e.g. organizations) are systems of meaning reproduced autopoietically: that is, through communication among its members the group creates its own autopoiesis which becomes independent from each of the group's members. The system acquires its own knowledge which is operationally closed regarding its internal organization; is self-referential in so far as it relies on its historical events to uphold its system of meaning; and becomes structurally coupled with its environment, that is, its internal structure is shaped and changed in the processes of accommodating recurrent 'perturbations' coming from the environment. Hence, for Luhmann the unit of analysis is the social system on its own and the individual becomes almost irrelevant, as an entity in the environment of the social system. Von Krogh and Roos have a problem with this particular feature of Luhmann's theory, as one of their main interests lies precisely in the mechanisms which allow individual knowledge to become socialized (or organizational) knowledge. The solution they have found for this particular difference lies in a theory of scaling which we will look at briefly ahead, but before doing so it is important to retain the main conclusion drawn by von Krogh and Roos, directly derived from Luhmann's ideas: that 'organizational knowledge, when socialized, has to be knowledge of the organization' (1995a: 64).

Drawing on many examples from the natural sciences, but especially from chaos theory and fractal geometry, von Krogh and Roos set out to demonstrate that 'like living systems the autopoietic knowledge development process is not only scaled in general, but similar across scale' (1995a: 74). They claim that a theory of scaling is appropriate as a linkage between individual and socialized organizational knowledge because knowledge is a process that is continuously brought forth on many scales in the organization. Examples of scales at the organizational level are the degree of departmentalization or the level of internatio-nalization or the level of vertical integration of the chain of production. Examples at the individual level are the 'degree of commitment' to the company or the level of education or the level of computer skills. Scaling at whatever level also implies self-similarity, that is, the same event is self-similar at whatever point of the scale one may wish to analyse the event. Self-similarity is defined by von Krogh and Roos as 'invariance over operations, any operations' (1995a: 81). Democracy is given as an example of a self-similarity: the concept is the same (or very similar), be it applied at the international, the national or the company level. Drawing on autopoiesis theory and on the self-similar nature of the various levels of autopoietic processes, i.e. first-, second- and third-order processes, von Krogh and Roos argue that the way new knowledge is produced (i.e. new distinctions are made) at the individual level is similar to the way that new knowledge is produced at the group, the department and the organization levels. Scaling and self-similarity become key concepts in the conversion between individual and organizational knowledge, in a very similar kind of analysis to Nonaka and Takeuchi's (1995) ontological dimension – and interestingly, also like Nonaka and Takeuchi, the 'engine' behind such conversion is language-based. In the case of von Krogh and Roos, however, the language dimension assumes much larger proportions in terms of its importance in the overall organizational knowledge system; and, in line with autopoiesis theory, they talk about languaging instead of language in order to emphasize the dynamic characteristics of the concept.

Von Krogh and Roos argue that 'the scale between socialized and individualized organizational knowledge is achieved by means of language' (1995a: 95). Language is what allows all action to be coordinated in the organization, and such coordination is achieved by means of organizational members making distinctions about the organization, starting with the first and broadest distinction of them all, which is the concept of 'organization' itself. Linguistically, the organization has to be distinguished from its environment. The simple emergence of a new entity, in this case the organization, presupposes languaging. Organizational members have to understand, in language, which organization they are working for, and from this very broad distinction other finer distinctions can start to be made. For example, what are the linguistic distinctions associated with the concept of 'product' in this particular organization? Thus, an organization develops its own unique languaging, that is, its own system of meaning which, according to Luhmann's theory, will develop its own autopoiesis. 'The organization has no substance except for being a self-similar, autopoietic system of knowledge and distinctions. Rather it has its tradition from which new conversations can take place. It demands of its members to continue to language about it on all scales in order for it to survive or, in other words, to continue its autopoiesis' (1995a: 98).

A very important part of von Krogh and Roos's (1995a) argumentation concerns the use of language in organizations, as this is an area through which a company may achieve business advantage. They build their argument based on the notion of language games, that is a notion whereby words are considered to derive their meaning from the content of their use rather than from the object or events they denote. To play a language game (i.e. for effective action to occur) it is necessary to know its rules, that is, the particular ways in which different uses may be made of the same word. According to von Krogh and Roos, 'to allow for rules and languaging that give way for effective action' (1995a: 101) becomes one of the main functions of socialized organizational knowledge. Thus, knowledge development in organizations will come about through the innovative use of old and new words and concepts as well as creating dynamics of meanings, in other words, through a managerial effort towards language development.

To sum up, according to von Krogh and Roos (1995a) organizational knowledge resides in both the individual organizational member and in the relations among organizational members, that is, at the social level. Organizational knowledge has the following properties: (a) it is shared among organizational members; (b) it is scalable and connected to the organization's history; (c) it both demands and allows for languaging. The expression 'organizational languaging' is intended to emphasize the dynamic properties of communication in organizations as it is created by and based on the experience of the individual organizational members. It is also pivotal in the organization's knowledge system that 'languaging may be understood as the "stuff" that the organization is made of' (1995a: 97). Given its dynamic nature, languaging fulfils a dual but conflicting function: on the one hand it contributes towards creating a unique identity for the organization in the form of its culture, and in that respect languaging can be instrumental in bringing about change. But, on the other hand, languaging becomes also the most important element in the maintenance of the status quo and resistance to change, given the self-referential nature of autopoietic systems, of which languaging is one.

Discussion and Conclusions

Towards an Integration of the Three Metaphors

First, organizational learning. The literature stream which has been labelled the individual view and which uses the organizational learning metaphor has not succeeded in providing convincing explanations for the transition of the learning from an individual state to an organizational state. This probably explains why the mainstream organizational learning movement avoids the issue of organizational knowledge and seems to treat learning as a concept which somehow is different from knowledge development (Duncan and Weiss, 1979). Centring the discussion around learning perhaps makes it more 'scientific' because measurement tools can be applied and the outcome of learning effort is measurable. However, this creates a narrow view of the problem as the discussion is often reduced to the level of skills measurement and the richness of the organizational dimension is lost. Individual learning cannot be isolated from the complexity of the social context where it takes place.

Second, organizational memory. Here there are problems of isomorphism. Memory is an attribute not only of human beings but also of lesser beings such as ants and of non-living beings such as computers. Both ants and computers have forms of memory, but these are totally different in nature from human memory. Hence, borrowing the 'memory' concept from cognitive psychology, from artificial intelligence or from sociology poses the problem of which type of memory is being borrowed. But there are also problems of anthropomorphism, in the sense that there is a danger of thinking of the organization as having the same memory capabilities as human beings. Some of the earlier attempts to deal with organizational memory were heavily influenced by the sociology of collective thought (Douglas, 1987) and did not achieve much more than to transfer to the organizational level the notion that individual and collective action are shaped and determined by social forces. In accordance with the social view, organizational memory is just another form of a collective memory, leaving unexplained phenomena such as organizational 'forgetting' (Hedberg, 1981) or the relationship between organizational memory and learning. A more recent attempt (Walsh and Ungson, 1991) has succeeded in conceptualizing the organization as a system of retention 'bins' (individuals, culture, transformations, structures and ecology) which is credible if one takes a static view of memory. However, if the organizational memory phenomenon is put in its dynamic social context, the notion of 'bins' becomes very restrictive and strongly resounding of 'storage', as in the information processing metaphor of organizational learning.

Third, organizational knowledge. Here, theories which have come mainly from the field of strategic management, in response to the view that competitive capability is obtained through the development of the organization's internal assets, bring new light to the debate. Without rejecting the need to consider and to measure individual learning (or knowledge development) these theories stress the interaction of the individual organizational members among themselves and as the locus of organizational learning. Von Krogh and Roos (1995a) explain how the concepts of individual and organizational knowledge are related using a theory of scaling, and also how knowledge development is dependent upon language-based managerial skills. Nonaka and Takeuchi (1995) detail the conditions necessary for knowledge to be created and developed and offer an organizational knowledge framework which brings together not only the individual and the organizational levels but also the inter-organizational dimension.

One of the major achievements of autopoiesis theory is in the tracing of knowledge from its biological roots (Maturana and Varela, 1992) and the way that it is naturally applied to both the individual and the social levels of analysis. Autopoiesis is therefore a very powerful theoretical framework to be applied to the study of knowledge and learning in organizations, as it bypasses the tensions between the individual learning and the social knowledge biases. The autopoietic view of languaging is one of the missing links between individual and organizational knowledge. The notion, derived from the sociology of Luhmann, that organizations are systems of meaning based upon communication among organizational members gives new strength to hitherto scattered voices claiming for an alternative view of the organization. Hence, autopoiesis theory and an organizational epistemology based on its theoretical framework afford the possibility of a common epistemological stance to be adopted around the concept of organizational knowledge, thus allowing the three metaphors of organizational learning, knowledge and memory to converge into a single all-encompassing metaphor.

However, in order to advance and achieve new roots, the whole discussion about organizational knowledge and learning has to be anchored on a new epistemological view of organization. This is what we have tried to do in introducing von Krogh and Roos's (1995a) seminal work to this discussion, in the hope that new light would be shed on a situation which can best be characterized as confusing as regards the literature, both academic and practice-oriented. And to consider a new organizational epistemology can have profound and decisive consequences in the fields of organizational behaviour and of business strategy which also show some signs of convergence, as we will see in the remainder of the discussion.

The New Organizational Epistemology and the Resource-Based Approach to Business Strategy: a New Role for Organizational Culture

Although the idea of the analysis of the firm from the resources side rather than from the products side had been around for a long time (Penrose, 1959), it received little formal attention from the business economics community for about three decades. 'The reason, no doubt, is the unpleasant properties (for modelling purposes) of some key examples of resources, such as technological skills' (Wernerfelt, 1984: 171). This situation is changing, however, and there is at present much interest in the resource-based approach, especially among the strategic management community, as an alternative to the analysis of firm growth and of the competitive advantage between firms (Conner, 1991; Barney, 1991; Grant, 1991; Schendel, 1994; Wernerfelt, 1995; Mahoney, 1995; Montgomery, 1995). We propose that in drawing attention to the autonomous, operationally closed and self-referential nature of systems, von Krogh and Roos's (1995a) organizational epistemology based on autopoiesis theory brings new support to the resource-based approach to business strategy.

If organizations are essentially closed systems, their internal growth in terms of knowledge and learning has to come from within. The environment as provider of new knowledge in the form of a constant flow of inputs into the system loses much of its previous relevance. Autopoiesis suggests that the two very basic characteristics of autopoietic systems are (1) the system's 'organization' which is not variable given that it is what defines the system itself, and (2) the system's 'structure' which can be changed through the structural coupling of the system with other systems. Translating this into organizational terminology, it can be said that the system's 'organization' is the organization's identity, and the system's 'structure' is all the structural and operational elements of the organization which are changed from time to time as a way of establishing more adequate 'couplings' both within the organization and between the organization and its environment. Von Krogh and Roos (1995a) put forward another basic element which forms the third corner of this foundation triangle: organizational languaging. Languaging has a pivotal function, in so far as it is the element which defines and maintains the organization's identity on the one hand, while it also restricts or enables the occurrence of any structural or operational changes in the organization on the other hand.

This distinction between a part of the organization which is almost monolithic (identity) and another part which can be changed (structures and structural couplings) by managerial action (language and languaging) is a powerful resource for the resource-based approach. The notion of the organization's identity as being fundamental in determining the limits to the growth of the firm had already been identified by several economists, in particular by Nobel prizewinner Kenneth Arrow, who states:

> the learning of a code by an individual is an act of irreversible investment for him. It is therefore also an irreversible capital accumulation for the organization. It follows that organizations, once created, have distinct identities because the costs of changing the code are those of unanticipated obsolescence. . . . Since the code is part of the firm's or more generally the organization's capital, the code of a given organization will be modified only slowly over time. . . . The need for codes mutually understandable within the organization imposes a uniformity requirement on the behaviour of the participants. They are specialized in the information capable of being transmitted by the codes, so that they learn more in the direction of their activity and become less efficient in acquiring and transmitting information not easily fitted into the code. Hence, the organization itself serves to mold the behaviour of its members. (1974: 55–6)

The issue of the organization's identity is central to resource-based thinking. Identity can also be construed as 'culture', and organizational culture has been pointed out as a key source of sustained competitive advantage (Barney, 1986; Fiol, 1991). The question which must be put, therefore, is: how can the new epistemological view help towards an achievement of the benefits of a more culturally oriented view of organizations? Organizational autopoiesis provides the necessary arguments to show that organizations cannot be modelled after an input–output paradigm and that organizational events are both emergent and enacted. The way to approach organizational research, therefore, is via the three basic components of any autopoietic organizational system: identity, structures and languaging. The first – identity – is the determining factor, the factor behind the organization's ethos. The remaining factors are dependent upon the organization's identity. Hence, organizational culture and all the other ways of operationalizing identity (for example, organizational frames, contexts or climates) must be at the forefront of any efforts to understand organizations and organizational life.

The adoption of epistemological stances different from organizational autopoiesis will lead to a perpetuation of the problems identified by Pondy and Mitroff (1979), that is, that organizational reality happens higher up on Boulding's hierarchy of systems complexity (at levels 7 or 8) while organizational research is carried out at lower levels (at levels 3 and 4). This, in turn, leads to confusion and dissonance between management practice and the literature closer to it, and academic research and publishing. An example of this can be seen in the issue of the 'learning organization'.

Let us go back to the questions put at the outset of this chapter regarding the 'learning organization' (i.e. what is it and how is it achieved?) and try to understand why this problem is of an epistemological nature. The whole conception of the learning organization is based on a cultural view of the organization (Morgan, 1986). Therefore, in order to achieve the desiderata of the learning organization, the discussion has be focused on identities, values, beliefs and perceptions which are all difficult to measure objectively. Meanwhile, the organizational metaphor which is still preferred in academia, regarding its research designs, its academic programmes and its textbooks, is not the 'culture' metaphor but the 'machine' metaphor (Morgan, 1986). To be more specific, we suggest that the learning organization will only become a viable proposition when management researchers and practitioners come to the realization that such an organization stands on the opposite side to the 'machine organization'. Machine organizations are most of those we see around us and which are still being created every day, based on the century-old command-and-control management paradigm (Drucker, 1988). It is not possible to create learning organizations out of machine organizations simply because the epistemological assumptions behind the latter are radically different from the assumptions that would be needed to create the former.

Organizational Autopoiesis as a Mid-Theoretical Approach: New Support for Managerial Action Perspectives

The second basic components of organizational autopoietic systems are the structural couplings (i.e. the organization's structures, systems, policies, procedures) which allow the organization to produce both internally, by giving it the basic rules for functioning, and externally, by linking it with other organizations. Structural couplings are, fundamentally, a static element of the organizational autopoietic system. They make up the organization's 'strategic intent' (Hamel and Prahalad, 1989), that is, all those aims and objectives the organization wishes to achieve and the means by which to achieve them, but they do not say much on the question of how to go about realizing such intent. Argyris and Schön (1996) claim that the literature on strategic management is 'inattentive' (1996: 253) regarding the gap between intent and realization and they suggest that the gap must be filled by a theory of action. A theory of action posits, first and foremost, that there is a behavioural world created by the parties to an interaction (Argyris and Schön, 1996) and rests upon language and on the use of language as its main tool of enquiry.

Going back to what was said at the outset of this chapter, the different views and intellectual biases about organizational knowledge and learning are a reflection of the tensions, on a wider scale, between views of management activity essentially based on rational thought versus approaches based on organizational power; a top-down view of business strategy as opposed to a bottom-up, emergent approach; a positivist approach to research versus a purely interpretivist stance; or the gap between intent and realization, just mentioned. In the literature on strategic management there seems to be a clear movement towards a *rapprochement* between these two extremes (see, for example, Schendel, 1994) and an active search for some 'middle ground'. Hence, *we propose that such middle ground must be filled by theories of managerial action and that organizational autopoiesis gives important epistemological support to such theories.*

In the resource-based approach to strategy, such middle ground has been explored by Mahoney (1995), who revisits Penrose's (1959) theory of the growth of the firm and puts forward a 'resource learning theory', as a synthesis of resource-based theory and of learning theories focusing on the development of human resources and of organizational capabilities in general. The theory may be summarized as follows: 'The accumulation of resources creates a base for organizational learning. Conversely, organizational learning and new organizational forms allow firms to increase their rate of resources accumulation' (1995: 97). Mahoney explains that, on its own, resource-based analysis is not sufficient as it is unable to articulate the management practices that enable firms to earn rents. But process-oriented models are also incomplete because they cannot make the distinction between what is strategically relevant and what is strategically irrelevant. The solution rests upon *managerial skills* which, jointly with other resources, produce rents for the firm.

The formulation above highlights the importance of the role of management in organizational performance, but it does not address the question of *how* such a role or such skills should be put into practice in order for organizational effectiveness to ensue. These issues have been addressed by Bartlett and Ghoshal (1993) and Ghoshal and Bartlett (1994) in a new managerial theory of the firm which these authors have began to craft and which is also positioned in the 'middle ground' mentioned above. Such theory is based on 'core management processes', a direct consequnce of the interactive development of managerial action and organizational context. Managerial action is the result of managerial choices which actors within firms have made over time, and organizational context is the consequence of managerial action. This stance is close to Argyris and Schön's (1996) theory of action perspective. Even though Ghoshal and Bartlett (1994) do not address themselves directly to the use of language by managers, they focus on value-oriented actions, such as 'shared ambition', 'equity', 'sanctions', 'involvement' and so forth, which are direct manifestations of language use. Organizational context is shaped by the presence of four dimensions of quality management, which are an outcome of managerial action – stretch, trust, discipline and support. The combination of these four dimensions, in turn, results in improved collective learning and in organizational effectiveness. These authors claim that although the concepts of stretch, trust, discipline and support have little relevance in existing theory, they believe that they are of 'central importance for the analysis of organizational effectiveness' (1994: 110).

Ghoshal and Bartlett's notion of organizational context is very close to Fiol's (1991) notion of 'identities' as a mid-theoretical construct which serves as a bridge between organizational culture as a set of beliefs and values, and observable behaviours such as the usage of words in organizations. In Fiol's own words:

> The reframing [of the organizational culture concept] recognizes cultural belief systems as the glue that binds the diverse aspects of the firm. However, we also suggest that in most cases it may be both difficult and ineffective to manage the gluing process at the level of behaviours. . . . Behaviour patterns reflect unique identities or contextual beliefs. . . . Those identities, rather than the discrete behaviours that drive them, are the keys to understanding and managing behaviours in relation to an overall belief system. (1991: 208)

Both Ghoshal and Bartlett's concept of organizational context and Fiol's notion of organizational identities, which tries to resolve the problem of how to overcome the gap between language as an unobservable set of rules and language as observable expressions in the form of words, have affinities with von Krogh and Roos's (1995a) construct of 'organizational languaging'. This languaging, which in a way also bridges the gap between a monolithic organizational identity and easily changeable organizational structures, is the third element of organizational autopoiesis. It is a powerful and highly dynamic element which keeps the organization together and has the power to change the other two elements – 'identity' and 'structures'. Hence, we see organizational languaging as being an exceptionally rich source of research in the future. Potentially interesting research questions are:

- What is the interplay between organizational identity, structures and languaging in the formation of organizational knowledge?
- How can languaging be operationalized so that clearer links can be established between managerial context and action?
- Can languaging be researched with methods other than ethnographies and action research?
- How can research on organizational languaging be turned into useful material for management education and practice?

It is hoped that these few questions and supporting arguments have contributed towards a complex undertaking, which is the understanding of organizations as knowledge systems or as cognitive entities. This contribution was given from the viewpoint of organizational autopoiesis, a new and very promising epistemological approach which, we hope, will reposition many of our current beliefs about human organizations and, in doing so, make them even more human. To end with the words of the creators of autopoiesis theory: 'Every act in language brings forth a world created with others in the act of coexistence which gives rise to what is human. Thus, every human act has an ethical meaning because it is an act of constitution of the human world' (Maturana and Varela, 1992: 247).

Notes

Acknowledgements go to the Portuguese Catholic University (Lisbon), to the Gulbenkian Foundation (Lisbon) and to EUROSTAT (Luxembourg) for the support given to the research project which has led to this chapter. A special word of thanks also to Professor Ian Angell, Dr L. Introna and Dr C. Avgerou of the London School of Economics (UK) for their support and advice, and to Professor Georg von Krogh of the University of St Gallen (Switzerland) for his helpful comments on a draft of the chapter.

References

Argote, L. (1993) Group and organizational learning curves: individual, system and environmental components. *British Journal of Social Psychology*, 32: 31–51.
Argyris, C. and Schön, D.A. (1978) *Organizational Learning: a Theory of Action Perspective*. Reading, MA: Addison-Wesley.
Argyris, C. and Schön, D.A. (1996) *Organizational Learning II: Theory, Method and Practice*. Reading, MA: Addison-Wesley.
Arrow, K. (1974) *The Limits of Organization*. New York: Norton.
Attewell, P. and Rule, J. (1984) Computing and organizations: what we know and what we don't know. *Communications of the ACM*, 27: 1184–92.
Barney, J.B. (1986) Organizational culture: can it be a source of sustained competitive advantage? *Academy of Management Review*, 11: 656–65.
Barney, J.B. (1991) Firm resources and sustained competitive advantage. *Journal of Management*, 17: 99–120.
Bartlett, C.A. and Ghoshal, S. (1993) Beyond the M-form: towards a managerial theory of the firm. *Strategic Management Journal*, 14: 23–46.
Bateson, G. (1972) *Steps to an Ecology of the Mind*. New York: Ballantine.
Berger, P.L. and Luckmann, T. (1967) *The Social Construction of Reality*. New York: Doubleday Anchor.
Boje, D.M., Fitzgibbons, D.E. and Steingard, D.S. (1996a) Storytelling at *Administrative Science Quarterly*: warding off the postmodern barbarians, in D.M. Boje, R.P. Gephardt and T.J. Thatchenkery (eds), *Postmodern Management and Organization Theory*. Thousand Oaks, CA: Sage.

Boje, D.M., Gephardt, R.P. and Thatchenkery, T.J. (eds) (1996b) *Postmodern Management and Organization Theory*. Thousand Oaks, CA: Sage.

Boland, R.J. (1987) The in-formation of information systems, in R.J. Boland and R.A. Hirschheim (eds), *Critical Issues in Information Systems Research*. Chichester: Wiley.

Brown, J.S. and Duguid, P. (1991) Organizational learning and communities of practice. *Organization Science*, 2: 40–57.

Bruner, J.S. (1990) *Acts of Meaning*. Cambridge, MA: Harvard University Press.

Cangolesi, V.E. and Dill, W.R. (1965) Organizational learning: observations towards a theory. *Administrative Science Quarterly*, 10: 175–203.

Cohen, M.D. (1991) Individual learning and organizational routines: emerging connections. *Organization Science*, 2 (1): 135–9.

Cohen, M.D. and Sproull, L.S. (eds) (1996) *Organizational Learning*. Thousand Oaks, CA: Sage.

Cohen, W.M. and Levinthal, D.A. (1990) Absorbtive capacity: a new perspective on learning and innovation. *Administrative Science Quarterly*, 35: 128–52.

Collis, D.J. and Montgomery, C.A. (1995) Competing on resources: strategy in the 1990s. *Harvard Business Review*, 73 (4): 118–28.

Conner, K. (1991) A historical comparison of resource-based theory and five schools of thought within industrial organization economics. *Journal of Management*, 17: 121–54.

Cyert, R.M. and March, J.G. (1963) *A Behavioral Theory of the Firm*. Englewood Cliffs, NJ: Prentice-Hall.

Daft, R.L. and Weick, K. (1984) Towards a model of organizations as interpretation systems. *Academy of Management Review*, 9: 284–95.

Douglas, M. (1987) *How Institutions Think*. London: Routledge.

Drucker, P. (1954) *The Practice of Management*. New York: Harper and Row.

Drucker, P. (1988) The coming of the new organization. *Harvard Business Review*, January–February: 3–15.

Duncan, R. and Weiss, A. (1979) Organizational learning: implications for organizational design, in B.M. Staw (ed.), *Research in Organizational Behavior*, Vol. 1. Greenwich, CT: JAI Press.

Durkheim, E. (1938) *The Rules of Sociological Method*. New York: Free Press.

Eccles, R.G. and Nohria, N. (1992) *Beyond the Hype: Rediscovering the Essence of Management*. Boston, MA: Harvard Business School Press.

Epple, D., Argote, L. and Devadas, R. (1991) Organizational learning curves: a method for investigating intra-plant transfer of knowledge acquired trhough learning by doing. *Organization Science*, 2: 58–70.

Fiol, C.M. (1991) Managing culture as a competitive resource: an identity-based view of sustainable competitive advantage. *Journal of Management*, 17 (1): 191–211.

Fiol, C.M. and Lyles, M.A. (1985) Organizational learning. *Academy of Management Review*, 10 (4): 803–13.

Flick, U. (1995) Social representations, in J. Smith, R. Harré and L. von Langenhove (eds), *Rethinking Psychology*. London: Sage.

Ghoshal, S. and Bartlett, C.A. (1994) Linking organizational context and managerial action: the dimensions of quality management. *Strategic Management Journal*, 15: 91–112.

Giddens, A. (1976) *New Rules of Sociological Method*. London: Hutchinson.

Giddens, A. (1984) *The Constitution of Society: Outline of the Theory of Structuration*. Cambridge: Polity.

Gioia, D.A. and Sims, H.P. (1986) Introduction: social cognition in organizations, in H.P. Sims and D.A. Gioia (eds), *The Thinking Organization*. London: Jossey-Bass.

Grant, R.M. (1991) The resource-based theory of competitive advantage: implications for strategy formulation. *California Management Review*, 33 (Spring): 114–35.

Hamel, G. and Prahalad, C.K. (1989) Strategic intent. *Harvard Business Review*, 67 (3): 63–76.

Hedberg, B. (1981) How organizations learn and unlearn, in P.C. Nystrom and W. Starbuck (eds), *Handbook of Organizational Design*, 1: 3–27.

Hedlund, G. (1994) A model of knowledge management and the N-form corporation. *Strategic Management Journal*, 15: 73–90.

Huber, G.P. (1990) A theory of the effects of advanced information technologies on organizational design, intelligence and decision making. *Academy of Management Review*, 15 (1): 47–71.

Huber, G.P. (1991) Organizational learning: the contributing processes and the literatures. *Organization Science*, 2 (1): 88–115.

Isaacs, W.N. (1993a) Taking flight: dialogue, collective thinking and organizational learning. *Organizational Dynamics*, 22 (2): 24–39.

Isaacs, W.N. (1993b) Dialogue: the power of collective thinking. *The Systems Thinker*, 4 (3): 1–4.

Jones, M. (1995) Organisational learning: collective mind or cognitivist metaphor? *Accounting, Management and Information Technologies*, 5 (1): 61–77.

Katz, D. and Kahn, R.L. (1966) *The Social Psychology of Organizations*. New York: Wiley.

Kochan, T.A. and Useem, M. (eds) (1992) *Transforming Organizations*. New York: Oxford University Press.

Lave, J. and Wenger, E. (1991) *Situated Learning: Legitimate Peripheral Participation*. Cambridge: Cambridge University Press.

Luhmann, N. (1986) The autopoiesis of social systems, in F. Geyer and J. Van de Zouwen (eds), *Sociocybernetic Paradoxes: Observation, Control and Evolution of Self-Steering Systems*. London: Sage.

Luhmann, N. (1990) *Essays on Self-Reference*. New York: Columbia University Press.

Lyles, M. and Schwenk, C. (1992) Top management, strategy and organizational knowledge structures. *Journal of Management Studies*, 29 (March): 155–74.

Magalhães, R. (1996) Organizational learning, organizational knowledge and organizational memory: new proposals towards a unified view. Working Paper Series 60, London School of Economics, Department of Information Systems.

Mahoney, J.T. (1995) The management of resources and the resource of management. *Journal of Business Research*, 33: 91–101.

March, J.G. and Simon, H.A. (1958) *Organizations*. New York: Wiley.

Markus, M.L. and Robey, D. (1988) Information technology and organizational change: causal structure in theory and research. *Management Science*, 34 (5): 583–98.

Maturana, H.R. and Varela, F.J. (1980) *Autopoiesis and Cognition*. London: Reidl.

Maturana, H.R. and Varela, F.J. (1992) *The Tree of Knowledge*. Boston: Shambhala.

Mintzberg, H. (1990) The design school: reconsidering the basic premises of strategic management. *Strategic Management Journal*, 11 (3).

Montgomery, C.A. (ed.) (1995) *Resources in an Evolutionary Perspective: a Synthesis of Evolutionary and Resource-Based Approaches*. Dordrecht: Kluwer.

Morgan, G. (1986) *Images of Organizations*. London: Sage.

Nelson, R.R. and Winter, S. (1982) *An Evolutionary Theory of Economic Change*. Cambridge, MA: Harvard University Press.

Nonaka, I. (1988) Creating organizational order out of chaos. *California Management Review*, 30 (Spring): 57–73.

Nonaka, I. (1994) A dynamic theory of organizational knowledge creation. *Organization Science*, 5 (1): 14–37.

Nonaka, I. and Takeuchi, H. (1995) *The Knowledge-Creating Company: How Japanese Companies Create the Dynamics of Innovation*. New York: Oxford University Press.

Normann, R. (1985) Developing capabilities of organizational learning, in J.M. Pennings (ed.), *Organizational Strategy and Change*. San Francisco: Jossey-Bass.

Orlikowski, W.J. (1992) The duality of technology: rethinking the concept of technology in organizations. *Organization Science*, 3 (3): 398–427.

Orlikowski, W. and Robey, D. (1991) Information technology and the structuring of organizations. *Informations Systems Research*, 2 (2): 143–69.

Orr, J. (1990) Sharing knowledge, celebrating identity: war stories and community memory in a service culture, in D.S. Middleton and D. Edwards (eds), *Collective Remembering: Memory in Society*. London: Sage.

Parsons, T. (1951) *The Social System*. New York: Free Press.

Parsons, T. (1956) Suggestions for a sociological approach to the theory of organizations – 1. *Administrative Science Quarterly*, 1: 63–85.

Parsons, T. (1957) Suggestions for a sociological approach to the theory of organizations – 2. *Administrative Science Quarterly*, 2: 225–41.

Penrose, E. (1959) *The Theory of the Growth of the Firm*. Oxford: Blackwell.

Polanyi, Ml. (1973) *Personal Knowledge: Towards a Post-Critical Philosophy*. London: Routledge and Kegan Paul.

Pondy, L.R. and Mitroff, I. (1979) Beyond open systems models of organization, in B.M. Staw (ed.), *Research in Organizational Behavior*, Vol. 1. Greenwich, CT: JAI Press.

Prahalad, C.K. and Hamel, G. (1990) The core competence of the corporation. *Harvard Business Review*, May–June: 79–91.

Robey, D. (1977) Computers and management structure: some empirical findings re-examined. *Human Relations*, 30: 963–76.

Robey, D. (1995) Theories that explain contradiction: accounting for the contradictory organizational consequences of information technology. Paper presented at the International Conference on Information Systems, Amsterdam, 1995.

Schendel, D. (1994) Introduction to competitive organizational behaviour: towards an organizationally-based theory of competitive advantage. *Strategic Management Journal*, 15, Special Issue: 1–4.

Senge, P. (1990) *The Fifth Discipline: the Art and Practice of the Learning Organization*. London: Century Business.

Simon, H.A. (1945) *Administrative Behavior*. New York: Macmillan.

Simon, H.A. (1977) *The New Science of Management Decision*. Englewood Cliffs, NJ: Prentice-Hall.

Simon, H.A. (1981) *The Sciences of the Artificial*. Cambridge, MA: MIT Press.

Spence, A.M. (1981) The learning curve and competition. *Bell Journal of Economics*, 12: 49–70.

Stalk, G., Evans, P. and Shulman, L.E. (1992) Competing on capabilities: the new rules of corporate strategy. *Harvard Business Review*, March–April: 57–69.

Stein, E.W. and Zwass, V. (1995) Actualizing organizational memory with information systems. *Information Systems Research*, 6.

Tenkasi, R.V. and Boland, R.J. (1993) Locating meaning making in organizational learning: the narrative basis of cognition, in R.W. Woodman and W.A. Passmore (eds), *Research in Organizational Change and Development*, Vol. 7. Greenwich, CT: JAI Press.

von Krogh, G. and Roos, J. (1995a) *Organizational Epistemology*. Basingstoke: Macmillan.

von Krogh, G. and Roos, J. (1995b) Conversation management. *European Management Journal*, 13 (4): 390–4.

Walsh, J.R. and Ungson, G.R. (1991) Organizational memory. *Academy of Management Review*, 16: 57–91.

Weick, K.E. (1991) The nontraditional quality of organizational learning. *Organization Science*, 2 (1): 116–24.

Weick, K.E. (1995) *Sensemaking in Organizations*. Beverly Hills, CA: Sage.

Wernerfelt, B. (1984) A resource-based view of the firm. *Strategic Management Journal*, 5: 171–80.

Wernerfelt, B. (1995) The resource-based view of the firm: ten years after. *Strategic Management Journal*, 16: 171–4.

Winograd, T. and Flores, C.F. (1987) *Understanding Computers and Cognition*. Cambridge, MA: Addison-Wesley.

Winter, S.G. (1987) Knowledge and competence as strategic assets, in D.J. Teece (ed.), *The Competitive Challenge: Strategies for Industrial Innovation and Renewal*. Cambridge, MA: Ballinger.

Yelle, L.E. (1979) The learning curve: historical review and comprehensive survey. *Decision Sciences*, 10: 302–28.

5

KNOWLEDGE AND THE CONCEPT OF TRUST

Lars Huemer, Georg von Krogh and Johan Roos

The notion of trust has in recent years received considerable attention. Trust has even been described as a business imperative (e.g. Davidow and Malone, 1992; Drucker, 1993; Sabel, 1993). In the 1994 summer special issue of the *Strategic Management Journal*, which focuses upon a search for new paradigms in strategy, Hosmer (1994) argues that trust is essential for success in a competitive global economy. In the same issue, Ghoshal and Bartlett (1994) suggest that trust is one of four primary dimensions of organizational context, which in turn influences the actions of those involved in a company. Contractor and Lorange (1988) and Lorange and Roos (1992) emphasize the importance of trust for strategic alliances, and Peters (1992) for project organizations; and industrial marketing scholars suggest that trust is 'the gateway to successful relationships' (Wilson and Jantrania, 1993: 5). In buyer–supplier relationships, single sourcing, outsourcing, early supplier involvement and the just-in-time philosophy are different phenomena that all have bearings on trust.

Trust is commonly regarded as crucial since its roles or functions for the wellbeing of business relationships are cardinal. The list is long: some examples include creation of benefits for all parties, reduction of complexity and the need for constant surveillance, reduction of opportunism, and production of positive attitudes (see e.g. Luhmann, 1979; Barber, 1983; John, 1984). Trust may furthermore lead to committed relationships, decrease transaction costs, and function as a significant determinant for managerial problem-solving effectiveness (Zand, 1972; Jarillo, 1990; Morgan, 1991; Ring and Van de Ven, 1994). Thus, besides being of growing concern within the realm of strategic management theory, trust is, or should be, a central matter for many firms today. In this chapter we argue that one of the most important roles of trust concerns issues related to corporate epistemology, i.e. how and why organizational knowledge may develop.

Knowledge has been stressed to be of utmost importance for business conduct, e.g. knowledge has been suggested to be crucial for developing and sustaining competitive advantage (e.g. Prahalad and Hamel, 1990). Firms increasingly compete on a differentiated stock of knowledge (Stinchcombe, 1990), where they succeed by developing, improving, protecting and renewing knowledge (Badaracco, 1991). Knowledge has previously been discussed in relation to e.g. power, dialogue and conversation (see Morgan, 1993). Brown and Duguid (1991) argue that to understand the way information is constructed and travels within an organization, it is first necessary to study the different communities of practice formed within it, and the distribution of power within those communities. Although power matters, we suggest an emphasis on the condition of *trust* among organizational members in the light of a corporate epistemology. Following the argument of Brown and Duguid, that what is learned is profoundly connected to the conditions in which it is learned, it seems plausible to suggest that there will be differences between communities 'tied together' and 'lubricated' by trust, and communities based on power. Our argument is furthermore in line with Giddens (1990) who regards trust as a function of imperfect information, and not primarily related to power. We suggest that trust facilitates learning between partners (cf. March and Olsen, 1990), and that decisions to exchange in knowledge under certain conditions are based on trust.

The objective of the chapter is to broaden the perspective on trust and to emphasize the link between trust and knowledge. This is accomplished by relating to trust according to the epistemologies of cognitivism, connectionism and autopoiesis. The chapter is divided into three sections. In the first section, recent views on trust from the strategy and management literature are discussed. A conceptualization of trust is furthermore suggested, which emphasizes the composite nature of trust. In the second section, trust is discussed according to the epistemologies of cognitivism, connectionism and autopoiesis. The final section addresses implications for theory development.

The Concept of Trust: a Brief Retreatment

Trust is being stressed to be of major importance in the contemporary economy.[1] The idea of trust, a user-friendly everyday expression with considerable appeal, is becoming an increasingly popular academic concept. But to mention a phenomenon is not the same thing as explaining or understanding the same phenomenon.

There are at least three main reasons why trust is not well understood. First, trust has been assumed away as a frictional matter in prior treatments of markets and hierarchies, where social relations between parties have been regarded as atomized and irrelevant (Dasgupta, 1988; Ring and van de Ven, 1992). Hence, business relationships, wherein trust is a crucial aspect, are phenomena that do not find convincing explanations in the traditional framework of economics and management (see Håkansson and Snehota, 1995). As pointed out by Rumelt et al. (1991), corporate strategy in the 1980s adopted the language and logic of economics. This explains the impact of assumptions such as self-interest and opportunism within the strategy field. But there are scholars returning to insights present in the work of e.g. Barnard (1938) and Follet (Graham, 1995). Second, there is a problem of reducing trust to only a part of its nature within e.g. economics, social psychology and political science. Psychometric scaling techniques or behavioural expressions in laboratory settings only focus upon the cognitive aspects of trust, and ignore its emotional aspects (Lewis and Weigert, 1985). Third, trust is a conceptually complex concept (see e.g. Kaplan, 1973; Corrazzini, 1977; Heretick, 1984; Lewis and Weigert, 1985; Young, 1992; Sitkin and Roth, 1993). One consequence of the variety of the existing literature is that the term 'trust' runs a risk of becoming a 'catch-all phrase' (Huemer, 1994).

The conventional assumptions of self-interest seeking with guile and opportunism in e.g. transaction cost economics seem unjustifiable. But so too do assumptions of trustworthiness (cf. Ring and van de Ven, 1992). The very idea of trust depends on assumptions that allow for uncertainty and diversity in human behaviour. This is in line with Ghoshal and Bartlett's (1994) view, which neither assumes a strict self-interest seeking behaviour, nor relies on a fundamental premise of stable altruistic behaviour. Instead, it reflects more a relativistic perspective on personal attributes, and more of a situationalist view on human behaviour. A theory with 'extreme' assumptions, in either direction, will not promote further understanding of trust. Although working within the tradition of organizational economics, Barney and Hansen (1994) depart from the assumption of opportunism in transaction cost economics, and also from the other extreme, by claiming that trust may vary. Moreover, it is this variance which can be a source of competitive advantage. Barney and Hansen further suggest that it may be possible to assess what kind of trust one may experience.

Until recently, trust had not received much explicit attention in the strategy and management literature. However, a number of contributions discussing different trust forms have been presented lately, as shown in Figure 5.1. Barney and Hansen (1994) discuss three trust forms and their relationship to competitive advantage. Weak form trust exists when there are no vulnerabilities from adverse selection, moral hazard, hold-up or other sources. Trust in this type of exchange emerges because there are only limited opportunities for opportunism. Weak form trust is primarily endogenous, i.e. it emerges out of a very specific exchange structure. Semi-strong trust in Barney and Hansen's terminology is trust

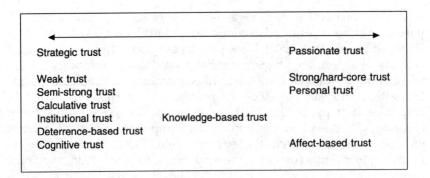

Figure 5.1   *Trust forms*

through governance mechanisms. This type of trust occurs when the vulnerabilities mentioned above exist, but trust still emerges owing to various governance devices. Hence, the costs of opportunistic behaviour will be greater than its benefits and it will be in the rational self-interest of exchange partners to behave in a trustworthy way. Contractual forms include complete contingent claims contracts, sequential contracting, equity joint ventures and hierarchical governance. Semi-strong trust is also endogenous. Finally, strong form trust or 'hard-core' trustworthiness is a trust which emerges despite significant exchange vulnerabilities and potential lack of social and economical governance mechanisms. Opportunistic behaviour would violate values, principles and standards of behaviour that have been internalized by parties to an exchange. This type of trust is exogenous.

Williamson (1993) also presents three types of trust: calculative, institutional and personal trust. Williamson's argument is that calculative relations should be described in calculative terms, where he believes the language of risk, not trust, is exactly suited. Calculative trust is thereby a contradiction in terms. Personal trust is normally only warranted for very special relations, if they are to obtain at all, and commercial relations do not qualify. This is in line, as Williamson himself notes, with March and Olsen's (1989) assertion that the core idea of trust is that it is not based on an expectation of its justification. Trust, they argue, is simply another version of economic exchange, if it is justified by expectations of positive reciprocal consequences. A third form of trust is institutional trust, e.g. politics, networks and corporate culture, which refers to the social and organizational context within which contracts are embedded. Each can be thought of as institutional trust of a hyphenated kind. However, calculativeness always appears, according to Williamson, since transactions are always governed with reference to the institutional context of which they are part.

Gulati (1995) presents a distinction between a knowledge-based trust and a deterrence-based trust. Knowledge-based trust builds on the idea of trust emerging from prior contacts based on the premise that through ongoing interaction, firms learn about each other and develop trust around norms of equity. Gulati refers to Lewis and Weigert's (1985) cognitive and emotional trust as strong bases for such trust. Deterrence-based trust emphasizes utilitarian considerations that may also lead to believing that a partner will behave in a trustworthy manner. Potential sanctions such as loss of reputation and of repeat business, which are perceived to be more costly than any potential benefits of opportunistic behaviour, may cause deterrence-based trust.

Finally, McAllister (1995) studies affect- and cognition-based trust as foundations for interpersonal cooperation in organizations. He discusses the nature and functioning of interpersonal trust relationships by distinguishing between cognition-based trust grounded in individual beliefs about peer reliability and dependability, and affect-based trust grounded in reciprocal interpersonal care and concern.

The Nature of Trust

The attention given to trust in recent years has resulted in a number of different perspectives, as was indicated above. A problem is that trust is a concept with clearly diverging traits. Moreover, this divergence is not always explicitly realized. For instance, Gulati (1995) refers to Arrow's (1974) argument that trust perhaps is the most efficient mechanism for governing transactions. Arrow's trust has however little to do with Gulati's trust. They are actually not talking about the same phenomenon, only the same label. Whereas Gulati's trust is calculative, even deterrence-based, Arrow's trust builds on a generalized morality.

This has led to a debate around the *nature* of trust. One key question is naturally what leads to a particular form of trust. Trust will, depending on what its bases are, and how it is communicated and manifested, take various forms. That is, different combinations of *components* and *levels* will create different trust forms, i.e. will affect the nature of trust itself. The notion of a mix constituting the trusting experience is in line with sociological accounts. Barber (1983) argues that both technically competent performance and fiduciary responsibility in fulfilling contracts are needed in different mixtures in different settings. Both types of trust are, however, always present. Lewis and Weigert (1985) suggest that various qualitative mixes of cognitive, emotional and behavioural contents make it possible to differentiate between different types of trust. They argue that trust in everyday life is a mix of feeling and rational thinking. Excluding one or the other leads to pure faith or cold-blooded prediction. Moreover, the practical significance of trust lies in the social attitudes and actions it underwrites (e.g. Lewis and Weigert, 1985; Moorman et al., 1993). The behavioural content of trust is reciprocally related to its cognitive and emotional aspects (Lewis and Weigert, 1985). Below follows a brief presentation of the suggested components and levels.

TRUST COMPONENTS   The most basic origin of trust as we have found it in the literature refers to *expectations*, i.e. expectations are the starting point for defining various meanings of trust (Barber, 1983). Hence, the concept of trust components departs from what one's expectations are based on. On the individual level, Luhmann argues that trust 'is the generalized expectation that the other will handle his freedom, his disturbing potential for diverse action, in keeping with his personality – or, rather, in keeping with the personality which he has presented and made socially visible' (1979: 39). The basis of all trust is claimed to be the presentation of the individual self as a social identity which builds itself through interaction and which corresponds to its environment. Trust depends upon sincerity in the sense that actors should be what they claim to be (Luhmann, 1979; Oakes, 1990).

Emphasizing the organizational level of analysis, Ring and Van de Ven (1994) argue that identity and inclusion are bases for an explanation of the development of inter-organizational relationships being grounded in the motivational and cognitive predispositions of individuals to engage in sensemaking and bonding processes. Sensemaking is, according to Ring and Van de Ven, an enactment process in which organizational participants come to appreciate the potential for transacting with others by reshaping or clarifying the identity of their own organization. Hence, we suggest that expectations based on identities, both individual and organizational, are crucial aspects of trust in business relationships.

Expectations are furthermore based on the trustor's perception of the motives and abilities of the trustee, i.e. the identity will be shaped by perceived motives and abilities. Barber (1983) distinguishes between the expectations that the other party will fulfil the requirements of technical competence (expertise), and that fiduciary obligations will be carried out. In social psychology and marketing, the ability to produce stated outcomes has been consistently suggested to be crucial for development of trust (e.g. Rotter, 1971; Andaleeb, 1989). Confidence in the other party's motives is another aspect of trust (Lindskold, 1978). Interpersonal characteristics have been suggested to involve ability and motivation, and expertise is argued to be a key factor affecting trust (Moorman et al., 1993). Focusing on learning, March and Olsen (1990) argue that varying degrees of trust depend on the belief in another person's ability and strength, together with the confidence in his motives. Therefore, we suggest that the trustor's perception of the trustee's identity, individual as well as organizational, is in turn affected by perceived motives and abilities.

However, trust cannot only be understood by these basic components. What below is described as trust levels and access points, where trust is communicated and manifested, should also be considered in order to understand the nature and hence the potential roles of trust in a business relationship.

TRUST LEVELS AND THEIR ACCESS POINTS   The literature points to two basic trust levels, i.e. personal and impersonal trust. Personal trust involves affective ties which induce individuals to place confidence in the viability of agreement and the calculability of others' behaviour (Luhmann, 1979). The affective component of trusting attitudes develops from an individual's interactions with other individuals over time (Holden, 1990). On this level, personal bonds may flow from congruent sensemaking and congruent psychological contracts may produce trust in the other party's goodwill. If the goodwill already exists, it will give the parties greater flexibility to transcend their organizationally specified roles in adapting to changing circumstances (Ring and Van de Ven, 1994). Personal relations are trust relations which are sustained by or expressed in social connections established in circumstances of copresence, i.e. what Giddens (1990) calls facework commitments. This is at least a plausible argument when a personal relationshiip is initiated. Copresence at all times may not be necessary in order to maintain a personal relationship, once it has been established.

However, as pointed out by Lewis and Weigert (1985), in the change from a face-to-face society to one of widespread anonymity in a demographically large and structurally complicated system, a person often interacts with others who are not known well or even at all. An impersonal trust therefore exists when formal mechanisms induce individuals to place confidence in the viability of agreements and the calculability of others' behaviour (Luhmann, 1979). Shapiro argues that impersonal trust arises 'when social control measures derived from social ties and direct contact between principal and agent are unavailable, when faceless and readily interchangeable individual and organizational agents exercise considerable delegated power and privilege on behalf of principals who can neither specify, scrutinize, evaluate, nor constrain their performance' (1987: 634). Impersonal relations are furthermore related to Giddens's (1990) notion of 'faceless commitments', i.e. the development of faith in symbolic tokens or expert systems, also called abstract systems.

Giddens (1990) takes the argumentation further and stresses that, in the majority of encounters, individuals or groups are involved also in abstract systems. These encounters are called *access points* of abstract systems. Access points in abstract systems are where facework commitments and faceless commitments meet. They are places of vulnerability for abstract systems, but also junctions at which trust can be maintained or even built up. A dynamic development of trust may take place, where encounters with representatives of abstract systems are regularized and successfully take the form and characteristics of trustworthiness associated with friendship and intimacy. Consequently, Giddens argues that 'all disembedding mechanisms interact with reembedded context of action, which may act either to support or to undermine them and . . . faceless commitments are similarly linked in an ambiguous way with those demanding facework' (1990: 80). Therefore, an adequate theory must offer a conceptualization that bridges the personal and the impersonal levels of analysis (Lewis and Weigert, 1985; Young, 1993), and it must further recognize the importance of access points between these levels.

PRESENT CONCEPTIONS OF TRUST There are different views on what actually makes trust occur, e.g. a trustor's perception of a trustee's motives and/or abilities. Likewise, there are also different views on the very nature of trust. Thus, one must consider trust's components in order to make some sense of what trust itself is. Basically, there are two major conceptions of trust present in the literature: one rational and calculative, founded on cognition; and one social and moral, founded on identification and affection as well as cognition.

Trust's nature may be instrumental, calculative and based on 'good rational reasons'. In this case, trust is taken to depend not on any particular reason of the trustee's intentions, but merely on credible reasons. Hence, a trusting environment is a pure strategic outcome, and does not include norms based on moral reasoning. However, another stream of thinking emphasizes the emotional and affective aspects of trust. This implies an affective component of trust which consists of an emotional bond between the participating parties in a relationship. As Dunn (1988) argues, when trust is a modality of human action, i.e. 'a more or less consciously chosen policy for handling the freedom of other human agents or agencies', then it is 'ineluctably strategic'. When trust incorporates 'the confident expectation of benign intentions by another agent', then trust is a human passion (1988: 73). Hence, it is possible to distinguish between 'strategic' and 'passionate' trust (Huemer, 1994), a distinction which corresponds quite well with the rational and social conception of trust employed in Tyler and Kramer (1996).

In summary, trust's nature depends on the perception and formulation of individual and organizational identities. These identities are in turn shaped by both motives and abilities. This mix of components, which form the basic expectations on which trust departs, can be communicated and manifested on personal and/or impersonal levels. The mix of components and levels will affect the roles trust will and can play in a certain context. The behaviour caused by a certain trust has, in turn, a reciprocal effect on the nature of trust itself. Thus, the nature and the role of trust are suggested to be interdependent. Trust may play many roles and fulfil various functions in intra- and inter-organizational relationships, as was indicated earlier. Trust may create benefits for all parties: for example, by reducing complexity and the need for constant surveillance, by restraining opportunism and by producing positive attitudes, it may lead to committed relationships, decrease transaction costs and be a significant determinant of managerial problem-solving effectiveness. Our argument is that *one of the most important roles played by trust concerns issues related to corporate epistemology.* We now turn to the perspectives on trust and knowledge according to this chapter's three theoretical settings, i.e. cognitivism, connectionism and autopoiesis.

Three Epistemological Perspectives on Trust

The central question asked in epistemology is how individuals or social entities come to know of the world (von Krogh and Roos, 1995). There are at least three distinct epistemologies in the literature on organization studies and strategic management: cognitivism, connectionism and auto-poiesis. Each of these epistemologies rests on a different set of assumptions regarding cognition. Because full treatment of these epistemologies can be found in von Krogh and Roos (1995), we will only provide a brief summary of them here. The notion of trust according to these perspectives is emphasized after each summary.

The Cognitivist Epistemology

Since the mid 1950s the ideas of Simon, Chomsky, Minsky, McCarthy and others have enabled the growth of cognitive science where the notion of 'human knowledge' holds a particular position (Varela, 1992). At the heart of the cognitivist epistemology is the idea that the mind has the ability to represent reality in various ways, that is, creating inner representations that partly or fully correspond to the outer world, be it objects, events or states. This is also frequently referred to as the 'intentionality of the mind'. 'Reality' and 'truth' hold privileged positions, reality being the point of reference for inner representations and truth being the degree to which inner representations correspond to the outer world (von Krogh and Roos, 1995). Learning in the cognitivist epistemology means to improve representations of the world through assimilating new experiences (von Krogh et al., 1994). The underlying assumption of an epistemology based on representationism is visual object recognition through perception, memory and processes of reasoning, i.e. logic and probability judgements. The cognitivist assumption is that, in addition to competence at logic, the human brain has some competence at probability judgements and heuristics. The combined competencies allow increasingly accurate representations to be developed. However, there is always uncertainty involved because the nature of the object, event or state to be represented may be more or less complex.

The cognitivist epistemology, with its cardinal idea of mirroring an objective reality, and its accompanying assumptions of transparency to information, ability to process information and competence at logic and probability judgements, can also be traced in studies of organization and management (von Krogh and Roos, 1995). Several seminal contributions assume that managers and organizations create representations of their environment (e.g. March and Simon, 1958; Argyris and Schön, 1978; Weick, 1979). In these works, knowledge has often been substituted with less troublesome notions, like information, data, resources, reputation etc.

Trust and Cognitivism

One interpretation of trust according to the cognitivist perspective is that it is a 'non-issue'. Trust may be viewed as a kind of heuristic, e.g. the description of trust as an intrinsically frail response to our ignorance, a way of coping with the limits of our anticipation (Shklar, 1984).

Trust according to cognitivism may furthermore be given and taken for 'good rational reasons' (see Lewis and Weigert, 1985). Prior experience is necessary for cognitive trust, i.e. it implies some level of familiarity and thus requires knowledge. Reliance on trust developed at an interpersonal level may be conditioned by legal systems or organizational role responsibilities (cf. Ring and Van de Ven, 1994). Actors are more conscious that everything that is accomplished is a product, that each action has been decided on after comparison with other possibilities (cf. Luhmann, 1979). Such instrumentality on the personal level may only decrease the level of trust between the parties. We suggest that 'passionate' trust is more spontaneous in nature, whereas 'strategic' trust is more perceptive. Perceptive trust demands more thought from the trustor, i.e. the object of trust is not trusted directly, but rather the trustor trusts the grounds on which trust functions regardless (see Luhmann, 1979: 68).

The cognitivist perspective emphasizes trust development which relies on many non-personal factors such as product quality and product delivery reliability, and if performance on those factors is poor, then trust will decrease (see Holden, 1990). The rational economist's opinion is that there is no internal reward in behaving trustworthily, i.e. 'I am willing to behave in a more trustworthy manner if everyone else does too' (Zeckhauser, 1991: 13). Economists are commonly supposed to argue that trust is associated not with moral expectations but with costs. Hence, the 'encapsulated interest account' opposes the writings on trust which often take the view that trust involves something beyond merely reasonable expectations based on self-interest. Many social and moral norms are primarily manifestations of encapsulated interest, as trust is suggested to be, e.g. 'most dealers are likely to share my interest, since they must share my interest to serve their own'. Trust is not taken to depend on any particular reason of the trustee's intentions, but merely on credible reasons. Hence, it is argued that a trusting environment is a pure strategic outcome, and not a norm based on moral reasoning (Hardin, 1991; Zeckhauser, 1991).

Following the conceptualization of trust presented in the previous section, trust according to cognitivism is strictly 'strategic', i.e. it is primarily a consciously chosen policy founded in expectations which are based on organizational identity and perception of abilities. Relations are primarily characterized as being more impersonal. These components are primarily communicated in a formal manner, not necessarily impersonal, but according to the roles designed by their organizational membership. This creates a technical, calculative or 'strategic' form of trust. An ability-based trust communicated impersonally is suggested to be less grounded in moral values than a trust based on motives. Concerning the relationship between trust and knowledge, the cognitivist perspective informs us that a certain amount of knowledge is necessary for a 'strategic' trust to develop.

The Connectionist Epistemology

The connectionist epistemology is centred around criticism of two 'deficiencies' of the cognitivist work. First, information processing is seen as sequential rule-based manipulation of symbols: one rule is applied after the other. Second, information processing is localized. If a rule breaks down or if a symbol is lost, this has serious implications for the global effectiveness of the system (Varela, 1992). The connectionist approach argues that rather than working sequentially starting with symbols, the brain seems to have dynamic global properties in a network of simple components, referred to as neurons. While cognitivists view learning as the increasingly accurate definition of representations corresponding to the external world, the 'connectionists' understand the brain as global states in a history-dependent system where the learning rules and the history of connections between components affect the present connections. When the brain recognizes patterns, events, objects, states etc., learning rules provide similarities in the emergent state of the system of components (von Krogh and Roos, 1995).

Contributions to organizational knowledge from the connectionist epistemology have as their focal points self-organization (Jantsch, 1980) of social entities, and evolving systems, structures and processes. Subtle but rarely touched upon implications of connectionist epistemology concern the emergent and the historical nature of knowledge. The connectionist approach has many insights to offer, but so far has had limited impact on theory building (see Weick and Roberts, 1993). Von Krogh and Roos (1995) indicate two studies which suggest that the individual organizational member is a component of the networked organization: Sproull and Kiesler (1991) suggested that connections among individuals are partly but effectively facilitated by information technology, and Weick and Roberts (1993) construed interpersonal connections as a social psychological problem. Organizational members construct their actions as contributions to a network of other contributions, and their actions are interrelated within the organization. Knowledge, according to Weick and Roberts, emerges and resides not only in the brains of each individual organizational member, but also in the connections among members through the rules of heedful interrelating.

Trust and Connectionism

One interesting issue in a trust perspective which is brought up by the connectionist perspective is that of networks. Trust in relation to group mind and collective action emerges as a particularly important issue in Weick and Roberts (1993). Trust ties together the complex and attentive system which forms the collective mind required for reliable performance. Cooperation is imperative for the development of mind, and trust, the authors suggest, is imperative for cooperation. Interpersonal skills enable people to represent and subordinate themselves to communities of practice. The emphasis on action is interesting, particularly in respect to collective or organizational action. Trust without a behavioural content has been described as a non-complete trust (cf. Lewis and Weigert, 1985; Moorman et al., 1993). Trust deserves to be studied further in this respect, in line with Luhmann's (1979) argument that lack of trust will cause withdrawal of actions, i.e. trust may be what makes collective action possible.

An interesting argument by Weick and Roberts (1993) is that certain organizational forms, like networks, have more capacity for developing 'organizational mind', i.e. a pattern of heedful interrelations of actions in a social system wherein trust is imperative, as was argued above. Moreover, they suggest that attention must be paid as much to social processes and microdynamics as is commonly paid to the statics of structure, strategy and demographics (Weick and Roberts, 1993). Bartlett and Ghoshal (1993) provide a similar argument when they claim that the management of 'new' multinational organizations builds on assumptions which differ from conventional views of organization structure, decision-making processes and ultimately human behaviour.

The network metaphor is also used by industrial marketers (e.g. Håkansson, 1982; Turnbull and Wilson, 1989; Hallén et al., 1991; Johanson and Mattsson, 1992). The interaction or network approach emphasizes social exchange, interfirm adaptations, mutual orientation and mutual trust. It is argued that trust is built through exchange of resources and will last over long periods of time. The basis for trust seems to be that the actors have certain norms and values in common. Trust has been defined in a network context as 'an assumption or reliance on the part of A that if either A or B encounters a problem in the fulfillment of his implicit or explicit transactional obligations, B may be counted on to do what A would do if B's resources were at A's disposal' (Thorelli, 1986: 38). Strategic networks (Jarillo, 1988) are relationships where the essential 'glue' is trust rather than pure price signals or command from above. Hence, Jarillo's notion of trust as a 'glue' corresponds with the view of Weick and Roberts (1993). An interesting comparison is Arrow's (1974) description of trust as a lubricant. Thus, it may be argued that trust may both tie a collective together, and simultaneously provide it with a certain smoothness.

Meyerson et al. (1996) change their focus of organizational form from networks to temporary systems. Most conceptions of how trust develops have emphasized that trust is a history-dependent process (e.g. Lindskold, 1978; Rotter, 1980) 'in which individuals operate like Bayesian statisticians, drawing inferences based on relevant but limited samples of experience' (Meyerson et al., 1996: 184). Trust builds incrementally and it accumulates. However, Meyerson et al. point out that there is not time in temporary systems to engage in the usual forms of confidence-building activities that contribute to the development and maintenance of trust in more traditional organizational forms. The swift trust emphasized in temporary systems by Meyerson et al. is a unique form of collective perception and relating that is capable of managing issues of vulnerability, uncertainty, risk and expectations. People in temporary systems deal more with each other as roles than as individuals, according to Meyerson et al. A form of depersonalized trust may develop based on category membership. People fall back on predispositions, categorical assumptions and implicit theories in order to reach a clearer view of either trust or distrust. Such a trust is swift, the authors argue, because to some extent it occurs independent of the object of perception. Consequently, Meyerson et al. suggest that the act of conferring swift trust concerns judgements more about the other's professionalism than their character. Trust in temporary systems is a cognitive and action form, not primarily interpersonal. It is less about relating than doing. This potentially 'cool' form of trust places less emphasis on feeling and commitment and more on action and cognition.

Hence, the connectionist perspective both broadens and complicates the concept of trust. Indeed, trust is, to begin with, an explicit topic. This perspective contributes to our understanding of the nature of trust by infusing social and emotional aspects of the concept. This affective component of trust consists of an emotional bond between participating parties in a relationship. Hence, 'passionate' aspects of trust may be present. In line with the notion of components and levels previously described, the connectionist perspective adds to the conceptualization by infusing individual identity, motives and intentions. Trust is communicated through informal channels, and individuals may rely less, ceteris paribus, on their organizational roles. In connectionism, trust and morals are interrelated. In an epistemological sense, trust may affect the quality of cooperation leading to a more reliable performance. However, depending on the organizational form in question, both components and levels may be affected, leading to trust forms which are related but not identical to the cognitivist epistemology. This may be the case in temporary organizations.

The Autopoietic Epistemology

Originally developed in the field of neuro-biology to characterize 'living systems', autopoiesis theory suggests the composition and structure of individual cognitive systems (Maturana and Varela, 1980; 1987). Through its application in the social sciences, autopoiesis theory also emerges as a new theory of knowledge of a social system (Luhmann, 1986; Teubner, 1991).

Following the line of reasoning in von Krogh et al. (1994), evoking autopoiesis theory implies rethinking some of the most basic assumptions behind the previous contributions on how and why organizations know. In doing this we suggest that autopoiesis theory emerges as an important contribution to these previous works in strategic management. Unlike the cognitivist perspective, autopoiesis theory does not suggest that the world is a pre-given state to be represented, but rather suggests that cognition is a creative act of bringing forth a world. Knowledge is a component of the autopoietic (self-productive) process; it is history-dependent, context-sensitive and, rather than being oriented towards problem solutions, enables problem definition (Maturana and Varela, 1987; Varela, 1992; Varela et al., 1992). Moreover, at the individual level, knowledge is not abstract but rather is embodied in the individual. Managerial cognition is altered in at least two ways by the claim that cognition is autopoietic: (1) knowledge is intimately connected to observation, and (2) the notion of information becomes redefined (von Krogh et al., 1994).

First, the proposition of 'embodied knowledge' suggests that everything known is known by somebody, e.g. a manager. More importantly, however, knowledge depends on the 'point of observation' of the manager. As pointed out by von Krogh et al.: 'Where you stand or what you know determines what you see or what you choose to be relevant' (1994: 10). In autopoiesis theory 'knowledge' and 'observation' are closely related, since observing systems are autopoietic systems. To be more precise, in autopoiesis theory distinctions and norms are two central categories (Varela, 1979; Luhmann, 1986; 1988). Knowledge is what makes managers able to make distinctions in their observations (for example between themselves and others) and, based on their norms, determine what they see. The distinctions made reveal the knowledge of the distinguisher.

New knowledge may develop by applying distinctions, a process described by the term 'self-referentiality'. Self-referentiality means that new knowledge refers not only to past knowledge but also to potential future knowledge (Varela, 1979; Luhmann, 1990). Managers use already established knowledge to determine what they see, and they use what they already know to choose what to look for in their environment. Knowledge is therefore highly dynamic, as managers make new observations, talk, use their fantasies to envision possible futures, and formulate problems.

A second implication of saying that cognition is autopoietic is the need to distinguish between data, information and knowledge (von Krogh and Vicari, 1993). In autopoiesis theory, information is not a commodity or a substance, as is often assumed in the cognitivist perspective and the strategic management literature. Rather, information is a process of interpretation, or, to use the words of von Foerster, 'information is the process by which knowledge is acquired' (1984: 193). As pointed out by Varela (1979), information means 'to put' data 'in form' (Latin *in* = in, *form* = form, *are* = doing). Books, movies, lectures, papers, computer programs, memos etc. are data in the environment of the manager – not information. They are simply fractions and may be vehicles for potential information. Information is dependent on the manager who makes use of it to create knowledge. The only way to describe this process is to say that individuals and social systems, like firms, are simultaneously open and closed: closed with respect to knowledge (also knowledge about the environment) but open with respect to data from the outside.

In summary, in autopoietic theory the world is not a pre-given state to be represented, knowledge is connected to observation, and the notion of information is redefined.

Trust and Autopoiesis

As was discussed previously, trust has not, until recently, received much explicit attention in the strategy and management literature. Nor has it received much attention in autopoiesis theory. However, we suggest that trust is an important issue in autopoiesis theory where it exists in a symbiotic relationship with both the autopoietic process and knowledge itself. Trust (we will return to the nature of this 'trust') may be viewed as a condition for the autopoietic process to continue. If the manager's cognition is the unit of analysis, the conditions for autopoiesis are biologically given and relatively unproblematic; he must be alive and the brain as well as the senses must be functioning. However, when the organization is the unit of analysis, organizational knowledge is highly dynamic, 'fragile', and developed through a self-referential, simultaneously open and closed process. Given this, how do organizations ensure that the autopoietic process continues and, hence, that knowledge develops? Trust, we argue, is a key issue in the environmental search process necessary for knowledge development. Autopoiesis theory implies that every living organism exists in order to maintain itself, and it does that by constantly interacting with the environment. It does it by embracing the environment and understanding that there is no boundary between itself and the environment. It uses the capacity for self-reference to notice how it should change in order to preserve itself. Trust spans boundaries, i.e. it affects the managerial reach, and embracement of distrustful environments/actors may be severely restricted. Hence, the knowledge creation process in which the manager is simultaneously closed for knowledge and open for information may be disturbed, since the manager will be closed also for data from the outside. Trust can further be assumed to facilitate the knowledge connections described by von Krogh et al. (1994). Knowledge connection is defined as the potential for individuals to convey messages about their observations. Without trust, knowledge at one point in time does not connect with new knowledge at a later point in time. When trust is lacking, the autopoietic process is terminated, which further leads to the termination of knowledge development.

There are, according to von Krogh et al. (1994), two conditions that need to be satisfied for knowledge to connect in the organization over time. The first condition concerns the availability of relationships, the second self-description. An organization consists of a set of relationships that may create immediate knowledge connections. Organizational members develop informal relationships over time that can ensure that the distinctions they convey are further built on and developed by others. Organizational members are also related to one another through organizational structures and reporting relationships. These facilitate communication among individuals and may therefore allow for organizational knowledge to develop (von Krogh et al., 1994). Organizational structures function as a set of 'expectations' (Deggau, 1988). Individuals, groups or subunits meet with structurally defined expectations to create or re-create the organizational knowledge, based on what they know or what others in the organization tell them. Similarly, March and Olsen (1990) argue that learning is a form of attitude formation. They further suggest a view of reality forming that 'emphasizes the impact of interpersonal connections within the organization and the affective connection between the organization and the participant on the development of belief, as well as the interaction between seeing and liking' (1990: 356). Here, trust is essential.

Second, knowledge connections require an adequate self-description of the organization (Luhmann, 1990). A self-description results from an 'observation' by the organization of itself. In fact, a 'self-description formulates the identity of the [organization]' (1990: 253). This provides criteria for selecting what passes for 'knowledge', and that as such should be further connected, as opposed to 'noise' that should not be connected. In many organizations, descriptions of the organization's identity include business ideas, mission statements, strategy documents, vision statements, management principles, guiding values etc. As was argued in the first section, formulation and perception of identities, individual and organizational, are crucial for trust to develop. Hence, in this case it is the autopoietic process which facilitates the development of trust, and therefore the argument that trust exists in a symbiotic relationship with the autopoietic process.

What insights does the autopoietic perspective provide for understanding the nature of trust? Autopoiesis does not provide, compared

Table 5.1 *Trust and knowledge according to cognitivism, connectionism and autopoiesis*

	Cognitivism	Connectionism	Autopoiesis
Nature of trust	Strategic	Mix of strategic and passionate	Mix of strategic and passionate
Trust and knowledge	—	Focus on the nature of knowledge	Trust ensures that the autopoietic process continues, whereby knowledge develops: • it facilitates knowledge connections • it ensures interaction with the environment The autopoietic process enables trust to develop through: • an adequate self-description

with connectionism, any further insights on the nature of trust *per se*. However, autopoiesis and trust each promote understanding of *the development of the other*. Moreover, they together provide insights on how knowledge develops and transfers in organizations, i.e. trust provides an open system necessary for knowledge development, and the autopoietic process enables trust to develop by an adequate self-description (Table 5.1). Autopoiesis emphasizes both the individual and the collective or organizational level. Examples are the notions of embodied knowledge and of knowledge connections. This may form different combinations or mixes of 'strategic' and 'passionate' trust.

Trust and Corporate Epistemology: Implications for Strategy Theory

It is important to recognize that the cognitive aspects are crucial for building trust in an initial stage of a relationship. This argument is in line with McAllister's (1995) finding that interpersonal trust builds on both cognitive and affective trust, where the former is necessary for the latter to develop. Similarly, Ring and Van de Ven (1994) discuss a subsequent substitution of inter-role relationships by interpersonal relations, where informal psychological contracts increasingly compensate or substitute for formal contractual safeguards as reliance on trust among parties increases over time. However, Ring and Van de Ven restrict their definition of trust to the 'passionate' aspects of trust. The process of trust development is a complex task, since it differs depending on its bases and how it is manifested. We suggest that aspects from both the cognitive and the connectionist perspectives should be considered, but the concept of trust does not reveal much when exclusively related to cognitivism (see Huemer, 1997). Hence, a mix of components and levels is likely to exist, forming certain relationship-specific mixes of 'strategic' and 'passionate' trust.

In order to understand the relationship between trust and knowledge, we turn to autopoiesis theory. Trust and knowledge share several properties and characteristics. Knowledge is a component of the auto-poietic (self-productive) process, i.e. it is history-dependent and context-sensitive (von Krogh et al., 1994), just like trust. Consequently, neither trust nor knowledge can be universally defined, but must be dealt with according to history, relationship and context. Trust is both a condition for as well as dependent on the autopoietic process. Both knowledge and trust may reduce uncertainty and complexity. Trust requires familiarity and contingency, which implies that knowledge is essential for trust. Knowledge can fulfil some of the functions of trust, but there are always margins for trust. Trust cannot entirely substitute knowledge, and vice versa. Hence, knowledge does not make trust superfluous. Trust cannot reasonably exist without knowledge, i.e. we might hope or even be ignorant, but we cannot trust. Neither can knowledge reason-ably exist, at least in a dynamic perspective, without trust. The dis-trusted environment will not be embraced, i.e. the information will not be made use of, or will be used in a restrictive manner. Hence, *no trust equals no action, equals no observation, equals no knowledge development, equals no knowledge transfer.*[2]

If trust is not part of our strategy, then some level of distrust is implied. But although trust in a sense is a simplification, so also is distrust. To distrust means to become more and more dependent on less information. Strategies of distrust often leave little energy to explore and adapt to the environment in an objective and unprejudiced manner, and hence allow fewer opportunities for learning (Luhmann, 1979). Luhmann further argues that 'Anyone who does not trust must . . . turn to functionally equivalent strategies for the reduction of complexity in order to be able to define a practically meaningful situation at all' (1979: 71). In some settings trust may be substituted by legal-formal integration or other forms of organizational 'life-jackets' (Ring and Van de Ven, 1994). These substitutes may not affect e.g. transaction costs in the same way as lack of trust will affect knowledge development. But there may not be any qualified substitutes for trust when it comes to issues related to corporate epistemology. This informs us even more of the necessity to better understand trust. However, the issue of trust finds little relevance in existing theories. Theories which currently dominate academic ana-lyses of business organization are based on assumptions of self-interest seeking (with guile) and opportunism (Bartlett and Ghoshal, 1993). Although theories with a microeconomic foundation contribute to the understanding of the 'strategic' aspects of trust, they do not provide much insight into the 'passionate' aspects. It seem plausible to suggest that only trust in the cognitivist sense will not lead to an atmosphere, or actions, which will facilitate knowledge development and knowledge transfer.

The distinction between survival and advancement activities described by von Krogh et al. (1994) is one feasible approach guiding future work. The overall goal of survival activities, e.g. product–market positioning, resource allocation, planning, organizing, human resource management, routinization and controlling, is to manage the input–output relationship between the firm and its environment. Advancement activities, e.g. development of distinctions and norms, processing data, scaling knowledge, ensuring knowledge connectivity, languaging and self-referencing, represent new activities for many organizations. However, there are few theories explaining them, and limited knowledge on how to address them, according to von Krogh et al. (1994). The key is to manage the firm's survival in a way that makes it able to engage in advancement activities. Central is that firms can be less different in terms of their survival activities and more different in terms of their advancement activities. This may explain differences in competitive advantage between firms. These differences may further be due to different trust forms in survival and advancement activities. A more 'strategic' trust may be found in survival activities, which are based on 'conventional rational' analysis, whereas a more 'passionate' trust may be needed in the advancement realm. Autopoiesis provides, and has the potential to provide, important insights into strategic management theory by emphasizing the relationship between trust and knowledge. Trust, more specifically the notion of the nature of trust, further informs us that strategic management theory needs more than a pure strategic content; it needs passion as well.

Notes

1 The section builds on Huemer (1994). For a more elaborate and critical approach, see Huemer (1997).

2 Plato had a similar view, which we believe illustrates the importance of trust in this perspective. He stressed that our experiences are part of our personal identity. We are the relations we live in. Plato warned one of his students *not to listen to a speaker which this student did not trust*. Plato's argument was that one must be careful about whom one listens to, since what enters our souls will remain there. Our experiences are not like water in glass which can be emptied and then refilled (in Flöistad 1993: 73). March and Olsen similarly suggest that 'a person is integrated to the extent which he accepts responsibility for the organization and feels that the actions of the organization are fundamentally his actions or the actions of those he trusts' (1990: 353).

References

Andaleeb, S.S. (1989) The strategic implications of trust for interorganizational exchange relations under asymmetric dependence. Dissertation, Graduate College of the University of Illinois at Urbana Champaign, order no. 9010794.

Argyris, C. and Schön, D. (1978) *Organizational Learning*. Reading, MA: Addison-Wesley.

Arrow, K.J. (1974) *The Limits of Organization*. New York: Norton.

Badaracco, J.L. (1991) *Knowledge Link: How Firms Compete through Strategic Alliances*. Boston, MA: Harvard Business School Press.

Barber, B. (1983) *The Logic and Limits of Trust*. New Brunswick, NJ: Rutgers University Press.

Barnard, C.I. (1938) *The Functions of the Executive*. Cambridge, MA: Harvard University Press.

Barney, J.B. and Hansen, M.H. (1994) Trustworthiness as a source of competitive advantage'. *Strategic Management Journal*, 15: 175–90.

Bartlett, C. and Ghoshal, S. (1993) Beyond the M-form: toward a managerial theory of the firm. *Strategic Management Journal*, 14: 23–46.

Brown, J.S. and Duguid, P. (1991) Organizational learning and communities of practice: toward a unified view of working, learning and innovation. *Organization Science*, 2: 40–57.

Contractor, F.J. and Lorange, P. (1988) Why should firms cooperate? The strategy and economics basis for cooperative ventures', in F. Contractor and P. Lorange (eds), *Cooperative Strategies in International Business*, Lexington, MA: Lexington Books.

Corrazzini, J.G. (1977) Trust as a complex multi-dimensional construct. *Psychological Reports*, 40: 75–80.

Dasgupta, P. (1988) Trust as a commodity', in D. Gambetta (ed.), *Trust: Making and Breaking Cooperative Relations*. New York: Basil Blackwell.

Davidow, W.H. and Malone, M.S. (1992) *The Virtual Corporation*. London: Harper Collins.

Deggau, H.G. (1988) The communicative autonomy of the legal system, in G. Teubner (ed.), *Autopoietic Law: a New Approach to Law and Society*. Berlin: de Gruyter. pp. 128–51.

Drucker, P. (1993) *Post-Capitalist Society*. Oxford: Butterworth-Heinemann.

Dunn, J. (1988) Trust and political agency, in D. Gambetta (ed.), *Trust: Making and Breaking Cooperative Relations*. New York: Basil Blackwell.

Flöistad, G. (1993) *Kunsten å omgås hverandre*. Gyldendal: Ad Notam.

Ghoshal, S. and Bartlett, C.A. (1994) Linking organizational context and managerial action: the dimension of quality management. *Strategic Management Journal*, 15, Special Issue (Summer): 91–112.

Giddens, A. (1990) *The Consequences of Modernity*. Cambridge: Polity.

Graham, P. (1995) *Mary Parker Follett: Prophet of Management*. Boston: Harvard Business School Press.

Gulati, R. (1995) Does familiarity breed trust? The implications of repeated ties for contractual choice in alliances. *Academy of Management Journal*, 38 (1): 85–112.

Håkansson, H. (ed.) (1982) *International Marketing and Purchasing of Industrial Goods: an Interaction Approach*. New York: Wiley.

Håkansson, H. and Snehota, I. (1995) *Developing Relationships in Business Networks*. London: Routledge.

Hallén, L., Johanson, J. and Mohamed, N.S. (1991) Interfirm adaptation in business relationships. *Journal of Marketing*, 55 (April): 29–37.

Hardin, R. (1991) Trusting persons, trusting institutions, in R.J. Zeckhauser (ed.), *Strategy and Choice*. Cambridge, MA: MIT Press.

Heretick, D.M.L. (1984) Trust–suspicion and gender differences in interpersonal functioning. *Journal of Research in Personality*, 18: 27–40.

Holden, R.K. (1990) An exploratory study of trust in buyer–seller relationships. Dissertation, Boston University, order no. 9022979.

Hosmer, L.T. (1994) Strategic planning as if ethics mattered. *Strategic Management Journal*, 15, Special Issue (Summer): 17–34.

Huemer, L. (1994) Trust in interorganizational relationships: a conceptual model. Paper presented at the 10th IMP Conference in Groningen, 29 September to 1 October.

Huemer, L. (1997) A critical inquiry into the notion of trust in business relationships. Dissertation, Umeå Business School, Umeå University.

Jantsch, E. (1980) *The Self-Organizing Universe: Scientific and Human Implications of the Emerging Paradigm of Evolution*. Oxford: Pergamon.

Jarillo, J.C. (1988) On strategic networks. *Strategic Management Journal*, 8.

Jarillo, J.C. (1990) Comments on 'Transaction costs and networks'. *Strategic Management Journal*, 11: 497–9.

Johanson, J. and Mattsson, L.G. (1992) Network positions and strategic actions – an analytical framework, in B. Axelsson and G. Easton (eds), *Industrial Networks: A New View of Reality*. London and New York: Routledge.

John, G. (1984) An empirical investigation of some antecedents of opportunism in a marketing channel. *Journal of Marketing Research*, 21 (August): 278–89.

Kaplan R. (1973) Components of trust: note on the use of Rotter scale. *Psychological Reports*, 33: 13–14.

Lewis, J.D. and Weigert, A. (1985) Trust as a social reality. *Social Forces*, 63 (4): 967–85.

Lindskold, S. (1978) Trust development, the GRIT proposal, and the effects of conciliatory acts on conflict and cooperation. *Psychological Bulletin*, 85: 772–93.

Lorange, P. and Roos, J. (1992) *Strategic Alliances: Formation, Implementation and Evolution*. Cambridge, MA: Blackwell.

Luhmann, N. (1979) *Trust and Power*. Chichester: Wiley.

Luhmann, N. (1986) The autopoiesis of social systems, in F. Geyer and J. Van der Zouwen (eds), *Sociocybernetic Paradoxes: Observation, Control, and Evolution of Self-Steering Systems*. London: Sage. pp. 172–92.

Luhmann, N. (1988) The unity of the legal system, in G. Teubner (ed.), *Autopoietic Law: a New Approach to Law and Society*. Berlin: de Gruyter. pp. 12–35.

Luhmann, N. (1990) *Essays of Self-Reference*. New York: Columbia University Press.

March, J.G. and Olsen, J.P. (1989) *Rediscovering Institutions*. New York: Free Press.

March, J.G. and Olsen, J.P. (1990) The uncertainty of the past: organizational learning under ambiguity, in J.G. March (ed.), *Decisions and Organization*. London: Blackwell. pp. 335–58.

March, J.G. and Simon, H.A. (1958) *Organizations*. New York: Wiley.

McAllister, D.J. (1995) Affect- and cognition-based trust as foundations for interpersonal cooperation in organizations. *Academy of Management Journal*, 38 (1): 24–59.

Maturana, H. and Varela, F.J. (1980) *Autopoiesis and Cognition: the Realization of the Living*. London: Reidl.

Maturana, H. and Varela, F.J. (1987) *The Tree of Knowledge*. Boston, MA: Shambhala.

Meyerson, D., Weick, K.E. and Kramer, R.M. (1996) Swift trust and temporary groups, in R.M. Kramer and T.R. Tyler (eds), *Trust in Organizations: Frontiers of Theory and Research*. London: Sage.

Moorman, C., Deshpandé, R. and Zaltman, G. (1993) Factors affecting trust in market research relationships. *Journal of Marketing*, 57 (January): 81–101.

Morgan, G. (1993) *Imaginization: the Art of Creative Management*. Newbury Park, CA: Sage.

Morgan, R.M. (1991) Relationship commitment and trust in marketing. Dissertation, Texas Tech University, order no. 9129401.

Oakes, G. (1990) The sales process and the paradoxes of trust. *Journal of Business Ethics*, 9: 671–9.

Peters, T. (1992) *Liberation Management*. London: Macmillan.

Prahalad, S. and Hamel, G. (1990) The core competence of the corporation. *Harvard Business Review*, May–June: 79–91.

Ring, P.S. and van de Ven, A. (1992) Structuring cooperative relationships between organizations. *Strategic Management Journal*, 13: 483–98.

Ring, P.S. and van de Ven, A. (1994) Developmental processes of cooperative interorganizational relationships. *Academy of Management Review*, 19 (1): 90–118.

Rotter J. (1971) Generalized expectancies for interpersonal trust. *American Psychologist*, 26: 443–52.

Rotter, J. (1980) Interpersonal trust, trustworthiness and gullibility. *American Psychologist*, 35 (1): 1–7.

Rumelt, R.P., Schendel, D. and Teece, D.J. (1991) Strategic management and economics. *Strategic Management Journal*, 12, Special Issue (Winter): 5–29.

Sabel, C.F. (1993) Studies trust: building new forms of cooperation in a volatile economy. *Human Relations*, 46 (9): 1133–70.

Shapiro, S.P. (1987) The social control of impersonal trust. *American Journal of Sociology*, 93: 623–58.

Shklar, J.N. (1984) *Ordinary Vices*. Cambridge, MA: Belknap.

Sitkin, S.B. and Roth, N.L. (1993) Explaining the limited effectiveness of legalistic 'remedies for trust/distrust'. *Organization Science*, 4 (3): 367–92.

Sproull, L. and Kiesler, S. (1991) *Connections: New Ways of Working in the Networked Organization*. Cambridge, MA: MIT Press.

Stinchcombe, A. (1990) *Information and Organizations*. Berkeley, CA: University of California Press.

Teubner, G. (1991) Autopoiesis and steering: how politics profit from the normative surplus of capital, in R.J. In't Veld, L. Schaap, and C.J.A.M. van Twist (eds), *Autopoiesis and Configuration Theory: New Approaches to Social Steering*. Dordrecht: Kluwer. pp. 127–43.

Thorelli, H.B. (1986) Networks, between markets and hierarchies. *Strategic Management Journal*, 7: 37–51.

Turnbull, P.W. and Wilson, D.T. (1989) Developing and protecting profitable customer relationships. *Industrial Marketing Management*, 18: 233–8.

Tyler, T.R. and Kramer, R.M. (1996) Whither trust?, in R.M. Kramer and T.R. Tyler (eds), *Trust in Organizations: Frontiers of Theory and Research*. London: Sage.

Varela, F.J. (1979) *Principles of Biological Autonomy*. New York: Elsevier North Holland.

Varela, F.J. (1992) Whence perceptual meaning? A cartography of current ideas, in F.J. Varela and J.P Dupuy (eds), *Understanding Origins: Contemporary Views on the Origin of Life, Mind and Society*. Dordrecht: Kluwer. pp. 235–64.

Varela, F.J., Thompson, E. and Rosch, E. (1992) *The Embodied Mind*. Cambridge, MA: MIT Press.

von Foerster, H. (1984) Principles of self-organization in socio-managerial context, in H. Ulrich and G.J.B. Probst (eds), *Self Organization and Management of Social Systems*. Berlin: Springer. pp. 2–24.

von Krogh, G. and Roos, J. (1995) *Organizational Epistemology*. London: Macmillan.

von Krogh, G. and Vicari, S. (1993) An autopoiesis approach to experimental strategic learning', in P. Lorange, B. Chakravarthy, J. Roos and A. Van de Ven (eds), *Implementing Strategic Processes: Change, Learning and Co-operation*. London: Blackwell. pp. 394–410.

von Krogh, G., Roos, J. and Slocum, K. (1994) An essay on corporate epistemology. *Strategic Management Journal*, 15, Special Issue (Summer): 53–71.

Weick, K.E. (1979) *The Social Psychology of Organizing*. New York: Random House.

Weick, K.E. and Roberts, K.H. (1993) Collective mind in organizations: heedful interrelating on flight decks. *Administrative Science Quarterly*, 38: 357–81.

Williamson, O.E. (1993) Calculativeness, trust, and economic organization. *Journal of Law and Economics*, XXXVI (April): 453–86.

Wilson, D.T. and Jantrania, S.A. (1993) Measuring value in relationship development. Paper presented at the 9th IMP Conference, Bath, 23–25 September.

Young, L.C. (1992) The role of trust in interorganisational relationships in marketing channels. Dissertation, University of New South Wales.

Young, L.C. (1993) A conceptualization of evolving interfirm trust. Paper presented at the 9th IMP Conference, Bath, 23–25 September.

Zand, D.E. (1972) Trust and managerial problem solving. *Administrative Science Quarterly*, March: 229–39.

Zeckhauser, R.J. (1991) The strategy of choice, in R.J. Zeckhauser (ed.), *Strategy and Choice*. Cambridge, MA: MIT Press.

PART II

MANAGING AND MEASURING KNOWLEDGE IN ORGANIZATIONS

6

THREE TALES OF KNOWLEDGE-CREATING COMPANIES

Ikujiro Nonaka, Katsuhiro Umemoto and Keigo Sasaki

Eliciting, anticipating and addressing customer needs have become an increasingly formidable task given shifting technological trajectories, shorter product life-cycles, expanded product offerings and increased competition. Conventional survey research methods are limited in their ability to provide useful information owing to time and uncertainty constraints. Getting new products to market ahead of the competition depends on firms' ability to manage and create knowledge. Reengineering extant business processes alone is not enough to cope with these changes in the market. Business firms have to develop knowledge in the form of business process innovations.

A recent summary of the current interest in the knowledge-creating organization points out that many organizations are now appointing chief knowledge officers (CKOs) (Davies, 1997). However, without an appreciation of the process of knowledge creation, it is unlikely that the adoption of new titles, procedures or technology alone will produce the sustainable competitive advantage that firms seek when they embark on efforts to improve the management of knowledge. In this chapter, we present our model of the knowledge creation process as well as three case studies which demonstrate the complexity and challenges of this process.

The three cases are of the Japanese companies Sharp, National Bicycle and Seven-Eleven Japan, all of which have successfully met the challenge of eliciting and responding to the needs of their customers through the use of knowledge-creating systems which tap into and transform knowledge flows within the customer firm as well as their own organization. The combination of both tacit and explicit knowledge, within and between organizations, leads to the timely development of new products and/or services. In other words, these firms are knowledge-creating companies. In the next section, we present our theory of organizational knowledge creation. We then describe the process of organizational knowledge creation, as it occurs at Sharp, National Bicycle and Seven-Eleven Japan. Sharp is an example of the prototypical knowledge-creating company. The latter two are examples of fusing information technology with face-to-face collaborative knowledge exchange to generate new products and/or services. We conclude with a discussion of the implications of these knowledge-creating systems for other organizations.

The Theory of Organizational Knowledge Creation

For us there are two types of knowledge: (1) tacit knowledge (e.g. intuitions, unarticulated mental models and embodied technical skills) and (2) explicit knowledge (i.e. a meaningful set of information articulated in clear language including numbers or diagrams).[1] Generally, Japanese emphasize the tacit type of knowledge, i.e. personal, context-specific and not so easily communicated. Westerners, on the other hand, emphasize explicit types of knowledge, i.e. formal, objective and codifiable.

In our view, these two types of knowledge are mutually complementary entities. They interact with one another and may be transformed from one type to another through individual or collective human creative activities. This is the key assumption of our dynamic theory of organizational knowledge creation. More precisely, we assume that new organizational knowledge is created by human interactions among individuals who have different types (tacit or explicit) of knowledge. This social and epistemic process brings about what we call four modes of knowledge conversion: socialization (from individual tacit knowledge to group tacit knowledge), externalization (from tacit knowledge to explicit knowledge), combination (from separate explicit knowledge to systemic explicit knowledge) and internalization (from explicit knowledge to tacit knowledge) (see Figure 6.1). Each of these four modes of knowledge conversion will be briefly discussed below.

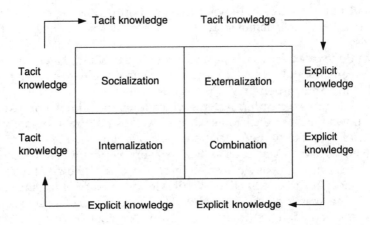

Figure 6.1   *Four modes of knowledge conversion (adapted from Nonaka and Takeuchi, 1995: 62)*

Socialization

Socialization is a process of creating common tacit knowledge through shared experiences. To foster socialization, we need to build a 'place' or 'field' of interaction, where individuals may share experiences at the same time and in the same space, thereby creating common unarticulated beliefs or embodied skills. In previous work we propose that tacit knowledge has two dimensions, i.e. technical and cognitive (Nonaka and Takeuchi, 1995). As for the technical dimension, traditional apprenticeship is a quintessential example of socialization. Young apprentices work with old master craftsmen, thereby acquiring technical skills through observation, imitation and practice. As for the cognitive dimension of tacit knowledge, Japanese companies often set up informal meetings outside the workplace, where participants chat over sake and meals. Through this informal process they create common tacit knowledge (e.g. a shared mental model or map) as well as mutual trust. In essence, they create the invisible bonds of community.

Externalization

Externalization is a process of articulating tacit knowledge into explicit concepts. Tacit knowledge becomes explicit through the use of metaphors, analogies, concepts, hypotheses or models. When we attempt to conceptualize tacit knowledge, we express its essence primarily through language. Yet, expressions are often inadequate, inconsistent and insufficient. Such discrepancies and gaps between expressions, however, help promote reflection and interactions between individuals. Externalization is typically seen in the process of concept creation and is triggered by dialogue or collective reflection. Deduction and induction are frequently used methods and are often combined for concept creation. When we cannot find an adequate expression for our image through deduction or induction, we have to use a non-analytical method. Externalization is, therefore, often driven by metaphor and/or analogy.

Combination

Combination is a process of assembling new and existing explicit knowledge into systemic knowledge such as a set of specifications for a prototype of new product. More often than not, a newly created concept should be combined with existing explicit knowledge to convert it into something tangible. Thus, this mode starts with linking different bodies of explicit knowledge. The so-called 'breakdown' can be included into this mode, since to break down a concept (e.g. one for a corporate vision prescribed by top management) is also to create deductively a systemic, explicit knowledge. It is critical for any organizational leader to create a thought-provoking and fertile concept, or what we call a 'mother concept', which gives birth to many 'offspring concepts'. The goal in this mode is to create an archetype (i.e. a prototype for a new product and a working model for a soft innovation such as a new business procedure) and promote justification throughout the organization.

Internalization

Internalization is a process of converting explicit knowledge into tacit, operational knowledge such as know-how. This mode is commonly triggered by 'learning by doing'. Explicit knowledge which has been documented into text, sound or video formats facilitates the internalization process. For example, engineering case studies help novice engineers to internalize explicit knowledge that has been externalized from veteran engineers' experience-based tacit knowledge of their design process. In addition to the provision of such explicit knowledge to organizational members, expanding the scope of direct experience and encouraging them to reflect upon the experience are equally important.

The Knowledge Spiral

Organizational knowledge is created through what we call a knowledge spiral across these four modes of knowledge conversion. A knowledge spiral may start from any mode, but usually begins with socialization (see Figure 6.2). For example, 'sympathized knowledge' about consumers' tacit wants may become explicit 'conceptual knowledge' about a new product concept through socialization and externalization. Such conceptual knowledge (i.e. a new product concept) guides the combination phase, in which explicit knowledge in the forms of newly developed and existing component technologies are combined to build a

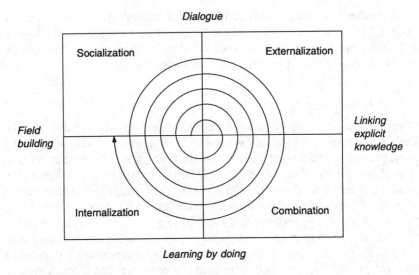

Dialogue

Socialization

Externalization

Field building

Linking explicit knowledge

Internalization

Combination

Learning by doing

Figure 6.2   *Knowledge spiral (Nonaka and Takeuchi, 1995: 71)*

prototype as 'systemic knowledge'. Systemic knowledge of a simulated production process for the new product turns into 'operational knowledge' for mass production through internalization. And users' tacit operational knowledge about the product and factory workers' tacit knowledge about the production process are often socialized and initiate the improvement of the product or the production process or the development of another product.

In addition to this epistemological dimension of the organizational knowledge creation process, the knowledge spiral can also be understood on an ontological dimension, namely, across the levels of knowledge-creating entities such as individuals, groups, organizations and collaborating organizations. Individuals' tacit knowledge is the basis of organizational knowledge creation. The organization mobilizes the tacit knowledge created and accumulated at the individual level and amplifies it at the upper ontological levels through the four modes of knowledge conversion. At the same time, organizational knowledge is utilized and internalized at the lower levels (see Figure 6.3).

The Five-Phase Model of Organizational Knowledge Creation

Thus far, we have presented the theoretical framework of organizational knowledge creation. In this section, we present a more practical, five-phase model of organizational knowledge creation (see Figure 6.4). The organizational knowledge creation process usually starts with the sharing of tacit knowledge, which roughly corresponds to socialization. Since tacit knowledge created and accumulated at the individual level is a rich

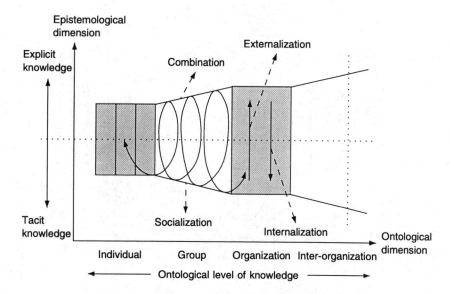

Figure 6.3   *Spiral of organizational knowledge creation (Nonaka and Takeuchi, 1995: 73)*

source of materials to be tapped for new knowledge, the key is to develop methods of sharing it and amplifying it at higher ontological levels.

In the second phase, tacit knowledge shared among group members is crystallized into concepts, gradually becoming explicit through metaphors, analogies and/or sketches. This is almost the same as the externalization process. The newly created concepts should be evaluated to determine whether they justify further investment of effort. The usual criteria are cost, profit margin and contribution to corporate growth, but the most significant criterion to determine further effort is a 'knowledge vision' that defines epistemologically a 'domain' that a company wants to inhabit. This provides members with a general direction regarding what kind of knowledge they should seek and create.

In the fourth phase, the justified concepts are transformed into 'archetypes', which are prototypes for new products and/or working models for procedural or operational innovations. They are built by combining newly created explicit knowledge with existing explicit knowledge possessed by people having such different expertise as research and development (R&D), production, quality control and marketing.

Organizational knowledge creation is not a goal to be achieved; rather it is an endless quest. It should be understood as a dynamic, unfolding process. It does not end once an archetype has been built. A new concept, which has been created, tested and realized in an archetype, moves on vertically to different ontological levels and horizontally across boundaries to different divisions of the same organization or to other

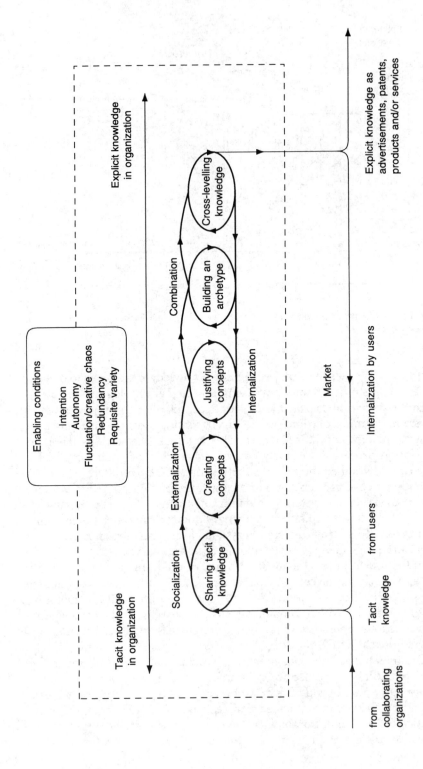

Figure 6.4 *Five-phase model of the organizational knowledge creation process (Nonaka and Takeuchi, 1995: 84)*

organizations, thereby starting new cycles of knowledge creation. We call this iterative and spiral process the 'cross-levelling of knowledge'.

In the following sections we use concrete examples from Japanese firms to understand how the knowledge creation spiral works. The example from Sharp demonstrates how a firm which has always recognized the importance of managing knowledge improves its ability to do so by creating teams and procedures to combine, transform and harvest knowledge. In contrast, the example from National Bicycle demonstrates how even mature, relatively low-tech industries can benefit from the knowledge creation process. Finally, Seven-Eleven Japan illustrates how innovation in the management of explicit knowledge can be as productive for a customer-oriented organization as collecting and transforming tacit knowledge can be for a technology-driven organization. Each example provides an illustration of how different segments of the spiral actually operate.

Sharp Corporation as the Prototypical Knowledge-Creating Company

Sharp began in 1912 when Tokuji Hayakawa, an inventor and tinkerer, set up a small metal works in Tokyo.[2] Hayakawa always told his employees, 'Don't imitate. Make something that others want to imitate'. He himself invented the first buckle that could adjust the length of the belt with no hole. He also engineered a mechanical pencil named 'Ever-Sharp' in 1915. It was an instant success and soon exported overseas. Hayakawa moved to a larger factory and hired more than 200 employees.

On 1 September 1923, however, the Great Kanto Earthquake destroyed his factory and took the lives of his wife, his children and many employees. Starting from scratch once again, he moved to Osaka. A year later, he founded the Hayakawa Metal Industrial Laboratory and developed Japan's first crystal radio after only three months of study and experimentation. Shortly thereafter he began mass producing the radio set. Although it sold very well, the passive receiver's range was limited. Therefore, Hayakawa began work on an active receiver that could amplify signals with a vacuum tube. In 1929, the company introduced a commercial model named 'Sharp Dyne' and became Japan's leading radio manufacturer. The company's rapid expansion in the following years necessitated its reorganization into a corporation in 1935, which was renamed the Hayakawa Electric Industries in 1942. Hayakawa Electric had been an outsider with no financial backing from zaibatsu and little connection with the government until it was forced to produce military devices during World War II.

Hayakawa Electric emerged from the war damaged but not destroyed. While other industrialists were purged from public life for their support of the militarists, Hayakawa was permitted to remain in business. The postwar recession was very difficult and the company only survived owing to its executives' personal guarantees of its liabilities and major underwriters' cooperation. In 1951, Hayakawa found television highly promising and started developing a TV set, even before the government prepared its official plan for TV broadcasting in Japan. When TV broadcasting began two years later, Hayakawa Electric introduced Japan's first commercial TV set under the brand name 'Sharp' in honour of the mechanical pencil. Throughout its history, Sharp has been quick to develop new products and bring them to market.

The implementation of 'quick product development' had been conducted traditionally by a small group of engineers on an *ad hoc* basis. In 1960, an organizational unit for development of technology (not product) was set up and in the following year emerged as the Central Research Laboratories. Until then, the company had no official organizational unit dedicated to medium- and long-term R&D. A small group of some 20 engineers was assigned to this R&D unit.

In 1970, the company was renamed Sharp Corporation and decided to mass produce semiconductors and liquid crystal displays for use in electronic calculators. This was a prescient decision because today Sharp manufactures and markets not only semiconductors and liquid crystal displays but also various other component devices. In recent years, Sharp's devices business contributed nearly one-third of its total sales. More importantly, as will be shown later, the essence of Sharp's strategy has been a combination of component technologies and product concepts to create a dynamic spiral between the two kinds of explicit knowledge.

Organizing for Knowledge Creation

In order to promote organizational knowledge creation, Sharp has developed a unique organizational structure, what we call the 'hypertext organization' (see Figure 6.5), which can be a model for every organization in the 'knowledge society'.[3] Knowledge in the form of new technologies and products is created at Sharp through the effective use of three layers: (1) a business system that is hierarchical and functionally departmentalized; (2) project teams organized flexibly for developing new technologies and/or products; and (3) a knowledge base consisting of tacit and explicit knowledge. The business system layer is what every manufacturing firm has in the traditional form of bureaucracy.

R&D at the Business System Layer

Sharp's day-to-day R&D activities are conducted at three levels: the Corporate R&D Group, Business Group laboratories, and Business Division laboratories. These are separated on the basis of the time frame

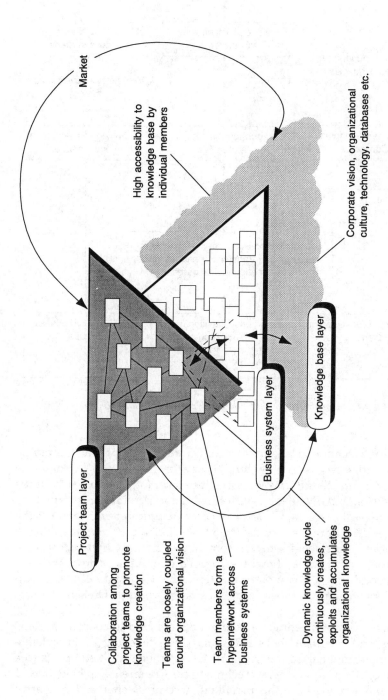

Figure 6.5 *Hypertext organization (Nonaka and Konno, 1993)*

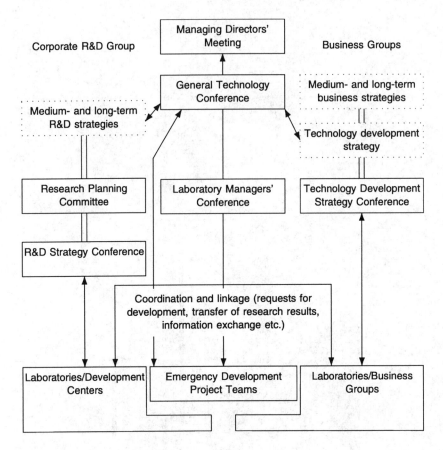

Figure 6.6   *R&D conferences within Sharp (Sharp Corporation, 1990)*

required for technological and/or product development. The Corporate R&D Group deals with long-term (three or more years) issues; the Business Group laboratories with medium-term (one and a half to three years) issues; and Business Division laboratories with short-term (one and a half years or less) issues. Concepts or prototypes created at the Corporate R&D Group are transferred to the Business Group or Division laboratories, whose engineers are sometimes relocated to the Corporate R&D Group for a couple of months. When the concepts or prototypes are found promising for commercialization, the Corporate R&D Group researchers sometimes move to the Business Group or Division laboratories.

Various types of meetings or conferences are held to coordinate R&D activities and facilitate the sharing and cross-levelling of knowledge across organizational boundaries and levels among the R&D units (see Figure 6.6). First, the General Technological Conference is held once a month and attended by the president, vice-presidents and executive directors, and the managers of the nine Business Group laboratories. They discuss what kinds of R&D themes should be focused on for an upcoming one-year period. These heated discussions about R&D strategy last as long as six hours with a break for lunch.

Second, the Laboratory Managers' Conference is held once a month and attended by managers of both the Business Group and Division laboratories, the director of the Corporate R&D Planning Office, and the director of the Intellectual Property Office. The Laboratory Managers' Conference makes specific, detailed decisions, including when and how to transfer a certain technology to the business groups and what links are needed with outside parties.

Third, the Technological Development Strategy Conference is held monthly at each Business Group. Its participants are not necessarily limited to members of a Business Group but include members of the Product Planning Department and the Engineering Department and selected individuals of the Corporate R&D Group. This conference is not only a medium for receiving technology from the Corporate R&D Group but also a locus for deliberating actively on what kind of key technologies should be developed at each Business Group.

Normally, new product development activities are carried out within each Business Division. Frequent meetings for product development are held to ensure cooperation among the engineering, production and marketing sections. In addition, the Product Planning Committee has been established to strengthen the link between marketing and product planning in each Business Division. The committee elaborates product concepts created by the planning side by reviewing them from the viewpoint of marketing. The committee also serves to enhance marketing people's sense of participation and involvement.

The Plans and Programmes Promotion Meeting, on the other hand, has been established to coordinate the efforts of the planning section with those of the production section. In addition, each Business Division holds a monthly meeting called the D&M Council, which is attended by R&D and marketing sections. The Council aims to prevent the marketing people from taking a negative attitude or saying 'It's just impossible' against technological possibilities, and to discover the potentials of an embryonic technology through frequent exchanges of ideas. During these meetings, consideration is given to how to convert product concepts into realities.

The Urgent Project System

In addition, important projects for product development are organized under the Urgent Project System independently of the above R&D organizations. Every member under the Urgent Project System wears the same 'gold badge', which is called *kin bajji* (*kin* means 'gold') in Japanese. Also, *kin* has the same sound as the first syllable in the

Japanese word *kin-kyu* which means 'urgent'. Wearing the 'gold badge' carries special significance not only for the project members but for other Sharp employees. The mission of an Urgent Project Team is to develop a strategically important product or technology within 18 months. An unlimited budget is available from headquarters. Also directly under the president, middle managers heading Urgent Project Teams are given top priorities in the use of company facilities or equipment and in the procurement of necessary items.

Members of an Urgent Project Team can be recruited from any section or department in the company at any time. Thus, a department may be deprived of its best people for over a year. Needless to say, every effort is made to ensure that the system is used as intended. Each urgent project proposed by a Business Division must justify company-wide support and indicate the feasibility of swift completion. Each proposal is reviewed at the General Technological Conference, the highest decision-making body regarding R&D at Sharp. To date, many successful products have been commercialized under the Urgent Project System. Examples include an electronic pocketbook and its more advanced model named 'Zaurus' or 'LC PenCom' using a liquid crystal display and a pen as the input device, and LC ViewCam or a video camcorder (camera and recorder) using an LCD instead of a viewfinder.

Extending the Idea of the Urgent Project System

The idea of the Urgent Project Team has recently been expanded into a product development system called 'concurrent engineering'. While each urgent project is terminated when product development is completed, concurrent engineering involves not only a product development team but also production, testing and design teams. This system aims to shorten the lead time from development to marketing as well as to prevent product defects and to increase production productivity. An example developed under this system is LC ViewCam.

Also, the success of the Urgent Project System led to two new kinds of meetings: (1) New Life Strategy Meeting and (2) Newing Product Strategy Meeting in order to apply the Urgent Project idea throughout the entire organization. The New Life Strategy Meeting is held monthly and attended by the president, vice-presidents and managers of the Business Groups and Divisions. Among new product candidates presented by Division managers, Super Excellent (SE) products are selected. Requirements for an SE product are rigorous. It must not only create a new market trend but also use a new technology, device and manufacturing method.

The Newing Product Strategy Meeting is held monthly and attended by some 20 members including the president, vice-presidents and managers of the Business Groups and Divisions. The word 'Newing' is a combination of 'new' and 'ing', and means 'efforts to create a new market'. Candidates for new product concepts are proposed by Business Group or Division managers and are reviewed for their originality and marketability. According to president Haruo Tsuji, a basic guideline for the meeting is that 'we start with saying yes rather than no' to the proposed new concepts in order to encourage idea generation. Each meeting reviews two proposals with discussions sometimes lasting more than six hours. Once a new product concept is approved as an SE product or a Newing product, development work starts at the division that proposed it. Authority given to the development team is similar to that of the Urgent Project Team, because development members receive direct support from the president and have increased access to company resources. However, it is different from the Urgent Project in that the members basically stay in their original positions in the business system layer and continue usual work during the development process.[4]

The latest programme intended to promote creativity at Sharp is STAR 21, which stands for 'Strategic and creative minds, Total customer satisfaction, Advanced technology, and Rapid actions toward the twenty-first century'. Under this programme, many cross-level, small-group projects aimed at developing STAR products have been initiated. For example, a spontaneous (i.e. self-organizing) group of people working on word processors came together to have brainstorming sessions. A technique used in the sessions is called *Sushi-neta hou*, which is explained metaphorically by Yukihiko Ueno, a manager of the Second Planning Section at the Computer Division, as follows:

> The taste of *sushi* is decided by the combination of fresh *neta* [such stuff as raw sea foods] and hand-rolled, vinegared *shari* or rice. Likewise, we write down each item of *shari* information (about technologies, or one that came from our database on users etc.) and *neta* information (about market trends, other companies etc.) on a card and make various combinations of them to find out tasty *sushi* (or promising product ideas), thereby conceiving more concrete images of new products.

This 'externalization' technique has produced, for example, word-processing software to print out original, illustrated postcards. In this case, a computer technology using a pen as an input tool to draw illustrations is *shari* and a postcard is *neta*.[5]

Tapping Tacit Knowledge in the Market

As suggested by the fact that it has given birth to many of the 'first products' in Japan or in the world, Sharp has carried out product development under the initiative of its technological departments.[6] That is, R&D at Sharp has long been technology-driven. Today, however, it is not only the Corporate R&D Group and Business Group and Division laboratories that take the initiative in product development. Sharp has established two additional organizations for concept creation and transmission. One is the New Lifestyle Planning Group and the other is the Corporate Design Group.

In 1985, the New Lifestyle Center was created chiefly by the incumbent president Haruo Tsuji, who was then managing director and the first director of the Center until his ascent to the presidency. The establishment of the Center was closely linked to changes within and outside the company around 1984–5. The changes then, as perceived by Sharp, can be summarized as follows. First, it was a period when performance gaps among Sharp's Business Divisions widened and their boundaries crumbled. This led to the creation of the Center to transcend levels and boundaries among the Business Groups and Divisions and to coordinate product lines from the users' perspective. Also, it was a period when products were being systematized from stand-alone ones into product groups or units for the benefit of users, e.g. the combination of audio and video equipment.

Second, at this time, many home appliance products reached maturity. The 1970s was a period when individualization and diversification became apparent among consumers' wants. By the mid 1980s, clear demands appeared not only for more colours and shapes but also for products that reflected new values and lifestyles. As a result, Sharp admitted that it could not cope with diverse consumer wants, merely with variations in colour and shape, and that it should create product concepts from the standpoints of users' value systems and lifestyles.

These environmental changes probably provided the continuity between the New Life strategy and the New Lifestyle Center. However, the Center was not merely an extension of the New Life strategy. There was an internal factor to its establishment. The Center was conceived about the time that Sharp started rethinking its business domain. The Corporate R&D Group reviewed the company's business domain from the technical viewpoint. At the same time, Sharp recognized the need to review its business domain from the consumer's viewpoint. It was for this reason that the Center was established.

The U's Series introduced in 1987 is one of the Center's initial achievements in incorporating a concept it had created into an entire product line. This series of 'new products necessary for a skilful use of time' was created for the benefit of women who value time. It was based on three approaches to household chores: (1) time flexibility (household chores can be done anytime); (2) labour substitution (they can be completely taken over); and (3) labour sharing (they can be done by any family member). In the case of the dishwasher, for example, a storage rack was added so that even a child can easily stack the dishes. Thus, the Center's unique contribution was the thorough review of existing products from the viewpoint of consumers who have certain values that govern their lifestyles.

The Center has developed various systems to create new product concepts based on consumers' needs, wants or values. The first is the Trend Leader System, which started in 1985. This system organizes about 600 'leading consumers', ranging from middle-school students to senior citizens in their 70s, as the Center's outside staff. The 600 people are divided into numerous clusters of students, married working women, retired senior citizens etc. When a product concept being created is reviewed by these 'leading consumers', each cluster is further divided into smaller focus groups to be interviewed, through which their specific needs, wants and values are narrowed down. Through these focus groups, the Center collects a large amount of high-quality information, from which it predicts consumer trends with time frames ranging from 1 to 10 years ahead.

The second is the Life Creator System adopted in early 1990. This system is similar to the Trend Leader System in that it organizes consumers as outside staff. The goal of the system, however, is to set up 'experiments in real-life situations'. The system provides consumers or corporate users with a prototype, allowing them to experiment with it as they like, thereby finding out how the prototype should be improved to become a product which meets their lifestyle demands. That is, the system aims not only to hire consumers as monitors but also to work with them to create a better lifestyle. Takuji Ohgawara, former director of the Center, characterized the organization as a 'guerrilla troop against the conventional concepts' and focused his efforts on creating better systems to listen to the voice of consumers. According to Ohgawara, 'Two things everyone in the company fears are the voices of consumers and the president'. He continued:

Important is to have as many contacts as possible. If you have a system for doing this quickly and inexpensively or have some sort of arrangement to make contacts with consumers, you will most naturally be inclined to listen to them. There are limits to surveys being conducted today because each survey has to begin with a survey design, and this requires substantial cost and time. One quickly spends one million yen or somewhere in that order on such surveys, and it often takes three months from survey design to tallied survey results. Considering the speed with which business is conducted today, a company would do away with any survey that takes three months. That's how the gap between consumers and business firms widens. Every company wants to know now, because it needs information right away. Another problem is that customers speak their own language while the business people who plan and develop products think in a totally different language. So, this Center's role is to bridge the two. We interpret what the customers say and relay the messages to Business Groups or Divisions.

The third system is joint research with companies in other industries. For example, when Sharp first developed the microwave oven toaster (a microwave oven with a toaster function), it used information and knowledge obtained through a joint research project with a food processing company. The accumulated know-how on food processing which resulted from this project was used by Sharp to create the microwave oven toaster, a new product category, and by the food manufacturer to improve products to be heated in the microwave oven.

The Center was renamed and upgraded to the New Lifestyle Planning Group in April 1991. Yet, its role continues to be to listen to consumers' voices, interpret them and create new concepts, which are then passed on to the relevant planning section of each Business Division. Moreover, the Group throws concepts back and forth not only to planning sections of Business Divisions but to R&D sections as well. Now, this group is taking the greater initiative in product development under the leadership of vice-president Atsushi Asada as its director. Staff of the group take consumers' views and transmit product concepts to relevant units.

The Corporate Design Group functions as an integrating link between the New Lifestyle Planning Group and the Urgent Project teams. It comprises 200 industrial design engineers who work together with planners and engineers from the Urgent Project teams on new product development. This is an unusual arrangement for non-Japanese firms who generally contract out for the services of industrial design engineers. For Sharp, however, this group serves an important purpose in the knowledge creation process. It is here that the tacit knowledge elicited from the external market is combined with the implicit technical knowledge gathered from within the organization.

The Knowledge Base at Sharp

Since 1986, Sharp has focused the company's future business development on optoelectronics.[7] The company believes that its business domain is where microelectronics merges with 'opto' (or light). Microelectronics alone is no longer sufficient in an advanced information society. As video information is increasingly important, the element of 'opto' is essential. Sharp has 20 years of experience in liquid crystal and numerous achievements in R&D and the production of electroluminescent (EL) displays, luminescent diodes, CCDs (charge-coupled devices that convert light into electronic signals) and solar battery cells (which convert light into electricity). Also, it has built the Optical Device Laboratories which are actively engaged in R&D in laser diodes, a key device in optical disk players and fibre optic networks.

This accumulated knowledge and experience in optoelectronics has become both the tacit and the explicit knowledge base for Sharp. Optoelectronics has actually affected R&D people's ways of thinking. Although optoelectronics is a technical term, it is also Sharp's 'knowledge vision'.

It has oriented not only the R&D sections but also Sharp as a whole. Optoelectronics provides a guide to the strategic domain that Sharp wants to inhabit and is a key concept guiding strategic decision-making. Sharp's grand vision of optoelectronics as part of its explicit knowledge base serves as a template for identifying the relevance and usefulness of new knowledge. In other words, optoelectronics designates the technological field in which Sharp wants to invest. All knowledge generated in the business system and project team layers is recategorized and recontextualized with the knowledge vision of optoelectronics in mind. Figure 6.7 shows applications of optoelectronics. The essence of Sharp's strategy based on optoelectronics is, in fact, to continue a dynamic spiral that it has long made between component technologies and product concepts (see Figure 6.8).

Optoelectronics has also affected the tacit understanding of the imperative 'Don't imitate' that the company has inherited from the founder Tokuji Hayakawa. It has permeated the organization, thus becoming part of the company's tacit knowledge base or corporate culture, and has influenced individual business behaviours. More specifically, the 'Don't imitate' doctrine serves as a guideline for Sharp's human resource strategy which emphasizes human creativity.

Creating Knowledge for Mass Customization at National Bicycle

In November 1986, Mitsuru Omoto became president of National Bicycle, Japan's second largest bicycle maker and a subsidiary of a consumer electronics giant, Matsushita Electric Industrial Company.[8] Until then, his career had nothing to do with the bicycle business. The mature industry gave him a challenge to make a breakthrough. Omoto focused his attention on the increasing demand for 'customized' sport bicycles which were gaining popularity in Japan owing to users' diversified wants and the physical fitness boom, while demand for mass-produced sport bicycles was decreasing. Manufacturing bicycles perfectly suited to users' bodily dimensions and personal preferences for colours and shapes coincided with the ongoing general 'individualization trend', that is, demand for customized products.

Major problems of the customized production of high-priced sport bicycles for users seeking high additional values are the possible overstock due to an overestimation of demand and the high-cost craftsmen-based production. To solve these problems, Omoto decided to computerize the company's business process for customized sport bicycles. With this business process innovation, he wanted to reduce production costs and the length of time from order taking to product delivery, thereby making the business profitable. He believed that such a new

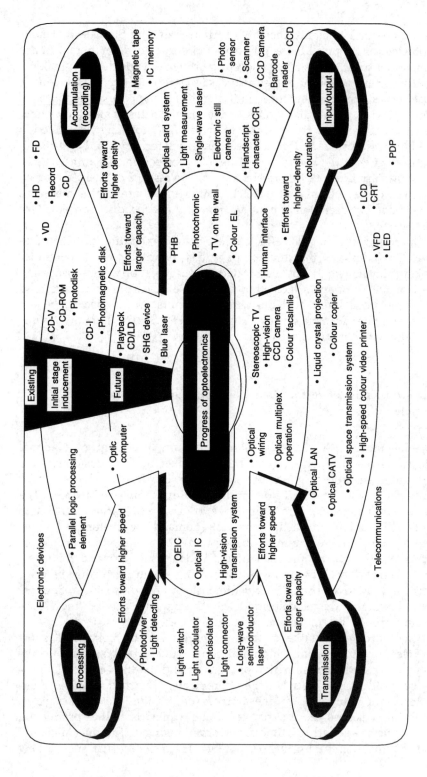

Figure 6.7 *Development of optoelectronic technologies*

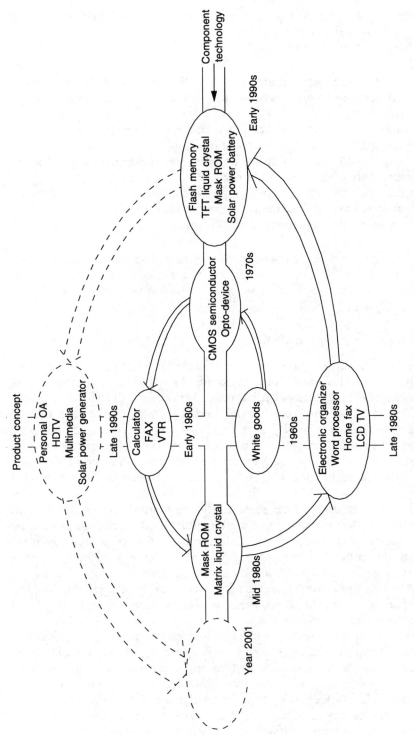

Figure 6.8 *Dynamic spiral of component technologies and product concepts (Sharp Corporation, 1990)*

system could successfully differentiate the company's customized sport bicycles from those of competitors.

Thus, Omoto aimed to:

1   develop high value-added products that truly fit each user's physical dimensions and his or her preferences for model features such as colour
2   build a plant to manufacture a customized product for each user toward the goal of 'mass customization'
3   implement craftsmanship-based, mass-customized production employing highly skilled workers
4   achieve no stock of finished products
5   differentiate its customized products through a computerized ordering, manufacturing and delivering system.

He announced that the new system should be completed in six months, and he himself became the project leader. On 1 June 1987 the new system went into operation as planned and it was named Panasonic Order System or POS.

Panasonic Order System (POS)

The POS system elicits a customer's 'subjective' feeling of the best ride (which is decided mostly but not entirely by his or her 'objective' bodily dimensions) and personal preferences for colours and shapes through 1000 POS agent stores across Japan. Each store is equipped with a fitting scale and a feature catalogue (e.g. colour patterns and handle shapes). Sizes of each POS customer's physical dimensions (lengths of leg and arm, width of shoulder and so on) are measured with the fitting scale. The device looks like a bicycle without wheels, on which a POS customer rides.

A customer and a POS store employee jointly find the most comfortable product sizes by adjusting the fitting scale and by discussing the customer's preferences. Then, the customer chooses product features from the 16 basic models and 190 colour patterns available, combinations of which make tens of thousands of colour variations. Finally the customer selects a logo type for his or her name to be printed on the top tube or stem of the bicycle. Overall, a customer can choose from about 8 million possible variations.

The fitting scale, feature catalogue and employee–customer dialogue are means to acquire users' tacit knowledge in the form of their systemic preferences for sizes, colours and so on (which can be expressed by a set of explicit information), and to externalize them into product specifications (i.e. explicit knowledge) through the socialization and externalization processes. Thus, the POS system can convert users' tacit knowledge into explicit knowledge effectively and efficiently.

The POS agent enters these data into an order form and faxes it to the POS factory, thereby reducing the order-to-delivery time to two weeks. The data on the order form are then input into the factory's host computer for computer-aided design and manufacturing (CAD/CAM) and, at the same time, a barcode for each order is printed and sent to the highly automated and robotized production line. The host computer memorizes the specifications of each ordered product by its barcode, thereby controlling the CAD/CAM system. Following the barcode, the CAM tunes production equipment for specified dimensions of each customized product, especially those for cutting, welding and building tube frames, and other processes prior to painting. Despite such extensive automation, highly skilled craftsmen must translate the unique specifications of each customer into finished products, using their tacit knowledge such as experience and expertise.

To make this system profitable, National Bicycle pursued efficiency thoroughly. Most important was the integration of all processes, from order taking to product delivery, into one system. This required many innovations. For example, integrating the painting process into the new system could have impaired the working environment of the shop floor. To solve this problem, project members from the Production Technology Department replaced a phosphoric solvent with a sulphuric acid-based solvent, and then developed a device that automatically covers a painting tank and a booth in which a powerful fan blows paint mist down onto water in a tub. Thus, they successfully built the 'POS factory', which includes all processes from fax order reception to highly automated production to finished product delivery in a 70-metre line.

Exploiting Tacit Knowledge of Skilled Craftsmen

National Bicycle has exploited the tacit knowledge of highly skilled craftsmen at the POS factory. The company has externalized their tacit knowledge into a computer language, which operates manufacturing robots and semi-automated equipment, by studying and observing their manufacturing skills. It has also instituted a policy to promote interaction between craftsmen at the mass-custom POS factory and workers at the adjacent mass-production factory. This interaction is critical, because knowledge creation depends on the interaction between tacit and explicit knowledge and the transformation from one to the other. Based on the policy, about 20 craftsmen are required to train semi-skilled workers at either the mass-custom factory or the mass-production factory, which is basically on-the-job training (OJT). This forces craftsmen to externalize their know-how or tacit knowledge by articulating their experience to the workers. In this process of externalization they also comprehend their tacit knowledge from a new dimension.

Seven-Eleven Japan as the Most Advanced Knowledge-Creating Retailer

The labyrinthine nature of the Japanese distribution and retailing sector is notorious.[9] But it is not well known that some large Japanese retailers enjoy higher labour productivity than their American counterparts owing to their efficient information-logistics system. Seven-Eleven Japan is considered to be the best at managing and exploiting information. As a result, the company has been the most profitable retailer in Japan in both absolute and sales–profit ratio terms. But it is not simply profitability which interests us here. More important to us is that this franchiser of convenience stores creates organizational knowledge systematically.

Seven-Eleven Japan originated in 1973 when Ito-Yokado, a Japanese supermarket chain, and Southland Corporation, the operator and franchiser of Seven-Eleven stores in the United States, reached a licensing agreement for convenience store operation. Ito-Yokado learned systemic knowledge about corporate policy, franchising and operation systems from Southland, but had to adapt this information to Japanese conditions. Since 1978 when the first store was opened, the number of stores has increased to over 6000.

Each Seven-Eleven store sells some 3000 goods, of which about 70% are changed every year. Out of total sales, 77% is foods; about 40% is processed foods (e.g. snacks and cup noodles) and about 20% is fast food such as rice balls and box lunches. In fact, Seven-Eleven is Japan's largest fast-food chain with sales greater than those of McDonald's Japan.

Critical to understanding Seven-Eleven Japan is the fact that it is a franchiser: it does not sell goods (although it runs several stores for experiments) but rather sells information and knowledge. The company charges its franchisees for the information and knowledge it provides them, royalties for trademarks, leasing fees for such equipment as the information system and display racks, refrigerated cases, 20% of utilities expenses etc.

Because of the necessity of providing materials to the various franchisees, Seven-Eleven Japan makes extensive use of manuals (i.e. quintessential explicit knowledge) for store operation, employee training and franchisee recruiting/training, which it learned from Southland and adapted to Japanese conditions. Also, to train part-timers, store owners use a guidebook and a 12-volume set of video tapes (i.e. explicit knowledge) on store operations. In this way Seven-Eleven Japan differs rather dramatically from most Japanese companies by relying heavily on explicit knowledge.

Creating Knowledge through Hypothesis Testing

The company has Japan's best retail information system, which may be accessed by store owners as well as part-time employees through hand-held computers called 'graphic order terminals'. When placing orders, they hypothesize what item will sell well, how many, and how to sell them, based on their intuition and experience as well as POS (point-of-sale) data, advice of field counsellors from Seven-Eleven Japan's local offices, information about weather forecasts, local events (festivals, school excursions etc.) and others. Each hypothesis is tested by an actual order and confirmed by POS data. Successful hypotheses are collected by field counsellors, and a selected one is reported at a weekly meeting at the headquarters, which is attended by all field counsellors, top management and headquarters staff. The hypothesis is tested throughout Japan in the following weeks. In this way, Seven-Eleven Japan converts front-line knowledge into organizational knowledge.

In terms of the four modes of knowledge conversion, organizational knowledge creation through hypothesis testing at Seven-Eleven occurs as follows:

Socialization   Observation of customers' buying behaviours and casual conversations with them (in-store information), plus tracking POS data to detect trends of particular items, plus information about local events.

Externalization   Making a hypothesis about sales of a particular item and a way to sell them.

Combination   Testing the hypothesis with the next day's POS numbers (explicit knowledge).

Internalization   Learning a lesson from the hypothesis testing, i.e. what was wrong or right.

Seven-Eleven Japan has another method for generating hypotheses. Its Merchandise Planning Section includes young 'antennae' people who spend most of their time 'town-watching', seeking information about what items are selling and why, and spotting lifestyle trends and changes. Through this participant observation process, they create hypotheses about a better assortment of goods and sometimes ideas for new products.

Creating Knowledge through Deductive Reasoning

Seven-Eleven Japan has a business creed: 'adaptation to environmental changes and adherence to four basic principles'. It considers the following four basic principles as the truth of the retailing business: (1) freshness of goods; (2) the best assortment of goods; (3) cleanliness of stores, goods and employee uniforms; and (4) friendliness to customers.

The business creed indicates that the company must adapt to changes in customers' preferences and needs, business cycles, and technologies in order to maintain the four basic principles. And top management always emphasizes the four basic principles at every meeting. Thus, the four basic principles provide criteria for deductively creating and justifying new knowledge in the forms of operational procedures, new products and/or new services, not only by store owners and part-timers but also by Seven-Eleven Japan employees. The new knowledge works in turn as a means to realize the basic principles.

In other words, the basic principles elicit or orient everyday actions, which change continuously according to changes in the market and technology, thereby realizing in turn the basic principles. A seventeenth-century *haiku* master Basho Matsuo argued that an excellent *haiku* tells what is constant (i.e. true) within what is ever changing. We suggest that an excellent company tells what is constant (i.e. its business principles) within what is ever changing (e.g. changes in the market and technology). Seven-Eleven Japan is such a company.

Multi-Organizational Knowledge Creation through Team Merchandising

Seven-Eleven Japan has also built multi-organizational knowledge-creating systems to develop new products through strategic alliances with manufacturers who possess complementary knowledge. The archetype of what the company calls 'team merchandising' is the Japan Delicafoods Cooperative, a consortium of box lunch and delicatessen makers, which not only cooperate for joint procurement of ingredients, quality control, joint distribution and new product development, but also share technologies and know-how to improve performance of member companies.

This idea of collaborative knowledge creation among (potentially competing) organizations has been applied so far to more loosely coupled teams of makers, trading firms and Seven-Eleven Japan. Examples include: (1) cooked noodles, a product line developed jointly by 20 companies, such as flour mills, soup makers, Seven-Eleven Japan and others, which share data, information and know-how; and (2) freshly baked bread to be delivered to Seven-Eleven stores three times a day for breakfast, lunch and dinner, which has been jointly developed by an alliance of Itochu Corporation (a general trading firm in charge of procuring ingredients and building a nation-wide system), Ajinomoto Frozen Bakery (which supplies frozen dough), local bread bakers (which have built bread-baking plants near stores) and Seven-Eleven Japan (which provides POS data on the best-selling items).

Conclusions

This chapter has shown how three knowledge-creating companies have coped with consumers' increasingly diversified and fast-changing preferences by creating new knowledge in the forms of organizational and/or technological innovations. In other words, they have built business process innovations as knowledge-creating systems to elicit consumers' needs, detect the first signs of incipient phenomena in the market, and develop new products and/or services based on such knowledge. These knowledge-creating systems are not the result of often inhumane reengineering, which overrelies on information technology, but the result of systems which rely on human beings' intellectual ability and mutual trust, while utilizing information systems to extend their capabilities.

More specifically, the three cases imply the following points. First, as Sharp's case clearly shows, task force teams (e.g. Urgent Project teams) organized independently of routine operations can be a major competitive advantage that helps a company establish a reputation for innovation. For such technology-driven project teams to be successful, however, emerging technologies have to match consumers' or users' wants or preferences which should simultaneously be externalized. Indeed, every product and/or service innovation is a confluence of technological capability and market demand.

Second, National Bicycle presents a case of a genuine organizational and technological innovation that has realized mass customization to meet diversified personal wants and preferences. Interestingly, the innovation makes the best use of seemingly irrelevant highly skilled craftsmen, who operate robotized or semi-automated manufacturing equipment. The case illustrates not only the essence of knowledge creation, i.e. externalization of tacit knowledge (embodied skills of craftsmen), but also the fact that such tacit knowledge cannot be entirely externalized and the remaining part is equally important and useful.

Third, as the cases of Sharp and Seven-Eleven Japan show, business creeds or basic business principles as 'true' knowledge for each business firm or domain help the company to create deductively new knowledge in the form of new operational procedures or new products and/or services, and to justify (i.e. evaluate) their truthfulness and relevance. These companies illustrate that successful knowledge management relies on the adoption of a total process, not on the adoption of individual components of the knowledge-creating organization.

Notes

1 For a detailed discussion on the theory of organizational knowledge creation, see Chapter 3 of Nonaka and Takeuchi (1995).

2 This description of Sharp's history draws on Numagami et al. (1991) and Sharp Corporation (1990).

3 This section draws on Numagami et al. (1991) and Nonaka and Takeuchi (1995: pp. 179–90).

4 Occasionally, the status of projects developing SE or Newing products is

raised to that of the Urgent Project, as in the case of the LC ViewCam, a best-selling video camcorder using a liquid crystal display as a monitor and an alternative to a viewfinder.

5 This paragraph draws on Hirabayashi (1994: 194–6).

6 This section draws on Numagami et al. (1991: 17–23).

7 This section draws on Numagami et al. (1991: 24–8) and Nonaka and Takeuchi (1995: 185–9).

8 This section draws on Nonaka and Sasaki (1996) and Kotha (1996).

9 This section draws on Umemoto (1995).

References

Davies, R. (1997) Reflections on knowledge. Working Paper, Management Centre Europe, Brussels.

Hirabayashi, C. (1994) *The Liquid Crystal Revolution by Sharp* (in Japanese). Tokyo: Diamond.

Kotha, S. (1996) Mass-customization: a strategy for knowledge creation and organizational learning. *International Journal of Technology Management*, 11 (7/8): 846–58.

Nonaka, I. and Konno, N. (1993) Knowledge-based organization. *Business Review*, 41 (1): 59–73.

Nonaka, I. and Sasaki, K. (1996) Business organizations as knowledge-creating systems (in Japanese). *Diamond Harvard Business Review*, December–January: 31-40.

Nonaka, I. and Takeuchi, H. (1995) *The Knowledge-Creating Company*. New York: Oxford University Press.

Numagami, T., Nonaka, I. and Otsubo, T. (1991) Sharp: Technological Management (in Japanese). Case Study SMIP-91-16(CN), Nomura School of Advanced Management.

Sharp Corporation (1990) *Entry in International Directory of Company Histories*. Chicago: St James Press. Vol. II, pp. 95–6.

Umemoto, K. (1995). Seven-eleven Japan: a knowledge-creating company (in Japanese). Unpublished manuscript.

7

KNOWLEDGE ENABLERS

Kazuo Ichijo, Georg von Krogh and Ikujiro Nonaka

Strategic management has a twofold purpose: to develop and sustain current competitive advantages for the firm (D'Aveni, 1995), and to build competitive advantages for the future (Hamel and Prahalad, 1994). Current competitive advantages hinge on the firm's command of, access to and effective utilization of resources and knowledge. These resources and knowledge allow the firm to implement cost advantages, differentiation advantages (Porter, 1980; Barney, 1991) or both (Hamel and Prahalad, 1994). According to resource-based theory of strategy, knowledge and resources that are unique, valuable, imperfectly imitable and impossible to substitute allow firms to sustain their competitive advantage, even facing attempts by competitors to duplicate the competitive advantage (Barney, 1991). To achieve this first purpose of strategic management, strategists must identify and analyse current use of resources and knowledge in existing markets, i.e. capturing and capitalizing on existing knowledge; invest in strengthening resources and knowledge that give rise to competitive advantages; and find new market opportunities in which resources and knowledge can be leveraged (Hamel and Prahalad, 1994).

The second purpose of strategic management is to build competitive advantages for the future, i.e. create new knowledge. This process is exposed to two types of uncertainty. First, any investment in developing new knowledge and new resources is uncertain (D'Aveni, 1995). The process by which to develop new sources of competitive advantage might be difficult to specify and difficult to conduct. The final form or shape of resources and knowledge is unclear as well. Second, development of resources and knowledge for future competitive advantage does not occur in a competitive vacuum. While the strategist's ambition is to develop knowledge and resources that turn out to be valuable, rare among competitors, imperfectly imitable and impossible to substitute, it should be expected that existing as well as possible future competitors engage in resource and knowledge accumulation and building that might have a strong impact on the future competitive advantages of the firm (Hamel and Prahalad, 1994). Competitors' resource and knowledge building might equalize competitive advantages in an industry, create competitive disadvantages, or render competitive advantages of other firms very incremental, and at best temporary.

The strategist must develop a balanced approach to strategic management; managing existing and developing new competitive advantages must be pursued concurrently (Hamel and Prahalad, 1994). Firms have a natural tendency to rely heavily on current sources of sustainable competitive advantage, however. Existing resources and knowledge, providing current superior industry performance, can develop into severe rigidities, making the development of new sources of competitive advantage highly difficult (D'Aveni, 1995). Relying on sources of superior industry performance alone can be fatal. In many industries sources of sustainable competitive advantages are becoming increasingly short lived as competitors erode them through aggressive knowledge and resource development, and whole industries are vanishing or undergoing large-scale restructuring through the introduction of radical innovations (Hamel and Prahalad, 1994). Simply renewing or adjusting resources and knowledge might not be enough to secure future competitive advantage (D'Aveni, 1995).

Thus, strategic management research should provide an answer to the following key question asked by strategists: while developing and utilizing current sources of sustainable competitive advantage, what does it take in terms of process to develop resources and knowledge for future sustainable competitive advantage?

So far, research on knowledge and competitive advantage has shared a particular set of assumptions about knowledge which can be grouped under the heading of 'cognitivism' (von Krogh and Roos, 1995). The cognitivist assumptions (March and Simon, 1958; Cyert and March, 1963) fit well with the context of current competitive advantages, but need to be rethought in the case of developing future competitive advantages. The reason is simple. Most strategic management research based on cognitivism views knowledge development as robust information processing in the firm about an externally pre-given reality, like an industry (Simon, 1989; 1993). It will be argued, however, that the development of knowledge cannot be adapted to an externally pre-given reality, since this really has yet to be created. Thus, the issue of creating future competitive advantages necessitates a new set of assumptions about knowledge, which we will term 'creational knowledge', seminally developed by Nonaka (1991; 1994). Under these assumptions, when knowledge is creational, knowledge development, contrary to what is assumed in most strategic management literature, is a highly fragile and subtle process fraught with complexity and uncertainty (Nonaka and Takeuchi, 1995). Strategic management becomes a process of enabling such knowledge development under a number of obstacles, and the key challenge for strategic management research becomes to identify these so-called 'knowledge enablers' which are key to this study.

The goal of this chapter is to develop a richer understanding of the problem of creating, capturing and capitalizing on knowledge-based competence in firms. Despite growing interests in the management of knowledge in firms, we still do not know the micro-level process of how knowledge is enabled in firms. Therefore this chapter, while providing insights on the subject, is overall still exploratory and at the stage of theory building rather than theory testing. We propose to study this topic – enabling the management of knowledge in firms – by pursuing the discovery of theory, i.e. grounded theory (Glaser and Strauss, 1967), intending to provide theoretical and management implications for knowledge management in firms from our case study on MYCOM.[1] The primary result of this approach is a conceptual model which highlights key knowledge enablers and shows how they will contribute to the management of knowledge-based competence in firms.

MYCOM as Sample

MYCOM, since its inception in 1924, has devoted itself to the accumulation of various know-how (including elementary, application and production technologies) and the development of new products, focusing on customer needs in the food and thermal technology industries as its most important goal. MYCOM was initially a company that developed and manufactured freezers for industrial use. Throughout its 70-year history, however, it has greatly broadened the domain of its technologies, products and services. In addition, the company has changed its organizational structure while making constant efforts to pursue innovations and respond fully to customer needs. It has also changed its management style so that the main focus is on decision-making systems, and its business domain effectively forecasts upcoming changes in the business environment. In other words, MYCOM is a corporate organization which has always been transforming itself before or after environmental changes while pursuing innovations.

Innovations entail the enrichment of tacit knowledge such as skills and a certain view of the world. Actually, tacit knowledge is the source of innovation (Nonaka, 1991; 1994). At MYCOM, all employees put great importance on tacit knowledge, and this emphasis on tacit knowledge is MYCOM's core value. Based on this value, MYCOM sees the pursuit of innovation in 'fields' (context, i.e. market where MYCOM can obtain competitive advantage) as its corporate mission. At MYCOM, its organizational structure, management, strategies and business domain are closely related with each other around these two key ideas of 'the pursuit of innovations in fields' and 'emphasis on tacit knowledge'. This study intends to show how the knowledge-based competence of a firm (Nonaka, 1991; 1994) can be developed by analysing the knowledge creation process at MYCOM, and its organizational structure and management system which support this process, especially focusing on knowledge enablers. What we want to emphasize in this chapter is twofold. First, we will reconfirm the knowledge creation views of the organization seminally developed by Nonaka (1991; 1994): namely, that the pursuit of innovations, or the pursuit of higher-quality knowledge, is the essence of the organization's activities and that the structure and management system of the organization are defined and established through such processes.

Second, we will contend that knowledge would not be created, captured and capitalized on in firms without its intentional development by means of knowledge enablers. Knowledge development in organizations should not be left unintentional. Otherwise, knowledge development in organizations will occur at random and will be unsystematic since knowledge is very fragile. To develop knowledge capital as one of its core competences, a firm should have knowledge enablers. Here knowledge enablers are defined as organizational mechanisms for intentionally developing knowledge in organizations. They will facilitate and preserve the development of knowledge in firms.

In this part, we will analyse the organizational structure and management system of MYCOM, focusing on its unique management system based on 'independent corporations'. We will describe the situation of MYCOM as of November 1996, where activities are conceptually characterized as 'the interactions in the world of tacit knowledge' in their own 'fields'.

Second, we will describe the TORIDAS project to illustrate actual knowledge development and management at MYCOM so that we will be able to have better understanding about knowledge and its fragility in firms, thus demonstrating needs for knowledge enablers. TORIDAS is a very innovative automatic chicken deboning machine. We will analyse the actual knowledge creation process at MYCOM by tracing the 14-year history of the TORIDAS project.

Third, we will discuss the theoretical and management implications obtained from the study on MYCOM. In this discussion, the challenge of developing knowledge for future competitive advantages will be highlighted, and a new set of assumptions about knowledge will be outlined. Based on these assumptions, obstacles to knowledge development will be highlighted. Finally, a number of knowledge enablers will be introduced and the description about their roles for knowledge creation will conclude the chapter.

Corporate Profile: Management Based on Independent Corporations

MYCOM has developed and manufactured industrial freezers continuously since its establishment.[2] Today, it is unequalled globally in this field. While MYCOM has continued to strengthen its position in the field of industrial freezers, it has also been responding to the needs of its customers for applying freezing systems and heat transferring technologies to other fields, and as a result has broadened the spectrum of its activities to services and technologies in the fields of energy, food processing and extremely low temperatures. MYCOM now manufactures several hundred types of freezers for industrial use. Well known by the corporate brand name MYCOM, they account for more than 90% of all industrial freezers exported from Japan. The company now has a 50% share of industrial freezers in the world market. Though the industry as a whole has suffered from the economic slump, MYCOM has continued to make a fair profit. The sales of the entire MYCOM group in 1994 were $1.1 billion (16.3% growth rate from the previous year), and its profit in 1994 was $54 million (58.5% growth rate from the previous year).

MYCOM is famous for its unique management system based on 'independent corporations'. These independent corporations, established and classified by product and market type, are small corporations which operate on a self-supporting accounting system. The group now has 80 such corporations in Japan and 23 in other countries. While the entire group has approximately 2500 employees, the average number of employees for each independent corporation is about 25. These corporations might be viewed as branch offices or subsidiaries, but not so at MYCOM. MYCOM employees share an idea that each independent corporation is a main constituent of the MYCOM group, and the MYCOM group exists only as a collective entity, comprising around 100 independent corporations. Each independent corporation is equivalent to a branch office or subsidiary at any other company; it has complete responsibility for its management with the ultimate goal of responding to the local needs of each region. The functional domains of each independent corporation (such as design, manufacturing, sales, marketing, service, general affairs, accounting and so on) are covered by a limited number of employees and each member is responsible for two or three functions. They are generalists as well as specialists in responding to local needs. In this way, a 'holonic' corporate culture has been fostered in the entire MYCOM group, in which all employees working for independent corporations are active 'entrepreneurs', but at the same time are mutually dependent on each other.

MYCOM's headquarters has only about 70 employees whose functions are limited to a minimum, such as tasks to provide its independent corporations with necessary information, financial and technical support.

Each independent corporation has complete control of its management and the headquarters never interferes with its tasks. The underlying feature of this management system based on independent corporations is thorough empowerment. This is why a large headquarters is not necessary for the group. The headquarters of MYCOM, located in the south-eastern part (Koto-ku) of Tokyo, is in a renovated condominium which also houses the offices of the group's various independent corporations. The impression is that the headquarters is just another tenant and these independent corporations are the owners of the building. At the entrance hall of the building, you see the nameplates of the 'tenant' independent corporations and headquarters' departments on a wall. Here, visitors are supposed to call up the persons they are to see. This building is very impressive as a symbol of the unique organizational structure of the MYCOM group, where the headquarters is subordinate to the independent corporations.

MYCOM's independent corporations are classified into two groups: (1) local independent corporations serving customers of each region; and (2) metropolitan independent corporations located in the Tokyo metropolitan area which devote themselves to particular categories of business. While local independent corporations respond to the needs of each region, metropolitan independent corporations develop technologies and products for their own markets of particular business categories. As of October 1995, there were 20 metropolitan independent corporations (6 for the food industry, 7 for industrial freezers and 7 for energy-related services) and 58 local independent corporations throughout Japan.

MYCOM has implemented this management system in order to allow each branch office to fully respond to the needs of each regional market without any interference from the headquarters.[3] The company thought that each branch office had to act as an independent corporation in order to accurately identify and fully respond to customer needs in its local activities. Each independent corporation is an autonomous organization. At the same time, however, it is also closely connected to the group's other independent corporations. Shun Murakami, director of MYCOM Food Process Engineering, one of MYCOM's independent corporations, says as follows:

> When you become a director of an independent corporation and devote yourself to responding to the needs of a particular region, you realize the limitations of your independent corporation. Then, you start thinking which other corporation(s) could complement your capabilities. In other words, you try to cooperate with other corporations in order to achieve your objectives.[4]

In many cases, such an independent corporation has its own market which is appropriate for its size and works only within it. However, this is not the way MYCOM's independent corporation actually operates. Since a local independent corporation has a limited number of employees, sometimes it cannot fully respond to the needs of its customers by itself. A typical case is when it has to develop a new product to solve customers' problems. Then, the local independent corporation decides which other corporations could help it satisfy its customers' needs and actively asks for the support of those corporations. Through the history of this unique management system, the members of each corporation 'instinctively' (to quote Murakami) know that they cannot fully respond to the needs of their customers without concentrating all the efforts of the entire MYCOM group. Now that the business environment surrounding MYCOM is highly complicated owing to political and economic factors, it is vital for the group to concentrate the knowledge of various independent corporations in order to solve complex problems. Consequently, the number of joint projects by different independent corporations has recently greatly increased at MYCOM. Murakami comments on this point by referring to his own experience with a meat supplier in Kyushu (southern part of Japan):

When you are doing business in Kyushu, you have a difficult time having access to certain information such as the future prospects of the Japanese meat industry and the latest technological development. However, when you are talking with your customer, you can picture the faces of various people at MYCOM in your mind, including one who devotes him or herself to the automation of meat processing work, one who is very familiar with various governmental agencies and one who is well versed in the practical aspects of meat processing plants. Then, you start responding to the needs of the customer by joining hands with them.[5]

The independent corporations of MYCOM aim at identifying and accurately and quickly responding to the needs of their customers by complementing each other. It is very common for them to exchange their managerial resources, particularly human resources, with each other. In this sense, MYCOM's independent corporations are closely related to and very flexible with each other while enjoying full autonomy. For example, there is only one employee working at the Tokyo head office of MYCOM Meat Planning, one of MYCOM's metropolitan independent corporations. The rest of its employees (approximately 15 people) work at other local independent corporations scattered throughout Japan. They are doing business by keeping in close contact with local meat suppliers in cooperation with the staff members of these local independent corporations. With these local independent corporations which are 'separated and united' at the same time, knowledge built up at each corporation can be easily shared with other corporations and then become the knowledge of the entire MYCOM group.

MYCOM's Corporate Mission and Values

Innovation in Fields as Corporate Mission

An interesting question about MYCOM is what truly underlies the activities of MYCOM's independent corporations which are 'separated and united' at the same time. It is MYCOM's mission to aim at creating new markets by developing new products and systems responding to customer needs, and MYCOM's value to emphasize the importance of tacit knowledge for innovation.

MYCOM's corporate mission is defined as innovation in fields. This mission has been repeatedly conveyed to all employees of the group, through slogans like 'the realization of society with no competition' or 'doing business within one's own territory' by company chairman Masao Maekawa, and more recently as a message encouraging employees to develop their own 'fields' (i.e. contexts) for the growth of MYCOM.[6] Through these messages from the top management, all employees share the company's mission and decide the direction of their organizational activities.

> Suppose sales of our freezers are slowed due to fierce price competition in the market. If we are involved in that price competition, we will be gradually losing our unique value added since tight competition means that our competitors are also able to respond to our customer needs. Then we will try to create a new market by developing a new product which responds to customer needs and which no other competitor can produce.[7]

Each independent corporation and the leader thereof are highly regarded when the corporation changes in an innovative way by pursuing its own unique 'field', i.e. market where MYCOM can enjoy competitive advantage in compliance with MYCOM's mission. In other words, each independent corporation is evaluated by the level of innovations it has made. Moreover, such an evaluation is made not by the headquarters but by the other independent corporations which are familiar with the business of independent corporations being evaluated. MYCOM believes that the changes of each independent corporation can be sensed and evaluated most accurately by the corporations around it. Murakami says, 'When you become the leader of an independent corporation, you feel extremely defenceless, being watched and examined by the independent corporations around you'. Each independent organization is constantly observed and evaluated by the other corporations as to whether it is effectively innovating itself by forecasting upcoming changes in the business environment. The relationship among different independent corporations is, however, mutually respective rather than antagonistic. Each independent corporation is ready to help other independent corporations to accomplish the mission of MYCOM. As explained below, each independent corporation is evaluated by how much it is cooperative in the activities of other independent corporations in this regard. Thus MYCOM's management system, which is inseparable from its mission, facilitates the field-based activities of its independent corporations.

As suggested above, the term 'field' here refers to areas where MYCOM can achieve competitive advantage and growth (Maekawa, 1994). More precisely, it means a certain business domain or market where each independent corporation of MYCOM can provide its own unique values. This field also means areas where MYCOM can make innovations. In other words, it is a field where MYCOM can react to customer needs more rapidly than its competitors by developing a new system or product without being involved in price competition. As mentioned before, each independent corporation of MYCOM is requested to constantly change itself in pursuing such a field.

Emphasis on Tacit Knowledge as Corporate Value

Incidentally, there is little verbal information in such a field. Today, many companies complain that they have a difficult time 'finding out customer needs'. It is now commonly understood that explicit, verbal or articulated information is becoming very scarce after the age of mass production. MYCOM is not an exception here. What their customers actually utter is 'a very vague anxiety or image'. They seldom make any specific suggestions like 'We want to do this using this and that', according to MYCOM chairman Maekawa. Words may express only 10% of an image which a customer has in mind. However, when any member of MYCOM grasps this inarticulated 'tacit idea', there is in-depth communication and mutual understanding between the customer and the company which will lead to the development of an innovative product. In this way, MYCOM's mission is closely related to its corporate value, 'emphasis on tacit knowledge'.

Tacit knowledge is embodied in or possessed by people. MYCOM's emphasis on tacit knowledge represents the company's basic philosophy in which tacit knowledge is regarded as the source of innovations. The company acquires 'tacit information' in a field through committed interactions with customers. Maekawa literally calls them 'interactions in the world of tacit knowledge'. On the other hand, Murakami refers to the same point, saying: 'It might sound a bit strange. However, I describe it as slipping into customers' minds.' More specifically, 'We come to see what our customers expect towards the future while we listen, consider various problems and forecast upcoming changes with them'. Through these interactions with their customers, MYCOM employees see into their customers' minds and grasp the vague, inarticulated ideas that lurk inside.

Such interactions in the world of tacit knowledge, however, cannot be accomplished overnight. In order to see into the world of tacit knowledge, a wide spectrum of knowledge is necessary about not only customers' business but also all relevant social, economic and environmental factors they may be facing. If they want to interact with their customers in the world of tacit knowledge, they must first be intellectually mature as individuals themselves. It is vital for them to foster and accumulate truly high-quality knowledge. In this context, MYCOM has trained its personnel with a long-term horizon in mind. However, the company has no specific training programmes as such. Instead, MYCOM focuses on self-learning on the job. At each independent corporation of MYCOM, even young staff members frequently visit the actual job sites of their customers, or their own fields. The company believes that 'young staff members can be enlightened through interactions with customers when they have opportunities to participate in the activities in these fields' (Maekawa, 1995). Their bosses, however, never give them any specific know-how for interacting with customers. They are asked to learn about the fields for themselves through repeated visits there, foster their own views on the world, and become mature enough to interact with customers in the world of tacit knowledge.

Engineers at MYCOM's independent corporations are also strongly requested to develop an 'ability to talk with customers' as an indispensable aspect of their field activities. Thus, engineers who can recognize the technical needs of customers by observing their production lines with them are trusted by customers more than those focusing only on technical specifications.

Systems to Facilitate the Sharing of Value and Information

In order to be 'separate and united' at the same time in compliance with the corporate mission and core value, it is indispensable for MYCOM's independent corporations to share information with each other. Unless all independent corporations grasp what information, skills and specialists exist in which independent corporation, the group cannot have them take appropriate actions. The information sharing at MYCOM is facilitated by three supporting systems: (1) various conferences such as bloc steering committee meetings; (2) positive personnel rotation according to the forecast of what may change in the business environment; and (3) business plans laid out at three different levels within the group.

Conferences and Personnel Rotation which Link Independent Corporations with Each Other

MYCOM's local and metropolitan independent corporations are respectively grouped into several blocs according to the regions and industrial markets they belong to. Each bloc comprises several independent corporations.[8] In each bloc, the presidents of the member corporations get together once a month to have the bloc's steering committee meeting, where information on the needs and activities of their customers are exchanged between the participants, and the trends of and general views on the relevant markets are discussed. At such meetings, the participants establish strategies for the bloc, by which they decide how to deal with the existing markets or cultivate new markets. They then lay out an exchange plan for human and technical resources within the bloc in order to achieve their objectives, and draw up the bloc's business plan for the year. Each of the participating independent corporations lays out specific plans for its activities in compliance with the business plan set at this meeting. In this way, different independent corporations which are 'separated and united' at the same time share the same information and thus strengthen the foundation for the cooperative relationship between them.

In addition to these bloc steering committee meetings, there are business conferences to facilitate information exchange and cooperative relationships between the independent corporations, development conferences and technical conferences. At business conferences, problems and solutions in connection with the establishment of certain independent corporations are discussed. Development conferences, held to develop new products and systems, start from the planning stages of development projects and continue to be held until the commercialization of the products. At technical conferences, each participant makes its own technologies open to the others, information on relevant problems is exchanged, and the results of research on new technologies are presented. In addition to technical conferences, technology-related information is conveyed to each independent corporation in order to further facilitate information sharing within the group. All these conferences are held as the occasion demands with the most appropriate members for their topics.

These meetings and conferences, which are held within the blocs or between different blocs including the headquarters, are effective mechanisms to concentrate the power of the entire MYCOM group in order to respond to the needs identified by each independent corporation. Through these meetings and conferences, information on the relevant markets and internal affairs of the MYCOM group is disseminated to all independent corporations. Furthermore, these meetings are very important opportunities for participants to have face-to-face interactions with the group's other corporations. With such face-to-face interactions, the effectiveness of such cooperative relationships as a mechanism to enhance the capability of each corporation is recognized, and the employees of the company feel that they live under the same roof even if they work at different independent corporations.

Personnel Rotation in Response to Environmental Changes

Information sharing between the independent corporations is also facilitated by personnel rotation between them. Personnel rotation often takes place between different corporations when the size of a certain corporation's business is about to be reduced or enlarged owing to changes in the marketplace. MYCOM's independent corporations constantly adapt themselves in compliance with the management philosophy of chairman Masao Maekawa: 'The corporation can survive only when it changes itself spontaneously, giving itself up to changes in the business environment'.[9] Thus the number of employees at each independent corporation is always changing. Personnel rotation between different corporations is carried out at the discretion of the concerned corporations without any interference by the headquarters, reflecting the full autonomy of each corporation: 'We must put greatest importance on the opinions of independent corporation employees who actually sense and experience changes in the business environment'.[10]

Communication Based on Tacit Knowledge through Business Plans

Information sharing between different corporations is also facilitated through the business plan of each independent corporation laid out once a year. In this business plan, the present situation of the independent corporation, an image of its business in the near future (three years ahead), a direction the corporation should take (a desired situation of its business a year ahead which is envisioned to realize the aforementioned image) and an implementation plan (plans of the corporation's activities for the year) are summarized on a piece of A4 paper. The business plan of each independent corporation is made open to the other corporations in the same bloc, and then thoroughly 'examined and criticized by them' (Yoshio Iwasaki of MYCOM Research Institute). The business plan for each bloc is also laid out by the presidents of the member corporations. Then, the business plans of all blocs are examined and compared with each other at the group level in order to realize consistency among them. In this way, business plans are laid out through discussions at three levels (each corporation, each bloc and the group) at MYCOM.

Since any of these business plans is written on a piece of A4 paper, the quantity of information contained therein is very limited. Here, statistical data are not very important. What MYCOM people consider the most important thing in these plans is, according to Iwasaki, 'communication based on tacit knowledge':

> Our business plans come from our heart. Even if the plan's presentation is clumsy, it is highly evaluated if it contains a certain belief. While I am reading it, such a belief is emerging in my mind. Something envisioned in the domain of their tacit knowledge must be accepted in the domain of our tacit knowledge. Otherwise we would face a complete breakdown in communication.[11]

Murakami explains Iwasaki's expression 'comes from our heart' more specifically as follows:

> We do not put great importance on data as such when laying out our business plan every year. What is most important for us is to keep in close contact with various customers and read into their thoughts and desires. We come to understand what they want to do while talking with them about various things.[12]

In other words, according to Murakami, interactions with customers provide MYCOM employees with prospects for the future. At MYCOM, people do not ask for statistical data to read market trends. What they truly rely on is interactions with customers. It is not very easy, however, to transform such interactions into a business plan. They must develop a certain 'belief' from interactions with customers, and then briefly summarize it on a piece of paper. Furthermore, such a belief must represent the belief of their corporation, not that of a particular individual. In short, all members of the independent corporation must share the same belief when laying out their business plan. They accumulate and share the same experiences with other members while committing themselves to their fields, constantly interact with customers, develop their own beliefs from these experiences, and articulate (externalize) and share them with other members. Then, they articulate these common beliefs about their perceptions of reality, namely their 'mental model' (Senge, 1990) into a brief text. In the process of these spiral interactions between tacit knowledge and explicit knowledge, the beliefs of an individual develop into the beliefs of the independent corporation, on which its business plan is based.

On the other hand, when they see the business plan of any other independent corporation, they try to read beyond the articulated text, or a tacit mental model. Thus, the beliefs of the independent corporation are integrated into the entire MYCOM group through the process of interactions between different corporations (and examination and criticism at the bloc level). MYCOM describes this process as 'approaching the whole by working together' (Maekawa, 1994). The transformation of tacit knowledge into explicit knowledge and the discerning of a tacit idea behind an explicit text is a process that every business plan at MYCOM goes through.

With these various mechanisms to facilitate the sharing of core value and knowledge mentioned thus far, the leaders of MYCOM's independent corporations 'know where a certain technology exists in the group and who is involved with it' (Murakami). Having studied the corporate profile of MYCOM, we will move on to our analysis of MYCOM's TORIDAS project, in order to understand how the group's unique management system can actually make innovations happen. We believe that the analysis of the knowledge creation process during an actual project provides a clearer understanding of MYCOM's management system based on its independent corporations which stimulate and inspire tacit knowledge.

The TORIDAS Project

TORIDAS, an automatic chicken leg deboning machine, has been well received by the food processing industry as an epoch-making product.[13] TORIDAS's deboning performance is considerable: it is able to debone a chicken leg in 4 seconds, that is to process 900 legs an hour. It is four times faster than manual deboning. In addition, TORIDAS has realized a considerable increase in the yield rate of the chicken deboning process, 1.8% to 2.0%, which translates to an additional output of approximately 43 tonnes per year. Because of this high deboning performance and yield rate, the machine has been acclaimed by the food processing industry whose main concerns were the reduction of production and personnel costs. TORIDAS was introduced to the market in May 1994. Nearly 100 units of the machine were sold during the first year. Considering the relatively high market price of 18 million yen per unit, TORIDAS has been remarkably well received by the market. The machine has also been highly rated from the technical viewpoint because it has made possible the complete mechanization of chicken deboning work which used to be done totally by human hand. For this reason, TORIDAS received the Minister of Agriculture, Forestry and Fisheries Award. It has also been acclaimed by overseas markets including those in Europe and America. TORIDAS has offered new prospects for the complete automatization of chicken meat processing plants and opened up the possibilities of fundamentally changing the chicken meat processing system.

The development of TORIDAS, however, was not easy: it took 14 years with an investment of more than one billion yen including labour costs. After repeated trial and error, however, the project members finally completed TORIDAS. In this machine, 'tacit knowledge' of chicken meat processing, obtained through the experiences of the project team members, is embodied in the form of mechanical specifications. In short, MYCOM's project team, through the development of TORIDAS, integrated human-based production technology into mechanical electronics knowledge and created 'new knowledge'. That is why TORIDAS is also an epoch-making product for MYCOM itself and is regarded as 'one of the group's greatest achievements' by MYCOM.

If a machine is defined as a device designed to repeat the same task over and over again, TORIDAS is not a machine. TORIDAS adjusts itself to the size of each chicken to be processed. This is the very feature which realized a deboning productivity four times higher than manual deboning. TORIDAS comprises a rectangular base (1 m × 1.27 m), a power control panel and a 2.24 m high cylindrical deboning device. TORIDAS debones a chicken in the following eight steps:

1 setting a chicken with two or three cuts on its flesh
2 cutting the tendon at the shank

3   cutting the tendon at the lower bone
4   measuring the joints
5   cutting the tendon at the joint of the lower bone
6   cutting the tendon at the joint of the upper bone
7   cutting the tendon at the upper bone
8   deboning.

First, a worker makes two or three cuts on a chicken and sets it on TORIDAS. Since TORIDAS can process chickens weighing 200 to 500 grams, the worker does not have to sort chickens according to size. He or she can set a chicken every 4 seconds using one hand. Once the chicken is set on the machine, TORIDAS follows the above eight steps, moving the chicken in a circular pattern.

TORIDAS was named after the Japanese verb *tori-dasu*, which is equivalent to 'take out' in English. TORIDAS's movement, however, might be described more correctly as 'stripping the meat from the bone'. TORIDAS cuts the chicken's tendons with its round cutters and strips the meat along the bone. In manual deboning, a deboner cuts the chicken's tendons with a knife and strips the meat from the bone. TORIDAS has displaced this manual labour with mechanical movements. Moreover, TORIDAS debones chickens much more efficiently than human deboners. In order to strip the chicken meat from the bone, the tendons on its joints must be cut first. However, deboners sometimes make improper cuts. This results in imperfect deboning that leaves meat on the bone (which causes a decrease in yield rate) or deboned meat with undesirable rips. In contrast, TORIDAS measures the positions of the joints accurately with its sensor and cuts tendons with its two round cutters. As a result, deboning using TORIDAS has made a considerably high yield rate possible without damaging the meat. In addition, deboning with TORIDAS is not only accurate but also quick, as mentioned earlier. It can debone 900 chicken legs an hour, and its performance is four times faster than manual deboning.

Background of the Development Project: the Chicken Processing Industry and MYCOM

MYCOM already had a very close relationship with the chicken processing industry prior to the TORIDAS project since the company had developed various freezers for the industry. As mentioned before, MYCOM employees are requested to identify the needs of their customers through interactions and observation with them, and develop new products according to such needs. The identification of customer needs through interactions with them is extremely important for MYCOM's activities in the food industry, where the company has to provide an original system for each customer's unique production procedure by combining freezers, automatic food production components and so on. MYCOM identified various problems of the chicken processing industry, solved those problems by developing new products and systems, and further strengthened its ties with the industry.

The chicken processing industry had long suffered from high costs due to labour-intensive processing work. At one time, deboning and finishing work for chicken meat was totally dependent on manual labour. At any chicken processing factory, deboners worked next to a long conveyer belt and deboned chickens using knives and chopping boards. Such manual deboning was not at all easy. Some deboners suffered from tenosynovitis because they had to cut the hard tendons of numerous chicken legs. Labour shortages and ageing deboners were also big problems for thousands of chicken processing factories throughout Japan. In addition, the market price of chicken had been decreasing. Faced with those circumstances, the chicken processing industry had long ago asked MYCOM to develop a system to realize the reduction of production costs and the automatization of deboning work. In short, the need for an automatic deboning machine was articulated. New and innovative knowledge was necessitated by these changes in the chicken processing environment.

Development Process of TORIDAS

The idea of developing a deboning machine emerged at MYCOM in 1980, and this idea finally came to fruition as the commercialization of TORIDAS in May 1994. There were two stages in this 14-year development process. The project was suspended for four years after the first model was introduced in 1986. This suspension divided the project into two stages. The project team's approach to the mechanization of deboning work in the second stage was completely different from their approach in the first stage. It was this change that led the project to success. The following sections explain how this change took place by tracing the development processes of the project at each stage.

FIRST STAGE OF THE PROJECT (1980–6)   The idea of developing a deboning machine was raised at MYCOM in 1980 by MYCOM chairman Maekawa. As early as 1977, Maekawa heard that the US Ministry of Commerce was interested in developing a deboning machine, and since then he had been thinking about whether MYCOM could develop a deboning machine or not. However, the project of developing a deboning machine did not start immediately for various reasons.

MYCOM finally initiated the development of an automatic deboning machine in February 1982. The first project team was organized with three core members, Manmoto (project leader), Iwasaki (electrical engineer) and Nagare (project manager). Some affiliated companies supported the project team in the development of mechanical parts. Since the project members had no idea how big the project would be, they decided to ask for outside financial support. They received a 15 million yen subsidy from the Livestock Modernization Technology Association, a public corporation under the control of the Ministry of Agriculture, Forestry and Fisheries. At this stage, however, it was not regarded as a project of the entire MYCOM group. It was a project of MYCOM Manufacturing Mechanization System, one of MYCOM's independent corporations, developing factory automation systems.

Soon after the project started, the three core members of the team discovered that the mechanization of deboning work was much more difficult than expected. The biggest challenge for them was to find an appropriate way to separate chicken meat from the bone. After repeated trial and error, they came to think that meat deboning could be realized by cutting (soft) chicken meat along the (hard) bone. Then, Nagare came up with the idea of using something like a string, such as piano wire, to scrape the meat off the bone. With this method, however, deboned meat looked messy because the cutting performance of piano wire was very poor. Thus, they thought up a method using a long, thin tape-like stainless steel cutter. But when the team members presented this idea to a group of people working at a chicken processing factory, they were told: 'You should not cut the meat off the bone. You must take the meat away from the bone.' At that time, the team members were not able to truly understand what the deboners meant by 'taking the meat away'. Therefore, they were not able to translate manual deboning ('taking the meat away from the bone') into mechanical movements.

In addition to this, the core members had another big problem. Since chicken legs came in various sizes, they could not apply any uniform mechanical movements. Deboners change the cutting position on chickens according to the size of each chicken. The team members thought and thought about how they could realize a machine with such flexible reactions, but did not come up with any good ideas. It was a particularly big challenge for Iwasaki, who had designed and manufactured various machine tools for a long time. For him, a machine meant a constructed device which repeats the same movement for the same task. He could not imagine any machine that could change its movements flexibly for different circumstances. To Iwasaki, such a 'machine' would not be a machine in the first place.

The core members repeatedly made cutting devices and experimented with these devices. Though they had been advised by deboners not to cut the meat, they still stuck to inventing a meat cutting machine. They believed it was the only way to develop a deboning machine, using their knowledge and expertise about mechanical electronics.

Ideas about mechanical electronics always came first, but they did not work at all. We concluded that we would not be able to achieve our goal with conventional methods.[14]

Though they noticed that conventional methods would not work at a relatively early stage of the TORIDAS project, they did not change the basic approach to the project, developing a mechanical electronics-based machine to cut chicken meat off. Besides, they did manage to separate chicken meat from the bone with this method. Furthermore, they were not able to come up with any alternatives. The first prototype was completed in the summer of 1983. They continued to improve the prototype for a higher yield rate, more compact size and reduced costs. In March 1986, the final version of the first prototype was introduced. Since the entire chicken processing industry had been longing for an automatic deboning machine, visitors who came to see the prototype showed an intense interest in it. While realizing automatic deboning, however, this prototype, which was a huge chunk of metal with a complicated mechanical structure, had not reached a level of commercialization at all. The machine clumsily cut chicken meat off the bone 'by force'. The productivity of this totally mechanical electronics-based machine only matched that of human hands. Furthermore, its cutters had to be replaced with new ones every 15 minutes. The production cost of the machine itself was also very high. Looking at the exhibited prototype, Manmoto, the project leader, thought:

> We based this machine on a faulty concept. We would never make it with this concept.[15]

Realizing their limits in developing a deboning machine, the core members decided to virtually discontinue the project in 1986, four years after its start.

SECOND STAGE OF THE PROJECT (1990–4) Even after the project was virtually discontinued, the team members continued to improve the prototype on a very small scale. The chicken processing industry still longed for an automatic deboning machine, their 'dream machine'. Since MYCOM had maintained a close relationship with the industry through its business of freezers, boilers and so on, it was not able to ignore those expectations.

MYCOM restarted the project in earnest in March 1990. Kodama, a young development engineer, told Manmoto, the project leader, that he wanted to get down to the development of a deboning machine. Kodama regularly visited some chicken processing factories for his tasks in developing freezers and other machines. Every time he visited those customers, they told him how eagerly they expected MYCOM to develop a deboning machine. Knowing about the processes of the virtually discontinued project, Kodama wanted to complete it by himself. He looked at the prototype which clumsily cut chicken meat off the bone by force. The machine's movements were completely different from the manual deboning work he had watched at chicken processing factories. He concluded that the development concept had been funda-mentally wrong and decided to experience deboning work for himself. He asked one chicken processing company to let him work at its factory. The idea was to master deboning skills, under the guidance of the factory's deboners, using his own hands and eyes. Through this 'training and practice' at the factory, he learned the knack of stripping chicken meat off the bone after cutting the tendons. The point was that deboners cut only tendons. The process that followed was best described not as 'cutting the meat off the bone' but as 'stripping the meat from the bone'.

Then, Kodama demonstrated manual deboning for Manmoto, saying: 'the chicken meat can be taken from the bone without cutting it off'. Manmoto, who was aware of the faulty concept and the limits of knowledge about mechanical electronics, saw Kodama's demonstration and thought 'he really had something!' He believed that it could be a highly viable alternative which he had not been able to find. Manmoto decided to officially restart the project. This conceptual change from 'cutting off' to 'stripping off' was a real breakthrough for the TORIDAS project which eventually led the project members to success.

Being convinced of success, Manmoto decided to upgrade the project as one to be tackled by the entire MYCOM group. At MYCOM, in order to start any group-level project, in which different independent cor-porations are involved, approval from the council members of MYCOM Technology Research Institute must be obtained. The council members recognized that there existed significant market needs for deboning machines and that MYCOM could only meet those needs if the entire group were involved in the development project. Thus, the deboning machine project was officially approved and upgraded to a group-level project. In response to this, a second project team was formed. Five core members were selected, which included two original members (Manmoto and Iwasaki), two young mechanical engineers (Kodama and Hayawaka) and an assembling expert (Hanaoka). In addition to these core members, independent food engineering corporations in Kagoshima, Miyazaki, Hachinohe and Sapporo, the four centres of Japan's broiler chicken processing industry, and another independent corporation in Osaka, joined the project. Thus, a project team of approximately 20 people was formed. Specific tasks in the development procedure were carried out mainly by the five core members. However, project general meetings were held occasionally, in which the progress and direction of the project were reported to and discussed by the participants.

At the beginning of the project's second stage, the project members, based on Kodama's experience, framed a hypothesis that deboning work could be mechanized by analysing the work of human hands and translating it into mechanical movements. First, deboning work by human hands would have to be fully grasped as prerequisite knowl-edge. Second, the work would be analysed into several very simple actions. Then, these actions would be translated into mechanical actions. If these mechanical actions could be combined in a single machine, the project members thought, they could realize their project of mechanizing deboning work. Unlike the first stage of the project which was totally based on mechanical electronics, the second stage focused on integrating human work skills into mechanical electronics. The project members started learning about chicken legs and experiencing deboning work for themselves. As prerequisite knowledge for understanding mechanized deboning work, they tried to understand deboning by human hands. Therefore, all the members of the project team including the five core members started learning deboning work from scratch alongside professional deboners at chicken processing factories in the Tohoku (northern part of Japan) and Kyushu (southern part of Japan) regions. The project members observed actual deboning work at those factories and tried to master deboning skills under the guidance of professional deboners. Most members were able to get the knack of deboning in three or four days.

After grasping the knack of deboning, the team members started breaking down manual deboning work into several phases. Through this procedure, deboning skills acquired by and embodied in the team members were articulated and transformed into explicit knowledge. They continued to translate production skills they experienced first hand into mechanical electronics technologies. They finally grasped the concept that deboning by human hands entailed stripping chicken meat from the bone, and deboners cut only the tendons of chicken legs. In the end, deboning work was broken down into the eight phases. They tried to make a system by combining different machine tools representing the eight phases of deboning work. The prototype was completed in 1992. Since it was a totally new invention from scratch, it took the project team a rather long period to complete the product. The product was completed and released to the market in May 1994.

Summary of TORIDAS Project

This section summarizes the two most noteworthy insights obtained through our study on the TORIDAS project: (1) interaction in the world of tacit knowledge, the critical factors which distinguished the dead-locked first stage and the successful second stage; and (2) MYCOM's management system observed in the TORIDAS project.

Interactions in the World of Tacit Knowledge through Dialogue with Customers

The TORIDAS project reveals that knowledge creation is not an easy task even for a firm which defines innovation as its corporate mission. At

MYCOM, interactions with customers are considered to be highly significant in identifying their needs. Even during the first stage of the TORIDAS project, there were certain interactions between the project team members and customers. Furthermore, people working at chicken processing factories provided the team with a very important piece of advice: 'You should not cut chicken meat off the bone'. However, the team did not follow the advice. According to Masao Maekawa, the chairman of MYCOM, the team members (i.e. engineers) and customers did not interact with each other 'in the world of tacit knowledge' at that time. Dialogue is defined as the interaction between two parties through explicit words. In order to create new knowledge (technology or system), the engineers should have taken one step beyond ordinary dialogue and shared a tacit, comprehensive thinking pattern with customers. Without the sharing of the same (tacit) mental models, dialogue between the engineers and customers in the first stage of the TORIDAS project stayed superficial in the world of explicit knowledge. Such dialogue did not stimulate innovation.

In other words, during the first stage of the TORIDAS project, interactions between MYCOM's engineers and people working at chicken processing factories were not on the level of mental model sharing. Production technology (human work skills) represented by the phrase 'strip chicken meat off', and mechanical electronics technology represented by the phrase 'cut chicken meat off', did not interact with each other. MYCOM's engineers were not able to grasp the world of deboners' tacit knowledge which lay behind their words 'strip chicken meat off the bone' and translate it into the language of the world of mechanical electronics. In other words, they failed not only in grasping tacit knowledge from explicit knowledge but also in externalizing tacit knowledge in the form of explicit knowledge. It was the biggest reason why they ended with a prototype still far from practical use in the first stage of the TORIDAS project.

Manmoto commented on this interaction in the world of tacit knowledge as follows:

> People often try to deal with current problems by referring to organized data of the past. However, it means that you try to look at the present situation through the colour of the past. The signs from the tacit world are very inconspicuous. If you try to find them through the colour of the past, they would become almost invisible. You have to be completely free from any prejudice or preconception when dealing with tacit knowledge. . . . Logic sometimes blinds you.[16]

To borrow Manmoto's expression, the first stage of the TORIDAS project ended in failure because the engineers looked at deboning work through the colour of mechanical electronics and missed the inconspicuous signs from the world of tacit knowledge represented by the deboners' advice of 'stripping chicken meat from the bone'. The logic of mechanical electronics blinded the engineers.

The TORIDAS project achieved its breakthrough in the second stage when a member of the project team mastered deboning skills through training and practice at a chicken processing factory. The reason for the breakthrough is symbolized in the product name TORIDAS (as mentioned, after a Japanese verb *tori-dasu* equivalent to 'take out' in English). In short, the second stage was successful because the project team engineers experienced production technology for taking out chicken meat at first hand and embodied it in their design. The engineers could not grasp the concept of 'taking chicken meat away from the bone' until they experienced it at first hand. They grasped what the deboners had wanted to say through experiencing, observing and copying deboning work. The first practical deboning machine was created when the engineers experienced a production technology for deboning which was totally new knowledge to them, and integrated it into mechanical electronics technologies.

In fact, the engineers devoted themselves to their deboning training and practice. Since they developed their deboning skills so seriously, they were told: 'Why don't you leave MYCOM and join our factory?' It was as if they had served their apprenticeship under professional deboners. Without such all-out commitment, any truly deep experiences could not be obtained. When such commitment is shown to others, trustful relationships will emerge among people. This trust improves the quality of dialogue and discussion as a basis for organizational activities, and thus facilitates the sharing of tacit knowledge.[17]

It is difficult to talk about tacit knowledge because tacit knowledge is personal and thus cannot be obtained away from its source.[18] Therefore, in order to grasp certain tacit knowledge, interactions between individuals are prerequisite. What underlies such interactions is independent, all-out commitment to the subject of concern. Such commitment nurtures mutual trust which facilitates constant, high-quality dialogue and discussions. In the second stage of the TORIDAS project, dialogue between the engineers and customers reached the level of 'interactions in the world of tacit knowledge' because there existed commitment and trust between the two parties based on shared experiences.

Management Based on Independent Corporations and Innovations

Some aspects of reality, which were overlooked or ignored by modern science, have recently been seriously discussed in the context of criticism of modern science based on its three principles: universality, logic and objectivity. The main idea of such criticism is that modern science, depending solely on its three principles, has overlooked the ambiguous nature of reality, and the inseparability of subjectivity and objectivity (the subject and the object) (Nakamura, 1992). Thus it has now become incapable of recognizing some aspects of reality based on physical experiences (Polanyi, 1966), or the reality of our daily life prescribed by interactions with others. When understanding the TORIDAS project from this point of view, the first stage of the project ended in failure because the engineers believed that the knowledge of mechanical electronics based on modern science was universal, logical and objective. Therefore, when they distanced themselves from the knowledge of mechanical electronics and went deeper into the reality based on physical experiences in the second stage, they discovered the key to success.

When we look at the TORIDAS project from the viewpoint of innovations, the project suggests that new knowledge for a new product is created when a development team enters the field where such a new product will be used (interaction with the field) and shares the same experiences with the people who will use it. Knowledge is unique to each field, or to the context in which it is created. In other words, innovations can be made when those who develop a new product share the same experiences as those who will use the product.[19] In order to make such innovations happen, the entire organization must recognize the significance of entering customers' fields (Brown and Duguid, 1991). There must also be a certain organizational system to encourage employees to do so. At MYCOM, the importance of 'tacit knowledge' and the significance of pursuing 'fields' have been repeatedly emphasized by the top management and disseminated to all members of the organization. In addition, MYCOM's independent corporations function as mechanisms for developing new products with customers. The strength of MYCOM's management system based on independent corporations lies in a greater number of such 'fields' which cannot be pursued at ordinary corporations.

Discussion of Theoretical and Management Implications

In the following, we will discuss the necessity of knowledge enablers for developing knowledge-based competence in firms. Our study on MYCOM reveals that knowledge is very fragile and the management and development of knowledge in firms is not an easy task even for a company which values innovation. In this regard, it is noteworthy that MYCOM has begun to emphasize tacit knowledge as its core value much more strongly since the failure and subsequent success of TORIDAS.[20] In other words, MYCOM has learned that organizational knowledge creation was fragile. Here our study on MYCOM suggests the necessity of knowledge enablers for organizational knowledge creation.

From this finding, we will argue that knowledge enablers are indispensable for organizational knowledge development. In order to demonstrate this argument, in the following, we will first explain the necessity for knowledge enablers, referring to the fragility of knowledge development in organizations. Then we will present the definition of knowledge enablers and introduce the knowledge enablers found from the study on MYCOM.

Fragility of Knowledge Development in Organizations

As stated in the introduction to this chapter, under the cognitivist assumption of knowledge, knowledge development, or more precisely knowledge acquisition, was not problematic. The reality is the reference point for representations, and if information processing works in the organization, those representations will be automatically secured.

On the other hand, according to the creationist assumptions (Nonaka, 1991; 1994), there are a number of factors making knowledge development for future competitive advantage a highly fragile process. The factors making knowledge management fragile can be conceived with regard to the following five aspects: (1) mindset of firm members; (2) communication in the firm; (3) the firm's structure; (4) relationship among firm members; and (5) human resource management.

First, with regard to the mindset of firm members, if the importance of knowledge as a crucial competence of a firm is not shared among firm members, the knowledge-based competence of the firm will not be developed since it is a social (collective) entity. The lack of a mindset supportive to knowledge management would impede the development of knowledge-based competence by firm members.

Second, with regard to communication in firms, if new knowledge is created by an individual organizational member, there might be no legitimate language in which this knowledge can be expressed (von Krogh and Roos, 1995). Even if there are forms of expression to be found for explaining the experience, other, more powerful, language practices will soon kill off the attempt of the individual to contribute (von Krogh et al., 1994).

Third, with regard to the firm's structure, it could impede the individual or collective knowledge development. Those structures in which organizational members look inward and which do not facilitate innovation in 'contexts' will have a negative impact on the knowledge development of a firm.

Fourth, with regard to the relationship among firm members, knowledge development is fraught with emotions, misunderstandings, misconceptions, rule-based entrapping etc. Therefore, if individual members of a firm are not eager to share their experiences with their colleagues on the basis of mutual trust and respect, individual knowledge development will not lead to the generation of social, collective knowledge.

Finally, with regard to the development of human resource management, if those who are willing to develop their experiences share those experiences with their colleagues, thus contributing to the development of the knowledge-based competence of a firm, are not highly evaluated and acknowledged by top management, they will be demotivated and discouraged. As a result, knowledge development by a firm will not be accelerated.

To sum up, given these five kinds of impediments, knowledge development and management in firms are highly fragile. Therefore, the need to identify enabling conditions for knowledge-based competence in firms is immanent.

Knowledge Enablers

Given the fragility of knowledge in organizations, knowledge development in organizations should not be left unconsidered and should not be ignored. Otherwise, knowledge development in organizations will occur at random and will be unsystematic. To avoid this situation, organizations should have knowledge enablers so that organizational knowledge is consistently and systematically developed. Here knowledge enablers are defined as organizational mechanisms for intentionally and consistently developing knowledge in organizations. Knowledge enablers have three significant roles. First, knowledge enablers should stimulate individual knowledge development. Individual organizational members should develop their range of activities so that they will have a variety of experiences, which will be sources for individual knowledge development. Second, knowledge enablers should protect knowledge development in organizations, tackling obstacles to it existing in organizations. Since knowledge is very fragile, it would not be nurtured in organizations without intentional facilitation and protection. Knowledge enablers are expected to play this facilitation and protection role. Third, knowledge enablers should facilitate the sharing of individual knowledge and experience among organizational members so that individual knowledge will be transformed into organizational knowledge. In the following, each knowledge enabler will be introduced and its function will be explained.

From the study on MYCOM, we developed five knowledge enablers (Table 7.1). They are: (1) creating a knowledge intent; (2) developing organizational conversations; (3) developing organizational structure and context facilitating knowledge development; (4) managing care relationships; and (5) developing knowledge managers. In the following, as the conclusion of this chapter, these five knowledge enablers will be explained.

Creating a Knowledge Intent

The importance of knowledge as the precious competitive advantage of a firm should be established if it wants to develop knowledge in organizations. This will be a crucial precondition for the knowledge develop-

Table 7.1 *Potential impediments to knowledge development and knowledge enablers*

Potential impediments to knowledge development	Knowledge enablers
Mindset	Creating a knowledge intent
Communication	Developing organizational conversation
Structure	Open to context for knowledge creation
Relationship	Managing care relationships
Human resource management	Developing knowledge managers

ment by a firm. Knowledge is defined as 'justified truth' (Nonaka, 1994). Organizational members individually as well as collectively should have a variety of experiences. These individual or collective experiences should be shared by other organizational members, who collectively interpret these experiences, reason the truth behind these experiences, justify this truth, referring to corporate values as justification criteria for organizational activities, and thus finally develop organizational knowledge. This process of developing organizational knowledge out of individual or collective experiences would be impossible if the importance of knowledge as one of the key competitive advantages of a firm is not well established in the firm and shared by its members.

At MYCOM, the importance of tacit knowledge is shared by all the members as MYCOM's core value. In addition, MYCOM's mission encourages MYCOM employees to pursue innovation by focusing on tacit knowledge in fields. By means of various mechanisms such as meetings and the statements of the president, the value and the mission are informed to MYCOM employees. MYCOM's strategy, management systems such as evaluation, and organizational structure are formulated so that its core value and mission will be actually carried out by its employees. In this way, knowledge intent as one of the knowledge enablers is firmly established in MYCOM.

Developing Organizational Conversations

As stated above, if new knowledge is created by an individual organizational member, there might be no legitimate language in which this knowledge can be expressed. Even if there are forms of expression to be found for explaining the experience, other language practices, more powerful, will soon stifle the attempt of the individual to contribute. Therefore, firms should focus on the role of language played in knowledge creation, and find the way to facilitate languaging (von Krogh and Roos, 1995; 1996) in firms and to use language which will be commonly shared and understood by organizational members.

At MYCOM, meetings are held very frequently and MYCOM employees are encouraged to have face-to-face conversation. In this kind of conversation, however, it is critically important to understand what idea, belief and feeling exist behind expressed words so that mutual understanding will be accomplished among people conducting conversation. For that purpose, at MYCOM, members are told to summarize an annual business plan on an A4 sheet of paper. People reading this business plan try to read what content exists behind the written words on a single A4 sheet. By continuing this practice, a foundation is built on which MYCOM employees will develop common understanding about language spoken by their colleagues. MYCOM has the system to encourage conversation among organizational members and to intentionally generate the foundation for understanding language spoken in this conversation.

Developing Organizational Structure Facilitating Knowledge Development

Firms should be being aware of, close to and actively penetrating into the 'context for knowledge creation' if they intend to pursue organizational knowledge creation as their competitive advantage. Here, 'context for knowledge creation' is defined as the market or domain where a firm can enjoy competitive advantage by offering unique values, i.e. socially created knowledge (Berger and Luckman, 1966), to their customers. It is where firms can accomplish innovation by means of creating, capturing and capitalizing on their knowledge asset. Firms' structures should be organized so that they are close to the context for knowledge creation and are able to act for knowledge creation.

There should be consistency between firms' structure and firms' knowledge intent. For that purpose, firms should know where they can accomplish a unique contribution to customers, actually penetrate into this context, be close to their customers and work with them so that knowledge will be created, captured or capitalized on (co-innovation with customers). At MYCOM, the pursuit of innovation in fields is defined as MYCOM's corporate mission. Its unique organizational structure, comprising many independent corporations, was developed to carry this mission in practice.

On the other hand, there is a large amount of empirical evidence from the group psychology literature supporting the general conclusion that integrating a variety of information and its interpretations is beneficial for groups engaged in complex problem solving (Tushman, 1977; Robertson and Wind, 1983). Therefore, firms should have such mechanisms by which a variety of information and interpretation will be facilitated among their members. In order to develop organizational knowledge in a turbulent environment, firms should have a variety of information sources, a variety of interpretation of this information, and a variety of perspectives developed from a variety of interpretation. Given this variety, the range of organizational activities will be enlarged and this wide range of activities will increase the possibility of developing organizational knowledge. Once it is shared among organizational members, a variety of information and interpretation will stimulate creativity among them, thus facilitating organizational knowledge development.

In order to make full use of variety and its integration, members of firms should be separated so that different information sources will be obtained. At the same time, however, they should be quick and eager to concentrate as soon as the integration of this variety is required for business activities, e.g. developing a new product. Although separate, the independent corporations of MYCOM are quick and eager to concentrate. MYCOM's independent corporations are characterized as 'separated but united'. This organizational structure enables MYCOM to enjoy the advantages of variety and its integration.

Managing Care Relationships

Tacit knowledge as a crucial source for innovation exists in individuals, groups or organizations in the form of individual experiences, images, skills, organizational culture, organizational climate and so on. Therefore, in order to grasp certain tacit knowledge, interactions between individuals are prerequisite. What underlies such interactions is independent, all-out commitment to the subject of concern. Such commitment nurtures mutual trust which facilitates constant, quality dialogue and discussions.

As we argue, knowledge development, especially social knowledge development, of the organization cannot be taken for granted, and relationships in the organization must be given more attention. Knowledge development is fraught with emotions, misunderstandings, misconceptions, rule-based entrapping etc. Mutually respective relationships must exist among members of firms since organizational knowledge creation is a social process. Patience, tolerance and emotional forbearance will be key features of this relationship. Care has the attributes of patience, tolerance, emotional forbearance and so forth. From the study on MYCOM, we see care as one particular quality of organizational relationships since the presence or absence of care will affect the development of individual and social knowledge.

Care characterizes a process of interaction between receiver and provider in firms, and should be understood as a quality of a relationship rather than in terms of roles and functions. When this relationship based on care is realized among organizational members, trust will emerge among people. This trust improves the quality of dialogue and discussion as a basis for organizational activities, and thus facilitates the sharing of tacit knowledge.

At MYCOM, in the second stage of the TORIDAS project, dialogue between the engineers and customers reached the level of 'interactions in the world of tacit knowledge' because there existed commitment and trust between the two parties based on shared experiences. This inter-action and the trustful relationship thus developed were crucial for the success of TORIDAS.

Developing Knowledge Managers

Those managers who value knowledge and its management (i.e. creation, capturing and capitalizing on knowledge capital) must be intentionally developed. How they are developed should be consistent with knowl-edge development and management. For example, an incentive system should be planned so as to evaluate those managers who actively pene-trate into the context for knowledge creation, collect various information, interpret it, share this information and interpretation with their col-leagues, establish a care relationship, and thus contribute to developing knowledge-based competence in the firm.

In order to enrich their experiences, which are the sources of indi-vidual knowledge creation by managers, job rotation can be used so that they may be faced with various information, various contexts and various employees whose expertise is diverse. These so-called 'knowl-edge managers' are expected to execute leadership with autonomy. If firms have plenty of these knowledge managers, they will be scattered in various parts of firms and will be ready to show leadership in devel-oping knowledge-based competence in firms. This redundancy of potential command will enable firms to be very agile in a turbulent environment. At MYCOM, the development of knowledge managers is conducted 'on the job'. However, we should not forget the fact that they are trained by various mechanisms, such as the value and mission statement by the MYCOM chairman, and active interaction with their colleagues in frequent meetings.

Notes

1 MYCOM is a corporate brand for Maekawa Seisakujo (Maekawa Manu-facturing Company).

2 This corporate profile was compiled from the following interviews and materials: interview with Masao Maekawa (President of Maekawa Seisakujo) conducted on 8 November 1994 (this interview appeared in *Business Review*, 42 (3): 71–9 as 'Management Inspiring Nonverbal Knowledge in the Market'); interview with Yoshio Iwasaki (Director of Maekawa Sogo Research Institute) conducted on 16 March 1995; interview with Shun Murakami (Director of Maekawa Food Process Engineering) conducted on 16 March 1995; *Maekawa Seisakujo Group* (company brochure); Imai and Kaneko (1989).

3 Maekawa Seisakujo began reorganizing its local branches/office as inde-pendent corporations in 1970. Before the current system based on independent corporations was introduced, Maekawa Seisakujo experienced a period of craftsmen (from the establishment to the end of the Second World War), a period

of area-based management (from the end of the Second World War to the early 1950s), a period of functional divisions (from the late 1950s) and a period of group-based management (from the early 1970s).

4 Interview with Shun Murakami (Director of Maekawa Food Process Engineering) conducted on 16 March 1995.

5 Ibid.

6 For example, Maekawa Seisakujo has held a regular forum called the Forum for Fields and Organizations in which participants exchange opinions about fields to pursue innovation. Knowledge creation in such fields will be explained later.

7 Interview with Shun Murakami conducted on 16 March 1995.

8 There are eight local blocs, one staff bloc and one service industry bloc at Maekawa Seisakujo as of November 1995.

9 Nikkei Business, 3 October 1994, p. 69.

10 Ibid.

11 Interview with Yoshio Iwasaki conducted on 16 March 1995.

12 Interview with Shun Murakami conducted on 16 March 1995.

13 This section on the TORIDAS project is written based on: interview with Shun Murakami conducted on 16 March 1995; interview with Shinzo Manmoto (the leader of the TORIDAS project) conducted on 8 August 1995.

14 Interview with Shinzo Manmoto conducted on 8 August 1995.

15 Ibid.

16 Ibid.

17 It seems that the significance of trust and commitment has recently been re-evaluated as internal cross-functional projects and strategic cooperation with outsiders, such as virtual corporation and modular corporation, have been promoted. Refer to Goldman et al. (1995: 312).

18 With respect to the nature of tacit knowledge, refer to Polanyi (1966).

19 This is related to the idea of local innovation (uncovering hints for new products through observing customer behaviour) proposed by J.S. Brown (1990).

20 Interview with Masao Maekawa on 18 September 1996.

References

Barney, J.B. (1991) Firm resources and sustained competitive advantage. *Journal of Management*, 17: 99–120.

Berger, P.L. and Luckman, T. (1966) *The Social Construction of Reality: a Treatise in the Sociology of Knowledge*. New York: Doubleday.

Brown, J.S. (1990) Research that reinvents corporation. *Harvard Business Review*, November–December: 35–41.

Brown, J.S. and Duguid, P. (1991) Organizational learning and communities-of-practice: toward a unified view of working, learning and innovation. *Organization Science*, 2: 40–57.

Cyert, R.M. and March, J.G. (1963) *A Behavioral Theory of the Firm*. Englewood Cliffs, NJ: Prentice-Hall.

D'Aveni, R.A. (1995) *Hyper-Competitive Rivalries: Competing in Highly Dynamic Environments*. New York: Free Press.

Glaser, B. and Strauss, A. (1967) *The Discovery of Grounded Theory: Strategies for Qualitative Research*. Illinois: Aldine.

Goldman, S.L., Nagel, R.N. and Press, K. (1995) *Agile Competitors and Virtual Organizations: Strategies for Enriching the Customer*. New York: Van Nostrand Reinhold.

Hamel, G. and Prahalad, C.K. (1994) *Competing for the Future*. Cambridge, MA: Harvard Business School Press.

Imai, K. and Kaneko, I. (1989) Holonic competing with many independent corporations: Maekawa Seisakujo, in *Organizations in Japan: Strategies and Organizational Forms*, Vol. 14. Tokyo: Daiichi Hoki. pp. 91–100.

Maekawa, M. (1994) Information and corporate activities (in Japanese). *Forum Communication*, 10 August.

Maekawa, M. (1995) Energizing individuals through benchmarking (in Japanese). *Diamond Harvard Business Review*, March.

March, J.G. and Simon, H. (1958) *Organizations*. New York: Wiley.

Nakamura, Y. (1992) *Clinical Knowledge* (in Japanese). Iwanami.

Nonaka, I. (1991) The knowledge-creating company. *Harvard Business Review*, November–December: 96–104.

Nonaka, I. (1994) A dynamic theory of organizational knowledge creation. *Organization Science*, 5: 23–34.

Nonaka, I. and Takeuchi, H. (1995) *The Knowledge-Creating Company*. New York: Oxford University Press.

Polanyi, M. (1966) *The Tacit Dimension*. London: Routledge and Kegan Paul.

Porter, M. (1980) *Competitive Strategy*. New York: Free Press.

Robertson, T. and Wind, Y. (1983) Organizational cosmopolitanism and innovation. *Academy of Management Journal*, 26: 332–8.

Senge, P. (1990) *The Fifth Discipline: the Age and Practice of the Learning Organization*. London: Century Business.

Simon, H. (1989) *Models of Thought*. New Haven, CT: Yale University Press.

Simon, H. (1993) Strategy and organizational evolution. *Strategic Management Journal*, 14, Special Issue (Summer): 45–65.

Tushman, M.L. (1977) Special boundary roles in the innovation process. *Administrative Science Quarterly*, 22: 587–605.

von Krogh, G. and Roos, J. (1995) *Organizational Epistemology*. London: Macmillan.

von Krogh, G. and Roos, J. (1996) *Managing Knowledge: Perspectives on Cooperation and Competition*. London: Sage.

von Krogh, G., Roos, J. and Slocum, K. (1994) An essay on corporate epistemology. *Strategic Management Journal*, 15, Special Issue (Summer): 53–71.

8

ERRORS AND LEARNING IN ORGANIZATIONS

Salvatore Vicari and Gabriele Troilo

The issue that has perhaps most stimulated debate and innovation in management studies in the last 20 years is the complexity of economic environments (Bell, 1973; Cohen and Axelrod, 1984; Frederickson and Mitchell, 1984; Huber, 1984; AA VV, 1990; Achrol, 1991; Eccles and Nohria, 1992; D'Aveni, 1994; Hamel and Prahalad, 1994; Stacey, 1995). Complex phenomena are difficult to interpret on the basis of *a priori* assumptions and forecasting their evolution is next to impossible. From an epistemological point of view, we can say that in a complex environment there exists no single reality, but rather a separate reality for each individual observer (Atlan, 1979; Prigogine and Stengers, 1979; Watzlawick, 1981; Bocchi and Ceruti, 1985; Varela et al., 1991).

The goal of this chapter is to explore how complexity affects some of the traditional concepts of managerial literature, with a specific focus on marketing management literature. Our assumption is that the firm is a cognitive system which enacts and makes sense of its environment from its own individual point of view. Following on this idea, we shall propose a model of innovation as a learning process, focusing on the concepts of error and error production. These topics raise many organizational issues which are briefly discussed in the last part of this chapter.

The Nature of Needs

A good way to examine the issue of complex environments is to try to answer the following question: is the market knowable? This is because today's markets are characterized by increasingly sophisticated customers, evolving lifestyles, ever more fragmented segments, and tastes that change at an unbelievable pace. Today's markets seem to be a very good example of complex environments (Glazer, 1991; Hamel and Prahalad, 1991; Mueller-Heumann, 1992; Glazer and Weiss, 1993; Blattberg and Glazer, 1994) and therefore it is possible to propose that there is not a sole market reality, but a number of realities coexisting at any one time (Firat, 1993; Brown, 1994).

The assumption that markets can be knowable (and known) lies at the very root of marketing theory. To quote some classics, Levitt maintains that 'The seller takes his cues from the buyer in such a way that the product becomes a consequence of the marketing effort, not vice versa' (1960: 83–9); and Kotler states that 'The company can often be more effective by adapting and adjusting its supplies to the needs of clearly defined buyers' (1967: 6). Therefore the assumption is that in the markets there are *given needs* which, once discovered, can easily be satisfied. In this respect, success is guaranteed by understanding these needs, forecasting their evolution better than competitors, and behaving accordingly.

This traditional view of marketing has succeeded quite well in describing and interpreting all market phenomena dealing with existing products/needs, for which it can be supposed that consumption models are stable and consumers are able to explain and communicate their needs. But the issue of new product development – and innovation in general – does not fit in well with this view (Kanter, 1988; Lindell, 1991). In effect consumers are not able to provide true indications of their new needs, because of the strong influence of their present product experience (Bennett and Cooper, 1979; 1981; Hayes and Abernathy, 1980; Hamel and Prahalad, 1991). So how can a firm develop new products with so little help from consumers? And how is it possible to justify the market success of products which market tests indicated as being unappreciated by consumers, or the market failure of products which, on the contrary, gained consumers' approval in the testing stage?

The solution has been found in the concept of *latent needs*, that is to say needs which customers are not able to articulate and communicate (Hamel and Prahalad, 1994). A new product is successful or unsuccessful according to its ability to transform latent needs into articulated needs.

Radical innovations have appeared in rapid succession in the last few years (colour TV, VCRs, cellular telephones, interactive media and so on) – and have sometimes been due to chance, or have even come as a surprise to the innovating companies themselves. The breadth and depth of these phenomena have shown that it makes no sense to speak of latent needs unless we place no limits on latency. Latent needs are infinite. To put it another way, we can say that they do not exist as a given. Therefore in our opinion *latent needs are not unarticulated needs but needs which exist only after their expression*. This can occur only when they have been made concrete by a supply bringing them into existence.

In a complex market situation, where the forecasting of needs becomes difficult and firms try to gain competitive advantage through innovation, most needs can be considered latent needs, according to the above definition. We thus propose that:

Proposition 1   Needs can exist only if and when a supply materializes, i.e. when there is a possibility for needs to arise.

What we are proposing is that a demand is determined only by the existence of a supply.[1] This proposition has a devastating effect on traditional marketing management paradigms. The logical and sequential structure of firm–customer orientation is undermined at its base.[2]

customer needs analysis	→	marketing mix planning	→	action	→	customer satisfaction analysis	→	remedial action

Until recently it was possible to expect a good manager to be able to understand the environment, detect weak signals ahead of others, and make and implement decisions enabling his firm's action to fit given needs – whether expressed or latent – as closely as possible. The manager's purpose was to lift the veil of ignorance covering something whose nature was clear: market and environmental needs. Nowadays, in complex economic and competitive environments, the task of a good manager has completely changed. The questions are no longer 'what is reality?', 'what is the right context?', 'what is the real market?', simply because these questions have become meaningless. Are traditional management paradigms therefore dead? And is the role of marketing itself nearing its end?

We do not think so, but management and marketing concepts must certainly be radically rethought. In effect the correct questions are: 'what is the new task of management?' and 'what should managers do in a context like the present one?'. Our proposal – which will be developed in the following pages – is that managers must not submit to the environment, but *must continuously generate the environment that is most compatible with their firm*. The marketing manager's task is to guarantee compatibility between his firm and the market it creates. Very often firms create expectations that they cannot satisfy completely, generate possibilities for their competitors, and open up paths they cannot explore. As a consequence, the problem becomes: how can a firm maintain its compatibility with an environment which does not have an *a priori* existence, but is the consequence of its own action?

To answer this, it must first be explained why a firm's relationship with its environment can be seen as an internal element of the firm itself, and second how it accomplishes the process of adaptation to an environment that is no longer objective, but takes its form from the firm's own actions. Our starting point is thus a reinterpretation of the relations between firm and market after the adoption of the theory of the firm as a cognitive system.

Firm–Market Relationships in the Theory of the Firm as a Cognitive System

As we are posing the problem of a firm remaining compatible with the environment it generates, we need to adopt a congruent view of the firm to expound our propositions. We can find help in the model of the firm as a cognitive system (Sims and Gioia, 1986; Weick and Bougon, 1986) because the basic assumption of this concept is that the firm is able to generate the reality in which it exists.

Viewing a firm as a cognitive system means maintaining that its existence, survival and evolution are based on its capacity to produce and develop knowledge (Vicari, 1991; von Krogh et al., 1994; Nonaka and Takeuchi, 1995; von Krogh and Roos, 1996). It means describing it as a set of schemata (categories, scripts, maps) which define the structure of its knowledge. Moreover it means considering the evolution of the firm as an evolution of its knowledge, that is to say as a learning process. So we are going to adopt the particular view of cognitive systems as auto-poietic systems,[3] whose existence and actions consist of the continuous production of knowledge starting out from knowledge itself, in a self-referential development process.

The following properties of autopoietic systems[4] are particularly relevant to our aim of understanding how it is possible for a firm to maintain compatibility with its environment:

- the capacity to generate an environment
- the capacity to evolve.

An autopoietic system is able to distinguish its own borders from the surrounding environment. The system defines its own identity and at the same time distinguishes itself from something external, represented by the environment. This means that the environment does not have an objective existence – from the system's point of view – but is generated through a distinction process carried out by the system itself. Every system *creates its own environment*. As a result of this generation process, a change in the distinctions applied by the system brings about a corresponding change in the system's environment.

An autopoietic system is further characterized by its capacity to evolve. Faced by disturbing events, that is to say events that are not knowable through the system's present set of distinctions, the system can produce new elements and relationships. In this way, the system is able to *learn*. It is evident that if the system creates its own environment, its evolution is necessarily concerned with the latter. This means that every time there is an evolution of the system there is a coevolution of system and environment, from the system's point of view.

The above are only some of the properties of a cognitive system and its relations with the environment. But they already allow us to infer some implications for the relations between a firm and its environment. In traditional strategic management literature the environment is defined objectively through certain characteristics: clients' needs, perceptions and preferences; the behaviours of companies competing to satisfy these needs and gain increasing market shares; regulators setting the rules for fair competition; financial companies providing resources; and so on. To be successful, the single firm must identify the characteristics of the environment, plan a series of actions and implement them accordingly (Abell, 1980; Day, 1984; Kotler, 1991). The following sequence represents the consolidated schema of the strategic management process:

analysis → diagnosis → planning → implementation → results	
of an	
environment	

Such a schema is not consistent with the concept of the firm as a cognitive and autopoietic system, because in this view a given environment does not exist: the firm cannot identify any objective characteristics of the market because the latter, being a part of the environment, is subjectively created by the firm itself. Therefore each company creates a different environment according to its own cognitive schemata. The concept of cognitive schemata is now widespread in organizational (Weick, 1979a; 1979b; Daft and Weick, 1984; Weick and Bougon, 1986; Sims and Gioia, 1986) and strategic management studies (Smircich and Stubbart, 1985; Porac et al., 1987; Stubbart, 1989; Huff, 1990; Reger and Huff, 1993; Calori et al., 1994; Hodgkinson and Johnson, 1994). Some pioneering studies are showing up even in marketing literature (Day and Nedungadi, 1994; Baker and Knox, 1995).

The premise of such studies is the following: if a company is a cognitive and autopoietic system, it must, by definition, have knowledge only of itself. Everything external to the company can be known only through its own cognitive structures. At the same time, the company needs to produce knowledge in order to survive. How can this apparent paradox be resolved? The solution is in the concept of *enactment* (Weick, 1979a). The company produces, through its actions, raw data which are monitored and then interpreted (Daft and Weick, 1984). Interpretation consists of transforming the data into information, that is to say, giving the data significance.[5] The firm makes a map which guides it in new, future actions. This map – the cognitive schema – can be represented by a 'network of causal sequences' taking the form of a causal map (Weick and Bougon, 1986). Thus the firm interprets reality as a sequence of causes and effects and acts on the basis of this sequence.

This does not imply a return to the concept of the 'environment fitting' model of the firm. The perception of the causality of events is, precisely, a perception of the firm. For the firm, the map of reality becomes reality itself. In Weick's (1979b) words, 'the map is the territory'. The environment therefore does not provide the firm with any objective input. By enacting an environment and by forming a cognitive schema, the company identifies itself within the environment. It unveils the environment by putting itself in relationship to it. If the network of causal sequences in the map is confirmed over time, that is to say the events the firm perceives are knowable through the set of distinction it possesses, the firm's knowledge becomes stable, according to a retention mechanism (Nelson and Winter, 1982; Prahalad and Bettis, 1986; Sims and Gioia, 1986; Warglien, 1990). Therefore a cognitive schema creates a system of expectations about the occurrence of events which, if confirmed, becomes the firm's reference environment.

At this point we can go back to the marketing management discussion, emphasizing the impact that the theory of autopoietic systems has on it. Our proposition is that:

Proposition 2   The market, being a part of the firm's environment, is a constructed reality. It consists of a set of clients, competitors and distributors enacted by the firms' actions.

This proposition affects many fundamental marketing constructs and has major managerial implications. One example is the reinterpretation of the construct of market segmentation. Traditionally, this term means a *subdivision* of the market on the basis of homogeneities with regard to *implicit* characteristics. The aim of a company is, according to the traditional formulation, to determine adequate segmentation criteria from which it is possible to infer customer behaviour. It should be noted that this interpretation urges the company to acknowledge that division exists in the market, and to 'discover' it.

In our formulation, however, market segmentation is a way of selecting those parts of the environment which react to given company signals. For example, when a company reduces its prices some customers will buy its products/services. Thus the firm makes a cognitive map representing the price-sensitive market segment. Had the company not decided to lower the price of its product, this segment would not exist or would exist only for other companies. Consequently the norm 'the market can be segmented with reference to price' enters the company's cognitive schema. Therefore, the firm's supply can *aggregate* customer needs. This concept of segmentation is opposite to the one previously described. Customers would remain an undefined set without company action. There are as many potential means of aggregation – and segmentation – as there are possible combinations in a market; this means that they are virtually infinite. The only limits to the possibilities of segmentation lie in the ability of the firm to aggregate demand, not in the structure of the demand itself.

The market is therefore not a given. The company interprets the relations between its possible actions and the actual reactions of economic subjects who play the role of buyers or producers. These *perceived* actions and reactions,[6] connected by causal links, constitute a cognitive schema of the market, which 'ties' the firm to specific clients and competitors and directs the firm's behaviour (Porac et al., 1989; de Chernatony et al., 1993; Reger and Huff, 1993).

Innovation as a Learning Process and the Importance of Making Errors

From what has been said so far, it appears that a cognitive schema, if confirmed and shared, creates a set of expectations about customer and competitor behaviour that acquires prescriptive value for the company. The consolidation of the schema, however, places large limits on innovation (Dougherty, 1992). The firm's cognitive system, like all stable systems,[7] in fact, tends to seek confirmation of its expectations in order to preserve its cognitive resources and maintain its structural stability by means of a homeostatic mechanism (Weick, 1979a). How then is company innovation to be achieved? What is it that encourages a firm to adapt its behaviour to the market? If reality is a firm's creation, the source of innovation cannot but lie in the firm itself.

The problem can also be considered from another point of view. The external environment, the one that is not known – unknowable and not yet created – is a source of disturbing events for the system's stability. This is because of new technologies, new regulations, changes in demand and so on. How can it confront such disturbances and ensure its own survival? If the environment is not knowable a solution has to be found within the firm itself. In our opinion, change and the maintaining of compatibility are possible through the transformation of the firm's cognitive maps. We define this phenomenon as innovation:

Proposition 3 Innovation is the means by which a company creates the conditions to maintain compatibility with its environment and to evolve.

Starting out from this definition, we can infer some properties of innovation. To begin with it must be *continuous*, if a firm is to remain constantly compatible with its environment. Those events which an outside observer might consider innovative are only the manifest signs of the firm's process of continuous adaptation to its environment, or – from the firm's point of view – of adaptation to its own generation of the environment.

Innovation is thus a *process* rather than a result. Furthermore, if innovation is a continuous process whereby the firm changes its cognitive schemata, it consists of a modification of *knowledge*. Given that a company changes its knowledge through innovation, it follows that:

Proposition 4 The innovation process is a learning process.

There is, however, an apparent contradiction which makes it difficult to realize that an innovation process is taking place. On the one hand, the cognitive system tends to be homeostatic in its behaviour. On the other, it is necessary to modify cognitive schemata in order to change and to survive. How can a firm solve this contradiction?

The solution lies in the concept of 'error' (von Krogh and Vicari, 1993). By 'error' we mean the distance between two cognitive schemata, the difference between expected events and perceived events, the deviation from the expectations of the firm. One example of such an error is the difference between the expected and the real behaviour of customers. The distance between cognitive schemata encourages the company to acquire new data, to interpret them, and to extract new meaning, thus creating new cognitive schemata. We can therefore say:

Proposition 5 Innovation and the learning process that constitutes it are made possible by the production of 'errors'.

In the following sections of the chapter we shall analyse the ways in which a firm produces errors and, in particular, their implications for managerial practice.

Error Production

Let us assume that the distance between the firm's expectations and perceived events – which we have called error – is brought about by a disturbance. Bearing in mind the distinction we made above, this disturbance can arise from two different sources:

- the external, unknowable environment
- the cognitive structure of the firm (the enacted environment).

Further, the invalidation of a cognitive schema can have the following causes:

- intentional behaviour of the firm
- chance.

The firm can actively search for events 'disturbing' its present mental frames. As many authors have recently pointed out there seems to be a strong need for this in today's hypercompetitive environments (D'Aveni, 1994; Hamel and Prahalad, 1994; Nonaka and Takeuchi, 1995). The company should call its own cognitive schemata into question in order to evolve and survive. Even if it has a strong dominant logic, the firm should learn to unlearn (Hedberg, 1981) creating new distinctions able to generate new realities. This is possible by applying the new distinctions to the – as yet unknown – external environment or to the present cognitive structure, that is to say by enacting them.

Chance plays a fundamental role in the firm's knowledge development processes (Barney, 1986). By chance we mean anything that is simply unexpected. Chance creates considerable opportunities for learning because it usually brings about chaos and disorder. As the experience of Japanese firms has demonstrated (Nonaka, 1988), disorder generates the stimulus for a new order. In the language of autopoietic cognitive systems, it means reaching a new level of stability through the generation of knowledge. Chance, too, is inherent in both the external environment and the present cognitive structure of the firm, but the necessary condition for error production to occur is that the firm perceives the event which causes the error itself.

By combining these two dimensions, we can define a matrix allowing us to classify the different ways in which errors are produced (see Figure 8.1). Through *experimentation* (the intentionality/external environment cell of the matrix) the firm enacts the still unknown environment in order to produce new data and information: for instance, in the case of acquisitions of companies operating in different sectors (Vicari, 1994), in the case of cooperative experimentation (Vicari et al., 1996), in the entrance into new industries or strategic groups or international markets. The firm aims in these cases to produce new information through the acquisition of new competences, differing from those belonging to the causal structures of its existing cognitive maps. The Japanese automobile and motorcycle producers in the US market initially entered small existing niches – jeeps and small motorcycles – to learn about US consumers' tastes and the distribution system, and then extended their supply to the whole market. Mediaset, Italy's biggest private TV operator, Banca Nazionale del Lavoro, one of the leading Italian banking groups, and British Telecom made an alliance, sharing their competences in different industries to become the third cellular telephone services provider in Italy.

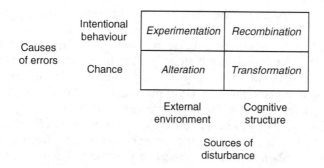

Figure 8.1 *Different means of error production*

There is a *recombination* (the intentionality/structure cell) when the firm makes a change in its components and/or in the relations which connect them, so as to increase the variety of producible information. This can be achieved, for example, by the introduction of new professional figures or new organizational roles not consistent with existing ones, by the creation of project teams, and by process reengineering. The purpose is to produce changes through disturbances to the organizational structure and consolidated management patterns. Barilla, the market leader in the Italian pasta and biscuit industries, hired the US company Procter & Gamble's CEO, who fired the company's whole top management team in order to change the firm's mindset and tackle the serious market crisis the company was passing through in an innovative way. Fiat, Italy's top automotive manufacturer and one of the largest in Europe, reengineered its product development process to face up to increasing competitive pressure and reduced its lead time from 60 to 22 months.

Typical examples of *alteration* (the chance/external environment cell) are macro-environmental disturbances (Ansoff, 1980): technological change, new regulations, social change and so forth. In all these cases, once they are perceived, the firm has to implement new procedures and create new knowledge to confront the disturbance, learning results from the new ways in which problems are solved. The European Union regulation about eco-packaging came as a surprise to many Italian package producers: at the moment some of them have perceived the potential threat of this event and are changing their production processes, whereas others do not seem to be very worried, in the belief that the Italian regulatory system will not be able to pass sound environmental laws and see that rules are kept to. The discovery and punishment of widespread corruption in the Italian pharmaceutical industry has led to general uncertainty in firms about what is correct and what is not in their business relations; some of them have adopted ethical codes and communicated this to their partners, thus achieving new success in the market.

There is *transformation* (the chance/structure cell) whenever the elements of the firm's cognitive structure do not behave as expected. For instance, employees alter their production standards, their motivation changes, shareholders are dissatisfied and so on. In this case, as well, the unexpected element generates a gap, an error, which helps the firm to create new distinctions to make sense of the events. In the last few years, the directors of many public agencies in the north-east of Italy – an economic area where the rate of unemployment is practically zero – were worried because many young people had been quitting high school. Since this phenomenon is typical of poor areas, where families need extra income to survive, it was most unexpected in a region where the average income is very high. Now they have made sense of it by learning that these young people consider attending school an opportunity cost and prefer to find employment very early in life.

Error Production in Markets

In our examples we deliberately left out the role of markets in error production, so we could focus on this aspect in more depth in the present section. To begin with it must be made clear that, on the basis of the subdivision of sources we have adopted, the market can belong both to the external environment and to the firm's cognitive structure. From the firm's point of view, the market behaves according to the expectations system of its own cognitive schemata. All consumers and producers who do not react to the firm's actions are part of the external environment.[8] Therefore they represent the background which does not directly interact with the firm in significant economic and competitive processes.

We assume that the four methods of error production described in the matrix in Figure 8.1 hold good also for the market:

Experimentation This occurs with a new product launch in a market as yet unentered, through the utilization of a new distribution channel, through brand extension to products not present in traditional competitive arenas and so on. In the Italian comics industry, for example, Sergio Bonelli, the market leader, experiments with new characters to enter new market segments without doing any market research. Every day they receive a considerable amount of mail from readers which allows them to modify their characters after the first stories. Swatch has expanded its brand into very different industries – telephones, cellular telephones, automobiles – making alliances with companies with very different competences.

Recombination This occurs when the company observes the gap between actual market behaviours and its expectations system. For instance, customer satisfaction measures are simply a demonstration of the gap between customer expectations and customer perceptions, attitudes and effective behaviour. It is worth remembering that customers have no objectivity in themselves, but are objective only in the representation system of the firm. Nevertheless they play the role of error activators whose function is revealed through customer satisfaction surveys.

Alteration   This occurs when a firm receives messages which do not belong to its expectations system: when the product is purchased by customers it was not originally aimed at, or new competitors from other sectors have entered the market, or new distributors add the product to their range and so on. Nearly 10 years ago Invicta, an Italian professional backpack producer, perceived that some young people used their small backpacks to carry books to school: they designed a new product line for this specific market segment and now they are the industry's market leader.

Transformation   This occurs when unusual behaviours are discovered: customers change their perceptions and/or their purchases, distributors eliminate the product from their ranges, competitors fail to respect the rules of the game and so on. Some years ago San Pellegrino, an Italian soft drink manufacturer, recognizing the need of many distributors to break Coca Cola's stranglehold on them, launched a new drink with a similar positioning to Coca Cola, expecting a good reception from these distributors. After getting off to a good start, sales began to decrease, and after a while the company discovered that the powerful Coca Cola Company had obliged its distributors to reject San Pellegrino or risk not having their orders filled.

In all these cases, error is the basis for change and learning. Whenever a firm becomes aware of the existence of something unexpected or unforeseen, something that is distant from its expectations system, it is obliged to develop a new expectations system and new knowledge, which eventually produce evolution. The subdivision of the matrix in Figure 8.1 does not allow for the fact that some errors can occur contemporaneously. For example, the creation of a system to survey customer satisfaction (which was classed as recombination) may generate an incremental product innovation which attracts unexpected consumers (alteration), or a brand extension strategy (experimentation) may determine a reduction in purchases by present consumers (transformation).

Organizational Conditions Fostering Error Production and Learning

If a firm decides to manage error production so that a cognitive gap between present and possible schemata can be created, the signal intentionally emitted by the firm itself or that created by perceiving environmental disturbances plays a fundamental role. The effectiveness of a signal for this purpose is directly proportional to its 'strength': the greater the strength, the more effective the signal. If the firm as a cognitive system produces knowledge by making distinctions, the causal cognitive schema from which it starts out must be well defined. A signal deriving from this schema is therefore linked to a system of expectations based on the occurrence of certain events. But what are the properties of a strong signal? And who should it be strong for?

If the environment had an objective existence, we might say that the signal should be strong for the environment. But, as we have supposed that both reality and the environment are created by the firm, the strength of the signal can only be evaluated in relation to the firm itself. Therefore:

Proposition 6   A strong signal must have the property of being 'perceived' by everybody involved in the innovation process, to generate tension and produce expectations.

To achieve this aim, *the firm can both detect and amplify the signal*. An effective detection and amplifying process must have certain characteristics. No event, whether occurring inside or outside a firm, can produce a signal if the firm does not have a detection system producing data continuously. If consumers are dissatisfied, for example, but there is no available system to detect their dissatisfaction, the firm continues operating unaware of the situation.

Once the firm receives a target signal, *the gap between cognitive schemata and present expectations must be defined precisely*. In cases where the market is used to produce errors, for example, benchmark indicators can be used effectively. These make the expectations system of the firm explicit (to be equal or superior to competitors, for example). They also permit clearer distinctions (what is the discrepancy compared with competitors?). Benchmarking allows both error recognition and learning to take place. It is also important to establish a metric for the measurement of error. In fact it is not enough to perceive and define error with respect to a yardstick. If error recognition is to result in action for change, some way must be found to assign weights to errors. To achieve this, *the most suitable measures must be found*, able to make errors meaningful: good examples are indexes of customer retention, of time required to carry out specific operations, of the cost of a given activity and so on.

If error is going to contribute to the learning process, *acknowledgement of error must be propagated throughout the organization*. The more widespread error recognition is, the more rapid and far-reaching the changes an organization can produce as a result of it. The dissemination of error recognition within a firm can invalidate present schemata, thus producing a generalized modification of schemata theselves. For this reason

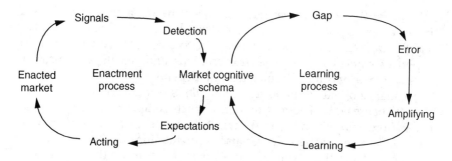

Figure 8.2 *Model of marketing innovation as a learning process through errors*

there must be transfer learning processes (Takeuchi and Nonaka, 1986) permitting a sharing of expectations and of their invalidation. Thus:

Proposition 7 In order to generate strong signals, the gap between detected target signals and the expectations system must be given visibility within the firm.

A good way to do this is *to clearly link the gap generated to firm goals.* If change is to be guided and not left to chance, the firm's goals and objectives must be made explicit. This means that there must be a shared vision of what the firm is and what it wants to become. For this purpose, it should be remembered that, once a gap between expectations and the present situation is detected, there are infinite ways in which the gap can be narrowed. The choice of one or another is fundamental in allowing corrective action to generate effective learning. In conclusion, the model of innovation as a learning process is represented in Figure 8.2.

Conclusion: Towards Postmodern Management

Now that we have come to the end of this chapter, some readers might hold that the introduction of the concept of error and that of learning through errors in the innovation debate does not necessarily contradict the traditional vision of a given environment and its objective needs. If there are errors which foster the learning process – some may argue – this must necessarily be so because a reality exists that must be taken into consideration. If the present work was concerned only with this proposition, it would add very little to what traditional management studies have already explained. As it happens, this is not the case. The concept of error we propose is not at all the idea of a deviation from an *a priori reality*, of consumers whose needs must be understood in order to provide a supply that can satisfy them. The error is not a supply which fails to satisfy given *a priori* environmental needs, as in the traditional management perspective. It is *the distance between the firm's expectations and the reality created by the firm itself*. This is a completely different idea: a perfect coincidence between expectations and results is impossible in any place or time. Results do not depend on reality but are the consequence of one of the *many compatibilities that can arise between a firm and its environment*. There is no end to such compatibilities, which can come from supplies and needs which generate each other in infinite variety. They are generable because compatibilities do not exist in the abstract but are the result of the actions of a firm or the market and the subsequent interlacement of actions and reactions triggered by the two. The idea we are proposing is that of a management process which *does not consist of a progressive reduction of uncertainty*, as in the traditional view. Management in the postmodern era has a much harder task: it must *promote a growing compatibility with the environment*, without certainties, without a clear point of reference, except for the certainty of its own errors, which provide the basis for a never-ending learning process.

Notes

1 The same conclusion is drawn in high-tech products marketing literature (Bourgeois and Eisenhardt, 1988; Weiss and Heide, 1993). In our opinion it depends not only on the complexity of the product but also on the complexity of the market environment.

2 Hamel and Prahalad (1994: 81–3) support a similar conclusion. The difference is that they focus on the difficulty of forecasting in a turbulent environment and we maintain the ontological indeterminacy of needs.

3 The theory of autopoietic systems, first developed in the biological field (Varela, 1979; Maturana and Varela, 1980; 1987; Zeleny, 1981) has spread to the sociological field (Roth and Schwegler, 1981; von Foerster, 1984; Luhmann, 1986; 1990; van Twist and Schaap, 1991) and finally to that of management (Morgan, 1986; Vicari, 1991; Kickert, 1993; von Krogh and Vicari, 1993; von Krogh et al., 1994; Nonaka and Takeuchi, 1995).

4 For a complete description of the properties of autopoietic systems, see the literature mentioned in note 3.

5 As von Krogh et al. note: 'Literally, information means "to put" data "in form". . . . Books, movies, lectures, papers, computer programs, memos, etc., are data in the environment of the manager – not information. . . . Information is dependent on the manager who makes use of it to develop knowledge. Thus, he is closed with respect to knowledge (also knowledge about the environment) but open with respect to data from the outside' (1994: 59).

6 Obviously perceived actions and reactions derive from the environments enacted by the firm through previous actions.

7 The concept of stability in system theory is quite different from that of equilibrium. In classical economic theory, equilibrium is a fixed point towards which the system strives (in a market, the point where demand and supply

intersect). In system theory, stability is the capacity to conserve relations among the parts of the system itself, also during change.

8 Researchers in relationship marketing hold a similar view, even if they adopt a structural network rather than a cognitive model of the firm. See Hakansson (1982; 1987), Johanson and Mattsson (1985), Hakansson and Snehota (1989), Achrol (1991), Webster (1992), Bucklin and Sengupta (1993), Lynch (1994) and Piercy and Cravens (1995).

References

AA VV (1990) *Complessità & Managerialità*. Milan: EGEA.

Abell, D.F. (1980) *Defining the Business: the Starting Point of Strategic Planning*. Englewood Cliffs, NJ: Prentice-Hall.

Achrol, R.S. (1991) Evolution of the marketing organization: new forms for turbulent environments. *Journal of Marketing*, October: 77–93.

Ansoff, H.I. (1980) Strategic issue management. *Strategic Management Journal*, 1: 131–48.

Atlan, H. (1979) *Entre le cristal e la fumée*. Paris: Seuil.

Baker, S. and Knox, S. (1995) Mapping consumer cognitions in Europe, in *Proceedings of the 24th EMAC Conference*, Paris. pp. 81–101.

Barney, J.B. (1986) Strategic factor markets: expectations, luck, and business strategy. *Management Science*, 10.

Bell, D. (1973) *The Coming of Post-Industrial Society*. New York: Basic Books.

Bennett, R.C. and Cooper, R.G. (1979) Beyond the marketing concept. *Business Horizons*, 22 (June): 76–85.

Bennett, R.C. and Cooper, R.G. (1981) The misuse of marketing: an American tragedy. *Business Horizons*, 24 (November–December): 51–61.

Blattberg, R.C. and Glazer, R. (1994) Marketing in the information revolution, in R.C. Blattberg, R. Glazer and J.D. Little (eds), *The Marketing Information Revolution*. Boston: Harvard Business School Press. pp. 9–29.

Bocchi, G. and Ceruti, M. (eds) (1985) *La sfida della complessità*. Milan: Feltrinelli.

Bourgeois, J. and Eisenhardt, K. (1988) Strategic decision process in high velocity environments: four cases in the microcomputer industry. *Management Science*, 34: 816–35.

Brown, S. (1994) Marketing and postmodernism: opportunity or aporia?, in M.J. Baker (ed.), *Perspectives on Marketing Management*, 4: 73–96. Chichester: Wiley.

Bucklin, L.P. and Sengupta, S. (1993) Organization of successful co-marketing alliances. *Journal of Marketing*, 57 (April).

Calori, R., Johnson, G. and Sarnin, P. (1994) CEO's cognitive maps and the scope of the organization. *Strategic Management Journal*, 15: 437–57.

Cohen, M.D. and Axelrod, R. (1984) Coping with complexity: the adaptive value of changing utility. *American Economic Review*, 74: 30–42.

Daft, R.L. and Weick, K.E. (1984) Toward a model of organizations as interpretation systems. *Academy of Management Review*, 2: 284–95.

D'Aveni, R.A. (1994) *Hyper-Competition: Managing the Dynamics of Strategic Maneuvering*. New York: Free Press.

Day, G.S. (1984) *Strategic Market Planning*. St Paul, MN: West.

Day, G.S. and Nedungadi, P. (1994) Managerial representations of competitive advantage. *Journal of Marketing*, April: 31–44.

de Chernatony, L., Daniels, K. and Johnson, G. (1993) A cognitive perspective on managers' perception of competition. *Journal of Marketing Management*, 9: 373–81.

Dougherty, D. (1992) Interpretive barriers to successful product innovation in large firms. *Organization Science*, 2: 179–202.

Eccles, R.G. and Nohria, N. (1992) *Beyond the Hype: Rediscovering the Essence of Management*. Boston: Harvard Business School Press.

Firat, A.F. (1993) Postmodernity: the age of marketing. *International Journal of Research in Marketing*, 10: 227–49.

Frederickson, J. and Mitchell, T. (1984) Strategic decision processes: comprehensiveness and performance in an industry with unstable environment. *Academy of Management Journal*, 27: 399–423.

Glazer, R. (1991) Marketing in information-intensive environments: strategic implications of knowledge as an asset. *Journal of Marketing*, 55: 1–19.

Glazer, R. and Weiss, A.M. (1993) Marketing in turblent environments: decision processes and the time-sensitivity of information. *Journal of Marketing Research*, November: 509–21.

Hakansson, H. (ed.) (1982) *International Marketing and Purchasing of Industrial Goods: An Interaction Approach*. New York: Wiley.

Hakansson, H. (1987) *Industrial Technological Development: a Network Approach*. London: Croom Helm.

Hakansson, H. and Snehota, I. (1989) No business is an island. *Scandinavian Journal of Management*, 5: 187–200.

Hamel, G. and Prahalad, C.K. (1991) Corporate imagination and expeditionary marketing. *Harvard Business Review*, July–August: 81–92.

Hamel, G. and Prahalad, C.K. (1994) *Competing for the Future*. Boston: Harvard Business School Press.

Hayes, R.H. and Abernathy, W.J. (1980) Managing our way to economic decline. *Harvard Business Review*, 58 (July–August): 67–77.

Hedberg, B. (1981) How organizations learn and unlearn, in P.C. Nystrom and W.H. Starbuck (eds), *Handbook of Organizational Design*. Oxford: Oxford Univerity Press. pp. 3–27.

Hodgkinson, G.P. and Johnson, G. (1994) Exploring the mental models of competitive strategists: the case for a processual approach. *Journal of Management Studies*, 4: 525–51.

Huber, G.P. (1984) The nature and design of post-industrial organizations. *Management Science*, 8: 928–51.

Huff, A.S. (ed.) (1990) *Mapping Strategic Thought*. Chichester: Wiley.

Johanson, J. and Mattsson, L.G. (1985) Marketing investments and market investment in industrial networks. *International Journal of Research in Marketing*, 2: 185–95.

Kanter, R.M. (1988) When a thousand flowers bloom: structural, collective, and social conditions for innovation in organization, in L.L. Cummings and B.M. Staw (eds), *Research in Organizational Behavior*, 10: 169–221.

Kickert, W.J.M. (1993) Autopoiesis and the science of (public) administration: essence, sense and nonsense. *Organization Studies*, 2: 261–78.

Kotler, P. (1967) *Marketing Management*. Englewood Cliffs, NJ: Prentice-Hall.

Kotler, P. (1991) *Marketing Management*. Englewood Clifs, NJ: Prentice-Hall.

Levitt, T. (1960) Marketing myopia. *Harvard Business Review*, July–August: 45–56.

Lindell, M. (1991) Developing new products – an action, interaction and contextual approach. *Scandinavian Journal of Management*, 3: 173–89.

Luhmann, N. (1986) The autopoiesis of social systems, in F. Geyer and J. van der Zouwen (eds), *Sociocybernetic Paradoxes*. London: Sage.

Luhmann, N. (1990) *Essays on Self-Reference*. New York: Columbia University Press.

Lynch, J.E. (1994) Only connect: the role of marketing and strategic management in the modern organization. *Journal of Marketing Management*, 10: 527–42.

Maturana, H.R. and Varela, F.J. (1980) *Autopoiesis and Cognition: the Realization of the Living*. Dordrecht: Reidl.

Maturana, H.R. and Varela, F.J. (1987) *The Tree of Knowledge*. Boston: Shambhala.

Morgan, G. (1986) *Images of Organization*. Newbury Park, CA: Sage.

Mueller-Heumann, G. (1992) Market and technology shifts in the 1990s: market fragmentation and mass customization. *Journal of Marketing Management*, 4: 303–14.

Nelson, R.R. and Winter, S.G. (1982) *An Evolutionary Theory of Economic Change*. Boston: Harvard University Press.

Nonaka, I. (1988) Creating organizational order out of chaos: self-renewal in Japanese firms. *California Management Review*, Spring: 57–73.

Nonaka, I. and Takeuchi, H. (1995) *The Knowledge-Creating Company*. New York: Oxford University Press.

Piercy, N.F. and Cravens, D.W. (1995) The network paradigm and the marketing organization: developing a new marketing agenda. *European Journal of Marketing*, 29: 7–34.

Porac, J.F., Thomas, H. and Baden-Fuller, C. (1989) Competitive groups as cognitive communities: the case of Scottish knitwear manufacturers. *Journal of Management Studies*, 26: 397–416.

Porac, J.F., Thomas, H. and Emme, B. (1987) Knowing the competition: the mental models of retailing strategists, in G. Johnson (ed.), *Business Strategy and Retailing*. Chichester: Wiley. pp. 59–79.

Prahalad, C.K. and Bettis, R. (1986) The dominant logic: a new linkage between diversity and performance. *Strategic Management Journal*, 7: 485–501.

Prigogine, I. and Stengers, I. (1979) *La Nouvelle Alliance: métamorphose de la science*, Paris: Gallimard.

Reger, R.K. and Huff, A.S. (1993) Strategic groups: a cognitive perspective. *Strategic Management Journal*, 14: 103–24.

Roth, G. and Schwegler, H. (1981) *Self-Organizing Systems: an Interdisciplinary Approach*. Frankfurt: Campus.

Sims, H.P. and Gioia, D.A. (eds) (1986) *The Thinking Organization*. San Francisco: Jossey-Bass.

Smircich, L. and Stubbart, C. (1985) Strategic management in an enacted world. *Academy of Management Review*, 4: 724–36.

Stacey, R.D. (1995) The science of complexity: an alternative perspective for strategic change processes. *Strategic Management Journal*, 16: 477–95.

Stubbart, C. (1989) Managerial cognition: a missing link in strategic management research. *Journal of Management Studies*, 26: 325–47.

Takeuchi, H. and Nonaka, I. (1986) The new new product development game. *Harvard Business Review*, January–February: 137–46.

van Twist, M.J. and Schaap, L. (1991) Introduction to autopoiesis theory and autopoietic steering, in R.J. Veld, L. Schaap, C.J. Termeer and M.J. van Twist (eds), *Autopoiesis and Configuration Theory: New Approaches to Societal Steering*. Dordrecht: Kluwer.

Varela, F.J. (1979) *Principles of Biological Autonomy*. Amsterdam: New Holland.

Varela, F.J., Thompson, E. and Rosch, E. (1991) *The Embodied Mind: Cognitive Science and Human Experience*. Boston: MIT Press.

Vicari, S. (1991) *L'impresa vivente*. Milan: EtasLibri.

Vicari, S. (1994) Acquisition as experimentation', in G. von Krogh, A. Sinatra and H. Singh (eds), *The Management of Corporate Acquisitions*. London: Macmillan.

Vicari, S., von Krogh, G., Roos J. and Mahnke, V. (1996) Knowledge creation through cooperative experimentation, in G. von Krogh and J. Roos (eds), *Managing Knowledge: Perspectives on Cooperation and Competition*. London: Sage.

von Foerster, H. (1984) Principles of self-organization in socio-managerial context, in H. Ulrich and G.J.B. Probst (eds), *Self-organization and Management of Social Systems*. Berlin: Springer.

von Krogh, G., Roos, J. and Slocum, K. (1994) An essay on corporate epistemology. *Strategic Management Journal*, 15: 53–71.

von Krogh, G. and Roos, J. (eds) (1996) *Managing Knowledge: Perspectives on Cooperation and Competition*. London: Sage.

von Krogh, G. and Vicari, S. (1993) An autopoietic approach to experimental strategic learning, in P. Lorange, B. Chakravarthy, J. Roos and A. van de Ven (eds), *Implementing Strategic Processes: Change, Learning and Co-operation*. Oxford: Basil Blackwell. pp. 394–410.

Warglien, M. (1990) *Innovazione e impresa evolutiva*. Padua: CEDAM.

Watzalwick, P. (1981) *Die erfundene wirklichkeit*. Munich: Piper.

Webster, F.E. Jr, (1992) The changing role of marketing in the corporation. *Journal of Marketing*, 56 (October): 1–17.

Weick, K.E. (1979a) *The Social Psychology of Organizing*. Reading, MA: Addison Wesley.

Weick, K.E. (1979b) Cognitive processes in organizations. *Research in Organizational Behavior*, 1: 41–74.

Weick, K.E. and Bougon, M.G. (1986) Organizations as cognitive maps: charting ways to success and failure, in H.P. Sims and D.A. Gioia (eds), *The Thinking Organization*. San Francisco: Jossey-Bass.

Weiss, A.M. and Heide, J.B. (1993) The nature of organizational search in high-technology markets. *Journal of Marketing Research*, 30 (May): 220–33.

Zeleny, M. (1981) *Autopoiesis: a Theory of Living Organization*. New York: Elsevier.

9

THE KNOWLEDGE SPIRAL

Jürgen Schüppel, Günter Müller-Stewens and Peter Gomez

As we approach the 'knowledge society' (Lane, 1966; Bell, 1976; Drucker, 1986), it is becoming clear that knowledge is a factor in value creation. Therefore this resource has to be managed like the classical factors of labour, capital and raw materials. In this chapter we describe a normative concept for the development of a knowledge management system and focus on a number of instruments which can be implemented to professionalize the use of knowledge in companies. Companies need to work on this approach, because in the future it will basically be the rapidity of the knowledge generating and applying process that forms competitive advantage. With both – the normative concept and the associated instruments – we contribute a very practical dimension to the discussion of knowledge management, which makes the whole discussion more adjustable to the competitive problems of companies.

The fundamental thesis is as simple as it is tempting: companies are 'filled to the brim with knowledge', but nonetheless use 'only around 20 percent of this resource' (Zucker and Schmitz, 1994). It has therefore become a significant consideration of companies to increase this proportion. Following this – empirical and not yet proven – thesis, companies have disdained the full use of knowledge, limiting their potential to their existing productivity. And when one follows this thesis to its logical conclusion, the question of the basis of competitive advantage of modern companies arises in the above mentioned way.

Based on this background, companies are increasingly drawn toward knowledge and learning as a way to a comparative advantage. Physical products and related services no longer dominate the competition; instead it is the capability to adapt most quickly to environmental and internal changes or to imitate new innovative changes. Under the label 'knowledge management' we go one step further. In areas in which only 5% to 30% of company activities are production processes, the value chains for these companies are in large part *knowledge-dependent value chains*, like research and development, design, marketing etc. Hence, the core elements of a company are *organizational knowledge* and the related *organizational learning processes*, and these have far-reaching consequences.

In the traditional understanding of organizations, 'the company' or 'the organization' was interpreted in a physical sense. Just think of the numerous metaphors which illustrate organizational models, for example the 'palace organization' (Hedberg, 1984). In this view one can enter and exit 'the organization' like a house with a tangible structure, which effortlessly guarantees the assignment of complex work processes. But in the end we must consider that this is just a simplified picture of an organization, and does not represent the real core of today's companies.

Organizations are originally *based on informational, intellectual and emotional processes*, such as knowledge, feelings, interests and behaviour patterns. The organization is therefore created and re-created daily by all its members and their interactions. Furthermore, by 'members of an organization' we mean not only its permanent employees, but also the temporarily 'docked' members of other organizations, for example suppliers, customers, partners in strategic alliances and all other stakeholders. Organizations can therefore be seen as *networks of intellectual and knowledge-based processes* – processes in which the relations and interactions between members are organized. Looking at the interplay of the material organizational structure and leadership, as well as communication processes, one main purpose therefore becomes apparent: the optimal formation of interaction patterns to enable effective and efficient cooperation *inside* the relevant network of the organization. The starting point for that lies in what we call an *invisible structure*. This invisible structure reflects the identity of the organization and its members and determines organizational rules, procedures and actions on the visible level (Gomez and Müller-Stewens, 1994).

We can now formulate the organizational pattern more clearly: the visible representations of organizations, such as structures, procedures, products, services etc., are in large part merely temporary materializations of the underlying organizational knowledge. In these knowledge-based systems, knowledge is a highly influential factor along with the traditional sociological concepts of power and money (Willke, 1995). From an economic perspective, knowledge is a key factor of value creation processes, substituting in large part for classical elements like labour, capital and raw materials. *Knowledge* can therefore be described as the *main principle in organizations* (Machlup, 1981; Stehr, 1994). Here are three examples (Drucker, 1986):

- The production costs for semiconductors are already made up of 70% 'knowledge' (through R&D, laboratory tests etc.) and only 12% 'labour'.

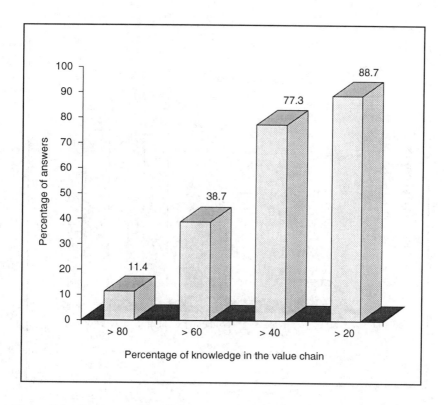

Figure 9.1 *Percentage of knowledge in the value chain of companies*

- This also applies to the pharmaceutical industry, where 'labour' accounts for only 15% and 'knowledge' accounts for over 50% of the total costs.
- Even in the automobile industry, 'knowledge' already dominates the production process, since design and engineering processes are the core value-creating activities.

An empirical study of knowledge management (Graßhoff, 1996) provides support for these examples. Almost 80% of the respondents said that *knowledge today comprises the most significant part of a company's value chain* (see Figure 9.1).

In addition, knowledge not only dominates in research-focused sectors like the chemical and pharmaceutical industries, but also plays a significant role in most of the other sectors. Looking at the future development of companies' value chains, almost 80% of the respondents expect a *strong increase in the amount of knowledge used* (see Figure 9.2).

From this empirical evidence that knowledge is – and will continue to be – the main factor in value creation, the *demand for an efficient management of knowledge is evident*. This demand steadily increases because of

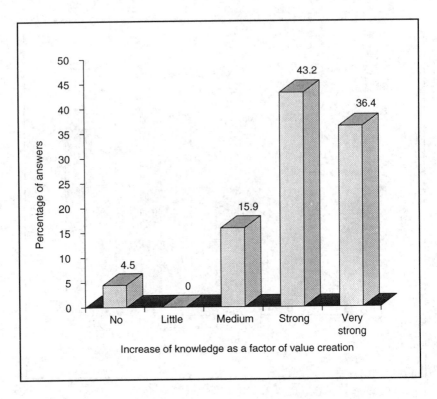

Figure 9.2 *Future development of knowledge as a factor of value creation*

large amounts of unused (and therefore 'wasted') organizational knowledge in every company. According to the empirical study (Graßhoff, 1996), in most cases 40% *of the given knowledge potential is left unused* within the organization and its value-creating processes. Even more surprisingly, in 46% of the cases, it was estimated that companies waste 60% to 80% of their knowledge.

Value Creation as a Process of Generating and Applying Knowledge

According to this empirical evidence, the demand for knowledge management (von Krogh and Roos, 1994; 1996; Nonaka and Takeuchi, 1995, Schmitz and Zucker, 1996) can also be illustrated along with the value chain of a company (see Figure 9.3). The elements of the value chain represent a systematically organized path of a product or service concept to a marketable product. Basically, *knowledge management is the organization of the flow of knowledge between the two poles of generating and applying organizational knowledge*. From this perspective, organiza-

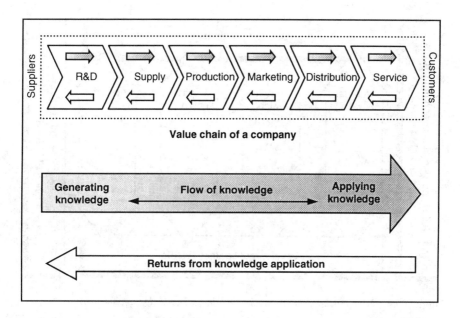

Figure 9.3 *The flow of organizational knowledge between generating and applying knowledge (Schüppel, 1996a: 50)*

tional knowledge is defined as the sum of individual knowledge used in the value creation process and the knowledge embedded in collective action.

Reversing this knowledge process which flows from an intangible to an increasingly tangible level, a *flow of potential returns out of the application of knowledge in goods and services* results. These returns can be reinvested into knowledge generation, so *the process is cyclically renewed* for product and service innovations.

The concept of an organization as a system of knowledge processes, with the reverse flow of returns to knowledge application, can be *reintroduced to the single parts* of the organizational value chain. For example, the R&D process can be characterized as a systematically organized flow of knowledge which ranges between the generation of ideas and the then marketable product concepts which have to be produced along the organizational value chain. In this context, the R&D department creates 'returns' to the application of its knowledge in the form of existing or future budgets etc. The structure also applies to all the other parts of the value chain.

It is implied in Figure 9.3 that the generation of knowledge does not always have to be an original element of the focal company or of the focal part of the value chain. Rather, in every part of the knowledge process, the pre-existing knowledge can be used as a starting point for their own generating process of knowledge. Therefore, the elements of

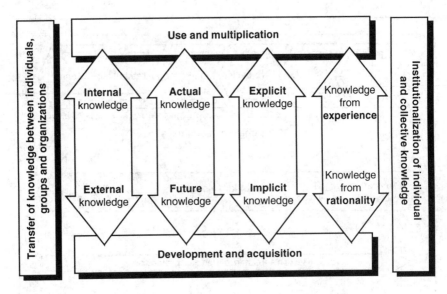

Figure 9.4 *Four bipolar dimensions for forming a knowledge management*

the value chain are interdependent with each other, as the whole value chain of a company is interdependent with its customers, suppliers, competitors etc.

The Constitutive Dimensions of Knowledge Management

Knowledge management is concerned with questions of knowledge production, reproduction, distribution, application and logistics, depending on who the specific bearer, mediator or multiplier of organizational knowledge is. The *goal of every action on the basis of knowledge management* is therefore (Schüppel, 1996a):

- *identifying and building* the essential competitive knowledge potentials
- *efficient use* of existing and established organizational knowledge
- *elimination* of knowledge and learning barriers.

Based on these goals, there are *four bipolar dimensions* to creating a knowledge management in managerial practice. Every bipolar dimension is a continuum with equal poles. Along with the bipolar dimensions, we can create options and install instruments for a knowledge management tailored to the specific situation of the focal company. Furthermore, the bipolar dimensions are strongly related to each other, which means that they cannot be managed in isolation from each other: in practice one has to jump from one dimension to another permanently (see Figure 9.4).

Knowledge management therefore tries to *optimize* the following *organizational knowledge potentials* along the four dimensions (Schüppel, 1996a: 197):

- First, the *inner* and *outer* knowledge potentials, answering the question: who is the relevant *bearer* of the necessary knowledge? Long-lasting competitive advantages can only be created if we professionally multiply the internal knowledge of the organization and all its individual members, and use the relevant external knowledge. Simply stated, within the value-creating process, the appropriate knowledge has to be 'in the right place at the right time'.
- Second, the *actual* and *future* knowledge potentials, answering the question: what is the *content* of the relevant knowledge? Actual knowledge ensures today's survival in competition; future knowledge opens up new fields for competitive advantages.
- Third, the *explicit* and *implicit* knowledge, related to the aspect of *visibility* and *communicability* of knowledge. Explicit knowledge 'on the surface' is usually bound to implicit elements of knowledge, so that the management of knowledge also has to focus on the underlying contextual framework. Nonaka (1991) has described the never-ending loop of externalization and internalization of knowledge within an organization. According to his view, the loop starts through the conversion of tacit individual knowledge to explicit knowledge through interactions. Explicit knowledge can then be combined to create new forms of knowledge and – even more important – be transferred to other individuals or groups.
- Fourth, the knowledge created out of *experience* and *rationality*, related to the aspect of *richness* and *validity* of knowledge. Knowledge management has to open up a wide field for personal and organizational experiences, but at the same time guarantee that these experiences can be systematically reflected. This dimension is also used by Nonaka, when he discussed quality and variety of individual knowledge.

The modelling of a *knowledge spiral* (Figure 9.5; see Nonaka, 1991; Nonaka and Takeuchi, 1995) along these bipolar dimensions aims at a *transfer of knowledge* between all individual members, groups, the whole organization and its environment. In addition, the main goal is the *institutionalization of individual and collective knowledge* within the focal organization. There are three possible levels of transferring knowledge: one is focused on the individual (from or to the individual), the second is focused on organizational subgroups (from or to groups), and the third is focused on the organization (from or to the organization). That implies that every action or instrument within the context of knowledge management should essentially support the intended transfer. On the other hand, knowledge has to be anchored in an organization independent of the original bearers.

Instruments to Establish a Knowledge Spiral in Practice along with the Constitutive Dimensions

There are numerous instruments in every bipolar dimension which can 'kick off' the above mentioned knowledge spiral. But before investing and implementing instruments of knowledge management in a focal organization, we must first examine the cultural situation. It is important to get the spiral started by using an instrument which fits each specific situation, and then accelerate it by using other instruments (see Figure 9.5). And before we look at the instruments it is appropriate to discuss what the *practical results* of the implementation of knowledge management instruments should be. These are:

- defending or developing market position
- improving performance
- ensuring competitiveness
- gaining an overview of existing organizational knowledge
- improving access to this knowledge
- efficient use of this knowledge.

Instruments for Using and Multiplying Internal Knowledge and for Acquiring External Knowledge

It is not surprising that we begin by looking at already existing organizational knowledge (Table 9.1). By managing *internal* knowledge, we take an *inside* perspective, focusing on:

- the evidence of individual and collective knowledge potentials and whether they are used and multiplied systematically
- whether problem-solving knowledge is used appropriately, in the right manner, quality and quantity
- the existence of measures to reduce the danger of individuals or groups leaving the company.

With the construction of a knowledge map, for example, companies try to get a systematic view on existing intellectual capital. In a reengineering project, Hoffmann LaRoche saw that the documentation within the licensing process of pharmaceuticals means more or less the 'mapping' of the knowledge flow within the product development. Adding an easy-to-use register, Hoffman LaRoche had something like the *Yellow Pages*, where they could identify relevant knowledge bearers according to the main problem fields of the company.

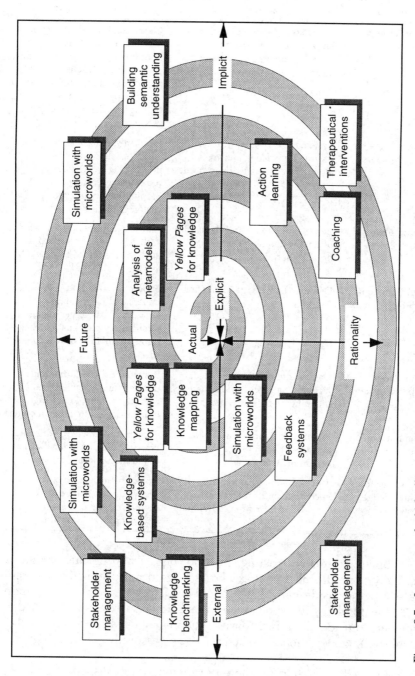

Figure 9.5 *Instruments for kick-off and acceleration of a knowledge spiral (Schüppel, 1996b)*

Table 9.1 *Instruments for the management of internal knowledge*

Instrument	Description	Intended effects
Knowledge mapping	Systematic review of existing knowledge potentials and mapping alongside the value chain	Clear visualization of present knowledge potentials; multiplying existing knowledge; elimination of 'useless' knowledge in core processes; finding opportunities for redesigning the knowledge process
Yellow Pages for knowledge	Systematic collection of problem-solving knowledge and tools alongside customer-driven needs	Problem-solving knowledge as an accessible resource; multiplying existing knowledge; recognizing redundancies; keeping the organization customer-focused
Knowledge brokers	Experts on supply and demand of knowledge within the organization	Professionalization of knowledge exchange, regarding speed and quality; creation of a knowledge market
Multifunctional project groups	Dynamic knowledge interaction in teams	Building shared and deeper understanding; creating new knowledge bases; increasing problem-solving capabilities through multiple knowledge bases
Knowledge-based systems	Database of existing knowledge; technical support for knowledge mapping and *Yellow Pages*	Systematizing, securing and documenting knowledge; institutionalizing knowledge independent of its original owner
Communication meetings	Platform for horizontal, vertical and lateral communication within the company	Support of knowledge diffusion; basis for the institutionalization of individual knowledge
Incentives for knowledge owners	Material and social incentives to encourage and preserve the knowledge flow from individuals	Protecting against loss of knowledge owners; basis for permanent use of existing knowledge

Mobilizing already existing internal organizational knowledge is certainly a promising way to elaborate significant productivity potentials. But the inside perspective could lead to a restrictive occupation with the focal organization, while there are also relevant knowledge elements outside their boundaries. By managing *external* knowledge (Table 9.2), we additionally take an *outside* perspective, examining:

- a focused mediation of internal, previously established knowledge and the necessary knowledge to survive in competition to detect knowledge leaks

Table 9.2 *Instruments for the management of external knowledge*

Instrument	Description	Intended effects
Knowledge benchmarking	Comparison of internal knowledge and market-relevant knowledge	Identifying 'knowledge holes'; basis for systematic acquisition of external knowledge
Mergers and acquisitions	Acquisition of external knowledge through insourcing (from cooperation to fusion)	Completing and enlarging the organizational knowledge base; revitalizing the business
Acquisition of consultant know-how	Temporary acquisition of external knowledge through insourcing	Completing and enlarging the organizational knowledge base regarding concrete problems; revitalizing the business
Stakeholder management	Acquisition of external knowledge through cooperation with all relevant stakeholders	Using external knowledge bases; systematically perceiving through other perspectives

- whether the knowledge potentials of the relevant stakeholders are used systematically
- whether there are supply strategies for transferring and institutionalizing external knowledge.

The Japanese company Toyota, for example, systematically uses the external know-how of its customers within the product development process. The R&D engineers for a minivan accompanied typical customers – carriers, drivers etc. – for up to six months through their daily work, *before* they designed the layout of the car. So they knew exactly, from customer experience, what the main success factors were, and they double-checked them in several car clinics.

Instruments for Using and Multiplying Actual Knowledge and for Building, Developing and Acquiring Future Knowledge Potentials

Actual knowledge is the basis for a company's survival in today's competition and for the cyclical renewal of its identity. Through the systematic multiplication of 'core competences' (Prahalad and Hamel, 1990) a company gets the chance to diversify its business and to open up its own market focus. By managing *actual* knowledge (Table 9.3), we then focus on:

- what knowledge is the core of our competitiveness
- in what way we can multiply this knowledge in different products and services.

According to that background, Sharp multiplies its core competence in LCD displays in different products like calculators, mini-television,

Table 9.3 *Instruments for the management of actual knowledge*

Instrument	Description	Intended effects
Actual knowledge profile	Listing the actual market-relevant knowledge for all products and services	Identifying core competences; identifying own market position
Building standard operating procedures	Standardization of existing knowledge in the form of replicable routines	Multiplying already successful knowledge procedures; institutionalizing knowledge independent of its original owner
Building centres of competence	Consolidation of core competences in organizational units	Market-oriented application of existing knowledge; basis for systematic acquisition of missing knowledge parts

laptops etc. In the same way, Honda uses its motor and gearing know-how in motorcycles, cars, lawnmowers, boat motors, generators etc. And Sony also takes the route of multiplying its actual know-how of miniaturizing products like cassette players, video cameras and CD players.

Looking at different ways to multiply actual knowledge in as many products and services as possible is only one side of the coin. To create and develop a sustainable competitive advantage, it is also necessary to envision future actions. By managing *future* knowledge potentials (Table 9.4), we therefore focus on:

- what we can do to develop a knowledge profile for future competitiveness
- procedures that keep cyclically renewing the knowledge base of an organization.

We can find a typical example within Daimler-Benz. The Research, Technology and Society Department organizes 'future-labs' in the company that aim at cross-functional dialogues to create a picture of what could be the market and consumer need in the future. Another example is the usage of the scenario technique, which enabled Shell to recover much better from the oil crisis than its competitors.

Instruments for Using and Multiplying Explicit Knowledge and for Making Implicit Knowledge Explicit

When we presented all the instruments for knowledge management, we used one hidden assumption: that knowledge is or can easily be encoded or materialized. We therefore always talked about a sort of knowledge, which is called explicit knowledge. By managing *explicit* knowledge (Table 9.5), we focus on:

Table 9.4   *Instruments for the management of future knowledge*

Instrument	Description	Intended effects
Future knowledge profile	List of necessary knowledge potentials for survival and future success	Identifying future customer needs; identifying future 'knowledge holes'
Continuous improvement	Permanent (also trivial or marginal) optimization of value creation processes	Actualization of the existing knowledge base; continuous improvement of core processes
Simulation with microworlds	Simulation of relevant environment conditions and their potential impact on the business	Sensitize for future developments and interdependencies; building already 'proven' options for quick reactions; building future knowledge potentials
Space for experiments	Free room, resources and fault tolerance regarding 'experiments' in the market	Encourage creativity and industriousness for future products, services and markets
Personnel and team development	Building future qualifications through all instruments of personnel and team development	Systematic, future-focused creation of knowledge potentials

Table 9.5   *Instruments for the management of explicit knowledge*

Instrument	Description	Intended effects
Materialization of knowledge in documents	Systematic collection of already explicit knowledge in distributable documents (knowledge maps, *Yellow Pages* etc.)	Basis for usage and distribution of knowledge and for standardization processes
Combination of materialized knowledge	Creation of new knowledge through 'endless' combination processes	Multiplying existing knowledge in different product and service contexts
Concepts for personnel integration	Familiarization with existing knowledge, procedures etc.	Internalizing already existing knowledge; reproducing standard operating procedures

- the factual materialization of explicit knowledge for everyone's use
- the widespread combination of single knowledge elements to new knowledge phenomena
- the internalization of collective knowledge.

Not all of the individual or organizational knowledge is explicit; a big part is not tangible, visible or expressible. This part of the knowledge often makes the difference. By managing *implicit* knowledge (Table 9.6), we examine for that reason:

Table 9.6   *Instruments for the management of implicit knowledge*

Instrument	Description	Intended effects
Learning by example	Perceiving, reflecting on and imitating existing procedures	Passing on implicit routines; standardizing procedures; socialization effects
Common sense in groups	Opening up horizons for collective actions	Passing on implicit knowledge through collective experience; building shared understanding
Metaphors, analogies, models	Using picture-like tools to represent implicit knowledge	Externalizing, articulating and passing on implicit knowledge; materializing knowledge
Shared vision	Discussion of central assumptions in groups	Externalizing, articulating and passing on implicit knowledge; building shared understanding

- the transfer of implicit knowledge through socialization processes
- the externalization or articulation of implicit knowledge
- the institutionalization of the articulated knowledge into the 'brain' of the organization.

Instruments for Using and Multiplying Knowledge from Experience and for Building and Developing Rational Knowledge

A majority of knowledge directly results from interactions with the environment. Through a cycle of acting, perceiving the results, building up options for potential new actions or reactions, then taking new actions, we build concrete knowledge from *experience* (Table 9.7). By managing that kind of knowledge, we examine:

- how we can foster the variety of individual and collective experiences
- measures to increase the fundamental and lasting impact of experiences.

The trainee programme of Goodyear focuses especially on the variety of experiences. All selected college students join a widespread rotation programme through all departments like R&D, sales, production, marketing etc. After this first part of the programme the trainees choose their specialization – but are still forced to extend their experience spectrum through several interfunctional courses.

Valid knowledge is built not only cyclically through experiences but also through careful analysis and reflection of experiences. By managing *rational* knowledge (Table 9.8), we focus on:

Table 9.7 *Instruments for the management of knowledge from experience*

Instrument	Description	Intended effects
Job rotation	Systematic change of workplace within and outside of the focal working team	Reducing monotony; support of integrative thinking and acting; increasing individual and collective flexibility; increasing individual knowledge
Teamwork	Delegating entire responsibilities to a self-regulating, partly autonomous team	Learning from one another in the team context; support of integrative thinking and acting; increasing individual and collective flexibility
Feedback loops	Creating a computer-based information system, coupled with existing knowledge-based systems	Scanning relevant reactions from the environment; making actions transparent
Arenas for action learning	Establishing project groups for concrete problems with systematic in-group feedback	Direct feedback on actions; improving feedback velocity and authenticity

Table 9.8 *Instruments for the management of knowledge of rationality*

Instrument	Description	Intended effects
Contemplative interactions	Allowing free room and organizational slack for 'non-action' interactions	Discursive reflection of actions, reactions, interactions, results etc.; learning from one another
Coaching	Systematic and professional consulting regarding individual personalities	Reflection on personal development; reframing own action patterns
Therapeutical interventions	Psychologically based interventions for individuals	Reflection on personal development; reframing own action patterns based on new attitudes and goals; reducing defensive routines
Reflecting systems archetypes	Explicit reflection of system patterns in workshops	Reflecting on the rules, norms, assumptions, values and the 'identity' of the whole system; positioning the system in its environment

- individual reflections
- collective reflections regarding groups or the whole organization.

According to that, Mercedes-Benz organized a series of 'workshops of change', where members of the management and employees discussed their form of leadership and other topics, like their own understanding of total quality management, customer orientation and the like.

Conclusion

In order to secure competitive advantage and to maintain a powerful market presence in the near future, companies will increasingly have to learn to manage their knowledge bases. This is certainly true as the service industry continues to grow more rapidly than ever, and knowledge becomes an integral part of every organization. Responsible knowledge management in the future will enable a dynamic and mutually beneficial transfer of information to all stakeholders in an issue. By actively using the different instruments described above, an organization will be able to start and successfully employ a knowledge spiral oriented toward increasing customer satisfaction, and, concomitant with that, increased productivity and innovation potentials.

The question now arises of how to have organizations implement these knowledge management strategies. It is important that every organization undergoes a rigorous and possibly painful analysis of its knowledge flows, so that all stakeholders understand the knowledge transfers among relevant groups. Future research should be dedicated to finding novel and effective ways of completing the transition to the knowledge society, and ensuring that every organization takes part in this vital shift of focus.

References

Bell, D. (1976) *The Coming of Post-Industrial Society: a Venture in Social Forecasting*. New York: Basic Books.

Drucker, P. (1986) The changed world economy. *Foreign Affairs*, 64: 768–91.

Gomez, P. and Müller-Stewens, G. (1994) Corporate transformation: Zum Management fundamentalen Wandels großer Unternehmen, in P. Gomez, D. Hahn, G. Müller-Stewens and R. Wunderer (eds), *Unternehmerischer Wandel: Konzepte zur organisatorischen Erneuerung*. Wiesbaden: Gabler. pp. 135–98.

Graßhoff, S. (1996) Nutzen, Einsatz und Gestaltung eines Wissensmanagements. Diploma thesis, Fachhochschule Kempten.

Hedberg, B. (1984), Organizations as tents: Über die Schwierigkeiten, Organisationsstrukturen flexibel zu gestalten, in H. Hinterhuber and G. Laske (eds), *Zukunftsorientierte Unternehmungspolitik*. Freiburg: Gabler. pp. 13–47.

Lane, R.E. (1966) The decline of politics and ideology in a knowledgeable society. *American Sociological Review*, 31: 649–62.

Machlup, F. (1981) *Knowledge and the Knowledge Production*. Princeton, NJ: John Wiley.

Nonaka, I. (1991) The knowledge creating company. *Harvard Business Review*, November–December: 96–104.

Nonaka, I. and Takeuchi, H. (1995) *The Knowledge-Creating Company: How Japanese Companies Create the Dynamics of Innovation*. New York: Oxford University Press.

Prahalad, C.K. and Hamel, G. (1990) The core competence of the corporation. *Harvard Business Review*, May–June: 71–91.

Schmitz, C. and Zucker, B. (1996) *Wissen gewinnt: Knowledge Flow Management*. Düsseldorf and Munich: Metropolitan.

Schüppel, J. (1996a) *Wissensmanagement: Organisatorisches Lernen im Spannungsfeld von Wissens- und Lernbarrieren*. Wiesbaden: Gabler.

Schüppel, J. (1996b) Wissensmanagement: Eine neue Dimension der Unternehmensführung? *Wissenschaftsmanagement*, May–June: 127–31.

Stehr, N. (1994) *Arbeit, Eigentum und Wissen: Zur Theorie von Wissensgesellschaften*. Frankfurt: Universitätsverlag.

von Krogh, G. and Roos, J. (eds) (1994) Knowledge in organizations, knowledge transfer and cooperative strategies. *International Business Review*, 3, Special Issue (4).

von Krogh, G. and Roos, J. (eds) (1996) *Managing Knowledge: Perspectives in Cooperation and Competition*. London: Sage.

Willke, H. (1995) Anschluß gesucht: Die Wissensgesellschaft und ihre Unternehmen. Paper presented at Workshop-Unterlagen zur Tagung 'Know-how flott machen' des Gottlieb-Duttweiler-Instituts, Rüschlikon, 9–10 February.

Zucker, B. and Schmitz, C. (1994) Knowledge flow management: Wissen nutzen statt verspielen. *Gablers Magazin*, 11–12: 62–5.

10

KNOWLEDGE AS A STRATEGIC RESOURCE

Gilbert Probst, Bettina Büchel and Steffen Raub

'In our view, the central competitive dimension of what firms know how to do is to create and transfer knowledge efficiently within an organizational context' (Kogut and Zander, 1993: 384). This statement not only points out that learning to manage knowledge is a source of competitive advantage, but also integrates two formerly separate streams of research: the resource-based view of the firm (Wernerfelt, 1984; Barney, 1991) and organizational learning (Fiol and Lyles, 1985; Huber, 1991).

One of the critical questions within the organizational learning field has been to establish a link between individual learning and organizational learning. Building on the idea that individual learning is not sufficient for organizations to be successful, organizational learning proposes that organizations need to be able to transform and distribute individual knowledge (Kim, 1993) and acquire new knowledge (MacDonald, 1995) in order to create a whole which is more than the sum of its parts. According to the resource-based view, those companies which secure resources such as knowledge that is rare, valuable, imperfectly imitable and non-substitutable obtain a competitive advantage (Barney, 1991).

The link between the resource-based view and organizational learning can be made by focusing on learning to develop organizational knowledge. While the resource-based view argues that the possession of strategic resources such as organizational knowledge leads to competitive advantage, the organizational learning literature suggests that the process of learning creates organizational knowledge. The question which follows is: how do organizations learn to develop organizational knowledge that leads to a competitive advantage? This chapter offers propositions which point towards the process of developing organizational knowledge.

Resource-Based View

One of the traditional foci of strategic management has been to explain sustained superior performance of companies and industries. Previously, superior performance was explained by analysing product–market positions (Porter, 1985). Industrial economists primarily focused on the environment and competition and paid little attention to the internal analysis of the firm. Contrary to the argument that industry structure is the determinant of competitive advantage (Porter, 1985), the resource-based view of the firm argues that the possession of unique resources within firms may be an important source of competitive advantage (Barney, 1991). The firm's unique capabilities in terms of distinctive knowledge and superior organizational routines are important sources of heterogeneity between firms that may result in sustained competitive advantage (Hitt and Ireland, 1985; Mahoney and Pandian, 1992).

The idea that resources can bestow a competitive advantage is not new. Various authors have discussed this issue under the terms 'distinctive' or 'firm-specific resources' (Hitt and Ireland, 1985), 'core competence' (Prahalad and Hamel, 1990), 'core capabilities' (Leonard-Barton, 1992; 1995) or 'strategic assets' (Dierickx and Cool, 1989). According to Barney, firm resources 'include all assets, capabilities, organizational processes, firm attributes, information, knowledge, etc.' (1991: 101). The above mentioned authors postulate that firms develop internal capabilities or knowledge over time which enable them to produce superior products. The unique aspect of such a perspective is its long-term orientation. The development of core competencies or capabilities is a long-term investment which results in improved performance in the future. Competencies are an interrelated mix of organizational knowledge which leads to an increase in the problem-solving capacity of an organization. It is the unique set of strategically relevant organizational knowledge which eventually leads to increased returns for a company (Hamel and Prahalad, 1994).

The resource-based view of the firm provides several criteria which indicate the necessary conditions for sustainable competitive advantage. In order to obtain a competitive advantage, this theory postulates that strategic resources must have four attributes: (a) they must be *valuable*, (b) they must be *rare*, (c) they must be *imperfectly imitable*, and (d) there *cannot be strategically equivalent substitutes* (Barney, 1991: 105–6). If organizational knowledge, one important element of a firm's strategic resources, fulfills these characteristics, the company is able to obtain a sustainable competitive advantage (Figure 10.1).

Valuable Knowledge

Valuable knowledge enables a firm to conceive of and implement strategies that improve its efficiency and effectiveness. This criterion is

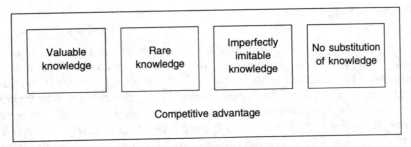

Figure 10.1 *Criteria for obtaining a competitive advantage*

fulfilled when organizational knowledge is able to exploit opportunities or neutralize threats in the environment.

Rare Knowledge

If a strategy has been implemented by few competitors and leads to a competitive advantage, then this strategy is considered to be based on rare organizational knowledge. Strategies demand a unique mix of knowledge in order to fulfil this criterion. Through a combination of physical, human and organizational elements, the firm is able to differentiate itself from its competitors. It is not a single element which allows a company to be competitive, but rather the combination of different elements of knowledge which allows a firm to fulfil the criterion of rare knowledge.

Imperfectly Imitable Knowledge

Imperfectly imitable knowledge is knowledge which cannot be possessed by competitors since the exact content or context of knowledge is unknown to both the owner and the potential imitator. The reasons for the lack of imitability frequently lie in (1) the unique historical conditions of development, (2) the ambiguity around the knowledge, and (3) the social complexity of knowledge (Barney, 1991: 107). Once organizational knowledge is distributed throughout the organization and difficult to localize, it frequently fulfils this criterion.

No Substitution of Knowledge

The last requirement for knowledge to lead to a competitive advantage is that it has no strategically equivalent substitutes. In order for a company to fulfil this criterion, it must have a resource that cannot be replaced by another resource of equal value.

There are two implications of the resource-based view. It recognizes that resources encompass tangible and intangible assets. Intangible assets are clearly the domain of organizational learning. Although these criteria indicate the necessary conditions for a competitive advantage, the resource-based view does not provide an explanation about how resources such as organizational knowledge develop over time.[1] Since questions of acquisition and development of organizational knowledge become increasingly relevant for the *management of knowledge*, the resource perspective essentially requires the organizational learning perspective to explain the development of organizational knowledge. The organizational learning perspective adds to strategic management by shifting the focus from a static view to a more dynamic view of organizations.

Organizational Learning

Essentially, the organizational learning concept has transported the idea of individual learning to the organizational level. Organizational learning has been presented from different angles. While some argue that it occurs at different levels – at the individual level, at the group level or over the whole organization (Probst and Büchel, 1996) – others have emphasized the learning processes, such as single-loop learning, double-loop learning and deutero-loop learning (Argyris and Schön, 1978) with different emphases on behavioural change and cognitive change. Although the variety of definitions of organizational learning may lead to scepticism regarding its value, a common denominator of the various definitions of learning seems to be the increase of knowledge and repertoire of action. Essentially, organizational learning is an increase of the organizational knowledge base[2] which leads to the enhancement of the problem-solving potential of a company (Probst and Büchel, 1996). This requires the development of organizational knowledge.

Companies differ in their organizational knowledge and these differences generally lead to persisting effects on relative performance. Owing to the existence of difference in performance, it is reasonable to assume that organizational knowledge has certain characteristics which hinder companies from replicating the knowledge and thereby make it a source of competitive advantage. The first characteristic refers to the complexity of knowledge. Complex knowledge involves a high number of parameters which constantly change. As the complexity of knowledge increases, it becomes more and more difficult to replicate all parameters involved. The second characteristic is the difficulty of codifying knowledge. Codifiability refers to the ability of a firm to structure knowledge into a set of identifiable rules and relationships that can easily be communicated (Kogut and Zander, 1993: 367). Since knowledge is context-sensitive and history-dependent, structuring knowledge into rules independent of both context and history is a difficult task. The third characteristic concerns the embodiment of knowledge in human beings, norms and values. Since knowledge is rarely independent of individuals, replication requires access to the individuals with the relevant knowledge. The fourth characteristic is the unique trajectories of knowledge development. Since the development of knowledge may take certain paths that cannot be traced back, it is difficult to replicate.

In the following section, three propositions are posited that attempt to explain the development of organizational knowledge with the above mentioned characteristics that make it rare, imperfectly imitable, valuable and lacking substitutes. These propositions highlight the *transformation, distribution* and *integration* of knowledge within the organization. The transformation of knowledge changes the structure of knowledge; the distribution of knowledge changes the concentration of knowledge within the organization; and the integration of knowledge changes the combination of existing and new knowledge.

Transformation of Knowledge

It is proposed that looking at the link between different levels of analysis – individual, group and organization – will provide new insight into the structure of organizational knowledge. The structure of organizational knowledge explains the complexity of knowledge.

According to organizational learning theorists (Fiol and Lyles, 1985; Huber, 1991), knowledge resides not only within individuals, but in the routines of the organization.[3] One of the most challenging steps for a theory on organizational learning is the transformation of individual skills into organizational routines. Although the organizational learning literature argues that the whole is more than the sum of its parts (Probst and Büchel, 1996), the connection between the individual level and organizational levels is perhaps the weakest link in the chain of arguments forwarded by organizational learning theorists.[4]

It is proposed that the development of organizational knowledge is mediated through multiple levels. At the individual level, interpretation of the environment leads to the revision of individual knowledge structures (Walsh, 1995). At the group level, individual knowledge structures are synthesized to create shared beliefs. At the organizational level, the routinization of shared beliefs leads to organizational knowledge.

Whereas learning at the individual level focuses on the *assimilation* of new information into past experiences, learning at the group level entails the transformation of individual experience into group knowledge. Since any single person's knowledge is incomplete, effective organizational action requires communicating and combining individual knowledge (Klayman and Schoemaker, 1993: 163). Organizational knowledge is not achieved by aggregating individual knowledge. Through social interaction between individuals, knowledge is synthesized. As Wiley states, 'intersubjectivity is emergent upon the interchange and synthesis of two, or more, communicating selves' (1988: 258). Through the process of interpreting actions and events, the group reaches consensus about action–outcome relationships which provide the negotiated norms based on which the group acts. The interaction creates agreements in a communication process and thereby leads to shared beliefs. It is not the aggregation or multiplication of individual interpretations which leads to group knowledge, but the *synthesis* of several interpretations.

The organizational level is the next level of emergence which Weick (1995) labelled 'interaction representation', referring to the process of consciously documenting the exchange between individuals. Put in different terms, this level results in the *routinization* of knowledge through representation of interactions manifested in organizational systems (Nelson and Winter, 1982). Organizational routines are a set of tasks that individuals and groups conduct in a coherent manner based on shared beliefs between group members.

The key feature of the transformation process is the complex relationship between the different levels. It is not a single level which allows a company to be competitive, but the combination of knowledge at different levels. Through exchange, individual knowledge is synthesized to arrive at group knowledge. This knowledge is routinized at the organizational level. By combining different levels of knowledge and different types of knowledge at each level, the organization can develop rare and imperfectly imitable knowledge.

Proposition 1   In order to develop organizational knowledge that leads to a competitive advantage, groups need to synthesize individual interpretations and routinize these at the organizational level.

Transforming individual knowledge into organizational routines leads to complex and embodied knowledge. Complex and embodied knowledge satisfies both the criteria of rare and imperfectly imitable knowledge. The transformation process makes knowledge difficult to imitate since the exact content is unknown. If this knowledge is the basis of a competitive advantage, competitors would want access to it. This demands replication or imitation. Once organizational knowledge has been imitated, the strategy based on rare knowledge will no longer lead to a competitive advantage. Thus rare and imperfectly imitable knowledge are closely linked.

Distribution of Knowledge

In order to synthesize and routinize individual interpretations into organizational knowledge, there is a need for a certain amount of consensus between individuals about the content of knowledge. Yet, organizational learning also implies that the development of different interpretations leads to an increase of the organizational knowledge base (Huber, 1991). Through the creation of a greater variety of interpretations, new ideas enter into the organization, thereby increasing the amount of knowledge. It is here that a controversial debate about the distribution of knowledge starts. The distribution of knowledge is the extent of overlap about the knowledge content at different levels.

While it can be argued that shared interpretations about the knowledge content will allow the organization to act in accordance with the consensus reached, different interpretations are said to increase the potential for problem solving in the future. As Huber argues, 'it seems reasonable to conclude that more learning has occurred when more and more varied interpretations have been developed, because such development changes the range of the organization's potential behaviors, and this is congruent with the definition of learning' (1991: 102). Yet, at the same time, Huber argues that there is a need for a common or shared understanding among the organization's units that various interpretations exist, thus requiring consensus about interpretations. This shows the relativity of the learning concept, since both consensus and diversity are necessary for learning to occur (Fiol, 1994). To summarize, one could argue that learning requires stable interpretations and a greater variety of interpretations at the same time. Balancing these two ends is a question of the organization's need for change and the desired stability.

Resolving the dilemma between shared and diverse interpretations demands differentiation between 'core knowledge' and 'peripheral knowledge' (Lyles and Schwenk, 1992). Whereas core knowledge refers to the goals of the organization, its vision and mission, peripheral knowledge pertains to the means–end relationships to achieve these goals. One can further distinguish between 'tangible core knowledge' (measurable goals) and 'intangible core knowledge' (goals of a qualitative nature). According to Bourgeouis (1980) organizations yield the highest performance when organizational members have shared interpretations about peripheral knowledge and tangible core knowledge.

In order for concerted action to take place, the firm has to decide on the right allocation of resources to achieve the desired goals. Internally consistent strategies demand agreement on the choice of means in order to avoid a clash between different functional areas. This requires agreement about 'the relative emphasis placed on a selected subset of goals for which measurable targets are easily established, and on the competitive strategies to be used to attain those goals' (1980: 244). There is, however, sufficient room for diverse interpretations about less tangible goals of the organization.[5] Donnellon et al. (1986) suggest that only minimal shared interpretations are necessary in order to produce organized action. Basically organizational members only need to share that knowledge which will continue exchange between organizational members (Donnellon et al., 1986).

Proposition 2   In order to develop organizational knowledge that leads
    to a competitive advantage, consensus about that knowledge which
    produces organized action is necessary.

By developing consensus about tangible core knowledge, the organization focuses on a jointly defined direction. At the same time, sufficient
space is left to increase the diversity of interpretations about less
tangible goals. Essentially, the organization needs to be able to increase
its knowledge base in order to avoid core competencies becoming core
rigidities (Leonard-Barton, 1995). This increase allows the organization
to select from a greater pool of strategies and the potential range of
strategies avoids the organization becoming blinded.

When organizational members have developed consensus about that
knowledge which produces organized action, they are guided by agreement about the anticipated consequences of their behaviour (Gray et al.,
1985). In this case, a rule governs behaviour. These rules are distributed
within the organization through repeated use and become embodied in
norms and values.

Once organizational knowledge is distributed throughout the
organization in the form of rituals and norms and is difficult to localize,
it fulfils the criteria of imperfectly imitable knowledge. The lack of
imitability lies in the unique historical conditions of development, the
ambiguity of shared interpretations, and the complexity of consensus.
These conditions of knowledge distribution enable organizations to
obtain a competitive advantage.

Integration of Knowledge

Notions of the learning organization have often emphasized internal
aspects of knowledge and neglected the external (MacDonald, 1995).
Other than the transformation and distribution of knowledge, the organization also learns when knowledge is acquired outside the boundaries
of the firm and integrated with existing knowledge. It is essential to
recognize that most information exists outside the boundaries of the
organization and needs to be integrated. In order to develop organizational knowledge leading to a sustainable competitive advantage, the
incorporation and integration of information which is available outside
the borders of the company are a necessary condition.

Yet, the integration of external knowledge is a challenge. External
knowledge does not always fit with the existing knowledge base of the
firm. Reluctance to consider knowledge not invented within the organization is a classic example of internal resistance to change. The need for
change connected with the acquisition and integration of external knowledge frequently leads to a preference for the use of internal knowledge. If,
however, the integration of external knowledge is required to exploit

opportunities or neutralize threats in the environment, then the obvious organizational response is to acquire the knowledge by capturing the source (MacDonald, 1995). 'It must bring home this new information to be mixed with resident information to shape a novel pattern of knowledge into a package that can be used' (1995: 562). By integrating external and internal knowledge, the company acquires valuable knowledge.

Proposition 3   In order to develop organizational knowledge that leads to a competitive advantage, the integration of external knowledge into the existing organizational knowledge base is necessary.

Through increased information gathering from the environment, the organization is able to gain greater awareness of the threats and opportunities in the environment and thereby increase its 'absorptive capacity' (Cohen and Levinthal, 1990). Absorptive capacity is a firm's ability to recognize the value of new external information, assimilate it and apply it to commercial ends, and is a function of a firm's existing knowledge. Organizational knowledge develops by recombinations of existing and new knowledge since a firm cannot separate itself from existing knowledge (Kogut and Zander, 1993: 392).

This recombination requires interpretation. Sufficient compatibility between existing knowledge and new knowledge is necessary in order for the external knowledge to be considered valuable. Compatibility requires organizational members to recognize the connection between existing and new knowledge in order to be able to integrate it. Languaging is the process through which the connections between existing and new knowledge are created (von Krogh et al., 1994). This process enables the development of valuable knowledge.

Different strategies may be employed to integrate external knowledge that exploits opportunities and neutralizes threats. Informal networks are a useful strategy for obtaining external knowledge. Informal networks of organizational members across different organizations allow for an exchange of information that may be integrated with existing knowledge. The likelihood that organizational members have received knowledge that is compatible with what is already in use is high in informal networks (MacDonald, 1995). Hence the importance of boundary spanners, individuals who provide the link between internal and external systems.

Implications for Research

The three propositions contribute to the strategic management literature by pointing out how learning to develop organizational knowledge can lead to a competitive advantage. Organizational learning contributes to the strategy perspective by conceiving the organization as a dynamic, integrated system that constantly changes. Within this context, organizational knowledge is not a physical product, but socially constructed. For this reason, knowledge itself is dynamic and cannot be easily imitated. This explains why firms may differ over time, as they have developed organizational knowledge through social interactions that cannot be replicated by other organizations.

While strategic management aims to explain survival and advancement of firms as well as striking a balance between the two, learning shows *how* developing organizational knowledge may explain differences among firms in their ability to advance. It may well be that the speed at which firms develop organizational knowledge is at the core of a firm's advancement capability. Yet, it is not only the speed of development, but also the speed of replication of that knowledge which determines the competitive advantage of a firm. If the organizational knowledge which lies at the core of a firm's competitive advantage can easily be replicated, then companies may only have a temporary advantage. The fundamental paradox with organizational knowledge is that the codification and simplification of knowledge induces replication which lowers the likelihood of a firm's ability to gain a sustainable competitive advantage. Long-term survival involves a complex trade-off between current profitability based on existing organizational knowledge and investing in developing new organizational knowledge to capture future opportunities. Yet, learning involves not only the development of organizational knowledge, but also deciding which knowledge to maintain or develop.

Although they represent only a modest attempt at integrating two formerly separate streams of research, the propositions nonetheless guide further research. The first implication of these propositions is to develop measures in order to empirically test the propositions. Developing measures involves operationalizing the organizational knowledge construct. This is probably one of the most difficult and challenging steps. Walsh (1995) has attempted to define knowledge structure[6] at different levels of analysis and classified knowledge structure into representation, development and use, yet his concept of a knowledge structure does not necessarily help to operationalize organizational knowledge. He nonetheless provides a list of methods and techniques that may be employed to operationalize organizational knowledge. Yet, operationalizing organizational knowledge is just the first step. What is equally important is to study organizations over time in order to be able to trace the development of organizational knowledge and its consequences for obtaining a competitive advantage. At this stage, the field is primarily establishing theoretical links. During this process, researchers have recognized that studying organizational knowledge development is a complex social phenomenon that may require revisiting existing research methods.

Implications for Management

Although there are still many unexplained questions in the area of knowledge development, we can nonetheless provide managers with some guidelines. Managers have to address the development of organizational knowledge in three areas. First of all, the transformation of individual knowledge into organizational routines demands increased emphasis on communication between individuals and groups. It is only through increased exchange between individuals and group members that individual interpretations are synthesized in order to create coordinated group action. Greater emphasis should be placed on institutionalizing the exchange between groups through increased communication.

The second management task is to create a collective understanding between decision-makers about that knowledge which leads to organized action. To promote the development of organizational knowledge, managers have to encourage the development of conflicting views about less tangible goals while striving for consensus about issues that either require immediate implementation or are broad enough to incorporate diverse views.

The third management task is to focus the organization on the acquisition of external information. For this purpose, boundary-spanning individuals and groups play a crucial role. Boundary spanners represent the link between the internal and external organization and contribute to the acquisition of external information. By fostering the participation of individuals and groups in networks across organizational boundaries, management increases the likelihood that relevant information is integrated with existing knowledge in the organization.

All of the above mentioned activities demand increased communication between organizational members. Since organizations and their members process information through a number of different channels, managers ought to consider the channels or media that are used for communication. This is an area that demands further research.

Conclusion

This chapter shows how the development of organizational knowledge will allow companies to obtain a competitive advantage. Knowledge needs to be transformed, distributed and integrated in order to fulfil the necessary conditions for companies to be successful. The propositions about knowledge development provide not only the beginning of further research about the organizational knowledge construct and its link to competitive advantage, but also guidelines for the management of knowledge.

Notes

1 Dierickx and Cool (1989) argue that strategic assests or core capabilities are accumulated over a period of time.

2 We assume that organizational knowledge is socially constructed, history-dependent, context-sensitive and shared by organizational members.

3 Nelson and Winter (1982) were the first to separate individual skills from routines whereby routines determine organizational behaviour and make the organization independent of individual contributions.

4 There are a number of authors who refer to learning at different levels of analysis (Sandelands and Stablein, 1987; Walsh and Ungson, 1991; Lyles and Schwenk, 1992). Although these authors provide arguments for the existence of learning at the organizational level, they refer back to the individual or group level to determine the criteria for learning at the organizational level.

5 As Bourgeois argues, 'assuming first that performance is the *dependent* variable, that is, that variations in strategy making lead to or "cause" performance, we can conclude that although *agreement* on *both* means and ends yields higher than average economic performance, the *greatest* performance occurs when strategy makers agree on means, agree on a narrow range of operable goals, and disagree on the less tangible goals' (1980: 243).

6 A knowledge structure is a 'mental template that individuals impose on an information environment to give it form and meaning' (Walsh, 1995: 281).

References

Argyris, C. and Schön, D. (1978) *Organizational Learning: a Theory of Action Perspective*. Reading, MA: Addison-Wesley.

Barney, J. (1991) Firm resources and sustained competitive advantage. *Journal of Management*, 17: 99–120.

Bourgeois, L.J. (1980) Performance and consensus. *Strategic Management Journal*, 1: 227–48.

Cohen, W. and Levinthal, D. (1990) Absorptive capacity: a new perspective on learning and innovation. *Administrative Science Quarterly*, 35: 128–52.

Dierickx, I. and Cool, K. (1989) Asset stock accumulation and sustainability of competitive advantage. *Management Science*, 35: 1504–11.

Donnellon, A., Gray, B. and Bougop, M.G. (1986) Communication, meaning and organized action. *Administrative Science*, 31: 43–55.

Fiol, C.M. (1994) Consensus, diversity, and learning in organizations. *Organization Science*, 5: 403–20.

Fiol, C.M. and Lyles, M.A. (1985) Organizational learning. *Academy of Management Journal*, 10: 803–13.

Gray, B., Bougon, M.G. and Donnellon, A. (1985) Organizations as constructions and destructions of meaning. *Journal of Management*, 11: 83–98.

Hamel, G. and Prahalad, C.K. (1994) *Competing for the Future: Breakthrough Strategies for Seizing Control of Your Industry and Creating the Markets of Tomorrow*. Boston: Harvard Business School Press.

Hitt, M.A. and Ireland, R.D. (1985) Corporate distinctive competence, strategy, industry and performance. *Strategic Management Journal*, 6: 273–93.

Huber, G.P. (1991) Organizational learning: the contributing processes and the literatures. *Organization Science*, 2: 88–115.

Kim, D.H. (1993) The link between individual and organizational learning. *Sloan Management Review*, 35: 37–50.

Klayman, J. and Schoemaker, P.J.H. (1993) Thinking about the future: a cognitive perspective. *Journal of Forecasting*, 12: 161–86.

Kogut, B. and Zander, U. (1993) Knowledge of the firm and evolutionary theory of the multinational corporation. *Journal of International Business Studies*, 24: 625–45.

Leonard-Barton, D. (1992) Core capabilities and core rigidities: a paradox in managing new product development. *Strategic Management Journal*, 13: 111–25.

Leonard-Barton, D. (1995) *Wellsprings of Knowledge: Building and Sustaining the Sources of Innovation*. Boston: Harvard Business School Press.

Lyles, M.A. and Schwenk, C.R. (1992) Top management, strategy and organizational knowledge structures. *Journal of Management Studies*, 29: 155–74.

MacDonald, S. (1995) Learning to change: an information perspective on learning in the organization. *Organization Science*, 6: 557–68.

Mahoney, J.T. and Pandian, J.R. (1992) The resource-based view within the conversation of strategic management. *Strategic Management Journal*, 13: 363–80.

Nelson, R. and Winter, S.G. (1982) *An Evolutionary Theory of Economic Change*. Cambridge, MA: Harvard University Press.

Porter, M. (1985) *Competitive Advantage of Nations*. New York: Free Press.

Prahalad, C.K. and Hamel, G. (1990) The core competence of the corporation. *Harvard Business Review*, 68: 79–91.

Probst, G.J.B. and Büchel, B.S.T. (1996) *Organizational Learning: the Competitive Advantage of the Future*. London: Prentice-Hall.

Sandelands, L.E. and Stablein, R.E. (1987) The concept of organization mind. *Research in the Sociology of Organizations*, 5: 135–62.

Von Krogh, G., Roos, J. and Slocum, K. (1994) An essay on corporate epistemology. *Strategic Management Journal*, 15: 53–71.

Walsh, J.P. (1995) Managerial and organizational cognition: notes from a trip down memory lane. *Organization Science*, 6: 280–321.

Walsh, J.P. and Ungson, G.R. (1991) Organizational memory. *Academy of Management Review*, 16: 57–91.

Weick, K.E. (1995) *Sensemaking in Organizations*. Thousand Oaks, CA: Sage.

Wernerfelt, B. (1984) A resource-based view of the firm. *Strategic Management Journal*, 5: 171–80.

Wiley, N. (1988) The micro–macro problem in social theory. *Sociological Theory*, 6: 254–61.

11

COMPETING WITH INTELLECTUAL CAPITAL

Donald A. Marchand

Not surprisingly, most managers agree that knowledge and information are critical factors for learning, changing and competing today in service and manufacturing companies alike. Yet, in many discussions of 'the learning organization', 'change management' and 'competitive advantage', the practical links between managers thinking about these concerns and how they manage knowledge and information are often weak to non-existent. Therefore, the managerial issue addressed in this chapter is, first, how to think about the interactions between information and knowledge and, second, how to use these interactions to develop and manage intellectual capital for competing more effectively.

My objective is to present a framework which demonstrates that the relationship between knowledge and information is continuously changing and interactive in companies. These continuous conversion processes between knowledge and information provide opportunities for improving the ways firms compete. To introduce the topic, I will clarify the relationships between learning, changing and competing with knowledge and information. Second, I will present a framework for the interaction of knowledge and information. Third, I will illustrate the business value of this linkage through one company's pioneering efforts to link its business strategy and performance with the measurement and management of 'intellectual capital', namely Skandia Group's Assurance and Financial Services (AFS). Finally, I will draw three conclusions from our discussion. One, managing the conversion processes between knowledge and information can lead to innovative business strategies for competing by leveraging these assets directly inside the firm and externally with partners and customers. Two, understanding the link between knowledge and information helps us avoid increased confusion about where one begins and the other ends. Most academic and managerial discussions of 'knowledge management' confuse the two terms or use them inter-changeably. Three, managing the conversion processes between knowledge and information can lead to innovative business strategies, structures and processes where companies use these assets better and faster than their competitors.

Linking Knowledge and Information to Learning in Business

We measure, use and manage knowledge and information to learn and change because they are critical to successful competition over time. For example, in defining the five main activities of a learning organization, Garvin lists: 'systematic problem solving, experimentation with new approaches, learning from their own experience and past history, learning from the experiences and best practices of others, and transferring knowledge quickly and efficiently throughout the organization' (1993: 81). Each of these activities must be accompanied by specific management processes to sense, acquire, organize and apply knowledge and information inside the company. As the vast and growing literature in this area shows, this is easier said than done. Some companies manage to balance a spontaneous, creative, dynamic and experimental mode and a more structured, codified, controlled and measured mode of working. Others do not.

In their study of some 40 companies, Graham and Pizzo (1996) found that those companies that managed the balance between the 'fluid' and 'institutional' modes most effectively had made knowledge management explicit, and central to their strategy, for instance by articulating and pursuing learning goals from their strategy. About a third of the companies interviewed fell into this category. The remaining companies studied did not find this balance.

Similarly, managing change involves at its core 'restructuring the information and knowledge people use to make decisions' (Jensen, 1996: 9). The process of implementing changes in the ways people learn and behave in the business to improve performance is not effective without redefining the ways individuals, teams and business units acquire, share, use and transform knowledge and information to compete more effectively.

Finally, the concept of competition incorporates directly the idea of using knowledge and information as sources of differentiation. Even under conditions of what classical economists call 'perfect competition', knowledge and information only cease to be sources of competitive differentiation because all market players are assumed to be competing on price and are 'equally' well informed and knowledgeable. In all other forms of competition – a monopolistic market, moderate competition among industry leaders or 'hyper-competition' (D'Aveni, 1994) – knowledge and information among competitors are critical resources for differentiation and value-creating activities with customers. Thus, every firm can be evaluated on the basis of how knowledge is developed, shared and applied to improve the firm's actions. The question is *not* whether or not a company competes with knowledge and information. The question is *how effectively* the company is in employing knowledge and information to learn and change continuously for competitive advantage.

The Relationship between Knowledge and Information

Understanding the relationship between knowledge and information is fundamental to my thesis. Although knowledge and information are often used interchangeably, most managers and scholars recognize that knowledge is different from but directly linked to information. Yet, the ways these two concepts are distinguished and yet related to each other are often unclear, and not explained.

Let me begin with the view that *data* are context free: they are the smallest differences that can be picked up by our senses. Data can always be shared among people because the receiver does not or cannot interpret them. An e-mail distributed to all employees in a company is just data to those who share no context for its interpretation.

Information, contrary to data, can never be context free or value neutral. Information includes all the documents and verbal messages that make sense or can be interpreted by organizational members. Moreover, information always encompasses an act of transfer or sharing among people.

Knowledge, finally, differs from information in that it resides in people; it is always personal. As has been pointed out by several authors, 'to know' means not only to understand or believe, but also to use or apply one's knowledge. In the context of organizations, it is obvious that knowledge depends on the interaction of people for its development (Nonaka and Takeuchi, 1995; von Krogh and Roos, 1995).

From this perspective, information use is the intermediate step and, therefore, essential to knowledge development, since it is through information represented in what we say, what we write and what we present that we develop new knowledge. Information involves the actions of sensing, collecting, organizing, processing, communicating and using expressions and representations of our or others' knowledge, whereas knowledge emphasizes personal interpreting and understanding.

Both knowledge and information are context-specific for their meaning: knowledge depends on context for expressing beliefs and commitments, whereas information depends on context for its use or application. Thus, it is not appropriate to use the terms 'knowledge' and 'information' interchangeably, since the terms refer to related but different ways of acting. We can use the distinction of Polanyi and suggest that

Knowledge   *to*   Information

	Knowledge	Information
Knowledge	Tacit to tacit Information transfer between people (conversation	Tacit to explicit A person transfers knowledge through documents, messages, data
Information	Explicit to tacit Documents, data, messages convey meaning to a person	Explicit to explicit Information about information: documents, data, messages are organized into indexes, maps, rules and repositories

from

Figure 11.1   *Converting knowledge to/from information*

whereas it is possible to *articulate* information, knowledge is *tacit*. Moreover, any attempt to 'manage' knowledge and information always involves understanding the context and content of the knowledge or information being used.

An important aspect of the relationship between knowledge and information is the *continuous conversion that goes on from knowledge to information and from information to knowledge in an organization*. In this context, Nonaka and Takeuchi's view of the conversion between tacit and articulated knowledge is a useful way of understanding the continuous conversion of knowledge and information between business units as well as within groups and among individuals in a business organization. Each of the quadrants in Figure 11.1 describes the four types of *conversion processes involving information and knowledge*.

Knowledge to Knowledge

The first quadrant of Figure 11.1 represents the transfer of information directly between people either on a one-to-one basis or in small groups. The primary mode of information transfer is 'conversation' where people interact through shared language, signs and symbols as well as expressions both facial and physical. In this form of knowledge transfer, individuals are able to express and convey their individualized knowledge through the 'shorthand' of expressions, metaphors, key phrases and emotions. Depending on how well individuals 'know' each other in terms of past experiences or relationships, the transfer or sharing of knowledge as well as its development through conversation is largely tacit – that is, intuitive and often metaphorical.

The limitations on converting knowledge to knowledge directly between people in conversations are primarily ones of time, geographic location and size of organizational unit. People do not have the time in their schedules to physically meet or speak over the phone. Geographic distances make it difficult to meet even in small groups. And, the number of people that a person must converse with quickly becomes too large for regular face-to-face contact. In addition, developing and maintaining a shared language over time between people to facilitate knowledge development and sharing may also be affected by similar limitations. Thus, managers and employees either quickly reach the limits of face-to-face knowledge exchange or must develop the means to represent knowledge and distribute it to those in the organization who 'need to know'.

Knowledge to Information

The second quadrant in Figure 11.1 represents the inevitable need that individuals have to transfer their knowledge into artefacts for communicating their knowledge (indirectly) to others. Paper is perhaps the most powerful and prevalent means in most organizations through which people create documents and messages to express their knowledge or beliefs. Today, we supplement the use of paper documents, records and faxes with e-mails and digital representations of our knowledge which can be shared asynchronously on a global basis with those whom we believe we must share our knowledge about customers, services, operations and change initiatives. Making explicit our tacit knowledge as individuals, as much as we can, has a powerful effect in organizations where efficiency and productivity require collaborative activities across time, space and levels of organizational responsibility.

The dangers that we as individuals face in turning our knowledge into various artefacts for broader distribution and sharing in our organizations are twofold. First, we must be willing to *trust* other members of the organization with our thoughts, beliefs and knowledge. This means that we believe that sharing our knowledge is more useful than retaining it. In this sense, we trust other people not to use our knowledge against us in a competitive sense and we believe that organizational goals are better served by expressing our knowledge rather than holding it to ourselves.

The second danger is that whenever we express our personal knowledge in artefacts such as e-mails, electronic documents or faxes, our knowledge becomes 'frozen in time' or reified in the document itself. Wherever that document is circulated or whoever accesses the document in paper or digital form will be reading a 'dated' expression of our knowledge. Given that our knowledge is constantly changing over time, the existence of information in the form of documents, messages and data means that we are constantly running the risk in organizations that people will decide or act on knowledge that is outdated or perhaps may be wrong at a later point in time.

Information to Knowledge

The third quadrant focuses on the processes whereby individuals access and interpret information in its many forms or expressions and seek meaning from the artefacts available to them. That is, they must decide explicitly or intuitively to search for and access other people's knowledge in the form of documents, messages and data, and incorporate or discard the information according to their view of its usefulness or value. Thus, the act of deriving meaning (i.e. adding to our knowledge) *from* information is as important as the act of conveying meaning *through* information.

However, several problems arise in seeking meaning from information. First, there may be too much information potentially available to us electronically and manually which we have neither the time nor the attention to interpret. Second, the information that is accessible to us over our desktops and workstations may be of variable quality and integrity. So, we must evaluate whether the documents that we see on the screen are valid, reliable or consistent. Third, our personal mindset may dispose us to select some documents as meaningful and ignore others, even though the documents ignored could have a major impact on our knowledge of events or people.

As time pressures, distance and the pace of events make organizational members more reliant on digital artefacts for sharing and gaining knowledge rather than personal contacts and conversations, the challenges of using information which others have produced affects the capability of an organization to learn and respond to change.

Information about Information

The final quadrant in Figure 11.1 deals with the need in most organizations for 'information about information' or meta-information. Stated simply, most organizations rely on many forms of directories, catalogues, indexes and maps to locate information or people in a physical sense. These forms of meta-information are so obvious to us that we often take them for granted except when we cannot find someone or some key document that we need. In the knowledge-based organization today, these forms of directories and maps for locating people or information are being supplemented by 'knowledge maps', *Yellow Pages* and other representations of who possesses what knowledge or expertise in the organization and how it might be accessed and tapped.

In addition, for selected areas of knowledge in the organization, if we can make explicit the knowledge and decision rules that people use, then we can develop an 'expert' system that replicates or incorporates in software the knowledge-based rules that people use to solve specific problems or perform complex tasks. Increasingly today, managing knowledge effectively in organizations involves shifting knowledge from the exclusive possession of individuals to an explicit, shared resource through the use of knowledge maps, repositories, databases and expert systems.

All business organizations are continuously converting knowledge to information and vice versa. However, few companies focus and manage these conversion processes as a key part of their business strategy for winning in the marketplace. In addition, even fewer companies have developed a view of 'intellectual capital' which includes a strategic focus on converting knowledge and information effectively not only inside the company, but also with suppliers, partners and customers. To illustrate how a company focuses on the conversion processes between knowledge and information as part of its competitive strategy, I will discuss the pioneering efforts of the Skandia Group's Assurance and Financial Services (AFS) unit to incorporate in its successful business strategy over the last few years an innovative way of managing 'intellectual capital' which depends on the effective and continuous conversion of knowledge and information among suppliers, employees, agents and customers to compete in the insurance and financial services markets. In addition, the case also shows how the AFS unit is continuously seeking to convert personal knowledge into what it calls 'structural capital' which permits knowledge to be retained in the form of information and meta-information and be reused by the company even after some employees have retired or left the company.

Company Illustration: Skandia AFS

With over US$35 billion in assets, the parent company is Skandia Insurance Company Ltd established in 1855.[1] The Skandia Group markets a wide range of products in the direct insurance and reinsurance markets, as well as in the savings market for individuals, businesses and the public sector. The Group is organized, as Figure 11.2 indicates, into four operating units.

Based in Stockholm, the Group employs approximately 10,000 people. The most rapidly growing division of the group, Skandia Assurance and Financial Services, manages some 70 billion Swedish crowns (approximately US$10 billion) worth of assets and operates in 15 countries including the UK and the US. AFS's products consist of flexible unit-linked insurance and pension plans, which are adapted to local legislation. In some markets, investment funds without an insurance component are offered. Customers are free to choose both the manager and the funds in which they wish to invest their life insurance savings. AFS

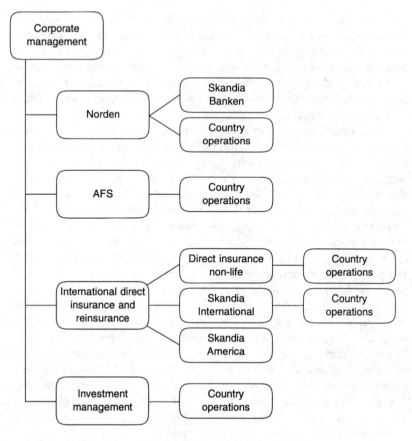

Figure 11.2 *Skandia Insurance Group organization chart, 1996*

offers customers over 500 different funds with leading managers around the world. Skandia AFS markets its investment funds and insurance plans through a non-exclusive partner network in each country in which it operates.

By most indicators Skandia AFS has grown aggressively in terms of gross premium income, number of alliance partners, customers and overall profitability. From 1991 to 1995, gross premium income grew from 5483 billion to 25,888 billion Swedish crowns. During that same time period, the alliance partners grew from 10,000 to over 25,000, while employees grew from 1106 to 1573. In addition, the company has expanded into 15 countries and is continuing to open new offices at a rapid rate globally. While the market for long-term savings products has also grown rapidly as a result of ageing populations in most of the industrialized world, combined with widespread concerns that government pension funds will not provide sufficient retirement income for all pensioners, nevertheless, from 1991 to 1995, Skandia AFS saw gross premium income rise 70% each year – a growth pace not generally associated with the insurance and financial services industries.

Business Concept

The focus of the AFS business concept is to be 'specialists in cooperation'. AFS's value added concentrates on fund management, product packaging and administration as well as distribution. On the upstream side of its value chain, AFS has developed a network of over 500 fund and pension plan providers; on the downstream side, AFS distributes its products to over 46,000 partners, including agents, banks, brokers and independent financial services in 15 countries.

To minimize indirect and fixed costs, AFS has developed a global growth model based on what is described as a 'federative structure' (see Figure 11.4) in which specialists are tied together through a common value system but operate autonomously to provide customer solutions.

At the centre of the federative structure are about 70 core 'competence leaders' or key executives. Surrounding the core are about 1700 AFS staff members, including employees handling information technology (IT), logistics and administration. At the next level from the core are over 46,000 partners (distributors) reaching the outer layer of over 1,000,000 customers who are mainly individual savers world-wide.

This federative structure leverages almost 20 customers for every AFS full-time employee and partner. AFS estimates that doing business this way saves the company several billion US dollars in working capital each year over competitors whose organizational approach is more hierarchical and country-based – either where the value chain of the company is replicated within each market, or where competitors have operated their own agent networks.

In addition, the company seeks to develop core competence in managing relationships at both ends of its value chain, but not owning the resources being leveraged. In this way, the company business concept seeks to add value though information sharing and knowledge acquisition and generation from its partners as well as employees. Information can be shared on products and customers across the value chain, while knowledge is generated inside the inner layers of the federative structure as well as at the outer layers with 46,000 partners and over 1,000,000 customers. Thus, the total business concept is aimed at managing information and knowledge flexibly, yet at the lowest cost possible, for continuous learning and change as the business structure responds to the environment of customer, partners, employees and stakeholders in over 15 countries in which AFS operates.

Visualizing the Hidden Value

During 1990 and 1991, Bjorn Wolrath, the president of Skandia Group, and Jan Carendi, the director of AFS, felt that there was a need to visualize for the board of directors and the financial community the 'hidden value' of the AFS business model. Like most publicly traded companies, the valuations of the corporation completed in a traditional manner did not evaluate carefully intellectual capital, the people investments in training and development and the supporting investments in processes, information and technology. Based on these concerns, Carendi decided in 1991 to establish a function under the direction of Leif Edvinsson, to develop a way of systematically assessing Skandia AFS's intellectual capital. To bring visibility to this responsibility, Carendi appointed Edvinsson as the first director of intellectual capital.

Edvinsson began his new task by devoting considerable time to articulating the 'hidden value' concept to colleagues throughout the company's offices around the world and by focusing on building awareness among the AFS board of directors concerning the need to systematically uncover the hidden value. Edvinsson explained the concept of hidden value using the metaphor of the 'black box': 'We had financial data on one sheet of paper, and in the middle we had a big space, like a black box, which we called the company's hidden values. Jan Carendi then asked the board if they would be interested in getting some information about some of these driving force items, such as customers, processes, human resources, innovations and new developments. Their response was very encouraging' (Oliver et al., 1996: 9).

Following the board meeting Edvinsson created the first reference to intellectual capital in the President's Statement of the 1992 Skandia AFS Annual Report. During 1992 and 1993, Edvinsson and a small team developed the first set of intellectual capital indicators which were summarized as eight major intellectual capital focus areas in the 1993 Balanced Annual Report Supplement. Also, in 1993, Edvinsson and his team developed the Skandia AFS Business Navigator (see Figure 11.3) which showed graphically how the focus areas fit together.

They simplified the eight focus areas to four: financial focus, customer focus, process focus and renewal and development focus. In each focus area, they developed appropriate metrics as indicators of performance. A fifth focus area – human focus – was added during 1994.

The original purpose of the Business Navigator was to show the outside world the hidden values by placing metrics on intellectual capital (IC). As the Navigator became more widely understood, it began to be perceived as a tool 'to steer the organization'.

From Measuring to Managing Intellectual Capital

During the mid 1990s, the focus of AFS's IC effort moved from awareness building and measurement to several management initiatives. First, Edvinsson was convinced that implementing an ongoing approach to collecting information for the measurement of IC required the refinement of the measures and their systematic reporting without adding an

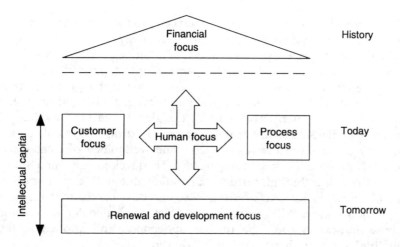

Figure 11.3   *Skandia's Business Navigator*

undue burden to the financial reporting system. Thus, AFS created the positions of Intellectual Capital Controller to begin collecting this supplementary information.

Second, Edvinsson communicated the Skandia AFS IC story broadly in the external media as well as inside AFS and the other Skandia Group companies. This strategy not only allowed outsiders to comment on the Skandia approach, but also built enthusiasm and pride among AFS employees as they saw the initiative highlighted in business magazines and periodicals around the world.

Third, the business units indicated that they wanted to integrate the IC indicators into a 'process model' aimed at linking IC with the strategic objectives and directions of each unit. Thus, the Business Navigator indicators became part of the planning and budgeting process for each business unit in AFS.

Finally, Edvinsson sought to move from IC 'indicators' to IC 'management' by emphasizing the need for executive leadership in developing appropriate core values such as a 'high-trust' culture among employees as well as by focusing on improving information systems and technology to permit better sharing of information and knowledge across AFS. In doing so, he sought to 'capitalize' on IC as an integral part of the corporate model of gaining long-term sustainability in markets through its federative, cooperative and global business approach. On leadership and values, Skandia AFS added 'intellectual capital development' to its list of 10 core values. In particular, AFS sought to implement this new value through the concept of 'work permits' where people are encouraged formally to gain and share knowledge and information in order to promote 'knowledge transparency' throughout the Skandia business structure.

To support these initiatives, AFS spends two to four times the industry average on information systems and technology, and fully 13% of Skandia's staff are employed in IS and IT. The strategic aim of Skandia is to evolve a global IT infrastructure capable of fully supporting a 'federative' or networked organization with information exchange using tools such as Lotus Notes for employee and partner collaboration. With global e-mail and information transfer tools, the global area network (GAN) permits Skandia AFS to lower the costs and lead time of opening new offices by using the processes, systems and technology of established offices. The company can also transfer IT development capabilities around the world through virtual cooperation among IS and IT specialists and users. Skandia AFS, during 1995, also developed a management information system (MIS) version of the Skandia Navigator so that the business indicators could be further understood and applied at the individual and team levels within the division.

As Skandia AFS has implemented its approach to managing intellectual capital over the last six years, the company has targeted and improved the four processes noted in Figure 11.1 for converting information and knowledge to compete in its markets. Indeed, it is clear that the success of the Skandia Business Navigator for managing intellectual capital is closely linked to the capability to improve the transformation of personal knowledge to 'structural capital' – information assets – to enable the federative business structure to work across fund managers, employees, agents and customers.

Knowledge and Information Conversion Processes at Skandia AFS

Converting Knowledge to Knowledge

The basic challenge of AFS is to develop a *global* organization where people cooperate and communicate directly with people: 'specialists in cooperation'. The core of the federative structure (see Figure 11.4) of AFS is a group of some 70 managers who act as the key levers between over 500 fund managers and 1700 staff and 46,000 agents. These 70 managers must share a strong common culture and vision as well as a common language developed through personal relationships and continuous conversations. They are the centre of Skandia's knowledge base in the sense that they represent the critical knowledge about AFS's business system and approach as well as the nucleus for developing AFS's change strategies.

However, it is also clear that without significant investments in communications and information technology, AFS's capability to leverage the values, expertise and time of these 70 core managers is limited. In addition, without the use of the Business Navigator at the corporate and

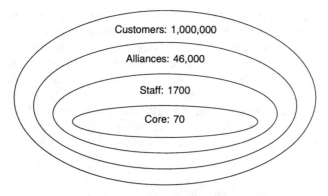

Figure 11.4   *Skandia AFS's federative structure*

individual level, the importance of identifying, developing and renew-ing intellectual capital in the 1700 employees beyond the core group is also limited.

Converting Knowledge to Information

The second conversion process at Skandia is critical to the extension of the collective intellectual capital of the core group of 70 managers to AFS's 1700 employees and 46,000 agents. The federative structure of AFS cannot function like a traditional insurance company with heavy use of paper for converting knowledge into useful information for others to share. For the federation to work efficiently, everyone must use infor-mation technology to document knowledge and share it across the boundaries of the federation. A critical ingredient for agents and employees in promoting the conversion of knowledge to 'sharable' information is a 'high-trust' culture. Unlike the traditional hierarchical insurance company where employees and agents are literally 'inside' the boundaries of the organization, the basis of the federation is the shared belief that non-exclusive agents and employees are better off cooperating and trusting each other to share their collective knowledge about customers, processes and products for mutual gain and sustainability. All these individuals must be willing to share their knowledge with each other and make it explicit through the use of tools like Lotus Notes and databases for others to learn from and use.

Converting Information to Knowledge

At Skandia AFS, the capability to leverage 500 funds through some 1700 managers and employees and a network of 46,000 agents in over 15 countries for over 1,000,000 customers requires a operating culture where individuals seek out and act on the information that they receive quickly and efficiently. In this context, the high-trust culture of cooperation extends to the confidence that people have in the quality and integrity of the information that everyone receives on a daily basis. In contrast to the traditional insurance company or investment bank where people operate on a 'need to know' basis and where there is limited sharing of information, especially with agents whom the company does not exclusively employ, the Skandia AFS business model places the widespread sharing and use of information and knowledge at the centre of its business values and culture. AFS is willing to run the risks of information 'leakage' to competitors to foster its high-trust, high information-sharing approach.

Converting Information about Information

Perhaps the most critical aspect of Skandia's approach to intellectual capital is the need to turn personal knowledge and information to 'structural' capital to benefit the long-term sustainability of the company. Like other knowledge-based companies, AFS faces the daily risk of critical knowledge leaving the company in the minds of its employees and agents. Like other 'knowledge workers' these people are able to seek employment with other insurance providers where their knowledge will be rewarded. Without seeking more effective ways of converting personal knowledge to some kind of *organizational* knowledge or meta-information, captured in different repositories, databases of best practices and expert systems, AFS is at constant risk of losing its most valuable knowledge, namely about how the business really works. To guard against these risks as well as to promote a constant turnover in personal knowledge being applied for the benefit of the federation, Skandia AFS has used the Business Navigator as the catalyst for the continuous conversion of personal intellectual capital into structural capital for the benefit of the company and its customers and shareholders. The Business Navigator also acts as a tool for measuring the success of this conversion to structural capital as well as a vehicle for communicating to shareholders the bottom-line value of this process of constant renewal.

Conclusions

Understanding the relationships between knowledge and information is the first step in focusing on the underlying processes for continuously converting knowledge into information and vice versa. In addition, by evaluating how well a company employs these four processes for improving the capacity to learn, change and compete effectively, we can begin uncovering new ways that companies can leverage knowledge and information internally as well as with their customers and partners in their value chains. In Skandia AFS, the focus on managing intellectual capital with the Business Navigator is its way of systematically examining and improving each of the four conversion processes among AFS's managers and employees as well as with its fund managers, agents and customers.

Second, with all of the academic and managerial interest in 'knowledge management' today, it is important that the role of information use and sharing in a company should not be overlooked or confused with 'knowledge development'. As important as knowledge development is to organizational learning and change, information is the means or vehicle that companies employ to express, convey and share knowledge retained among their people. Thus, a company's capabilities to manage information provide the means through which knowledge development and management are possible. Within Skandia AFS, information management to enable the development and sharing of knowledge is critical to the ability of the company to operate in a high-trust, high information-sharing, 'federative structure' with fund managers and agents. This style and mode of operation contrast sharply with the more traditional functional organizations of banks and insurance companies where information is highly controlled within the boundaries of the company, since trust in agents and fund managers as well as lower-level employees is limited or non-existent.

Finally, if competitive success in the 1990s depends on learning and changing faster and better than one's competitors, then managing effectively the conversion processes between knowledge and information will position companies to improve both the velocity of conversion and the quality of the knowledge and information that will be shared and employed throughout the company. Companies such as Skandia AFS represent a new breed whose business strategy and approach to customers and markets require excellence in growing and deploying knowledge and information more effectively and quickly than their competitors – the essence of effective learning, changing and competing in the 1990s.

Notes

1 Section based on Oliver et al. (1996).

References

D'Aveni, R.A. (1994) *Hyper-Competition*. New York: Free Press.
Garvin, D.A. (1993) Building a learning organization. *Harvard Business Review*, July–August: 80–91.
Graham, A.B. and Pizzo, V.G. (1996) A question of balance: case studies in knowledge management. *European Management Journal*, special issue on *The*

Epistemological Challenge: Managing Knowledge and Intellectual Capital, 14 (4): 338–46.

Jensen, B. (1996) Was change management ever necessary? *Focus on Management*, July–August: 9–18.

Nonaka, I. and Takeuchi, H. (1995) *The Knowledge Creating Company*. Oxford: Oxford University Press.

Oliver, D., Marchand, D.A. and J. Roos (1996) Skandia Assurance and Financial Services: measuring and visualizing intellectual capital. *International Institute for Management Development*, Lausanne, Switzerland.

Skandia (1994) *Visualizing Intellectual Capital*. Supplement to Skandia's 1994 Annual Report.

von Krogh, G., and J. Roos, (1995) *Organizational Epistemology*. London: Macmillan.

12

THE LEARNING–KNOWLEDGE–VALUE CYCLE

Valery Kanevsky and Tom Housel

The fundamental building material of a modern corporation is knowledge. The engine of wealth in the 'third wave' is creation and utilization of knowledge. Understanding how to accelerate the conversion of knowledge into money is the real challenge in the information age. This 'knowledge payoff' occurs when a corporation's most valuable intangible asset – knowledge – is converted into bottom-line value in the form of a concrete, saleable product.

If we can track this conversion process in an objective way, we will have the beginnings of the new finance of the digital economy. Existing accounting methods do not help us track this conversion process because they are based on 'second wave', industrial revolution era approaches tied to tracking the cost of converting raw materials into final goods. The economics of scarce resources does not hold in the digital age where inventories do not deplete by application of the digital resource (in the form of data, information and/or knowledge) to the production of the finished product. We need a new source of raw accounting data that will allow us to count the amount of knowledge contained within final products in terms of the processes which used the knowledge to generate the finished products. This new raw data is knowledge.

The problem is to describe knowledge in a way that makes it countable in equivalent units so that we can track the investment required to convert knowledge into bottom-line value. Just as a genome represents the knowledge required to 'build an organism', corporate knowledge represents the knowledge required to reproduce the corporation's value-creating structure. In this context, the knowledge embedded in a corporation's structure (processes, technology, people) can be viewed as the genome which represents the code required for reproducing corporate products. This 'code' is virtually equivalent to the value added by the corporation because it is what is necessary and sufficient to reproduce the corporation's products.

Knowledge can be measured in the common units of bits (in the Shannon information theory sense). Therefore, all production processes and the products they produce can be measured in the same units.

These instructions then are a virtual representation of the product, just as a genome is a virtual representation of an organism. If a product can be represented as a given number of bits (or virtual genetic structure), and the product sells for a given price, we can determine the virtual price paid per bit. Knowing the price per bit it is possible to backward allocate the price to those activities in the production process which executed the knowledge required to make the product in proportion to the amount of knowledge each activity contains. This approach allows us to ascribe an observable, objective value to each activity.

It takes a variety of types of corporate knowledge to produce its products. This knowledge is distributed throughout the company's processes, technology and organization. And this is where we must look to begin tracking the 'knowledge payoff'. What we need is a way to establish the monetary representation of the value of corporate knowledge. As accountants will tell us, bottom-line value is established when a market price is realized by selling something. So, to measure the value of pieces of corporate knowledge, we need a way to associate each with the revenue it generates.

If we ask customers to tell us how valuable our corporate knowledge is, they might have trouble understanding the question, let alone giving us a consistent answer. One thing is for sure, the customer speaks loudest when he/she buys one of our products and in effect pays us for the knowledge we used to produce it. Being a bit on the conservative side, we are wont to speculate about our customers' perception of the value of our knowledge: we would much rather make the reasonable assumption that if they bought our product (i.e. the knowledge embedded therein), this knowledge must have been of value. And the price they were willing to pay tells us just how valuable it was when they purchased it – remembering that customers can change their minds in the future about how valuable our products are, based on a wide variety of factors (e.g. introduction of competing products, supply/demand, fads).

Given that the customer established the value of the product/knowledge, the problem is to determine the relative values of all the different pieces of corporate knowledge that the product contains. This becomes critical when corporate executives make their decisions to invest in knowledge.

Let's be honest, customers are only willing to pay for the corporate knowledge that allowed the production of a product they wanted to buy. All the other implicit corporate knowledge contained in employees' heads, or elsewhere, may prove valuable over time, but its value can only really be ascertained when it shows up in a product that gets purchased.

Backward Allocation Problem

The problem is to define our product in such a way that the purchase price (or other revenue surrogate) can be allocated back to all the separate pieces of corporate knowledge it contains. If we can solve this problem, then we can track our return on investment in the various pieces of corporate knowledge contained in our products. More importantly, we can measure the return we receive on our investments in the learning necessary to generate new corporate knowledge and hence new or changed products.

Many, many approaches exist to help us determine what changes should be made to our product line; however, we also need to objectively track the cycle of learning to knowledge to value. Our prosperity, not to mention survival, ultimately will rest on our ability to keep track of that corporate knowledge which is unambiguously valuable to the customer.

Inherent Value

We also need to recognize that it is the knowledge required to change raw materials into a final product which becomes valuable because it represents the product's inherent characteristics (e.g. features and functions) and ultimately is what the customer pays for. Purchase price is a convenient way to represent the financial value of this knowledge when the product which results from its application is sold.

The market prices of products are not constant; they can vary based on a wide variety of factors (e.g. fads, supply and demand). However, products, once produced, do not vary; their inherent characteristics are fixed. If we want to take advantage of our corporate knowledge about products, we have to understand the relationship between that which is valued (i.e. the product) and the market's response to it (e.g. purchase price).

We need to recognize some fundamental truths about products and the marketplace:

1   Purchase price is one way to measure the financial impact of corporate knowledge. It cannot be used to create new corporate knowledge.
2   Products have value by virtue of their inherent characteristics, and these characteristics are embodied in the corporate knowledge needed to produce them.

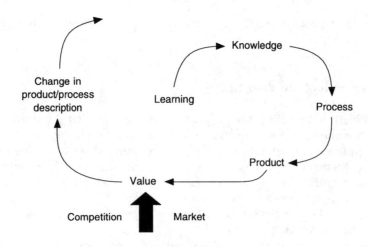

Figure 12.1   *Learning–knowledge–value spiral*

3   Corporations can only create new value by creating new or better
    products. Playing a financial 'shell' game by manipulating cost
    structure will not result in long-term knowledge creation and hence
    value.

Learning–Knowledge–Value Chain

Ultimately, we have to understand that learning from the market must
be translated into knowledge that can be applied to our company
production processes resulting in changes in our products. This learning
to knowledge to new value cycle must spiral upwards if our company is
to flourish, not to mention survive (see Figure 12.1).

To ensure that it is spiralling upwards, we must constantly measure
the market's response to this cycle. This can be accomplished with a
measure we call return on investment in knowledge (ROK). Getting
ROK requires that we draw the linkage between products, knowledge,
learning and value.

Valuable Corporate Knowledge = Production Processes

We can tie revenue to corporate knowledge by recognizing that
knowledge is embedded in production processes and that all processes
can be described. Being descriptions, they are made up of comparable
units of information (or in the strict information theory sense, bits of
information). These units of information can be counted. This approach

provides a means to proportionately allocate purchase price back to all the pieces of knowledge necessary to produce our final products.

Imagine the entire product process description as a 'virtual' representation of the real product. It is possible to think of the product then as synonymous with the various elements of process knowledge required to create it. In this sense, the customer is paying as much for the company's knowledge about how to build a product as he/she is paying for the actual product. In a virtual reality amusement ride, a child pays for an entertainment service which is almost entirely the product of the computer code required to create it.

When we establish a common unit of process description (i.e. unit of information at some level of aggregation) across all processes, especially the component or subprocesses, it is possible to count the total amount of knowledge required to make a sellable product. A simple way to get these process descriptions, as a first cut, would be to ask component process subject matter experts how to reproduce the outputs of each of their component processes based on some finite set of instructions. Common sense would help us determine who was being repetitive and who was being too general. With a little patience and general discussion, we would arrive at reasonably comparable process descriptions which represented the amount of knowledge contained in each component process.

Of course if you have a process which is automated, you can use computer code as a process description and count lines of code using the same kind of common-sense redundancy/generality rule. Each line of code represents an element of the knowledge that is required to produce the output. By totalling the lines of code, we have a first-order estimate of the knowledge embedded in each component process.

It also stands to reason that, on average, the time it takes to learn is proportionate to the amount of new knowledge there is to learn. Hence, learning time is another way to estimate the amount of knowledge present in process descriptions. So, learning time itself becomes a way to estimate the distribution of new knowledge within production processes. Tracking the speed with which learning translates into new knowledge in the form of new or modified products is a way to measure our corporation's nimbleness in turning learning and knowledge into bottom-line value.

Since it is not always easy to generate (or find) process descriptions or estimate learning time, another way to estimate amount of knowledge is something we call the binary query method. All processes can be represented as a series of yes–no decisions. In essence, this approach breaks all processes into a series of binary choices or bits. Since bits are universal units, this approach allows comparisons among all processes in terms of bits of knowledge produced per dollar of investment.

Armed with these three options in estimating the amount of knowledge embedded in processes it is possible to calculate the ROK for all

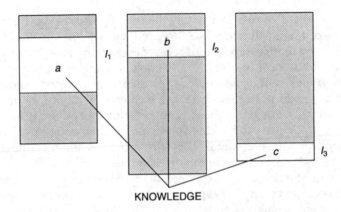

Figure 12.2 *Component process description. A particular piece of knowledge is distributed among three component processes. The relative value of this knowledge is proportional to the total number of instructions in its description. Thus, if a, b and c are the number of instructions necessary to describe the knowledge as parts of the description of the processes I_1, I_2 or I_3, then value added by this knowledge is proportional to a + b + c*

production processes. The key here is that all three approaches generate comparable measures of knowledge for our ROK calculation. By obtaining the three measures, we can cross-check the consistency of our estimation of amount of knowledge in the processes.

It is possible to make a first approximation of how well our company is doing in converting existing knowledge into value. And, it is possible to identify the effect of the introduction of new knowledge on our bottom line. Fortunately, we have numerous case studies using our methodology that have demonstrated the viability of our approach in practice in obtaining this critical process–knowledge performance information.

We can see how the new knowledge is distributed among the component processes required to make the product (see Figure 12.2). This 'knowledge accounting' provides management with a new view of how the investment in knowledge and learning is paying off – not just how much it costs.

Market Change = Need for Learning

When a customer purchases our product, he/she changes the market forever. Corporate success largely rests on the ability to translate learning from these changes into knowledge that will result in new or modified products. Lest we forget, the competition also can learn from this market perturbation and, if it is smart, will respond accordingly. Our ability to quickly translate this critical learning into new knowledge, and hence new products, will largely determine whether we win in the marketplace.

The market 'organism' responds like any other living creature. To survive, the company must adapt to the new market condition created when it sells a product. It must adjust its product description, and consequently its processes, to maximize its potential for long life – namely by making sure it has the knowledge necessary to make products that will continue selling. Hence, learning is a critical element in ensuring that our corporation makes the necessary adjustments to the new market environment by continuing to produce valuable products.

The effectiveness of our process adjustments to the market and competition can be determined through real-time, learning to knowledge to value, performance feedback in the form of ROK. And this kind of performance feedback is critical in the information age where hyper-competition is evolving in most markets.

Process Cost and Knowledge Execution Cost

If we know the value of knowledge, then we have the upper half of the equation. But we also need the lower half, i.e. the cost to execute the knowledge. There are several well-established ways to calculate these costs, e.g. activity-based costing, generally accepted accounting practices. However, it may be easiest to measure process execution time which would include the time required to learn the new process by workers or automated systems (in the form of the time required to introduce or change computer code) as well as the actual product manufacturing execution time. This approach would ultimately yield a cost per bit for every component process.

Knowledge = Value

In our approach, knowledge and value are both derivatives of the same thing – process description. Since knowledge is the value generator and both are derived from the same category, they are virtually equivalent to each other. In this sense, knowledge accounting is really a form of 'value accounting'. As such it supplements the information provided to decision-makers through cost accounting in a way that allows them to better understand the relationship between cost and value in their production processes (see Figure 12.3). In sum, as long as the value derived from new knowledge exceeds its cost, by an acceptable margin, then the corporation is winning.

Winning here means more than just a bottom-line number. It means that we are really creating new value through turning our learning into

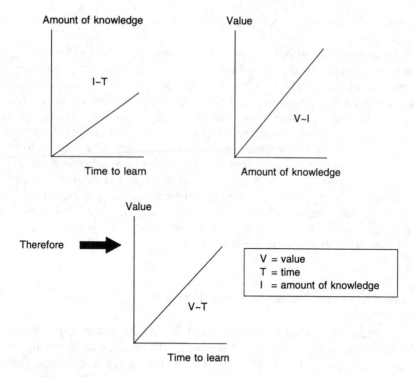

Figure 12.3   *Learning time, knowledge and value*

new corporate knowledge. It means that not only will our company ultimately produce greater shareholder value, it will provide concrete new value to our customers in the form of new or improved products. This value accounting also allows our employees to understand what contribution their knowledge is making to the bottom line.

Given the need to stay ahead of the competition and adapt quickly to a changing market, we must keep track of the effectiveness with which our corporations change learning into knowledge that is valuable to customers.

Kolmogorov Complexity and Value Added

Kolmogorov complexity (K-complexity) is both a universal measure of changes in the form of matter and a universal property of matter (just as weight is a universal measure of gravity's influence on matter, and also a universal property of matter itself). Creation of K-complexity (and the equivalent information) can be viewed as the universal activity of people, such as in the creation of value in business processes. K-complexity itself can be seen as the universal product of their activity.

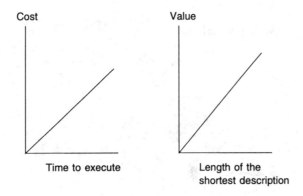

Figure 12.4 *Value–cost duality principle: value is proportional to the length of the shortest description (Kolmogorov complexity); cost is proportional to the time to execute the shortest description (computational complexity)*

The focus of this approach is on those processes which have predetermined outputs (i.e. given the same inputs, the outputs will always be the same). For example, the approach will not apply to creative activities such as art, or, at the other extreme, destructive activities such as demolition. Processes with predetermined outputs represent the majority of core business processes which produce sellable outputs in the form of products/services. In this context, processes with predetermined outputs are isomorphic with computer algorithms and therefore the processing itself is virtually identical to computing.

The Fundamental Metaphor: Business Processing = Computing

In what follows, we will show that the value added by business processes should be measured in terms of the length of the shortest program for the corresponding computer. On the other hand, this parallel goes even further such that the cost to execute a business process is essentially equivalent to the time to execute the shortest computer program corresponding to a given business process, i.e. computational complexity. This completes the fundamental metaphor (Figure 12.4):

1 The value added by a business process equals the length of the shortest program (i.e. Kolmogorov complexity).
2 The cost to execute a business process equals the time to execute the shortest program (i.e. computational complexity).

This focus allows us to draw the parallel between business processes and computation (Figure 12.5). The advantage of this parallel is that it

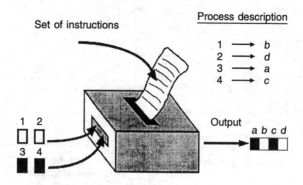

Figure 12.5 *Computer analogy of business process*

enables us to apply the framework of computer science to business process analysis. Specifically, this parallelism will enable us to find the corresponding concepts in computer science for such fundamental notions as value added and cost. Given that, at present, objective methods for backward allocating value to processes do not exist, this approach provides a consistent, rigorous way to compute these two performance characteristics allowing ratio analysis at the core and component process levels.

Thermodynamics of Business Processes

Businesses are open systems – systems that exchange information, substance and energy with their environments. As such, businesses have the capability, through their processes, to change the structure of raw material inputs (i.e. substance, energy, information) into final products/services. In the language of thermodynamics, this change in structure can be measured in terms of the corresponding change in entropy, when an input state a is transformed into output state b by process P (i.e. $b = P(a)$). Assume that this change can further be represented as a set of 'elementary' changes that are minute enough to become identical in terms of the corresponding amount of entropy they cause. This assumption about the equivalence of elementary changes can be expanded across any finite number of processes with predetermined outputs. This allows comparison in terms of entropy among any set of processes by means of the number of elementary changes. To eliminate a potential misinterpretation of this concept, it is important to emphasize that a change in entropy when state a is transformed into state b depends only on a and b and does not depend on process P. This means that any process P that changes a into b introduces the same change in entropy or, in a business context, adds the same value. However, it is reasonable to assume that the minimal set of instructions which allows the execution of process P reflects the corresponding change in entropy given the current state of technology. In other words, we believe that the length of the shortest description provides an acceptable approximation to the change in entropy given the current state of technology.

Given the relationship between entropy and change, the concept of value added can be addressed with the following assumption:

If business process P is such that output b is equal to input a, i.e. $b = P(a)$ = a, *no value is added by process P.*

In other words, no changes: no value is added. Consequently, it is possible to infer that the amount of value added by process P can be associated (proportionally) with the corresponding change in entropy. This relationship, while fundamental, does not provide a practical way to calculate the value added by process P, i.e. the entropy increment.

Within the framework of thermodynamics, a fundamental parallelism between transformation of substances and information processing has been established (Li and Vitanyi, 1993). If a substance is transformed from state a to state b, then the difference of the entropies, i.e. $\Delta E = E(b) - E(a)$, is proportional to the amount of thermodynamic work required for the change. In parallel, the amount of thermodynamic work required to transform string ('word') x into string y by the 'most efficient computer' equipped with the 'most efficient program' is proportional to the length of the shortest program to execute this transformation, i.e. to $K(y/x)$, the conditional Kolmogorov complexity of output y given input x (see Li and Vitanyi, 1993; Cover and Thomas, 1991). Conditional Kolmogorov complexity, $K(y/x)$, can be viewed in the business context as the shortest description of the process, i.e. effectively the value added by the process.

This concept can be applied to calculating the value added by business processes by calculating the entropy or K-complexity caused by the process to transform an input to its process output. To accomplish this, we will employ the parallelism between business processes and computations.

Assume that process P can be fully specified, i.e. can be formally described as a set of instructions in a formal language:

1   There is a universal computer U equipped with program p.
2   There is a one-to-one map from $\{a\}$ to $\{x\}$, where $\{a\}$ is the set of all possible inputs to process P, and $\{x\}$ is the set of all possible inputs to computer U.
3   There is a one-to-one map from $\{b\}$ to $\{y\}$, where $\{b\}$ is the set of all possible outputs from process P, and $\{y\}$ is the set of all possible outputs from U acting on $\{x\}$ by virtue of p, such that $U(p, x) = y$, if and only if $P(a) = b$.

Second, we must define the value added by process P using the established correspondence between processes and their computer representations. Since there is a duality between processes and their computer representations, it is possible to reduce the problem of the value added by process P to a problem of calculating the value added by its computer representation. It follows that the value added by process P when it transforms a into b is proportional to $K(y/x)$ where x and y correspond to a and b as previously defined. The value added by P will vary owing to the level of detail in the description of P captured by the maps defined in point 2 above.

The description of any process can be viewed as texts written in a formal language. It has been proven that the K-complexity of a text is nearly equivalent to the Shannon amount of information in the text: a unit of K-complexity is identical with a unit of Shannon's information. (For a detailed description of the mathematical reasoning of this relationship see Cover and Thomas, 1991: 153–5.) Therefore, amount of information will be used as a substitute for K-complexity when appropriate.

K-Complexity Conditioned by Level of Language

Description of outputs of all components within the compound process will be determined by the language used to describe the original inputs to the compound process. Therefore, all K-complexities calculated along the value-added chain will be conditioned with respect to the language used to describe the original compound input.

The length of the shortest description is dependent upon the formal 'vocabulary' used. The more powerful or comprehensive the vocabulary used, the shorter would be the shortest description. An example of this phenomenon in human languages is the use of acronyms to shorten texts.

The description of a product can be shorter or longer depending on the formal vocabulary 'building blocks' (i.e. inputs) used to describe it. This implies that the complexity of a product is conditional upon the level of aggregation of the process inputs. For example, the description of a car in terms of inputs such as doors, engines, transmissions, bodies etc. would be much shorter than the car described in terms of position of nuts, bolts, pistons, sheet metal, welds etc. At each point in the car assembly process, value is added as the output of one component process serves as the input of the next higher-level component process output. Oversimplifying a bit, nuts, bolts, sheet metal etc. are transformed to become engines, doors, transmissions etc., and finally the engines, doors etc. are assembled to become a car. To approximate the K-complexity of the car in terms of the raw material inputs, it is necessary to accumulate the estimate of increments in K-complexities along all components of the value-adding chain between the raw materials and final assembly.

Comparing K-Complexity across Compound Processes

Theoretically, Kolmogorov complexity is not computable because it is impossible to prove that a given description (i.e. computer program) is the shortest possible. In spite of this, it is possible to find an approximation to the ratio of K-complexities by calculating the actual length of the computer programs which represent the processes because it is reasonable to expect that there is a relatively narrow, unimodal distribution of performance among computer programmers. The program length ratio will better approximate the ratio of K-complexities the narrower the distribution of programmer performance with regard to redundancy.

In other words, practically speaking, the ratio of K-complexities of two processes is approximately equal to the ratio of the lengths of the corresponding programs. This approach allows comparison of the value added not only between component processes within one compound process but also across processes and therefore across industries.

Component and Compound Processes

To understand how K-complexity can be used to measure value added, the value-adding process must break the compound process down into its component processes. Component processes are those interim processes (e.g. subassemblies) whose outputs provide the inputs to other subsequent value added steps in the production chain. The compound process is the representation of the overall process, including all the component processes (and their outputs) necessary to produce the final product/service.

As the output of each component process makes its relative contribution to the final output product/service, these changes in structure can be measured via K-complexity. The compound process output, then, is the accumulation of all the K-complexities introduced at each step of the value-adding process. Formal descriptions can be created, or programs which describe the processes can be used to calculate the K-complexity of component processes.

Having identified the component processes of a compound process, it is possible to formally describe the outputs of these processes in terms of the original compound process inputs. The computer programs used to represent (as per instructions 1–3 given earlier) the actual process can be viewed as the description of the processes outputs. The K-complexity contained in these formal descriptions/programs reflects the changes in structure brought about by the value-adding process. The compound product/service is the total accumulation of the K-complexities manifested in the component process output descriptions/programs. Measuring the K-complexity of different output descriptions/programs provides a formal way to quantify the intuitive understanding that an automobile is a more *complex* structure than any of its components.

A Calculus for K-Complexity in Business Processes

The ROK methodology is designed to measure value creation for processes with predetermined execution paths. These processes can be effectively mapped in terms of their computer representations (as in instructions 1–3 earlier). In a sense they are a real-world analogue to the well-known concept of computable functions in computer science. For example, in the telephone service provisioning process, the output of a sales contact is a service order that represents the result of negotiating potential features with the customer. The output of this process can be created from a well-defined algorithm applied to a formal description of the customer request for service. Flexible manufacturing systems are another example of software applications that predetermine what, how and when component processes will be executed in the manufacturing process to produce a given set of outputs.

These kinds of processes represent a large percentage of the work of business. Any process that ultimately can be automated is a process with a predetermined execution 'path'.

Complexity-Based Process Performance Measurement

We will define the internal performance V of this kind of process as

$$V = I/C \tag{1}$$

where I is the amount of K-complexity (information) and C is the cost to produce this amount of K-complexity. It follows that the K-complexity I of a compound process can be expressed as

$$I = \Sigma I_i \tag{2}$$

and the cost C as

$$C = \Sigma C_i \tag{3}$$

Here I_i and C_i are the amount of K-complexity produced by component process P_i, and the cost associated with this component; $i = 1, \ldots, n$, where n is the number of component processes.

Let $V_i = I_i/C_i$ be the performance of component process P_i. Then

$$V = I/C = \Sigma I_i / \Sigma C_i = \Sigma (C_i / \Sigma C_i) V_i \tag{4}$$

That is, the V performance of the compound process is equal to the weighted (by relative costs) average of the component process performance.

Along with V, we must have an external process performance measurement which accounts for the market value of the product/service. Purchase price is one objective measure of the market value of a product/service. V_m represents the purchase price of a unit of K-complexity/information in a given product/service. V_m for a compound is defined as

$$V_m = M/I \tag{5}$$

where M is the purchase price of the output of a compound process and I is the amount of K-complexity/information in the purchased product/service.

Formula (5) can be applied to component processes when M is allocated along the outputs of the component processes. The problem is to establish an objective way to allocate the purchase price using a method that is consistent with an ROI (return on investment) approach. This can be done in the following way. Let P_i represent an arbitrary component process ($i = 1, \ldots, n$, where n is the number of component processes) of the compound process P. Then M_i is calculated as (i.e. allocation formula)

$$M_i = (I_i/I)M \tag{6}$$

As the following formula shows, the price per unit of information does not depend on a given component process. The customer pays for the output of the compound process in the form of a final product. The customer is paying the same price for each unit of information, regardless of which component process produces it.

$$V_{m,i} = M_i/I_i = [(I_i/I)M]/I_i = M/I \tag{7}$$

It follows that $ROP_i = \text{constant} \times V_i$, where the constant $= M/I$.

Given formula (6), ROP for a component process P_i can be defined as

$$ROP_i = M_i/C_i \tag{8}$$

Now it is possible to calculate ROI for the compound process in terms of the component ROPs:

$$ROI = M/C = \Sigma M_i/\Sigma C_i = (C_i/\Sigma C_i)ROP_i \tag{9}$$

That is, the ROI performance of the compound process is equal to the weighted (by relative cost) average of the component ROPs.

Therefore, the application of the ROP for a given compound process can be reduced to the calculation of V for all the components of that compound. So, V is the critical measure in making comparisons of the value-producing capabilities of the various components of a compound process. This conclusion is also consistent with operational managers' intuitive belief that the key to adding value lies in an understanding of processes.

ROP allows decision-makers to predict value creation or 'value adding' throughout the production process, not just on the results of the compound process. As such, this approach allows them to make more precise investment allocations in the operations of a company based on a market-dependent estimator, V_m, and a market-independent estimator V.

In this context, creation of K-complexity is a metaphor of the same sort as 'making money'. Measures of productivity become the amount of K-complexity produced per dollar of cost. Measures of profitability can be represented as the price per unit of K-complexity. Indexes of productivity based on ROP can be used as new indicators of company, industry and an economy's performance.

References

Cover, T.M. and Thomas, J.A. (1991) *Elements of Information Theory.* New York: Wiley. pp. 153–5.

Li, M. and Vitanyi, P. (1993) *An Introduction to Kolmogorov Complexity and its Application.* Berlin: Springer.

INDEX